THE COMPANION GUIDE TO EDINBURGH AND THE BORDERS

THE COMPANION GUIDES

*It is the aim of these guides to provide a Companion
in the person of the author; who knows
intimately the places and people of whom he writes, and is able to
communicate this knowledge and affection to his readers.
It is hoped that the text and pictures will aid them
in their preparations and in their travels, and will
help them remember on their return.*

BURGUNDY · THE COUNTRY ROUND PARIS
DEVON · FLORENCE · GASCONY AND THE DORDOGNE
GREECE · GREEK ISLANDS · ISTANBUL
KENT AND SUSSEX · LAKE DISTRICT · LONDON
MADRID AND CENTRAL SPAIN · NEW YORK
PARIS · ROME · SICILY
SOUTH OF SPAIN · VENICE

THE COMPANION GUIDE TO

EDINBURGH
AND THE BORDERS

A. J. Youngson

Illustrated with new photographs by
Graeme Youngson

COMPANION GUIDES

First published 1993
Reissued 1996
Companion Guides, Woodbridge

New edition 2001

ISBN 1 900639 38 6

Companion Guides is an imprint of Boydell & Brewer Ltd
PO Box 9, Woodbridge, Suffolk IP12 3DF, UK
and of Boydell & Brewer Inc.
PO Box 41026, Rochester, NY 14604–4126, USA
website: http://www.companionguides.com

A catalogue record for this book is available
from the British Library

Printed in Great Britain by
St Edmundsbury Press Ltd, Bury St Edmunds, Suffolk

Contents

Illustrations

Maps

Preface

A HIGH PROPORTION OF Scottish history and what for want of a better word one must call Scottish culture is concentrated in Edinburgh, East Lothian and the Borders. Each of these parts of the country, although perfectly distinct from the others, occupies a prominent place in the mainstream of Scottish history, and each exhibits a certain grey sombreness which lies beneath its more cheerful and inviting characteristics and which adds substance and serious interest to almost every scene.

Edinburgh is one of the world's remarkable cities because it contains both an old town, rebuilt on the medieval street plan after being burned by an English army in 1544, and right alongside the old town a new town, a planned concentration of eighteenth and nineteenth century classical buildings which is more extensive than anything else of its kind in Europe. Oliver Wendell Holmes wrote of 'the incomparable loveliness of Edinburgh;' evidently he missed the point. Edinburgh is a city of variety; it is surprising, challenging, spectacular; it can be gloomy, mysterious, even forbidding; above all, it is historic; but loveliness is not its forte.

The modern city encloses both the Old Town and the New Town. In total it spreads, as do all modern cities, for considerable distances, and the spread is mostly of no particular interest. This book concentrates on the historic central areas, although there are also chapters which deal with excursions to outlying parts where there is something interesting to see.

After London, Edinburgh is the most visited city in Britain. At Festival time, in August, it is packed with action; all the convenient as well as many inconvenient places are appropriated for plays, concerts, exhibitions, happenings and every other conceivable kind of public attraction. The crowds in August are part of the fun. At other times of the year there is room for everyone, for there is much to see. But should the visitor grow tired of human company, some of the emptiest and most beautiful country in these islands is at Edinburgh's door. Space and quiet are the priceless assets of East Lothian and the Borders. These happy lands are all but untouched by modern developments. From the rocky coast of Berwickshire to the high fastnesses of Liddesdale there is very little industry, no great town, no international holiday centre to pull in the crowds and the caravans.

The whole of the south-east of Scotland is steeped in history. Scotland was an independent kingdom before the year 1000, and Edinburgh was its capital from around 1450 until 1603. It still has the air of a capital. It was Sir John Vanbrugh who said that old buildings give rise to 'lively and pleasant reflections on the persons who have inhabited them, and on the remarkable things which have been transacted in them'. True enough. But not everywhere does one find buildings where kings were born, or where some of their more prominent subjects were assassinated; or streets once trodden by persons as diverse and famous as Mary Queen of Scots, Bonnie Prince Charlie, Dr Johnson and Sir Walter Scott, to name only a few. In the countryside it is much the same; abbeys destroyed by invading armies, castles that withstood countless sieges but have crumbled at last, great houses still owned by families 'that the Flood could not wash away'. History is everywhere, although not all of it gives rise to 'pleasant reflections'. I have tried to indicate some of this history, but it is very complicated.

Central Edinburgh is described in chapters which are arranged so that the reader can walk through sections of town without having repeatedly to turn aside or retrace his steps in search of some item of note but inconveniently located.

East Lothian has a chapter to itself. A circular tour is outlined which could just possibly be managed – but not very well managed – in the course of a day.

For those who have enough time to see the Borders, the final chapters suppose the visitor to begin in Edinburgh, and to take any of four routes to the Tweed. Then, starting from Berwick-upon-Tweed, successive chapters take the reader on a tour to the source of the Tweed and from there back eastwards to Jedburgh. The final chapter deals with the remote hilly areas that lie close to the Border itself.

No guide book can cover everything, and like other authors of guide books I have picked and chosen. So there are omissions, some of which I regret. But I believe that there is enough here to convey the style and spirit of this part of Scotland, and of its people. For the reader who wants to know more, there are countless other books to read. Or better still, live here.

Gullane, East Lothian
1992

Preface to Second Edition

THIS EDITION INCLUDES new material, principally because Edinburgh has altered and expanded since 1992. New constitutional arrangements for Scotland have demanded a Parliament House and related buildings; there are new museums, a large new conference centre in the very heart of the city, and new uses have been found for several existing buildings, some of them unoccupied for several years. It seems that Edinburgh has changed more in the 1990s than in the previous thirty or forty years put together. In the countryside, change has been far less, as is the way of things. But many will say, none the worse for that.

A. Youngson, 2000

EDINBURGH

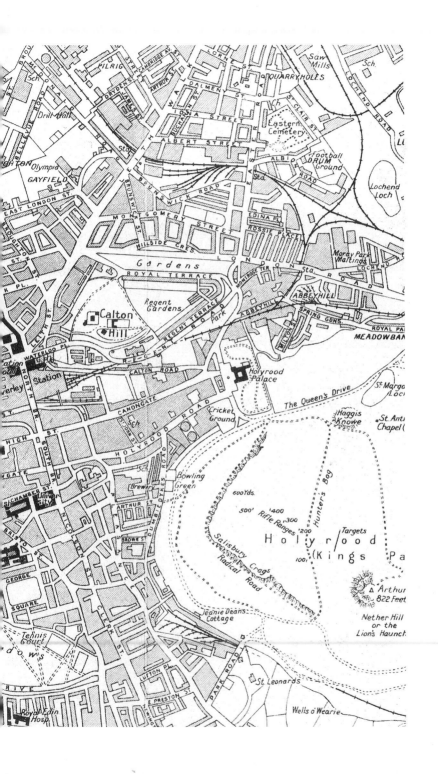

1

The Castle

WHEN AN INCREASING number of adventurous travellers began to come to Scotland in the second half of the eighteenth century (Johnson, with Boswell for company, made his celebrated journey in 1773) they invariably visited Edinburgh, and were amazed at the dramatic appearance of what we now call the Old Town, which was then the whole of Edinburgh. Thomas Pennant, distinguished naturalist and traveller, reported in 1771 that the city

> *possesses a boldness and grandeur of situation beyond any that I had ever seen. It is built on the edges and sides of a vast sloping rock, of a great and precipitous height at the upper extremity, and the sides declining very quick and steep into the plain. The view of the houses at a distance strikes the traveller with wonder; their own loftiness, improved by their almost aerial situation, gives them a look of magnificence not to be found in any other part of Great Britain. All these conspicuous buildings form the upper part of the great street (the High Street), are of stone, and make a handsome appearance; they are generally six or seven stories high in front; but by reason of the declivity of the hill, much higher backward. Every house has a common staircase, and every story is the habitation of a separate family. The castle is antient, but strong, placed on the summit of the hill, at the edge of a very deep precipice.*

Late in the eighteenth century, by which time the New Town was beginning to take shape, a sporting gentleman from Yorkshire visited the city. Thomas Thornton was making for the Spey valley, where he was to shoot almost anything that moved, but he stayed long enough to admire both the New Town and the Old:

The appearance of Edinburgh is wonderfully romantic, and must strike every traveller. On the left hand extends Princes Street, forming a most elegant vista of magnificent new buildings. To the right, rising as it were from the depth of a vast fosse, called the North Loch, stands the old city, fantastically piled on the summit of an immense rock, nearly two miles in length, and abruptly terminated by the ancient castle, which impends, in sullen grandeur, like the stronghold of some giant of romance.

Since these passages were written Edinburgh has expanded enormously. The North Loch has given place to Princes Street Gardens, and many of the old lofty tenements have disappeared. Yet the spectacle of the Castle and the Old Town on the 'vast sloping rock' and the New Town beside them remains much as it was, and 'romantic' is still the word that comes to mind.

No one knows when the **Castle Rock** was first fortified. Long before Caesar invaded Britain there may well have been a walled enclosure on the summit, with timber-framed buildings, the scene of Celtic feasts as described by the Irish bards; conventions, says Stuart Piggot, of 'swaggering, belching, touchy chieftains and their equally impossible warrior crew, hands twitching to the sword-hilt at the imagined hint of an insult ... wiping greasy moustaches that were a mark of nobility'. It seems probable that in the seventh century the British kingdom of the Gododdin (identified by the Romans as the Votadini) was centred on the rock, and that the royal hall of King Mynydogg, whose capital was called Din Eidyn, was on the rock itself. The site was used also for the halls of later Anglian chiefs. But it is not until after the death in 1093 of St Margaret, Queen of Scotland and wife of Malcolm III (who defeated and killed Macbeth) that the Castle first appears in recorded history.

As it now stands, the **Castle** is an assemblage of buildings and fortifications which date from early in the twelfth century to early in the twentieth. It is very extensive, covering almost seven acres, but it used to be much smaller; early sixteenth century drawings show that although there were at that time defences round a considerable area, the Castle buildings were confined to the higher part of the rock, towards the south-east side. Little remains of these earlier buildings, which were on a fairly modest scale. Their size was determined partly by the poverty of the country, but also by the fact that until the later fifteenth century Edinburgh had not established its position as the capital of Scotland; Perth, Stirling and Dunfermline were also important. It was James III, who came to the throne in 1460 (he was a monarch 'wondrous covetous'), who formally acknowledged Edinburgh as his capital. He also gave the Castle a new function, that of ordnance factory. This cannot have made the place any pleasanter to live in, but its importance was further enhanced. Building on a new and grander scale began with James IV (1488–1513), Scotland's renaissance king, and it was he and his successor James V (1513–1542) who established the basic outlines of the Castle's subsequent development.

To enter the Castle you must walk or drive across the esplanade. At one time this area was used as a parade ground, but when it was enlarged and given a parapet-wall and decorative railings in 1816 everyone recognised that the Castle's fighting days were over. There are several monuments here, and good views of the city, but we can leave these until after exploring the Castle itself.

You enter across a drawbridge and through a rather too tasteful gatehouse built in the 1880s. (The ditch below the drawbridge dates from the 1650s). A pair of statues in canopied niches flank the entrance arch; their date is 1929. One is of William Wallace, the other of Robert the Bruce. These are the great heroic figures of Scottish history, the leaders in Scotland's War of Independence. Wallace was captured in 1305 and taken to London, where he was hanged, drawn and quartered, and Bruce defeated the English at the Battle of Bannockburn in 1314, the most famous of all Scottish battles, and thus ensured the continuation of Scotland as an independent kingdom. In a sense, the war dragged on for another two hundred and fifty years, for the English did not abandon their ambition to control or absorb Scotland, and the Scots did not depart from the spirit of the Declaration of Arbroath, a letter sent to the Pope in 1320 which stated that 'so long as a hundred of us remain alive we will never be subject to the English'. Scottish life, even today, is unintelligible without reference to these and similar facts. In all this prolonged warfare, Edinburgh Castle played a vital part.

The road into the Castle itself curves to the right, below the sheer curving stone face of the Half Moon Battery, which seems to grow out of the rock, then past the nineteenth century guardhouse (now the Castle shop) and on to the **Portcullis Gate**. This used to be the defensive gateway into the Castle, overlooked by heavy fortifications. The lowest stage of the Portcullis Gate as it now exists was completed in 1577. It replaced a fourteenth century tower which was shot to pieces in 1573 when the Castle was held by Sir William Kirkaldy of Grange for the exiled Mary, Queen of Scots. Kirkaldy and his men were the last who fought on Mary's behalf. The siege lasted for two years, and ended only when Queen Elizabeth sent English artillery to batter down the defences. Two upper storeys were added to the Gate a few years after this, terminating in a crenellated parapet and a flat roof where guns could be positioned. Although emphatically designed to withstand attack, the gate is decorated with pilasters and hood-moulds, and above the string-course there are two absurdly small lions and a pedimented aedicule. The shield with the royal arms is a replacement, done in 1887. These sixteenth century embellishments were no doubt intended to reflect the Castle's role as an occasional royal residence. In the relatively peaceful eighteenth century the top floor was rebuilt with a pitched roof, and in the 1880s it was rebuilt again with a corbelled parapet and a stone-slabbed pitched roof in more or less medieval style.

Beyond the Portcullis Gate the road rises, with the Argyle or Six Gun Battery and the Mills Mount Battery on the right, and a low building which is now the visitors' centre, and the Governor's House ahead. Except for fortifications, this area, known as Hawk Hill, was a rocky, uneven, desolate hill-top – it is not quite the very top, which was and is occupied by the heart of the Castle – until almost the middle of the eighteenth century when the Batteries were constructed.

You are now almost four hundred feet above sea level, and there is a magnificent view over Edinburgh to the Firth of Forth, and, if the day is clear, to the hills of Fife beyond. (If the day is especially clear, you can see, fifty miles to the north-west, some of the high mountains of the Highlands). Enjoy the distant view, and then take the opportunity of a preliminary look at the New Town. What is properly called the New Town covers an area approximately one square mile in extent, now surrounded by the rest of Edinburgh. It was almost all built between 1770 and 1840. In scale and consistency of style it is unique, an astonishing feat of imaginative and artistic planning, and sustained enterprise. Later we shall see it in detail; but from the Castle one has an overall view.

To your right is the Calton Hill, with a most extraordinary assemblage of objects scattered across it. The principal of these are as follows. Farthest to the right is the Royal High School (a school no more), long, low, and Doric; the tall column is the Nelson Monument, and beyond it are the twelve columns of what was intended to be a full-scale replica of the Parthenon; to the left of these are two observatory domes and a mock-Gothic house, and a little nearer, but still on the hill, there rises a circular, colonnaded Grecian monument. It is all perfectly absurd, but wonderfully fanciful and free. Directly below you, at the foot of the 'beetling cliff', lie Princes Street Gardens and the railway line, both of them the legacy of nineteenth century improvers; there are lawns and tree-lined paths and rosebeds – extensive lawns and regiments of roses, most of them keeping as far away from the railway as they can manage; a railway alongside arcadia; and on the far side of the Gardens runs Princes Street itself, alive with vehicles and pedestrians. This is the furthest south of the three long parallel streets that comprise what proved to be the first instalment of the New Town; geometrical not fanciful. Building in this section began late in the 1760s. To the right a street leaves Princes Street and climbs up towards the Old Town. This is called the Mound (for reasons to be explained later) and where it leaves Princes Street there are two large Classical buildings which are the National Gallery of Scotland (nearer to the Old Town) and the Royal Scottish Academy (nearer to Princes Street). Looking down on them like this they do not look their best; but they are both very handsome. Finally, and unavoidably, there is the towering Gothic structure that rises two hundred feet from Princes Street Gardens on the far side of the Mound, a Victorian extravaganza, pinnacled, buttressed, and recently partially cleaned; the Scott Monument, completed in 1846. After the Castle, it is the very sign and symbol of Edinburgh.

So much, in the meantime, for the New Town; let us return to the old one. The guns on the **Argyle Battery** are six 30-pounders. They are naval guns, brought there, it is said, on the suggestion of Queen Victoria, who thought that the place looked rather bare. **Mill's Mount Battery** is reserved for the one o'clock gun, a 25-pounder fired every day of the week. It startles pedestrians in Princes Street and the local pigeons have never got used to it; they fly on the instant, in a great sweeping arc over the gardens. Below the batteries there are some angular artillery outworks that were apparently constructed in the sixteenth century and were reconstructed in the eighteenth, and below and beyond them the rock. This north face is very steep. But in 1313 a band of resolute men is supposed to have climbed up here at midnight and captured the Castle for Robert the Bruce. They were led – so the story goes – by a young man who while previously stationed in the Castle had often had recourse to this route when returning from a visit to his girl-friend in town. The 1313 assault party carried up a ladder to scale the wall, overcame the watch, took on the rest of the garrison, and (in the words of the fourteenth century poet to whom we owe the story) 'slaw of them dispitwisly'. It is a sort of David and Goliath story, but may be true nevertheless.

Forbear a visit to the tea room, which began as an eighteenth century cart shed, but pause a moment to admire the **Governor's House** on your right, built in 1742. It used to be three houses; the Governor lived in the centre, the Castle's storekeeper in one wing and the master-gunner in the other. It is quite small but excellently proportioned and very dignified, especially the central block with its pedimented porch and rusticated pilasterstrips that lead up to huge crowsteps on the gables. It shows how well a fairly simple stone-built house can look. The lime tree and the oak tree beside it – the only trees within the defences – are quite a surprise. Continue up and left and go through the seventeenth century round-arched gate called – for reasons unknown – Foog's Gate, carefully positioned so that anyone approaching it had to cross open ground which could be covered by small arms fire from the gun-loops in the adjacent wall. You are now in the upper enclosure of the Castle, and straight ahead of you is the oldest building in Edinburgh.

St Margaret's Chapel stands on the very summit of the rock. It used to be thought that in this small chapel St Margaret frequently worshipped before her death which took place in the Castle in 1093; but now we are assured that this cannot be so, and that the chapel must have been built some time in the twelfth century. It is a rectangular building not much more than thirty feet long and fifteen feet wide, with only five small windows, one wall being blank. For several hundred years it stood unregarded, joined to other buildings and at one time used as a storehouse for gunpowder. In 1845 a local antiquarian discovered that the storehouse was a medieval chapel, and restoration began. The work has been very well done, the form of the building remaining just as it was. The interior (now, alas! whitewashed) is not as simple as the exterior suggests, for there is a vaulted apse, completely concealed by the outer form of the church (as at Durham Cathedral), and a beautiful arch leading into it, decorated with zig-zag ornament. The shafts of the arch are mid-nineteenth century as is the tunnel vault of the nave. Restoration work has also had to be carried out to the base of the chapel, and the north door was renewed in 1939. The stained glass is superb. It is the work of a Scottish artist, Douglas Strachan, and the date is 1922. The five tiny windows depict, in jewel-like colours, William Wallace, Saint Andrew, Saint Columba, Saint Ninian, and Queen Margaret herself.

Although the chapel was never hers it is not unworthy of her. A grand-niece of Edward the Confessor and thus a member of the old Saxon royal family, she was born in exile in Hungary. When the Saxon monarchy was restored in 1054 she came to England with her father, to be brought up at the Confessor's court. But her father died almost at once, in mysterious circumstances, probably murdered by Harold or his supporters. Margaret remained at court, and was educated under the pious guidance of the Confessor. But when Harold became king she fled from England, intending to return to Hungary. Her plan failed, because the ship taking her to the Continent was wrecked in the Firth of Forth (some say on the coast of Northumberland, where a Scottish army was operating at the time), and she and her party were taken to Edinburgh. All seemed lost. But through this chance of fate the well-educated princess of 23 met the King of Scotland, and became his Queen. It sounds like a plot from Shakespeare.

Margaret seems to have been a remarkable woman. She has been described as 'one of those strong, interfering, pious and persistent women of whom England has successfully bred a considerable number'. Her husband looked up to her, and she exerted a strong influence in europeanizing and civilizing her adopted country. She was canonized in 1249.

From the chapel – which, by the way, is still occasionally used for weddings; on account of its small size they must be very exclusive – the road continues towards the buildings around Crown Square; these constitute the heart of the Castle. To reach them, you pass two batteries on the left, overlooking the Gatehouse and the Esplanade. These are the Forewall Battery and the cliff-like Half Moon Battery. They are massive fortifications, raised on the line of the original curtain wall.

When the Castle was smaller and simpler, it was surrounded by the curtain wall, in which were set several towers. The largest of these was the tower-house or donjon of the Castle, built by David II in the later fourteenth century, and hence known as David's Tower. This tower was partly destroyed during the siege in 1573, and it finally disappeared during the work of reconstruction which began immediately afterwards. This was when the great walled semi-circle of the **Half Moon Battery** appeared, wrapped round the remains of the two lower storeys of David's Tower. Buried inside the Battery there is still some medieval work – fourteenth century passages, walls, footings and a privy (disused), as well as a series of vaults which once served to contain the garrison's water supply. (The original well of the Castle is in the Forewall Battery; its parapet dates from 1913). The enormous curved wall of the 1573 Half Moon Battery is one of the Castle's dominant features, almost as majestic as the rock itself. It is pierced only by one sixteenth century gun-loop, and surmounted by a parapet with segment-headed gun embrasures rebuilt late in the seventeenth century.

From these gun embrasures there is a commanding view to the east. The start of the Royal Mile is seen as a narrow defile between the nearest buildings. Its further course is marked by a series of spires; the Tolbooth Church spire, dark and Gothic; the crown spire of St Giles; and the octagonal tower and short spire of the Tron. Defenders of the Castle could keep an eye on the town from the Half Moon Battery and they obviously had a wonderful field of fire. An attack on the Portcullis Gate below the Battery must have seemed suicidal. Nevertheless, the Castle was taken by Cromwell in 1650 (defence half-hearted) and again in 1689 when it was in the hands of a Roman Catholic, the Duke of Gordon, and was assailed by the Protestant forces of William III and the Glorious Revolution.

From the Half Moon Battery it is only a few yards to the entrance of Crown Square. As you approach it, the Palace is to your left and the Scottish National War Memorial to your right; the other sides of the Square are made up of the Great Hall, next to the Palace, and Queen Anne Barracks, next to the War Memorial. These are the substantial core of the Castle, all replacing earlier buildings on the same sites.

Crown Square itself is above the rock. Its surface rests on a series of vaults and sub-vaults, probably built in the late fifteenth century so as to provide as large a level area as possible in front of important buildings. **The Palace**, also raised on vaults, is on the site of the Great Chamber, built in the 1430s as a residence for the King. Its first occupant was James I, who was assassinated shortly after the Great Chamber was completed, but it was kept in use and then replaced by a larger building, probably late in the fifteenth century. The present Palace is basically this rubble-built fifteenth century building, although only a few medieval features remain. It is joined to the Great Hall by an angle building, possibly put up at much the same time.

The east face of the Palace, which rises from the rock and looks towards the Old Town, is much as it has always been, decorated only by the stumps of three fifteenth century oriel windows. The north-facing part of the Palace, which you pass on the way into Crown Square, was re-modelled in 1617 when James VI briefly returned from London and held court in the Palace block; he slept, however, at Holyrood. There is a central octagonal stair-tower, with official accommodation to the right. The distinction between the two parts is plain to see; the upper floor of the royal apartments has large mullioned and transomed windows and pediments decorated with royal emblems, whereas the official block is lower and plain. There is one blocked medieval window. On the west front facing Crown Square there is again a central stair-tower. It looks as if it only partly belongs to the building, and this is in a way true because the two upper storeys of smooth ashlar were stuck on top in the early nineteenth century in order to give the flagstaff a more exalted position. As before, the stair-tower marks off the royal lodgings, which this time are to the right, and official accommodation to the left. The stair leads to a room which seems to have been built as a vaulted strong-room and which now appropriately contains the Scottish Regalia. Further to the right the roof-line drops and the much-reconstructed medieval Palace reappears. The entrance doorway is round-arched with rusticated quoins, and above it is a cartouche with the date 1566, the year of James VI's birth, and the monogram M A H which stands for Mary, Queen of Scots, and Henry, Lord Darnley.

Going through the Palace is a must. There are several huge stone fireplaces, two of them (in the north-east ground floor rooms) possibly dating back to the fifteenth century, and there is an aumbry in the outer chamber. Other notable items are a large portrait of Charles II by Kneller and a fine study of Mary herself by Clouet. But the real attractions are the Regalia room, and **the room in which James VI was born**.

When in Edinburgh, Queen Mary usually resided at Holyrood, but in 1566 she was advised to await the birth of her first child at the old Palace in Crown Square. This was an event of great political importance. But political events in Scotland and the course of Mary's personal relationships were so interconnected that it is impossible to understand the one without at least trying to understand the other. In 1565 Mary had married Henry Darnley, who was her first cousin. He had been brought up in England, and was suspected of Roman Catholic sympathies. (Mary herself, of course, was an avowed Roman Catholic, but most of her subjects were not). To say that the marriage was imprudent and unpopular would be putting it mildly, and to make matters worse it did not take Mary long to find out that Darnley was weak, treacherous, and good for nothing. Except that he was tall and handsome, no historian has ever found a single favourable thing to

9

say about him. But he was next in succession to the throne of England only after Mary herself, and the marriage therefore strengthened Mary's always dangerous claim to succeed Queen Elizabeth. The birth of an heir, however, was doubtfully to her advantage. A prince or princess would provide the Protestant party in Scotland with a possible alternative sovereign, and would make loyalty to the Queen seem less necessary. The situation was so unstable that at this point no one could tell whether the next development would be civil war in Scotland, an uneasy peace between England and Scotland, or the Union of the Crowns. Marriage and motherhood were part of a game played by princes for very high stakes in the 1560s.

The birthplace of the future King of England, Scotland and Wales is a remarkably small ground-floor room opening off what was the Queen's bed-chamber, at the south-east corner of the Palace. This room, which is not quite rectangular, has a high medieval wooden ceiling divided into four compartments, with painted thistles at the corners of each compartment. The initials MR and IR appear in alternate compartments. The upper parts of the walls are covered with wide boards on which are painted the date of James VI's birth and a large royal coat of arms of Scotland with the following inscription:

> *Lord Jesu Chryst that Crounit was with Thornse*
> *Preserve the Birth quhais Badgie heir is borne.*
> *And send Hir Sonce Successione to Reigne still*
> *Lang in this Realme, if that it be Thy will*
> *Als Grant O Lord quhat ever of Hir proceed*
> *Be to Thy Glorie Honor and Prais sobeid.*

The panelling below the boards may be of the seventeenth century, but it was not put here until 1848. From the window there is a great commanding view to the south over long miles of hills towards England, the rock dropping directly two hundred feet to the road below. The room is perched high as an eagle's eyrie, and it seems to symbolize the perilousness of princes.

The **Crown-room**, as it used to be called, is on the first floor, guarded by a yett, or iron gate. The **regalia** – the Scottish crown, sceptre and sword of state – are not the grandest in the world, nor the oldest (although far older than those in London, which are post-Cromwell), but they must surely have the most extraordinary history. The sceptre was a gift from Pope Alexander VI to James IV in 1494; the sword of state was a gift to the same king from Pope Julius II (the patron of Raphael and Michelangelo) in 1507; the origin of the crown is uncertain, but it was remodelled for James V in 1540. One hundred years after this, for fear that the regalia would fall into the hands of Oliver Cromwell who had invaded Scotland, they were taken from Edinburgh to Dunottar Castle on the rocky north-east coast some twenty miles south of Aberdeen. Hardly had they arrived when the Cromwellians laid siege to Dunottar, so they were smuggled out of the castle by the wife [or possibly the servant] of a local minister, who buried them under the floor of his small kirk at Kinneff. In 1662, after the return to the throne of Charles II, they were brought back to Edinburgh.

But this is not the end of the story. When the final Act of Union between Scotland and England was being negotiated in 1707, the Scots became concerned that these symbols of national identity would be removed to London, so a clause was inserted in the Act declaring that the regalia would be 'kept constantly in the Castle of Edinburgh'. They were accordingly put in an oak chest and locked up in the Crown-room. Years passed. The inhabitants of Edinburgh, and Scotland, did not quite forget about them, but they partly forgot, and then they became increasingly suspicious as to their exact whereabouts – perhaps the English had taken them after all. In 1794 a search of the Crown-room was carried out, but nothing was found, because the searchers believed that they would exceed their powers if they forced the locks of an old chest, which in any case appeared to be empty. In 1818 a more thorough search was made, and the regalia were brought to light (Sir Walter Scott in attendance) 'in a state of perfect preservation'.

The crown is of gold, adorned with precious and semi-precious stones, and there are crosses and fleurs-de-lys. It is trimmed with ermine. The sceptre is of silver, double gilt, with a capital of embossed leaves on top of the stalk, and surmounted by a crystal globe and a large pearl. The sword, which is five feet long, is a fine example of Italian workmanship. The handle and pommel are silver gilt, very elaborate, and on the blade is indented in gold letter Julius II P. The scabbard is of crimson velvet. They are a remarkable treasure.

The south side of the Square (except for a small building put up in the 1540s and since altered) is occupied by the **Great Hall**. The Hall, like the Palace, rests on a series of vaults built above the steeply sloping rock. This is the last of many halls that must have been built in the Castle; they were an indispensable feature of medieval life, used for all sorts of purposes from everyday eating and drinking to masques and other displays. No one knows when this hall was built. It may have been by James IV, who died at Flodden (a disastrous battle with English forces fought in 1513), and whose monogram IR4 is on one of the corbels that support the roof. On the other hand, the Renaissance character of the architectural ornament here and there makes so early a date seem unlikely, and some scholars prefer a date around 1540. It has even been suggested that James V modernised a hall built by James IV, inserting the IR4 monogram in recognition of his father's work; or that he took down the roof built by his father and re-erected it on raised walls – there is some evidence which would support this idea. The fact is, that it is all too difficult, too much like deciding who really wrote *Henry VIII* or who was the dark lady of the sonnets. All we know for certain is that the Great Hall was standing before 1550, and that it has had a rough history. In 1650 it became a barracks. In 1737 it was extensively subdivided. In 1799 it was turned into a military hospital. It had to be rescued, and rescuing was the work of Hippolyte J Blanc in 1887–1891. As a result, it is now scarcely possible to be sure what the appearance of the Hall was in the sixteenth century.

It is a fine building nonetheless. The four windows facing the Square are larger than the originals and the parapet has been changed. The wide door in the centre, now blocked up, seems to have been the original entrance, but now there is a smaller Gothic door at the west end. These are significant but not overwhelming changes. The Hall must always have looked handsome in an unostentatious way. And it has probably always looked like a Renaissance rather than a Gothic building. Internally it is not so convincing. The hammerbeam roof is its glory, but has been altered, both by cutting away some timbers and adding some new ones. The effect is rather fussy, and this is made worse by the use of relatively thin square-sectioned timbers; one critic has gone so far as to say that the roof now possesses 'more than a passing resemblance to a matchstick model'. The large hooded fire-place in the east wall is a nineteenth century copy of a fifteenth century original, while the screen at the west end and the elaborately carved panelling are likewise Blanc introductions, based on Late Gothic work to be found elsewhere in Scotland.

There is a good display of weaponry; armour and lances, swords and pistols, and numerous small eighteenth century bronze trench mortars, still in their original wooden mounts. There is also an exceptionally well-preserved 1676 cannon made in Holland for Charles II.

The Castle

Leaving the Great Hall, the building on your left is the Queen Anne Barracks, which now houses the **Royal Scots Museum**. At one time there would have been kitchens here to serve the Great Hall. In 1708 the site was selected for an officers' barracks and the present building was erected. It consists of two parallel ranges with a very narrow space between them. The range to the rear, like much else in this part of the Castle, is supported on medieval vaults.

From an architectural point of view, almost nothing about the Museum deserves comment; the fenestration has been messed about and the interior has been gutted. The contents of the Museum illustrate the history of the Royal Scots. The Regiment was begun by Sir John Hepburn of Athelstaneford (*see* p. 276) in 1633. At first it fought for Louis XIII, but since these early days it has taken part in British campaigns all over the world. The history of the Regiment is illustrated by drawings, photographs, uniforms, medals and weapons of all kinds.

The vaults, entered from the rear of the Museum building, should not be missed. They are a labyrinth of large and not so large, lofty stone vaulted spaces, on two levels, with stone stairs, most of them now closed off, ascending or descending mysteriously through the immense thicknesses of the walls. The whole place has a medieval, almost a primeval air. Nowhere else in the Castle do you feel so strongly that you are in a powerful fortification belonging to a long past age.

In one of these vaulted spaces stands Mons Meg, a siege-gun of the fifteenth century. Few such guns are still in existence. This one was made in the 1440s, at Mons in Belgium, and was presented to James II in 1457. It is a massive contrivance, about fifteen feet long, hand-made. When supplied with enough gunpowder, and enough luck, it could project a stone ball nineteen inches in diameter for a distance of over a mile. Mons Meg is known to have gone to war once, in 1497. She was hauled fifty miles south to the Tweed (it must have been a herculean task) and fired at the walls of Norham Castle, causing considerable damage. In 1680 this very dangerous bombard exploded when firing a salute. It was later taken to the Tower of London, and returned to Edinburgh in 1829.

Next comes the **Scottish National War Memorial**, opened by the Prince of Wales in 1927. It stands on the site of a barracks built in 1755, which made use of the masonry of a medieval church previously on the same site; a good part of the present building is in fact the rubble masonry of the barracks. The architect, Sir Robert Lorimer,

13

retained the length of the 1755 building, and also the wings projecting to the Square; he then added a much more elaborate central entrance which leads straight across the long Hall to a semi-octagonal apse built out on the north side. The style is strong Gothic, and all the ornamentation, inside and out, is part of Lorimer's design.

Discussing this building is not easy. We live today in a secular age in a non-elegiac mood, whereas there was something of a pious war memorial cult in the early 1920s. People were very emotional about the war, much more so than they were about the 1939–45 war when that holocaust ended. Perhaps the difference stems partly from the fact that whereas the civilian population was directly involved in hostilities from 1940 to 1945, death and destruction from 1914 to 1918 took place somewhere else, and non-combatants felt shamefully safe. However that may be, there was a perfect rush to build war memorials after 1918. This is not to say that respect and honour for the dead were not sincerely felt. But a change in attitude makes it difficult for us, in the twenty-first century, to approach a 1920s war memorial in the spirit that once would have been expected. How do we respond, and why? Let us first see what there is in this case to respond to.

The exterior is far from plain. Facing Crown Square, there are broad canopied niches in the wings, each cradling a small statue. This device is repeated at the rear. All arches are heavily segmented, including the cavernous arch above the porch, which contains a very large statue. A semi-circular flight of steps leads to the porch, which is flanked by a lion and a unicorn, both of which look as if they had strayed in from a different, smoother world. At the rear, the apse is strongly vertical, with tall buttresses. (This must be one of the few buildings which looks as well from the back as from the front). The statues are all abstractions. The very large one above the porch represents the Survival of the Spirit, and others represent Peace, Mercy, Justice, Freedom, Truth and so on. The interior consists of the transverse tunnel-vaulted Hall of Valour, the two wings which are to be regarded as chapels, and the Shrine directly across the Hall from the porch. The Hall, divided into nine bays by octagonal piers, contains regimental memorials in various forms, stone or bronze, and pale stained glass windows. The chapels are similar. The Shrine, entered through wrought-iron gates, is elaborately vaulted, and from the central boss there hangs a huge painted wooden figure of St Michael. Below this figure is a granite altar, upon which rests a steel casket containing the Rolls of Honour, with the names of all Scots men and women killed in the 1914–1918 war. The windows are stained glass, in sombre colours, and the floor is of Ailsa Craig granite. Natural rock rises through the floor, and the altar rests upon it. What do we feel about all this? We cannot feel what the people of the 1920s felt, for several reasons. They thought that they were commemorating the war that ended war, sacrifices heroic, terrible, but infinitely worth while; whereas we know that it was only stage one in a vast disaster. And they believed that a great victory had been won, paving the way to a better world. We, alas! know too much about the military mistakes that led to needless slaughter, and the disappointments of the post-war years. And they, more than we, were Christian people, for whom suggestions of the Resurrection and salvation were easy to accept. No wonder this building is so hard to judge! And yet we must respond to it. It is not trivial; that is one of its virtues. There are some beautiful and moving things in it. The stained glass windows by Douglas Strachan; some of the bronze reliefs – nurses with a stretcher party, or in the shrine the seemingly endless procession of combatants of all ranks. Perhaps it is the overwhelmingness of it all. It is so archaic and so elaborate, so – dare one say? – rhetorical. For many people there is as much feeling in a well-designed village war memorial, and far more mystery in Queen Margaret's chapel. One remembers the comment about Tennyson's 'In Memoriam'; when he should have been broken-hearted he had many reminiscences. The War Memorial is an admirable, even a noble effort; but it is not a building for all tastes. And perhaps we should let it go at that.

Now leave Crown Square and retrace your steps through Foog's Gate. Ahead of you is the gable end of the Military Prison, and on your right the very large New Barracks. **The Military Prison** was built in 1842, the forestair and the top floor being added in 1880. The place was designed with the happy thought of providing solitary confinement for everyone, and has been described as 'a gem of an early Victorian prison'. There are cells on two levels, arranged round a central open space, with a central stair leading to the cast-iron gallery which runs round the upper level. No one could call it a building of elegance or charm, but the internal iron-work and the round-arched window at gallery level give it undeniable architectural quality.

Of the **New Barracks** little good can be said. Regimented and dreary, this enormous block of building was put up in the 1790s. The barracks have served a useful military purpose for almost two hundred years, but have had few if any admirers. 'Look at the west side of the Castle and shudder,' wrote Lord Cockburn. (The barracks look their worst from the west); and Sir Walter Scott compared them to a cotton mill. Nineteenth century improvers were keen to knock them down and do better, according to the superior ideas of an over-confident age; one plan was to replace them with something that looked like a French chateau, and another idea was to use the site for a memorial to Prince Albert. Neither scheme came to anything, which is just as well. At least the barracks prevent the Castle from being purely an historic monument.

This west end of the rock is less steep than the north and south faces, and defences were therefore built along it. They can be seen from Old Back Parade, behind the barracks, and from nearby Butt's Battery. There are pepper-pot sentry boxes at the corners, and martial-looking garderobes. It has been suggested that these add a touch of romance; and if a garderobe can be romantic, perhaps they do.

The final building worth noticing in the Castle is the **Hospital**. It is rather a fraud, with a two-hundred year history. It originated as a powder magazine, built in 1748 to replace an earlier seventeenth century powder magazine. This second version at least had the distinction of having been built (although not designed) by John Adam. It was extended in 1753 so as to form a courtyard, but the result was not inspiring and in the 1890s, when the urge to 'improve' and romanticize the Castle was at its height, the authorities resolved to reconstruct the entire building as a baronialized military hospital. The magazine was demolished, and the north block was heightened and given tall pedimented windows, a corbelled parapet and crowsteps. The originally arcaded ground floor and the first floor were less altered. The overall effect is sort-of-early seventeenth century, an obvious mongrel, not uninteresting. It is instructive to compare it with the severe, consistently Classical Governor's House.

You may leave the Castle either by the way you came in or down the steep winding flight of steps known as the Lang Stairs. During the Middle Ages this was the normal route to and from all the important castle buildings. It passes along the upper storeys of the Portcullis Gate. Go through the Gatehouse (taking a peep into the dry ditch across the east front which was completed in 1742) and step onto the **Esplanade**. This began to be used as the parade ground in 1753, when the rocky slope was first levelled and made smooth – a sure sign that the Castle was becoming more ornamental than military. There are extensive views to the south and the south-east. The high dome of the University in front of Arthur's Seat and the shallow dome of the Usher Hall are easily picked out, and there is an unimpeded view of the entrance front of George Heriot's School, splendidly and genuinely Jacobean.

The Esplanade has been the scene of the Tattoo since the Edinburgh Festival began in 1947. Every August tiers of wooden seats supported on vast tubular scaffoldings arise to overlook the Esplanade, and guns, bands, bagpipes and uniformed men (and women) bring martial sounds and excitement to the scene. Eight thousand people climb nightly to their aerial balcony seats (don't forget your rug and cushion) to witness this military extravaganza. Fully floodlit, the Castle is a more spectacular backdrop than was ever contrived for Wagner. The emotional impact of the Massed Pipes and Drums, flooding onto the Esplanade from the Gatehouse like coloured silk handkerchiefs from a conjuror's sleeve, wave after wave of them, finally creating a sea of different tartans and filling the night with the alarming, thrilling sounds of Celtic music, is irresistible. And when joined by the Massed Military Bands the scene, the sound and the setting are heroic. It is a tournament at full tilt – or, as someone said, at full kilt. All ends with the Last Post, only a solitary piper to be seen, high on the battlements, as the Castle illuminations gradually dim to darkness.

At other more prosaic times of the year, when the Esplanade is half-deserted, only the monuments (besides the view) are to be noticed. The first of these, to the 78th Highland Regiment, appeared in 1861, a Celtic cross with an elephant in low relief at the base; and the last, to Ensign Ewart of the Royal North British Dragoons (now the Scots Greys), who seized the standard of the French 45th Regiment at Waterloo, was erected in 1938. Perhaps the best, and certainly the best-known, is an equestrian bronze statue of Earl Haig, British Commander in Chief from 1915 to the end of the war three years later. He was born in Edinburgh and buried near his home on the Tweed. He is now, alas, something of a fallen idol. The statue was erected in 1923.

Seen thus at close quarters, the Castle is a curious mixture of military and domestic, utilitarian and romantic, old and pseudo-old. Seen from a distance, it looks marvellously picturesque; and at night, floodlit, it hangs in the air, complete and enormous, as if part of another and far more romantic world. But in its day – and its day was a long one – it was a formidable fortress. To see it as it was, think away the Gatehouse and everything else in front of the Portcullis

Gate, and in your imagination transform the smooth esplanade into a rough hillslope. Think away also the whole surrounding town except the High Street and the houses clustered along it. Then turn down a flight of steps on the side opposite the monuments and walk a little way down the street there (Johnston Terrace). Looking up, you see rough almost vertical rock, the enormous rounded front of the Half Moon Battery, and the Palace and the Hall, far overhead, facing out to the distant hills. Surely, one exclaims, this fortress was never taken! But it was, a few times; some have been mentioned. Successful defence, however, was more common. In 1400 the weather helped. Henry IV appeared before the Castle with a numerous and well-appointed army and laid siege to it; but, says the chronicler, 'cold and rain, and absolute dearth of provisions' (in August!) compelled him to depart unrewarded. The last attempt to coerce the Castle (it could hardly be called a siege) was in 1745, when Prince Charles Edward seized control of the town and called upon the Castle to surrender. But the response consisted mostly of cannon and musket fire, and there was really no contest. (The Governor of the Castle at the time was General Guest, who was not very well and eighty-two. But he proved to be perfectly capable of looking after George II's interests).

The Castle likewise held firm during the most terrible of all the English invasions of Scotland, that by the Earl of Hertford in 1544. The *casus belli* was Scotland's repudiation of an agreement to marry the infant Queen Mary to Henry VIII's son and heir, Prince Edward. This arrangement would have secured Scottish neutrality when Henry invaded France. Instead, war between England and Scotland once again broke out, and Henry's orders to his northern commander were of a savagery surprising even in so cruel and bloated a tyrant as Henry had become. Hertford was instructed

> *to sack Leith and burn and subvert it and all the rest, putting man woman and child to fire and sword without exception ... and extend the like extremities and destruction in all towns and villages whereunto ye may reach conveniently ...*

Hertford was aghast; he 'could not sleep this night,' he recorded, 'for thinking of the King's determination for Leith'. Nevertheless, he and his mercenaries carried out their orders. Mary was whisked out of the way to safety, but Leith and Edinburgh were sacked and burned, as were many of the Border abbeys and villages. The destruction was appalling, nowhere worse than in Edinburgh. This is why the Old

The Castle

Town is not a medieval city, except in its plan; no building now standing there, except the ruined abbey, existed before 1544. Only the rock, and Queen Margaret's chapel, unaltered over the centuries, have looked down upon it all.

2

The Royal Mile: I

THE **ROYAL MILE** is the spine of the Old Town, the thorough-fare and great processional way of Old Edinburgh; kings and queens have passed along it since the twelfth century. It follows the ridge of a hill, not quite straight in its descent from the Castle at the top to the gates of Holyrood Palace almost exactly one mile further east. The Royal Mile begins as Castle Hill, becomes the Lawnmarket, then the High Street, and finally the Canongate (street of the canons). Many narrow lanes and alleys, in Edinburgh called wynds and closes, branch off to right and left, down the sides of the hill. Before Nash built Regent Street and Haussmann drove his boulevards through Paris, the High Street was often referred to, and not only by Scotsmen, as a very grand street, 'perhaps ... not equalled in grandeur by any street in Europe'. Its grandeur was felt to reside in its length and its width – and it is very wide, remarkably wide for a medieval street; by contrast, Castlehill and the Canongate are fairly narrow. The High Street was also deemed imposing because of the astonishing height of many of the houses, built eight or even nine storeys up from the lower slopes of the ridge. This style of building arose from the fact that for many centuries Edinburgh was a walled town, offering some security in a country where warfare was endemic. But space within the walls was limited, so houses were built high and for several hundred years people of all ranks lived closely packed together; Defoe believed 'that in no City in the World so many people live in so little Room as at Edinburgh'. This concentration of people has left a superb assemblage of old buildings, although with some rather awful modern additions and repairs. There are sixteenth and seventeenth century houses built for nobles who attended the court, for merchants who traded inland and overseas (mostly to France and the Low Countries), for lairds, lawyers and divines. There are lofty tenements of the seventeenth century which by the nineteenth had become some of the most appalling slums on earth. There are wynds and closes worn and stained by dark deeds and dark days. There is a cathedral (a presbyterian cathedral!) dating from the Middle Ages, a Parliament House now used by the lawyers, and a sequence of approximately twenty pubs, including the World's End, which was once the last tavern in the High Street before the traveller passed through the city gates into the unsafe countryside. To walk down the Royal Mile (walking up is harder) is a remarkable experience, for there are nine centuries of history between the Castle and Holyroodhouse.

To leave the Castle and enter the Royal Mile is to find less contrast than might be expected, partly because the Old Town, like the Castle itself, and the New Town as well, are all built of stone; brick was not much used in Scotland until the twentieth century, and wood was for many centuries scarce and dear. So Edinburgh is a sandstone city. The quarries are all worked out now, but in the nineteenth century there were still several within the city bounds, perhaps the most famous of them at Craigleith, near the Queensferry Road. Other sandstones were imported from Fife, and yet others, later in the nineteenth century, from Northumberland. Colours varied, but over many years they have all been subdued to a solemn, crepuscular hue, a stern but pleasing uniformity; lately, however, this uniformity of appearance has been somewhat reduced by cleaning, and several wayward shades of fawn and pink have emerged to startle the pigeons and the passers-by. These novelties are not to be confused with the red colour of the sandstone brought from Dumfriesshire and used in a few places. Likewise the roofs, or at any rate those built before 1900, are consistently slate, most of it transported by sea from quarries near Oban, on the west coast north of Glasgow. The twentieth century suburbs and housing estates, admittedly, are like suburbs and housing estates everywhere else. But the rest of the city, seen from afar, is all stone, a re-ordering of local nature, not a thing imposed. Trees and open spaces are scattered about this hilly town, and spires and glistening roofs relieve the predominant stoney greyness.

In view of all this, the Royal Mile begins rather strangely. Leaving the Castle Esplanade, you see immediately on your left a very singular building, **Ramsay Garden**, red-roofed and half-timbered and quite unlike any other building in the vicinity. It is a rambling five-storey block of flats which was completed in 1894 and has been variously described as outrageous, absurd, ultra-picturesque, folksy and Flemish. The projector was Patrick Geddes, who was a botanist, a sociologist, a town planner and above all a crank. He dreamed that he might guide mankind along the right evolutionary road by a socio-biological-environmental approach, otherwise known as 'orthogenic evolution'. He first put his ideas, such as they were, into practice by trying to bring respectability back to the then seriously dilapidated Royal Mile. This was where Hume and Adam Smith and other great thinkers of the eighteenth century had lived, and Geddes had some hopes that the 'Golden Age' might come again if the right people could be attracted to the ancient wynds and closes. For a time he went to live in a slum tenement himself, with his wife and child. As a result of his efforts the tenements improved but the inhabitants did not, so the next step was the building of Ramsay Garden in order to bring back professional people to the area. It is his greatest success. Geddes made no significant contributions to either science or town-planning, but it was he who began the reclamation of the Royal Mile, and it was *via* Ramsay Garden that the Old Town renewed its connections with the cultural and intellectual life of Edinburgh. The style of Ramsay Garden is eccentric to the point of perversity; but it proves something: it proves that a building need not resemble its neighbours in order to 'fit in'. Despite its red tiles and red sandstone, its half-timbering and fancy iron-work and clamorously Scottish detail Ramsay Garden is an accepted, even a valued part of the Edinburgh scene. It fits in because it is different. And if it seems to be a little like Disneyland before Disney, we may remind ourselves that it is, after all, 'genuine' in part, for it incorporates Ramsay Lodge, built around 1740 by the poet Allan Ramsay for his own use. The Lodge, which is on the north side of the complex, looks directly down on the poet's statue at the foot of the Mound.

On the opposite side of the street (here called Castlehill) another rather odd building faces the Esplanade. This is **Cannonball House**. The building is old – the date 1630 on the south wing refers to the wing itself which was an extension to the main part of the house – and has been a good deal altered. It would attract no more attention than a hundred other buildings in the neighbourhood were it not for the cannonball (far from obvious) in the west gable. How did it get there? Was it inserted by a Victorian promoter of tourism? or was it – as some fondly believe – fired from the Half Moon Battery in 1745, when Prince Charles occupied the city but the Castle held out for George II? We shall never know. Whatever its history, it serves the cause of tourism today.

A few yards further down, on the opposite side of the street is the **Outlook Tower** or **Camera Obscura**. The building itself dates from the early seventeenth century but has been much altered. Its use for a camera obscura began in 1853, when the original device was installed, surprisingly, by a woman, Maria Theresa Short; almost equally surprising, she is described as an Edinburgh optician. In this technological age there is nothing very wonderful about a camera obscura, except that it is wonderfully simple. Not many remain in public use. The present instrument was installed by Geddes, who bought the building in 1892, intending to establish 'the world's first sociological laboratory, nucleus of the University of the Future for all neo-technic thinking' etc. etc. These were mere dreams. Only the peep-show survives, providing at least one view which cannot be seen in any other way – a close-up of the Gothic detail on the 240 foot high steeple of the nearby Tolbooth Church.

The **Tolbooth Church** (1839–44), which has also been known as the Victoria Hall and as Highland Tolbooth St John's and is now called **The Hub**, has always made a notable contribution to Edinburgh's famous skyline; recent changes have turned it into one of the city's most remarkable buildings. It was designed by James Gillespie Graham, a local architect who built much in Edinburgh, usually on a large scale, and A.W.N. Pugin, the apostle of the Gothic Revival and author of *The True Principles of Christian Architecture*. As would be expected from Pugin, the whole building is richly and correctly detailed in the style of the early fourteenth century. The internal arrangements were most unusual. It was planned to be used both as a local church and as a meeting place for the General (i.e. national) Assembly of the Church of Scotland – a very large gathering of ministers of the Kirk. This is why it was built to very high standards, and was provided – exceptionally for a church – with two floors, a ground floor divided into committee rooms for the Assembly, and an upper floor which could be used by the local congregation but was sufficiently large and sufficiently grand to meet the greater and grander needs of the Assembly.

All went well for many years, but nothing lasts for ever. Use by the Assembly ended in 1929, and by congregations a few decades later. Time had by now blackened the exterior, diminishing the effect of the hoodmoulds, the pinnacles, the gablets, the crocketing, and the other high-class Gothic ornamentation with which Pugin had endowed it. The church fell into disuse, and by 1980 was approaching a state of dereliction. It looked, and was, dark, dismal, decaying – and locked up.

Then someone had an idea. Why not turn the old place into a public venue for artistic activity as well as an administrative headquarters for the Festival itself? Why not make it Edinburgh's Festival

Centre, complete with ticket office, (there are others in town), specialist CD and book shop, café, and information counter and allow it to be used for wedding receptions and other jollies? Why not spend a little money to employ genuine artists and craftsmen – as they did in the 1840s – to convert the Gothic Revival masterpiece into 'a building for people' – as it originally was – 'and a glorious celebration of the creativity and fun of Edinburgh's festivals'? Renovation began in the later 1990s, and in 1999 The Hub was officially opened by the Queen.

Leave behind the coal-black exterior and enter the outer vestibule (there are two) beneath a stone rib-vault. Ahead stretches the original barrel-vaulted stone corridor, now flanked by yellow walls and a double track of cast and polished glass, soft green, lit from below. The café is on your left, golden yellow with handsome Gothic windows and multi-coloured terrazzo panelling to dado level. At the end of the corridor you reach the stair-hall, and before you rises the original imperial stair with its ornate cast-iron balustrades. The stair-hall is boldly red with a blue ceiling, and is enlivened by 150 small tableaux of slightly strange (and carefully lit) figures; there are dancers, singers, musicians with their instruments of many kinds; a few outlandish other-wordly creatures; other figures close to the flat-ribbed stone ceiling survey the scene. Even this scarcely prepares you for the main hall. It is very large – over 350 square metres, sufficient for 250 people to sit down to dinner – roofed by a single span of flat-arched rib-vaulting ten metres above the floor. The floor is unstained wood, the roof is painted blue with the ribs picked out in red, yellow, blue and green. All around there is much carved wood and panelling; at the east end a tall and intricately carved pulpit with a lofty spire, at the west end an intricately carved screen by Pugin and Gillespie Graham. A gallery circles the hall. Below the gallery the walls are generously hung with a striking woollen fabric which has a blue background which supports a geometric scheme of triangles in red, gold, blue and green, matching the ceiling.

No words can do this interior justice. It banishes gloom and defies mediocrity. It is all song and sunshine. The whole place cries out to be made use of and enjoyed. It proves that there is life in old Edinburgh yet. And it is a standing reproach to all those – and they are many – who believe that the right thing to do with an old building is to return it, as near as possible, to what it is supposed to have looked like one, two, three or half a dozen hundred years ago. That is the dead hand of conservation. This is life.

Leaving the erstwhile church, there is a fine prospect looking down the hill towards Holyrood: a façade of tall eighteenth century tenements on the south side with crowstepped gables, St Giles cathedral further down, John Knox's house beyond it on the north side (these two are the most visited buildings in the Royal Mile) and in the distance – if the day is good – the blue waters of the Firth of Forth, over five miles away. This possibility of looking from the centre of the city to the distant sea or countryside, which recurs in several places, is one of Edinburgh's most delightful features.

You have now left Castlehill and are in the **Lawnmarket**, which used to be the Landmarket, the place where the landward or country people set out their produce on market days. This is the Royal Mile at its widest, and here it was once most fashionable to live. The last great housing scheme in the Old Town before Princes Street and the New Town were begun in the later eighteenth century is here, on the north side of the Lawnmarket. In 1690, Robert Mylne, master mason to Charles II, James II, William and Mary, and Queen Anne, demolished several narrow closes in order to create a new kind of development, a relatively spacious courtyard enclosed by tall tenements: **Milne's Court**. Two of Mylne's tenements remain, the taller of them, six storeys plus an attic floor, facing the Lawnmarket. The Court is not large, the fenestrations are regular, and the buildings are rather plain. They were deemed very grand in their day, but what is now chiefly remarkable is that they have been turned into halls of residence for Edinburgh University. Private money helped to save and convert them in the 1960s (much of the internal planning in both tenements has been retained) and they must be two of the most characterful halls of residence in Europe, with marvellous views from many upper windows.

Next door to Milne's Court is **James Court**, built in the 1720s. Its layout is genuinely spacious, with a few small rowan trees (called mountain ash in England) looking very young and somehow out of place in these ancient surroundings. Were there trees here in the eighteenth century? It is very unlikely. The double tenement on the north side, which is five storeys high facing the court, is higher than it looks, for it has no less than eight storeys and an attic floor facing Princes Street; even the nineteenth century wrote of it as 'that vast pile of tall houses'. Boswell once lived in James Court, and it was here that he entertained Dr Johnson, for whom Mrs Boswell conceived a strong and immediate dislike. Another resident in the 1760s was David Hume, historian and philosopher of genius, who described his 'house' (i.e. flat) as 'very cheerful and very elegant, but too small to display my great talent for cookery, the science to which I intend to addict the remaining years of my life'. The buildings in James Court have unfortunately been much altered, and the 'houses' once occupied by Boswell and Hume have disappeared. But something of the dignity and the elegance remains.

One building, however, which backs onto James Court is still much as it was a hundred years before Boswell was born. This is **Gladstone's Land**, named after Thomas Gladstone (or Gledstane) who bought the property in 1617. Seen from the street, Gladstone's Land ('land' meaning a tenement or block of flats) is a tall narrow building with two unequal arches at ground-floor level and a forestair rising from the pavement, four upper floors, and an unequal pair of attic gables. It stands out from its neighbours, chiefly on account of the arches. But in Gladstone's day it was much more a typical Edinburgh tenement, for arcading along the High Street used to be common. It was a good practical arrangement, because stalls were set up within the arcades, receiving protection from the weather, and this facilitated both trade and gossip. Before the seventeenth century most Edinburgh arcades were of wood, and the fronts of houses were often faced with wooden galleries, possibly on several floors. If Gladstone's house was like this when he bought it, as seems most likely, he removed the timbering and extended his house forward into the Lawnmarket. (So, in the course of time, did everyone else). The two stone arches and forestair and the whole front of the house were built between 1617 and 1620, giving a new front room on every floor, and a new facade to a basically sixteenth century building.

This much enlarged house was a valuable property, for Gladstone could and did let the several floors as self-contained flats. He himself probably lived on the third floor, where the ceiling is decorated with a *gled* or hawk. The first floor seems at one time to have been rented by a knight with the splendidly Scottish name and title of Sir James Creichton of Fiendraucht, and another floor was occupied by a merchant who traded from the booths on the ground floor and from a little ramshackle lean-to shop somewhere near the forestair. A minister of the Kirk lived on another floor, while the attics and the cellars were reserved, as was usually the case, for poorer folk.

In the course of time Gladstone's Land, like much other property in the High Street, became a slum and was condemned. It was rescued by a private citizen in 1934, in the nick of time, and restoration began. In 1978 it was acquired by the National Trust for Scotland, and it is now open to visitors, furnished as a high-class seventeenth century town house. Although the rooms are rather dark by modern standards, it is a most attractive property. The cloth merchant's booth, which now serves as an entrance, is conjectural but convincing, and the inner hall is a marvellous space of unexpected angles and openings, not at all cramped; the window here, like those on the floor above, is a reproduction of the original, having fixed leaded glass above and double wooden shutters below, the usual arrangement in Gladstone's day. A sixteenth century turnpike stair at the rear, which gives access to all the flats, leads to the 'little chamber' on the first floor, furnished with late seventeenth century pieces, and to a flagged kitchen, which boasts a huge seventeenth century grate. There is also a neat fold-away wall-bed, which proves that space-saving devices are nothing new.

The front room on this floor, the 'painted chamber', is delightful. It is part of Gladstone's extension, for the wall opposite the windows is the original front wall of the house. The pair of doors in this wall must originally have given access to a wooden gallery, and it is these twin doors, plus the decoration on walls and ceiling, which give the room its outstanding character and charm. Above the doors there is a painted frieze of vases of flowers in an arcade of coupled pilasters; this frieze has been continued recently on the west wall; and the beamed ceiling is generously decorated with coloured designs of fruit, flowers, birds and arabesques. The huge bed by the fireplace was made in Aberdeen early in the seventeenth century, and the massive cupboard opposite the fireplace probably came from Holland. These items tend, in one way, to spoil the room, making it seem smaller than it really is. But at the same time they help to show that the seventeenth century, even the early seventeenth century, was not all plain fare and discomfort for prosperous citizens. Here is a house of informality and ease, artistic in a robust sort of way, masculine and reassuring. The pictures on the walls are all Dutch; they include a Ruisdael, two winter scenes by Molenaer, and a very fine moonlit river scene by Van de Neer.

From Gladstone's Land down to the first traffic artery which cuts across the Royal Mile, coming up from Princes Street, there are numerous old closes and tall, gabled tenements of the seventeenth century and eighteenth century. Until the 1770s or 1790s this neighbourhood was where most of Edinburgh's prosperous and distinguished citizens chose to live. There were the lawyers, working in the refined judicial system of Scots law; in the eighteenth century many of the pioneers of modern medicine; writers and philosophers who welcomed Dr Johnson and later Burns into clubs and coteries of European reputation. A gay and cultured society lived in those days in the tall lands and narrow closes. The mode of living for almost everyone was very communal. The well-to-do family occupied the same tenement, with its narrow dark entrance and gloomy stone stair, as caddies – water-carriers – and kailwives (it might be) on the ground floor, tradesmen and lawyers' clerks further up, then lawyers and 'bonnet lairds' and persons of title in the fresher air still further up, and in the attics (less convenient and might leak) possibly a dancing-master and a repairer of old furniture. Everyone rubbed shoulders with everyone else. Birth and death, family rows, every variation of fortune would be known at once to the entire stair, and then to the entire street. Privacy is a modern invention. Places that seem to us very un-private and therefore very 'downmarket' were home to generations of the great, the wealthy and the fastidious.

Boswell and Hume have already been mentioned as residents, and a long list of other distinguished and respectable persons could easily be drawn up. The town house of the Duke of Buccleuch, grandson of the Duke of Monmouth, was to be found in Fisher's Close in the 1730s. The Earl of Louden lived in Gosford's Close (now demolished) in the 1770s, as did the son and daughters of the Marquis of Tweeddale. In 1783 the Misses Preston kept a boarding school for young ladies in nearby Liberton Wynd, advising parents that their daughters would be well cared for: 'the greatest attention will be paid to their morals, behaviour, and every branch of education'. Most of these dwellings have been very much knocked about – over-enthusiastically 'restored' or 'given the Geddes picturesque treatment' (Geddes's activities in the Royal Mile were not confined to Ramsay Garden and the Outlook Tower), and not a few have been demolished. Many now contain shops on the ground floor, selling woollen and other goods, and these are often well worth a visit.

Only one building stands out from the rest, well advertised; this is **Lady Stair's House**. It is not visible from the Lawnmarket but is set back a little, in Lady Stair's Close. It was built in 1622, and 'restored' in the 1890s, when a great deal round about it was demolished. Scraps of the old house remain. Lady Stair was a great lady of the days of Queen Anne, and later. She experienced two tempestuous marriages, the first to Viscount Primrose, who fortunately for her died in 1706, when she was still a young woman, and the second to the Earl of

Stair, General of the Marines, Governor of Minorca, Colonel of the Greys and Knight of the Thistle, who drank. The Countess, however, seems to have been well able to look after herself. She was given to occasional 'ebullitions of temper', and sometimes used language which even today would raise eyebrows in what is left of polite society. The house has been unsparingly restored, and its interior chills the imagination. It is now a rather dreary museum containing mementoes of Sir Walter Scott and Robert Burns. The latter, during his visit to Edinburgh in the winter of 1786–7, lived for a time in a nearby close, now destroyed, paying eighteen pence a week for his accommodation.

Two other closes deserve a mention. There are interiors in **Riddle's Court**, at the south end of Riddle's Close, which recall mercantile high life three hundred years ago or more. And **Brodie's Close** is worth a visit, described by one authority as the most atmospheric of Edinburgh closes. It is connected with a curious piece of history, for this close was renamed late in the eighteenth century in memory of Deacon Brodie (his name has also been adopted by a pub next to Lady Stair's Close) who was a prominent merchant in Edinburgh in the days of George III and a respected member of the Town Council. For reasons that are not clear he took to burglary in his spare time, and in the winter of 1787 terrorised the citizens whose peace and prosperity were supposed to be his especial concern. After many audacious and successful robberies he and three other men broke into the Excise Office, but were disturbed; and soon after this Brodie was betrayed by one of his accomplices. He fled to Ostend and then to Amsterdam, where he was arrested by the King's Messenger for Scotland on the eve of sailing to America. He was brought back to Edinburgh and hanged in the Lawnmarket in the autumn of 1788. His activities and sudden end aroused intense and enduring interest. Robert Louis Stevenson wrote a play about him, and Edinburgh still seems inclined to be proud of his memory.

Crossing the top of the Mound from Deacon Brodie's Tavern (here the last public hanging in Edinburgh took place in 1864) one's attention is immediately caught by the west front and famous crown of St Giles. **St Giles** is one of the most complex, and in part one of the oldest buildings in Edinburgh, and it stands in what may fairly be called the most historic part of the city. This is the very centre of old Edinburgh, the Heart of Midlothian, where the Royal Mile 'expands to a noble width, and the buildings rise to a great height'. Until Victorian order and a measure of Victorian sobriety descended upon it, this was always a scene of noise and bustle, 'clanging with the voices of óyster-women and the bells of piemen'. When darkness fell it must have been spectacular, for 'the extraordinary height of the houses was marked by lights which, glimmering irregularly along their front, ascended so high among the attics that they seemed at length to twinkle in the middle sky'. Many prominent structures once stood here which have long since vanished, and along with them many dark and furtive closes which tumbled down the slopes on each side of the High Street. **Advocates Close**, facing the church, survives, now visited chiefly because of the view it provides looking to Princes Street; but in the eighteenth century it was a centre of activity for the legal profession; members of the bar lived, carried on business, and drank much claret in the gloomy taverns of what was then a dark and steep alley.

In the middle of the High Street once stood the **High Cross** or **Market Cross**, built in the Middle Ages, rebuilt in 1617, removed to another site in 1756, reconstructed in Parliament Square (*see* p. 32) in 1885. At the Cross royal proclamations were (and still are) read out, offenders of superior status were executed nearby, and the Edinburgh 'caddies' – a species of porter, street-messenger and water-carrier, 'a ragged, half-blackguard looking set of men' – congregated there in the eighteenth century and no doubt earlier. Not far from the Cross, and within a few feet of the north side of St Giles, stood the old **Tolbooth** prison, once the Town House, and the **Luckenbooths** (i.e. locked booths). This single block of building, five storeys high, was so positioned as to leave only a narrow lane for foot passengers between it and the church, and it extended so far into the High Street as to reduce the width of what was supposed to be the finest street in Europe to little more than four metres. The Tolbooth, in the words of Sir Walter Scott, was 'gloomy and haggard in aspect, its black stan-chioned windows opening through its dingy walls like the apertures of a hearse", and it was usually in a filthy state. The outline of a heart in the paving stones marks its location. The Luckenbooths, on the other hand, contained both superior shops and superior dwellings, and at the east end, looking down the Royal Mile towards Holyrood, Allan Ramsay established the first circulating library in Scotland in 1752. This innovation did not meet with universal approval. 'Profane-ness is come to a great height!' wrote one contemporary. 'All the villainous, profane, and obscene books of plays printed at London by Curle and others are got down from London by Allan Ramsay, and let out for an easy price to young boys, servant women of the better sort, and gentlemen, and vice and obscenity dreadfully propagated.' Perhaps so. On the other hand, it should be noted that Sir Walter Scott in his younger days was an enthusiastic user of this library.

In 1771 Ramsay's premises passed into the hands of William Creech, publisher to Adam Smith, Burns and many others, and at once became a kind of literary lounge for Edinburgh. All around it were booths and shops of every description – jewellers, goldsmiths, shoemakers, clothiers – and in daylight hours the street was thronged with people. Old prints show women pushing barrows, traders selling from stalls and tables, horses and carts, dogs, bairns and soldiers, barrels of ale being rolled along, loungers in every doorway. Smollet, who lived with his sister in the Canongate in 1776, tells us in *Humphrey Clinker* that 'all the people of business in Edinburgh, and even the genteel company, may be seen standing in crowds every day, from one to two in the afternoon, in the open street, at a place where formerly stood a market cross'. Rich and poor were not much separated in those days. The idlers and gossips who hung about the windows and stairheads of the tall lands in the Lawnmarket, keeping an eye on the whole busy area round the Market Cross as well as on the entrances to the principal taverns in the vicinity, must have become as well-informed about the doings of the fifteen judges of the Court of Session (the highest Criminal Court in Scotland) and their wives as those of the City Guard, the shop-keepers, the poets, the apprentices, the children and the beggars. What with the dogs and the horses and the general inadequacy of sanitation it cannot have been very salubrious; but it was certainly lively.

Reconstruction of the area around St Giles began in 1753, when it was resolved to build a merchants' **Exchange** and thus put an end to buying and selling in the street. Several ruinous tenements on the north side were pulled down, and John Adam produced a scheme for 'a New design'd Square to serve as an Exchange'. Adam's plan was accepted, but it was almost at once revised by a local architect called John Fergus. The resultant building (which is the only eighteenth century public building in the Royal Mile) is now part of the **City Chambers**. It forms a three-sided courtyard, arcaded on the ground floor, with a one-storey arcaded screen on the High Street. The most striking features are the centrepiece, which has a pediment with urns and sculptured tympanum in the middle, and fluted Corinthian pilasters below; and the sculptured coat-of-arms above the screen, added in 1901. There appear to be only four floors, but due to the abrupt fall of the ground there are twelve storeys to the rear. The whole has been considerably altered, especially the screen on the High Street, and the interior has a general air of stuffiness and tedious grandeur. While the Exchange was building – it was completed in 1761 – the Market Cross was removed, as mentioned above, and the area was then left in peace for forty years, until plans were hatched to provide more accommodation for the majesty of the law. This meant, in the end, extensive alterations to all the buildings near St Giles.

Parliament Square, across the street from the City Chambers, is the enclosing backdrop for St Giles. In the seventeenth century, when the Old Town was still densely inhabited, the area immediately south of St Giles was partly a churchyard and partly occupied by **Parliament House**, built between 1632 and 1640. This building exhibited a very Scottish style of architecture. It appears to have been part late-Gothic, part Scottish vernacular, yet not uninfluenced by Renaissance ideas. It boasted a circular angle tower with a conical roof, pedimented windows, an ornamental balustrade, and a lavish display of carved ornamental detail; pictures of it remind one of Falkland Palace in Fife, or of Glamis Castle in Angus. This architecture was engulfed soon after 1800 in a series of additions and improvements by Robert Reid which provided Scotland with more space for litigation but hemmed in St Giles with a long facade of what has been called 'ponderous Adamesque wallpaper'. The obliteration of all external trace of the old building was condemned by Lord Cockburn who saw the work being carried out.

> *No one who remembers the old exterior can see the new one without sorrow and indignation. The old building exhibited some respectable turrets, some ornamental windows and doors, and a handsome balustrade. But the charm that ought to have saved it, was its colour and its age, which, however, were the very things that caused its destruction. About 170 years had breathed over it a grave grey hue. The whole aspect was venerable and appropriate; becoming the air and character of a sanctuary of Justice. But a mason pronounced it to be all 'Dead Wall'. The officials to whom, at a period when there was no public taste in Edinburgh, this was addressed, believed him; and the two fronts were removed in order to make way for the bright freestone and contemptible decorations that now disgrace us ... there was such an utter absence of public spirit in Edinburgh then, that the building might have been painted scarlet without anybody objecting.*

Robert Reid's law courts are certainly remarkably dull. There are Ionic columns, stony-breasted sphinxes, pedimented windows, balustrades, an Ionic pedimented centrepiece and several loggias. The whole is derived to some extent from Robert Adam's design for Edinburgh University (*see* p. 32); but it lacks character and it goes on too long. In spite of this, the law courts are not to be passed by, for behind their facade lie two of the finest rooms in Scotland.

The first of these, open to the public, is the **Great Hall of Parliament House**, preserved amid all the changes that have gone on around it. The Hall is over 120 feet long and almost 50 feet wide, and it was originally hung with tapestries and portraits of Scottish kings. It possesses a simple antique grandeur, perhaps not unsuited to the judges and advocates whose domain it now is. Its most splendid feature is the dark but magnificent hammerbeam roof, rising to 60 feet above the floor, made of Danish oak (1637–39) by John Scott, Master Wright to the Town of Edinburgh. The roof has a low pitch, and is supported on stone corbels which are boldly carved with portraits, castles (including Edinburgh Castle), and beasts. The enormous stained glass window in the south gable is almost equally remarkable. Designed by Wilhelm von Kaulbach and executed by Maximilian Ainmiller, both of Munich, it was installed in 1868 at a cost of £2,000. It depicts the inauguration of the College of Justice, the Supreme Court of Scotland, by King James V in 1532. The young king (the father of Mary, Queen of Scots), surrounded by nobles and officers of state, presents the charter of institution to the first Lord President, the Abbot of Cambuskenneth, who kneels to receive it, watched by other judges in their robes. The Archbishop of Glasgow, with upraised hand, invokes a blessing on the act. The scene is imaginary, the costumes are authentic, and the faces of the judges are reputedly portraits of some who were on the bench in the later 1860s. The effect is rather overwhelming, but such large clear areas of brightly coloured glass, making up a very distinct scene, are not often to be found. On the west wall are three heavily varnished chimney-pieces of the 1880s, one with Madonna-and-Child caryatids and another with a bas-relief of scenes from *The Merchant of Venice*.

The statues are not to be ignored. One, by William Brodie, is of Lord Cockburn, whose remarks about Parliament House have already been quoted. Cockburn was a judge, and a much respected one; but he is chiefly remembered as the author of *Memorials of His Time*. This book, brilliantly written, is indispensable for an understanding of Edinburgh in the early decades of the nineteenth century; and besides being indispensable, it is most entertaining. Cockburn was an acute observer of men and affairs, and a most clubable man – 'one of the most popular men north of the Tweed'. No one who wishes to understand the Athens of the North can do without Cockburn. Of the other statues, three are by Chantrey: Lord President Blair (who possessed, says Cockburn, 'a great taste for contemplative repose,' not to be confused with laziness), 1815; Lord Chief Baron Dundas (his 'abilities and acquirements were both moderate ... a little, alert, handsome, gentleman-like man'), 1814; and Henry Dundas, Viscount Melville ('well calculated by talent and manner to make despotism popular ... the absolute dictator of Scotland'), 1818. And there is a superb statue of Duncan Forbes, Lord President of the Court of Session, by Roubillac, 1752. The figure is seated, leaning forward, intensely alive. Duncan Forbes deserves to be remembered, for he was the great organiser of resistance in Scotland against Prince Charles in 1745–6, and by his efforts, it has been said, he 'preserved the throne for the House of Hanover, chiefly at his own expense, and for no reward but that which Charles Esmond found customary among princes'.

The Great Hall is thus a very singular room, and one moreover that is steeped in history. Here the Scots decided to intervene in the Civil War on behalf of Parliament, and here they later resolved to hang the Marquis of Montrose, who had supported the King. Cromwell's troopers (now the enemy) were in the Hall in 1650, and ten years later the future James II and the future Queen Anne were entertained in it. And as every Scotsman knows – or should know – it was in the Great Hall in 1707 that the Scots Parliament, its members not uninfluenced by £20,000 worth of bribes from London, voted to terminate its own existence and to accept the Articles of Union with England. The Union was not popular, and many of the required signatures, it is said, were discreetly appended to the hated document in a cellar on the other side of the High Street, after dark.

Below the Great Hall is the Laigh Hall (low hall), which retains its original arcade of octagonal piers, and its original fireplace.

The second splendid room in Parliament Square is the **Signet Library**. The Society of Writers to Her Majesty's Signet is probably the oldest society of lawyers in the world. Its members, most of whom practice law in Edinburgh, and whose brass plates gleam from the doors of countless houses in the New Town, have, for many centuries, had the exclusive right to affix the Royal Signet or Seal to legal documents, and thus to authorise the commencement of civil actions in the Court of Session. They own and maintain the Signet

Library, which is adjacent to and west of Parliament House. It was begun when Parliament received its new façade, and the shell of the Library was completed in 1811. The interior, which is what matters, is basically by William Stark, a Glasgow architect and planner about whom not much is known; he died in 1813. The ground floor was originally the whole Signet Library, but in 1833 the Writers to the Signet obtained possession of the upper floor also, and they then commissioned William Burn to build a new imperial stair leading up to the first floor, opening through a corinthian-columned screen by W.H. Playfair. These form a suitably impressive approach to Stark's superb Upper Library. This room, which occupies the whole length of the building, is no less than 136 feet long, but beautifully proportioned, with nave and aisles separated by Corinthian columns, a vaulted ceiling, and anthemion-balustraded balconies running behind the columns. Lighting is excellent, thanks not only to the windows north and south, but also to the central saucer dome, painted by Thomas Stothard in 1821 (Apollo and the Muses, poets, philosophers etc.). When George IV visited Edinburgh in August, 1822, this room was used as a drawing-room on the occasion of the royal banquet in the Parliament Hall. It would be hard to think of two rooms so different, so splendid, and so convenient to one another. The King is said to have exclaimed, as he entered the Library, 'This is the most beautiful room I have ever seen'.

Before we finally enter St Giles, two other items should be noted. The older is the equestrian **statue of Charles II**, on the south side of the cathedral. Charles is shown as Caesar – a rather unsuitable similitude for so urbane a monarch. Erected in 1685, close to where it now stands, this statue is perhaps the finest work in lead of its date in Britain. It seems to have been made in Holland, possibly in Rotterdam, and it has required frequent repair. Just round the corner, to the east of the cathedral, is the **Market Cross**. Erected in 1885, this is a replica, in general terms, of the 1617 Cross. The drum is slightly smaller than the original, but there is still room for heralds to read proclamations from the parapet. The capital on the octagonal shaft (shorter than the original) is early fifteenth century, and the unicorn was added in 1869. It is a praiseworthy effort, but a patchwork; and it looks too new.

Turning at last to **St Giles**, do not be put off by the exterior. Except for the late medieval tower and its famous crown, everything external is dull nineteenth century work. But this exterior bears almost no relation to what goes on inside. The interior is old, complicated and surprising; it cannot be taken in at a glance; and the overall impression is of a church that is not beautiful, but is elemental and indestructible.

St Giles church – it is often referred to as a cathedral – is built on the only piece of level ground between Holyrood and the Castle. Throughout the Middle Ages it was the only parish church in Edinburgh, and a building certainly stood here in the twelfth century. It was entirely rebuilt some time in the fourteenth century, and then was burned although not destroyed when Richard II sacked Edinburgh in 1385. Restoration soon followed the fire, and two chapels were added south of the existing nave, which had five bays (as it still does) and stood west of a low central tower. Transepts were added in the 1390s, the choir was completed a decade or two later, and this cruciform church still stands, although it is obscured by many later additions.

The lower stage of the tower also dates from around 1400; but the upper stage and the energetic Gothic crown with its flying buttresses were built about a hundred years later. The only other surviving crown steeples in Scotland (there is only one in England, the spire of St Nicholas, Newcastle-on-Tyne) are those of King's College Chapel, Aberdeen, and the Tolbooth Steeple in Glasgow. In these two the cupola is carried on four arched supports springing from the corners of the tower; at St Giles there are four additional supports springing from the middle of each side, and the central feature is a lofty pinnacle surrounded by a pinnacled gallery. The weathercock was added in 1567, and the pinnacles half way up the flying buttresses, by John Mylne jun., in 1648. The crown is a truly extraordinary construction, rugged, complex and commanding. In any view of the city's skyline it at once attracts the eye, so different from the slender spires that accompany it. The crown of St Giles confidently proclaims the kingdom of God – and perhaps also the kingdom of Scotland; and you are bound to listen to it.

Other alterations and additions mostly took the form of chapels; five were built between 1395 and 1518, some on the north side, where expansion was difficult because of the High Street, and some on the south side, where space was available in the churchyard. Their construction was an act of piety, or possibly of repentance. One of these was the Albany Aisle. (In Scottish usage, an aisle is a wing or private part of a church, probably for the use of the local laird and his family). This was built as a chapel soon after 1400. The capital of the central pillar bears two shields, one with the arms of Robert, Duke of Albany, and the other with those of Archibald, Earl of Douglas. Both men were implicated in the starving to death of the Duke of Rothesay at Falkland Palace in 1402, and it is possible that the chapel was erected in expiation of this crime.

Further changes were made in the second half of the fifteenth century. It was decided to alter the choir, which was of four aisled bays with a vaulted roof, and make it more splendid. The two west bays, built about 1400, remain as they were; they have tall octagonal columns and plainly moulded capitals. But the two east bays were made into more elaborate Late Gothic, with carved foliage and abaci, and the roof was raised to allow taller windows in the clearstorey. On one of the pillars, known as the King's pillar, are the arms of James II (James of the Fiery Face, so-called because of a birthmark) facing west; of his son who became James III facing east; of Mary of Gueldres, Queen of James II, facing north; and the Fleur de Lys of France facing south. As the young prince was not born until 1453 and his father was killed by the explosion of a cannon at the siege of Roxburgh in 1460, the reconstruction must have been carried out between these dates, because the label on the Prince's shield indicates that his father was still alive. In spite of belonging to two different periods, the choir is an admirably unified piece of design, and is undoubtedly one of the best examples of late medieval ecclesiastical architecture in Scotland.

Still more alterations were carried out in the later fifteenth century; these included extending the transepts and adding another large chapel south of the choir. To do this, part of the south wall of the church had to be removed and replaced by three arches opening into the new chapel. Now known as the Preston Aisle, this addition was built to commemorate the gift by Sir William Preston of an arm bone of St Giles, which Sir William had obtained from France at great expense. Early in the sixteenth century the width of the church was further increased by the addition of two more chapels, both adjacent to the south transept. One of these, by Walter Chepman, who introduced printing to Scotland in 1507, was formally dedicated in August 1513 to the welfare of the souls of James IV and Queen Margaret, nineteen days before the king was killed at the battle of Flodden. (See p. 318).

The Reformation brought on an orgy of ecclesiastical destruction, which affected St Giles as it did almost every other church in Scotland. The medieval screens, altars, images and relics were all broken up and cast out. Much of the work was done systematically, and paid for by the Town Council. John Knox thundered from the pulpit, and the church was suddenly deemed fit to hold two congregations instead of just one; after all, Presbyterianism had no need for an altar, and church processions, which took up space, savoured of popery. Around 1561, stone walls were built so as to divide the ancient edifice into three churches, and uses were discovered for various parts of the building which were no longer, or not always, required by religion; thus the three west bays of the nave became an annexe to the Tolbooth, the town clerk found space for an office, a school was occasionally housed in another part of the building, and in due course the guillotine used for the execution of criminals, called the Maiden (now to be seen in the Museum of Scotland, *see* p. 103), was also kept within the walls. (In 1699 a fourth church appeared, called New North, or Haddo's Hole Church. This took its name from a small room above the north porch having been used at one time as a place of confinement for Sir John Gordon of Haddo, a notable royalist. He was subsequently beheaded at the Cross).

These strange proceedings were interrupted, although not entirely reversed, when Charles I came to Scotland for his coronation in 1633, and began his attempt to convert the Scots to episcopacy. St Giles again became a cathedral, the dividing walls were taken down, and a worshipper by the name of Jenny Geddes gained immortal fame by throwing her stool at the dean (or perhaps it was the bishop) who dared to say mass in her church and in her presence. (Replicas of the stool used to be available in the St Giles shop. For what purpose they were to be used was not stated). Episcopacy did not catch on, and in 1637 St Giles ceased to be a cathedral, although it resumed this role from 1661 to 1688.

Throughout the eighteenth century the church remained, architecturally speaking, a mess. And then a worse fate befell it, for it began to be tidied up and 'restored'. Most of the damage was done by William Burn, who in later life became the great exponent of the Scottish Baronial style of architecture. He commenced work in 1829, removing chapels, demolishing porches, altering windows, building new doors and standardising the buttresses. All this, and much else, is Burn's work. He aimed to make the church more uniform and symmetrical, more like a 'real' cathedral. Mercifully, he left the tower alone.

The furnishings within the church, sad to say, are almost all of the late nineteenth century, and few are of artistic interest. There are seemingly endless war memorials, monuments, bronze reliefs and plates. The pulpit, second-rate carving in Caen stone, dates from

1883, and the canopied oak screen and reredos from 1927–32. There is a depressing statue of John Knox executed in the early years of the present century by a sculptor whose name sufficiently proclaims his nationality: J Pittendrigh MacGillivray. There is a canopied effigy of the Marquis of Montrose by R Rowand Anderson (1887–9) in Jacobean Renaissance style, and a languid Robert Louis Stevenson by Augustus St Gaudens (1904). The sole relief from all this Victoriana and after is above the east crossing arch, a large painted Royal Arms of George II, dated 1736.

With two exceptions, the stained glass windows are not much better. Scotland lost almost all its old stained glass at the hands of the Reformers in the years around 1560. No more of the idolatrous stuff was produced for the next three hundred years, and what came then was studiously prosaic. But in an inspired moment the elders of the church commissioned Burne-Jones to design and Morris and Co. to execute a new window for the north aisle of the nave. This depicts the Israelites crossing the Jordan, and some Old Testament heroines, and is a superb swirl of truly glowing colour. It was inserted in 1886. Almost exactly one hundred years later a new window for the west end of the nave was commissioned from an Icelandic artist, Leifus Breidfjord. It commemorates Robert Burns and the brotherhood of man, and is not unworthy of its setting.

The Thistle Chapel remains to be noticed. Designed by Sir Robert Lorimer and built 1909–11, it is a private chapel for the Dean, the Knights, and the Heralds of the Thistle; there is no room in it for anyone else. Very small and very high, it is crammed with wood and stone carving of every kind. In general terms, it follows the style of the fifteenth century, and there are echoes of St George's Chapel at Windsor Castle. It was enormously admired in its day, but as that day recedes the visitor is more and more likely to see it as an absurd archaic extravagance. The twenty-two stalls are over-carved, the roof is over-bossed, and the whole thing is overdone. In any case, it is totally historicist. The Thistle Chapel makes no contribution to either religion or art, for it was dead when it was built.

The High Kirk of St Giles, however, is not dead; it is a lesson in ill-use and survival. It began as a nave and a central tower; it became cruciform; a succession of chapels made its plan almost rectangular; meanwhile, it nearly disappeared behind a muddle of shops, tenements, and a prison; for over two hundred years it had to accommodate almost anybody and everybody except money-changers; it emerged haggard and divided, and forthwith became a text-book example of how not to 'restore' an old building. It has lost much, and could do without some of what it has gained. Yet the interior is immensely impressive. There is a fortress-like quality about the massive octagonal piers, the rugged stonework, the tunnel vaulting. Because it has so irregular and unpremeditated a plan, it provides numerous surprising vistas of variety and complexity. And the tower, holding aloft the massive ornamented crown, makes a masterly contribution to Edinburgh's extraordinary skyline.

3

The Royal Mile: II

FROM ST GILES Cathedral it is only a couple of hundred yards down the High Street to the Tron Church. The Tron (named after the public weighing-machine which in the seventeenth century stood in the street nearby) is no longer a church but serves a variety of purposes. This stretch of the High Street has little to attract the visitor. If it is August, he may seek out a booking office for 'the fringe', that cornucopia of mostly dubious delights that floods the town during the annual Edinburgh Festival; if it is New Year's Eve (and not pouring with rain or snowing) he may be able to get a ticket and join the many thousands of citizens who throng the centre of Edinburgh to sing and shout – revel is the right word – and enjoy a magnificent display of fireworks launched from the heights of the castle. But the street hereabouts seems rather bleak; it seems to comprise little else than tall lands, diminutive shops selling tartan, and very uneven granite setts which test the suspension of the passing cars and buses. Once the Guard House stood where the traffic now goes: it was a low gloomy building, and according to Sir Walter Scott 'it suggested the idea of a long black snail crawling up the middle of the High Street'. The City Guard, whose headquarters it was, consisted of a few score ex-soldiers armed with muskets, bayonets, and Lochaber axes. Their duty was to keep the peace, and a hard time they had of it, for sword-fights and affrays used to be as common here as in Verona.

Notice though, how many closes there are. They used to be a major feature of Edinburgh life. Most of the population, including 'the rank and fashion', must have lived in one close or another, until in the later eighteenth century the wealthier families began to drift away and occupy the New Town to the north. Came the twentieth century and it seemed that the day of the close was over. Closes were unhygienic and unwanted, save by those who were too poor to live anywhere else. They began to crumble and disappear. A guide book to the Royal Mile, published in 1928, lists 73 as being of special note, but most of those have been destroyed or have been reduced to passages only a few yards in length. The fragments that remain, however, are often surprisingly interesting. Some have been rehabilitated and are lived in – Warriston Close, for example, and Roxburgh's Close, both opposite St Giles. But if you like the unexpected there is scarcely an opening in the Royal Mile that is not worth looking into – you may find a handsome doorway, or a carved inscription, or a stair tower, or a small interior court, or a flight of steps going down precipitously towards the railway station or, on the south side, to the Cowgate far below.

It is a pity, certainly, that so many closes have been lost; Old Bank Close, for example, where the senior judge in Scotland was shot in the back and killed by an unsuccessful litigant in 1689. But much remains. On the north side there is still **Anchor Close**, where Dawnay Douglas's Tavern stood, familiar to Burns, its kitchen 'a dark fiery Pandemonium, through which numerous ineffable ministers of flame were continually flying about;' just below it is **Old Stamp Office Close**, where Susanna, Countess of Eglinton, and her seven beautiful daughters lived in the early part of the eighteenth century in a house that later turned into Fortune's Tavern; and beyond the North Bridge lies **Carubber's Close** where Allan Ramsay opened a theatre in 1736 and the clergy and the magistrates promptly closed it. On the opposite side of the street is **Old Assembly Close** where the Old Assembly Hall was once the venue for dancing assemblies and fashionable balls. Nearby this centre of pleasure there is **Old Fishmarket Close**, which in the years around 1800, according to Lord Cockburn, was 'a steep, narrow, stinking ravine' where the fish 'were generally thrown out on the street at the head of the close, whence they were dragged down by dirty boys or dirtier women; and then sold unwashed ... from old, rickety, scaly, wooden tables'. The flesh market, not much more salubrious, used to be at the back of the Tron, and the meal market was where the law courts now stand.

Such a concentration of closes and of food markets meant also a concentration of population. This part of the Royal Mile was the most densely occupied part of the old city, very densely occupied indeed, with some unfortunate consequences. One was the smell; Edinburgh was early distinguished for its magnificent High Street and its abominable smells. 'I never came to my own lodgings in Edinburgh,' wrote an Englishman in 1636, 'or went out, but I was constrained to hold my nose'. A hundred years later, it was no better – it was probably worse. At ten o'clock at night, wrote one disgusted visitor, 'every-body is at

Liberty to throw their Filth out at the Windows'. Returning to his lodgings 'through a long narrow Wynde or Alley,' he was provided with

> *a Guide ... who went before me to prevent my Disgrace,*
> *crying out all the Way, with a loud Voice, Hud yer Haunde.*
> *The opening of a Sash, or otherwise opening a Window,*
> *made me tremble, while behind and before me, at some little*
> *Distance, fell the terrible Shower.*

Still later in the century the evening aroma of the High Street embarrassed Boswell. Conducting Johnson 'to my house in James's Court,' he walked with the Doctor 'arm-in-arm up the High Street; it was a dusky night: I could not prevent his being assailed by the evening effluvia of Edinburgh'.

The second disadvantage was the terrible danger of fire. Many of the houses had wooden frontages, built out into or over the street, and this, coupled with the narrowness of the wynds and closes, made fires extremely dangerous. In 1824 a fire began near Old Assembly Close which devastated much of the area, and after burning from Monday evening until Tuesday forenoon finally set light to the Tron steeple.

Christ's Church at the Tron was begun in 1636, and in 1647 its doors were opened to receive its first congregation, one which had been ejected from St Giles when that building became a cathedral. The Tron was originally much larger than it is now; in the 1780s, when the road that here crosses the High Street was built, the original T plan disappeared with the removal of the south aisle, and the number of bays was reduced from five to three. As first constructed, the new church was very up-to-date in design and a curious mixture. It was in general, as it still is, severe and Classical in appearance. But Dutch influence – which, like Dutch trade, was important in seventeenth-century Scotland – is apparent in the fluted Ionic pilasters on each side of the entrance door, and in the door itself, round-arched and corniced; and there used to be buttresses and a large internal gallery, giving a touch of Gothic. Above all, there used to be a different tower and a steeple made of wood, iron and lead – the steeple that caught fire in 1824. It burned well. 'The outer covering boards were soon consumed' wrote Cockburn, 'and the lead dissolved. The conflagration was long presided over by a calm and triumphant gilded cock on the top of the spire, which seemed to look on the people, and to listen to the crackling, in disdain. But it was undermined at last, and dived down into the burning gulf'. A new tower and steeple were built in 1828, different in design and higher, but the architectural mixture much as before. The upper octagon and the stone spire have been compared to St Martin's-in-the-Fields.

The interior has now been gutted but the roof remains, and it is worth entering the building to see it. It is a hammerbeam roof, similar to that in the Great Hall of Parliament House, but not nearly so flat. This roof, like the other, was built by John Scott, Master Wright to the Town of Edinburgh, and was completed in 1647. The walls have been stripped bare, and excavations below floor level have revealed the stoney surface of Marlin's Wynd and an ancient drain, neither of them seen for a century and a half or used for a couple of centuries before that. They look mysterious and very ancient, more evocative of the past than much that is every bit as old, but tended to and tidier.

Cross the busy main street to reach the next section of the Royal Mile. (You may, if you choose, look down the slope to the north and see the splendid front and dome of Robert Adam's Register House. This used to be a noble prospect. But early in the 1970s it was ruined by the insertion of a modern monstrosity to contain shops and offices, an angular concrete commercial block, a monument – let us hope not an imperishable one – to the tasteless folly of the Town Council. Of which, more anon.) What about the corner building? A hotel, certainly; the **Crowne Plaza**. But could it belong, as it seems to claim, to the seventeenth century? Were there hotels in the High Street in the seventeenth century? Could the Marquis of Montrose have slept here, or, not to go quite so far back, Bonnie Prince Charlie? The answers to these questions are rather obvious; for this is a steel and concrete construction of the late twentieth century, made to look antique. For twenty years we had a vacant building site growing willow herb and thistles, one of Edinburgh's several 'holes in the ground'; and making use of it posed the great problem of style. A modern design to fit the High Street would have had to be of very high quality and of great discretion and sensitivity; a replica of the old frontages and of the geometry behind them would have been exceedingly expensive, and perhaps not very practical. So what we have is a reproduction style hotel with 250 bedrooms, or in other words a large grid-plan structure masquerading behind what look like tenement fronts. It is a sham, of course, and shams are rarely satisfactory. The massive scale, and the lining up of the windows (although they vary a little in size) on five floor levels across the full width of the High Street frontage spoil the pretence that this is a series of several high, narrow houses. It has flat roofs, which are incongruous, and a hefty corner turret – the only one in the Royal Mile. Yet the whole has been so well arranged, with projections and recesses, one section a different colour from the rest, a small outside stair, and the entrances to three old closes preserved and incorporated into the building that it must be declared a qualified success. For example, what used to be Cant's Close has been done away with, but where there was the old entrance there is a new one, which leads to 'a form of Old Town Court', where alcoholic drinks are sold and consumed – this at least is in the genuine High Street tradition.

The whole site, although not what now stands on it, has known violent times. It was at the head of **Blackfriars Street** (once Blackfriars Wynd), just beyond the hotel, that the celebrated affray known as 'Cleanse the Causeway' began. During the minority of James V (he did not assume power until he was fifteen) the country was governed by feuding Regents, and in 1520 two of them came to blows in the High Street. Each seems to have had several score, if not several hundred followers. Positions were prepared, weapons were brought out of the houses of sympathisers, and the windows were crowded with spectators. After a savage struggle, the Earl of Angus ('a witless young fool' who had married the widow of James IV; her matrimonial adventures were almost as remarkable as those of her brother, Henry VIII) drove the vanquished down Blackfriars Wynd, 'and the dead and wounded began to cumber the causeway in every direction'. Perhaps as many as a hundred men were killed. One of those who managed to get away was the Archbishop of Glasgow. The story goes that before the fight began he made a speech in favour of it, which ended by his striking his breast and declaring 'There is no remedy!' He was wearing ecclesiastical robes over armour, and the armour rattled. 'How now, my lord?' said the Bishop of Dunkeld, 'I think your conscience clatters'. To this the archbishop is supposed to have replied that 'he had merely provided for his own safety in these days of continual turmoil, when no man could leave his house but at the hazard of his life'. Another affray took place on the same spot seventy years later. One of the combatants killed a man but in doing so lost his sword. He fled down Blackfriars Wynd but was pursued by the Earl of Bothwell, who 'strake him in at the back and out at the belly, and killed him'. These 'street disturbances' as they were euphemistically called, continued into the early nineteenth century.

Strichen's Close (its line now preserved as a passage within the hotel) has slightly less gruesome associations. Beside it there stood at one time a tenement, seven storeys in height and burnt to the ground in 1825, where once lived Primrose Campbell of Mamore, widow of Simon Fraser Lord Lovat who was beheaded on Tower Hill in 1747 for his part in the Jacobite Rebellion. If ever there was a double-dealer it was Lovat. In 1703 he intrigued in Scotland on behalf of Louis XIV of France, but he betrayed his employer and spent ten years in a French gaol. In 1715 he supported the Government. In 1745 he at first supported both Prince Charles and the Government by words, then, after the Prince took Edinburgh, he sent his son and his clan to join the rebellion. As the campaign progressed and the Jacobites' fortunes declined, he continued to keep a foot in both camps. When the 'fatal catastrophe' at Culloden took place he was in the Highlands. He was captured soon after the battle. Hogarth's splendid portrait of the old rascal is in the National Portrait Gallery in London.

Opposite the new hotel are two items of greater interest. One of them is quite small, a sculptured face above a doorway and the words 'Heave awa' chaps, I'm no dead yet'. The date this time is 10th November 1863, when an ancient tenement in Baillie Fyfe's Close collapsed without warning at midnight, burying thirty-five people in the ruins. Some were dug out alive, including the boy whose words to his rescuers are here recorded. Elsewhere in the Royal Mile other carved sentences of a pious nature are to be found, carved above doors or windows: *The feir of the Lord preservith the lyfe*; *O Lord in The is al my traist*; *Blissit be God in al his giftis*.

The second item of note is **Trinity College Church**, down Chalmers Close, founded by Mary of Gueldres, widow of James II of Scotland. It was built between 1460 and the middle of the next century, and stood in the valley between the Old Town and Calton Hill. But in 1848 it was taken down to make room for the onward march of civilisation in the shape of the North British Railway. Sheds, offices and railway sidings took the place of the church, and for twenty five years the resultant pile of pinnacles, gargoyles, Gothic windows and the rest lay unused on Calton Hill. Rebuilding on the present site began in 1872, by which time many of the carefully numbered stones had vanished, their new owners finding an imme-diate use for them in other parts of the city. The church as it now stands, converted to a brass rubbing centre, is no more than the orig-inal choir; the aisles, the transepts, the crossing tower and the flying buttresses have all disappeared. (No nave was ever built). To make matters worse, rebuilding did not always put the available material in the original places. It is therefore not surprising that to the passer-by

Trinity College Church seems a dismal affair, or that few Edinburgh citizens have ever been in it. But the interior has the true impact of Gothic architecture. It is enormously lofty, vaulted, and arcaded to a considerable height. There are foliage capitals with shields and grotesque masks. In the west wall is a large window with early sixteenth-century tracery (it was originally in one of the transepts) and below it is a very fine fifteenth-century fireplace from a High Street house which was demolished when the church was being rebuilt; the figures on the fireplace capitals are splendidly medieval and delightfully domestic. There is also a fifteenth-century canopied piscina. Nothing of the original furnishing remains, but the church once contained a set of painted panels known as the Trinity Altarpiece. Four of the five original panels survive – the fifth, central panel is thought to have been destroyed at the Reformation – and are kept safely in the National Gallery of Scotland. Copies are here. They show Sir Edward Bonkil, the first Provost of the church, kneeling in prayer beside two angels, one of whom is playing an organ; James III with St Andrew beside him and his son James IV behind; James III's Queen, Margaret of Denmark, with a knight in armour, evidently St George; and the Holy Trinity (Christ, God the Father, and the Holy Spirit as a dove). The original panels were commissioned in the 1470s. In style they resemble the Portinari altarpiece by van der Goes which is in the Uffizi.

Continue down the High Street, and John Knox's House is directly ahead, its west front facing towards the Castle. It attracts all eyes, but **Moubray House**, just before you come to John Knox's is worth more than a glance. It is very like Gladstone's Land, and is about as old. The rubble-built rear wing almost certainly dates from the first half of the sixteenth century, and what is now the front part of the house was added around 1630. Moubray House has a shop on the ground floor, a forestair (as used to be common), and four storeys and an attic. The attic is jettied (that is, projects forwards), and is gabled with a timber front; inside, it has a wooden barrel-vaulted ceiling painted with designs similar to those in Gladstone's Land. This was once a very grand house, and it is pleasant to record that one of the best early portrait painters in either England or Scotland once lived here; George Jamesone (1588–1644) who had studied in the atelier of Rubens at Antwerp, and who knew van Dyck.

John Knox's House likewise dates back to the sixteenth century. It was part of the Edinburgh that Knox knew, but there is no proof that he ever lived in this particular house, or had any particular connection with it. Because it was once the property of a man named Knox, it has become romantically (that is to say, falsely) associated with Scotland's most famous churchman. In the 1840s it was threatened with demolition, but was restored and is now the property of the Church of Scotland. It serves as a Knox museum, and contains a sixteenth century Geneva bible and a copy of Knox's *History of the Reformation of Religion in Scotland*, the work which purports to record some of his conversations with the Queen. In many respects Knox has been seriously misrepresented. He is depicted as the great reformer, whereas he was one among many; as a severe Calvinist, but he did not 'utterly condemn' dancing and his farewell advice to the Kirk was that it should continue to have bishops; as a dyed-in-the-wool Scotsman, although before he finally settled in Scotland in 1559, when he was approaching fifty, he was at least as well known in England (where he refused a bishopric) as in his own country. What is correct is that he was an implacable enemy of the Queen, because he feared that her settled policy was to re-introduce Roman Catholicism, sooner or later. For what was said during his interviews with Mary we have only his own account; but we know that on at least one occasion he reduced her to tears.

The external appearance of the house is wonderfully picturesque. The shapes, sizes and disposition of the windows; the advance and retreat of the façades; the large isolated gabled attics that look as if they had grown out of the building; the rambling irregularity of the whole composition – it looks like a stage set, almost too fanciful to be true; yet it is all perfectly genuine, very much now as when it was built. Begun in the Middle Ages, the old house was extended forwards some time around the middle of the sixteenth century, and the front block, which is what one sees, was built into the High Street. The main work must have been completed before 1573, because the garlanded coat of arms on the west front is flanked by the initials J M and M A, which stand for James Mosman and Mariota Arres, who owned it; and James Mosman, goldsmith to Mary Queen of Scots, was executed for treason in 1573. Like Gladstone's Land and Moubray House, it is a good example of a sixteenth century Edinburgh town house. Above the entrance door at street level is an entablature inscribed with the words *Lyfe God abufe al and yi nychtbour as yi self*, and on the corner is a sundial beneath a carved relief of Moses pointing to the sun hidden in a cloud inscribed 'God' in Greek, Latin and English. On the south front, facing the High Street, there are shallow timber galleries of the kind treasured in the sixteenth century because they gave 'a fair and pleasant prospect' and access to fresh air. Those that existed on the west front were replaced (in the seventeenth century) by an ornamental façade, including an elaborate first floor window flanked by small garlands. The forestair is not the original. Inside, there are two main rooms on each floor, and two turnpike stairs which give access to different parts of the house. By comparison with Gladstone's Land it all seems rather plain, but there are sixteenth-century wooden panels (some of them unfortunately 'improved' in the nineteenth century), a painted ceiling on the second floor, and fireplaces with Dutch and Flemish tiles; the south fireplace on the first floor has a motif of three large and handsome vases of flowers. If John Knox ever sat in the first floor gallery he had an unrivalled view of all the doings and mis-doings in the High Street.

Now cross the street to something different. Since the 1930s numerous attempts have been made to restore and rehabilitate the old houses in the Royal Mile. Slum conditions have disappeared and population has been attracted back, but the results have often been visually depressing. How it should be done is demonstrated behind the façades of Nos. **14–42 High Street**. Enter through Hyndford Close or Fountain Close or South Gray's Close. Here is sheltered housing in 72 self-contained up-to-date flats, along with seven shops and even some car-parking.

Integrated into the development is the relocated and enlarged **Museum of Childhood** (no charge). The entrance is through a double-storey glazed archway which conceals the original eighteenth century archway, set back a little from the street. The Museum occupies several rooms at several levels, and in one of them there is a decorative plaster ceiling –confirmation that this was once a theatre. The contents, Victorian or twentieth century, are for all tastes and ages; children's clothes, dolls and dolls' houses, railway trains, motor cars, the lot. Looking out through the small windows, you see that in spite of re-development you are in a world of closes (four of the five original closes remain, although altered), and tall tenements. There are gablets and balconies and an irregular roofline and perhaps some washing hung out to dry – very traditional. Many buildings have been demolished, but frontages and parts of frontages have been retained, and listed tenements of the seventeenth century (Nos. 14–16) and of the nineteenth century (No. 24) have been rehabilitated. New elements have been skilfully integrated with the old, equally well with the rubble stonework of the eighteenth century as with the dressed stone of Victorian times. Where buildings have been demolished there is hard landscaping – paving stones, heather, poplars, rowan trees, a garden setting; and so light comes in, and sunshine when available. The old closes used to be very dark, and narrow; but here they are made to turn, and widen, and narrow again, and run into one another, and so down the slope to the Cowgate. A little town is here. It is not the Old Town, but it is sympathetic to the Old Town, and better to live in. And after the noise of the High Street, it is *so* quiet.

This development of the 1980s is helped by the inclusion within it of Tweeddale Court. Tweeddale Court is a considerable open space, larger than it used to be, and it is partly enclosed by **Tweeddale House**. This mansion was begun in the sixteenth century and several times extended. In 1670 it was bought by Lord Yester, subsequently Marquis of Tweeddale, a resolute royalist who had held Neidpath Castle on the Tweed (*see* p. 355) against Cromwell after every other stronghold south of Edinburgh had been given up. After he bought it, Tweeddale incorporated into the old house the three-storey north wing, which had begun as a separate tenement built about 1600. In 1750 John Adam reported that the entire building was in a severe state of dereliction: 'There is not one single thing within the Doors of it that can be of use in the repairs ... Floors, Ceilings, Doors, Sashes, Shutters and everything must be made new, so that nothing would be saved but the walls'. As a result, the house was virtually rebuilt in the 1750s. In 1791 it became the head office of the British Linen Bank, and the Doric porch was added a few years later. The interior has a good plaster ceiling of the 1780s, and handsome nineteenth-century Classical bookcases.

Return to the High Street through **Tweeddale Close**. This Close was the scene of a notorious murder in 1806. On November 13th, an hour after sunset, a little girl whose family lived in the close was sent by her mother to get water for tea from the well in the High Street. In the dark archway she stumbled over the body of a man – a messenger of the bank – with a knife in his heart 'up to the haft'. Several thousand pounds had disappeared and the murderer was never caught. Wherever you go in the High Street there is the same smell of blood.

Next to Tweeddale Close is **World's End Close**, so-called because at the cross-roads here the High Street ends and the Canongate begins. The distinction is an important one, for whereas the High Street was inside the city wall the Canongate was not. For many centuries the wall spelt safety of a sort, and the traveller who emerged from the city at dusk and heard the gate clang behind him must have looked round the darkening countryside and checked his cudgel or his sword. For the same reason building in the Canongate was never nearly so dense as in the High Street. There were not many houses in the Canongate before 1600. Those that came later tended to be larger and grander than the houses inside the wall, with gardens extending behind them for considerable distances.

The wall here is to be seen only by entering the World's End pub and descending to the cellars; we shall find small portions of it above ground in other parts of the city. In the roadway, however, brass plates have been inset to mark the outline of the **Netherbow Port**, one of the six gates which gave access to the old town. Built in 1606, it was demolished in 1764. This demolition was one of Edinburgh's great architectural disasters (as even the nineteenth century admitted) for the Netherbow Port was a remarkable building. It was two storeys high, and completely blocked the roadway. It had heavily corbelled battlements both east and west, and round towers with conical roofs, facing east. From the central roof rose a tall decorated tower surmounted by a spire with a cock on top. There was a central rounded archway, with a portcullis, for wagons and carriages, and a wicket for foot-passengers.

On only one occasion was this antique structure put to the test. In September 1745 Prince Charles and his army approached the capital and demanded its capitulation. Negotiations took place. At five o'clock in the morning of September 17th a hackney coach containing the emissaries of the city returned from Charles' camp and the Netherbow Port was opened to let them into the city. But when it was opened again to allow the coachman to drive back to his home in the Canongate, 800 Highlanders (so it is said; 80 would seem a more likely number), led by Cameron of Lochiel, rushed in, made the guards prisoners, and occupied their posts as quietly as one guard relieves another. When the inhabitants of Edinburgh awakened in the morning, they found that Charles was master of the city.

The **Canongate** begins, not too promisingly, with a grim Victorian Gothic church. On the south side St Mary's Street plunges down to the Cowgate. It was at this corner that Boyd's Inn stood, 'at the sign of the White Horse', where Boswell met Dr Johnson when the latter arrived in the middle of August 1773 . A few days later the two men set off on their famous journey to the Hebrides. On the north side, the **Morocco Land** scheme of the 1950s, with coloured frontages and arcading along the pavement, is neither modern nor vernacular; it is

51

no better than the church, but it seems to demand attention. Morocco Land itself (No. 267) is a fairly close copy of the eighteenth-century tenement which stood nearby. The name demands explanation, but the preferred explanation is hard to summarise and still harder to believe. Briefly, a young man about to be hanged at the Cross for taking part in a riot in 1625 escaped from the Tolbooth on the day before execution. Twenty years later, when Edinburgh was in the grip of the plague, an Algerian pirate vessel anchored in Leith Roads. The leader of the pirates entered Edinburgh with his men, cured the Provost's daughter of the plague, and then revealed himself as the condemned fugitive, and a distant relation. Needless to add, he married his patient, and they came to live in the Canongate, adorning their house 'with an effigy of his royal patron, the Emperor of Morocco'. There may be this much truth in the story, that Morocco Land was in some way connected with deliverance from the plague.

Hereabouts there are some interesting shops. On the south side redevelopment has been extensive, but the eighteenth-century façades have been respected. **Chessels Court** is behind the arcades of nos. 234–240. This was where Deacon Brodie made the fatal mistake of breaking into the Excise Office (*see* p. 29). The Excise Office has disappeared, and the court is now dominated by Chessels Buildings, a three-storey block built as flats about 1745, and currently provided with a setting so arboreal as almost to give the impression that you are looking at a country mansion. The frontage is very handsome, with a short flight of steps leading up to a heavily rusticated door. The central windows are round-arched and also rusti-cated, and there is a chimneyed gable (not uncommon in Edinburgh houses) and an octagonal stair-tower in the west wing. Many rooms have their original panelling, painted overmantels, and doorcases with swags of fruit. The buildings on each side of the court were put up in the 1960s.

After Chessels Court, on the other side of the street, there is another 1950s redevelopment, starting with **Shoemaker's Land**, a large handsome block. The most interesting feature is a panel high above the door carved with the emblem of the Cordiners (shoe-makers) – the rounding knife of St Crispin – and inscribed with the words 'Blessed is he that wisely doth the poor man's case consider'. The word 'wisely' is a good clue to some date early in the eighteenth century. Older and more interesting is **Bible Land** (nos. 183–187). It is a double tenement erected in 1677 and almost entirely rebuilt. Above the main doorway, however, is a pedimented cartouche dated

1677, again with the Cordiner's emblem, a crown above it flanked by cherubs' heads, and below an open book inscribed:

> *Behold how good a thing it is*
> *and how becoming well*
> *Together such as brethren are*
> *in unity to dwell*
> *IT IS AN HONOUR FOR MEN TO CEASE FROM STRIFE*

Presumably it is the book that has given the name to the building.

Opposite stands **Moray House**, built about 1625 by Mary, Dowager Countess of Home, and inherited in 1643 by her daughter Margaret, Countess of Moray; Lady Home's arms are in one of the pediments above the upper windows. Defoe described it as 'very magnificent', but its external appearance is angular and stern. It is L-shaped, with a tall gable to the street, having an iron balcony carried on massive carved corbels. In the middle of the west front of this wing there is a semi-octagonal stair-tower flanked by tall pairs of chimneys. The east wing to the street is of three storeys. There used to be a door here, and small windows; but when the house became a school in 1849 these were built up, the first-floor windowsills lowered, and extra windows inserted. The gateway is flanked by two remarkably tall obelisks set on very large piers. No one could say that Moray House is a beautiful building, but the interior contains some panelling with allegorical paintings, and two fine dome-shaped plaster ceilings. One of these has low reliefs of lions, griffons, sprays of flowers, figures and fleurs-de-lis, while the other goes so far as to include a naked lady standing amid trees.

All this now houses a College of Education, but it has seen stirring times. Cromwell stayed in Moray House for a few weeks in 1645 and is said while there 'to have come to the terrible conclusion 'that there was a necessitie to take away the king's life''. In 1650 the Marquis of Montrose passed by in a cart, on his way to be hanged in the Lawnmarket. He had won some brilliant victories on behalf of the King during the Civil War but was subsequently defeated and betrayed. On the night before he mounted the scaffold he is reputed to have scratched the following poem on the window of his cell:

> *Let them bestow on ev'ry Airth a Limb;*
> *Open all my Veins, that I may swim*
> *To Thee my Saviour, in that Crimson Lake;*

Then place my pur-boil'd Head upon a Stake;
Scatter my Ashes, throw them in the Air:
Lord (since Thou know'st where all these Atoms are)
I'm hopeful, once Thou'lt recollect my Dust,
And confident Thou'lt raise me with the Just.

Montrose always fought for what he believed to be right, and his memory is now greatly respected. But as he was carted up the Royal Mile he was jeered at and spat upon from the balcony of Moray House by a bridal party which included the first Marquis of Argyll (executed soon after the Restoration), Argyll's son, the Earl of Moray's daughter, and various other noble persons. To continue the list of notable events only a little longer, some signatures to the Treaty of Union are said to have been obtained in the privacy of the garden that used to exist at the rear of Moray House.

We have now come almost to the end of a rather dull stretch of the Royal Mile. It is grim and over-trafficked here, and the knowledge that Smollett wrote *Humphrey Clinker* while staying with his sister in St John's Street in 1766 is insufficient compensation. The same can be said of the **Canongate Tolbooth**, with its ostentatious clock, dated 1884, sticking out over the street on scrolled wrought-iron brackets. The building is respectably ancient, the tower and probably the block to the east of it built in 1591; this date is on a panel above the pend arch, which also carries the motto of Canongate Burgh, 'Patriae et posteris', and the initials of Sir Hugh Bellenden, who became Superior of the Burgh after the Abbots of Holyrood were dismissed. The tower has conical-roofed turrets or bartizans over the street, with gunloops, and a conical spire. The east block has a forestair and an oriel window at the east end, and in the centre of the block a large pedimented frame with thistles at the corners and what has been described as 'a blowsy crowned thistle' on top; the inscription is

> *I R 6 IUSTICA ET PIETAS VALIDE SUNT PRINCIPIS*
> *ARCES*
> *(King James VI Justice and religion are truly the sure*
> *foundations)*

The rest of the Tolbooth was heavily reconstructed in the 1870s, and the interior is scarcely at all original. It is now a museum of local history, but is apt to come across as an assemblage of soulless glass cases, obtrusive electric lights, miscellaneous objects from the past, and background noises. It transmits neither history nor mystery.

Beyond the Tolbooth, however, the street opens out (at last), and the **Canongate Church and churchyard** come in sight behind a screen of cherry trees. The churchyard is a large open area and the church is a big surprise. It was begun in 1688 and opened for worship in 1691. It is un-Scots in appearance and, for its date, remarkable in plan, because it is cruciform. Some of the explanation of this may lie in its origins. In 1687 James II and VII gave instructions that the nave of Holyrood Abbey was to become the chapel for the Knights of the Order of the Thistle, an Order which he himself had re-erected. Hitherto, the Abbey church of Holyrood had served as the parish church of the Canongate, so a new church was now required for that congregation. The task of designing this new church was entrusted to James Smith, Overseer of the Royal Works in Scotland. Smith had been a master mason at Holyroodhouse, and in 1680, when he was arbiter in a building dispute, he was referred to as 'Mr James Smith, architectour, a man who has the repute to be very skilled in works of this nature'. He was over 80 when he died in 1731, active to the last, and the self-declared father of 32 children. More to the point, he was reputed a Roman Catholic. The king, his master, was an avowed and zealous Roman Catholic. Could this conjunction have influenced the designing of the new church? The question arises because the plan is a Latin cross with nave, transepts, a short chancel and an apse. No other church built in Scotland in the seventeenth century is of this form. Scottish Presbyterians regarded the practice of dividing a church into these distinct parts as an obstacle to fully congregational worship. Their principal requirement was a single-chambered building in which the whole congregation could equally and simultaneously take part in acts of worship. A cruciform church plan was rightly felt to be associated with Roman Catholic churches on the Continent. Perhaps this is why the Canongate Church has often received a bad press in Scotland. Thus one hundred years ago, when religious feelings ran higher than they do now, it was dismissed by one author as 'a most unpicturesque-looking edifice, of nameless style, with a species of Doric porch'.

The style is admittedly a combination of styles, Classical with Gothic; it has also been called Baroque. The multi-curved gable is very striking, especially in the Royal Mile; at its apex rise a pair of antlers, a reference to the foundation of Holyrood Abbey (*see* p. 62). The portico is Roman Doric, its pediment echoed above the doors to left and right, and there are two tall round-arched windows and a circular window. Between the windows are the arms of Thomas Moodie, whose bequest of 1649 met much of the cost. Above the round window are the royal arms of William III, generously carved. In the apse there are two lights below a tracery motif of the Decorated style. Inside the church the nave arcades are round-arched and the columns are Roman Doric. All the windows have clear glass. The overall effect is one of simplicity, very carefully contrived. The lines are flowing, easy and relaxed. The external whitewash is bright and cheerful, the interior spacious and well lit. The whole building is reminiscent of Holland, from which country many craftsmen, as well as shiploads of Dutch tiles, came to Scotland in the seventeenth century. Holland, after all, was only a short sea voyage away, and, unlike England, was a friendly neighbour.

The churchyard is also of interest, one of three churchyards in Edinburgh worth a visit. (The others are Greyfriars and the Old Calton Burying Ground). In this case, the view is one major attraction; the Royal High School and the Burns Monument (a circular Greek temple) on Calton Hill are nowhere better seen than from the Canongate churchyard. But that apart, the display of monuments is immense: urns, busts, tablets, pedestals, mausoleums, aedicules, obelisks, columns, headstones, along with cherubs, angels, garlands, skulls, bones and crossbones – all tastes are catered for here. The connoisseur of cemeteries is bound to linger.

For those whose curiosity lies more in other directions, some of the choicer items may be picked out. In the west part of the churchyard probably the most celebrated monument is the headstone to Robert Fergusson, who died in 1774, at the age of 24. He spent his short manhood drinking heavily and writing incessantly. He played an important part in the revival of Scots vernacular poetry, and it is for his monument, which was set up by Robert Burns in 1789, that Burns wrote the inscription:

> *No sculptur'd Marble here nor pompous lay*
> *No storied Urn nor animated Bust*
> *This simple Stone directs Pale Scotia's way*
> *To pour her Sorrows o'er her Poet's Dust.*

Not far away is a pedimented headstone erected by the Society of Coachdrivers in Canongate, dated 1765. Besides a skull and inscription, it has a highly unusual relief of a coach, a coachman and two horses crossing a bridge. In the northern part of the churchyard, at the north-west corner, stands the mausoleum of Dugald Stewart, a philosopher of some consequence who at various times of his life taught philosophy, mathematics, economics, logic and Greek in Edinburgh University. At the foot of the slope there is a monument to soldiers who died at Edinburgh Castle. It was erected in 1880, and was described by the *Scotsman* newspaper, in a rash moment, as Byzantine. There are verses. Finally, before you depart, there is the wall monument to Adam Smith, built into the back of the Tolbooth, just west of the gate. Large and severe, it commemorates one of the most famous of all Scotsmen. Like most economists, he was an earnest man. His conversation, says a contemporary, 'was not colloquial, but like lecturing'; if you could persuade him to attend to the subject of conversation, 'he immediately began a harangue, and never stopped till he had told you all he knew about it, with the utmost philosophical ingenuity'. The monument, however, sticks to a very plain record of what he wrote, when he was born, and when he died.

Leave the church, but spare one more moment for Adam Smith. In Little Lochend Close stands **Panmure House**, a solid, white-washed L-shaped building with crowstepped gables. Here the great economist lived from 1778 until his death in 1790. During these years he was one of the Commissioners for Customs in Scotland, and must often have travelled up and down the Royal Mile between his home and the Customhouse, which was in the rear part of the recently-built Exchange. Panmure House is not visible from the street, concealed by some rather nasty developments of the nineteenth and twentieth centuries.

The area hereabouts was described a hundred years ago as one of 'ancient grandeur and modern squalor'. It has been much tidied up, with varying degrees of success. But it does contain, facing the church, one of the finest groups of old buildings in Edinburgh. This comprises Huntly House and Acheson House, standing one on one side and one on the other of Bakehouse Close, with a small seventeenth century tenement (which boasts a balustraded parapet) on the street between them.

See **Bakehouse Close** first because it affords intimate views of the two adjacent buildings. Bakehouse Close is probably the best preserved close in Edinburgh. It no longer extends very far, but what there is of it combines the genuinely old with the very well restored. You enter through a vaulted pend which runs underneath the eastern-most part of Huntly House. It is best to go to the foot of the close and look back. On your left are two three-storey tenements of 1648, with timber-clad gable projections, which were incorporated into Huntly House in 1932. Straight ahead is a house which was rebuilt over the pend in 1570, when it and the next two small houses up the Canongate were united to make the original Huntly House. This rear elevation is most attractive. The tri-partite window with small sidelights; the irregular sizes and disposition of the other windows; the rough stonework; the steps leading up to the door; the flattened arch of the pend; the projecting attic; the granite setts; all these are brought together into a fascinating jumble of seventeenth-century Scots domestic architecture. It *is* a jumble; but it is architecture nevertheless. Return towards the street, and on your right is Acheson House, begun in 1633, and restored in the 1930s. Acheson House faces Bakehouse Close, and there is a moulded door here, dated 1679, which leads into a small forecourt; but the entrance is now from the Canongate, so let Acheson House wait for a moment.

The original **Huntly House** was bought by the Incorporation of Hammermen (smiths, or metal workers) in 1647, and it was they who appointed Robert Mylne to enlarge it. So above the corbelled-out first floor he raised two timber-framed and harled storeys, also corbelled out, with three broad gables facing the street, which define the three pre-1570 house widths. (These upper storeys were replicated in the 1930s). Inside there is a labrynth of panelled rooms and changing floor levels. There are moulded stone fireplaces and late sixteenth-century painted beams brought from a now-vanished mansion near Edinburgh. It is an interesting house to walk through, and now a museum. The contents include pre-historic, Celtic and Roman items; four late seventeenth-century bells which are all that are left of the great carillon of twenty-three bells that used to ring in St Giles; and there is a very fine collection of eighteenth-century Scots silver, along with a seventeenth-century silver quaich (a shallow drinking vessel with two handles, once common in Scotland). The great fire of 1824, described at the beginning of this chapter, is recorded in six dramatic watercolours by William Turner. (It is curious that exactly ten years later William Turner's great namesake, J M W Turner, recorded the burning of the Houses of Parliament in London). Six other items of particular interest relate to the New Town. Two are portraits, one of George Drummond, the Lord Provost who laid the foundations for Edinburgh's expansion in the eighteenth century. and one of James Craig, who provided the initial plan of the New Town. Craig's plan is on show, along with an extraordinary cast-iron model made in 1829. Also worth noticing are a

1780 view looking along the valley between the Old Town and New Town (now all railway line and gardens) and a painting (again by William Turner) of George IV entering Edinburgh in 1822. There is a good deal to see, and all in an appropriately historical setting.

Unlike Huntly House, **Acheson House** was built as a single dwelling, begun in 1633 for Sir Archibald Acheson, who held several high offices under Charles I, including that of Secretary of State for Scotland, and who was a friend of the poet Drummond of Hawthornden. It is an attractive four-storeyed building set back from the Canongate behind a wall and beyond a small informal court where roses grow, some jasmine, and a couple of rowan trees. Many of the better houses in the Canongate were likewise set back from the hurly-burly of the street; John Taylor, the water-poet (he was a Thames waterman, and his many journeyings included a walk from London to Braemar, which is forty-five miles west of Aberdeen) visited Edinburgh in 1618 and observed that 'the gentlemen's mansions and goodliest houses are obscurely founded in the ... by-lanes and closes'. This side of the house, where is now the entrance, has a crow-stepped gable and a wooden balcony, the latter rebuilt in the 1930s. The crow-stepped gable above the original rectangular stair tower, which projects towards Bakehouse Close and is best seen from there, was also built in the 1930s.

The house, which is at present unused and closed, is of considerable interest. The room on the ground floor has a very large fireplace, and the ceiling beams mostly came from the roof. The stair is a stone turnpike of the eighteenth century, with a 1930s wrought-iron balustrade. On the first floor there is another large room with another huge seventeenth-century fireplace, as well as moulded plasterwork of seventeenth-century style on the ceiling, done in 1937. The smaller room facing Bakehouse Close, has a stone chimney-piece, the arabesque frieze on the lintel repeated in the decoration of the timber ceiling (1937). It is especially worth looking out of the windows here, because at the foot of the stair tower the original front door can be seen. It has a pediment, broken by the Acheson crest of a cock standing on a trumpet. The date is 1633 and the monogram bears the initials of Sir Archibald and his wife Margaret Hamilton. These initials appear separately on the pedimented dormerheads above the forecourt.

The next building of genuine antiquity is **Queensberry House**, further down on the same side of the street. It does not look very old, or in the least attractive; a white-painted quadrangular monster. Its history has been white-washed away, and the excitements of the past have vanished in the confusion of dilapidations and repairs, and soon perhaps it will vanish altogether. (*see* p. 59) Yet Queensberry House was once a very grand mansion. It was begun in 1681 for Lord Hatton, later the third Earl of Lauderdale, who was Master General of the Mint. His office was a profitable one, but he seems to have thought it not profitable enough, for in 1683 he was tried for 'irregularities' at the Mint and fined £20,000. Having thus fallen on evil days, he sold his splendid new house to the first Duke of Queensberry. In 1803 it became a barracks (bought, it is said, for £900), in 1853 a House of Refuge for the Destitute, and then a hospital for the old and infirm. It seems that it once had a mansard roof, and some people thought that it resembled Versailles.

Queensberry House would not be worth noticing except that it is so large and was once the home of the second Duke of Queensberry. This Duke was the chief promoter in Scotland of the Act of Union, and he received the enormous sum of £12,325 from the Lord Treasurer in London when his efforts were crowned with success. Fearing for his life in his native country, he then fled to England. It was his father the first Duke who built Drumlanrig Castle in Dumfriesshire (by the designer of the Canongate Church), and on the day of whose death (so the story went in Edinburgh) a Scottish ship's captain, being in Sicily, saw a coach and six driving furiously towards the crater of Mount Etna and heard a terrible voice call out, 'Make way for the Duke of Drumlanrig!' The family was not always popular. Perhaps it should be added that the rules of boxing were drawn up by a Victorian descendent.

For something more light-hearted, cross the road to **Whitehorse Close**. The west side is unremarkable, the east side makes more of an effort. But these merely serve as introductions to the stage-set composition which looks down the court. It began as an inn in 1623, and prospered in the later eighteenth century, when stage-coaches for Newcastle and London left from Calton Road, which is just behind the Close. (The service was rudimentary. In the 1780s a coach left every two weeks or so and was scheduled to take 'thirteen days without any stopping (if God permit)'). In 1889 the inn was reconstructed as working-class housing, and it was again renovated and altered in the 1960s. It has everything, or nearly everything, that the guileless visitor could desire; jettied bays, wooden beams, crow-stepped gables, an irregular fenestration, an arched doorway and a rather handsome external staircase which led to the main rooms;

servants and horses were on the ground floor. It drives purists wild, but it is rather fun. Perhaps this is what the seventeenth century ought to have looked like, even if it didn't. Restoration went a little too far, however, when a datestone which read 1523 was taken from somewhere else and recut to read 1623 so as to make the whole thing appear more plausible. Being hoodwinked is not the same as being lied to.

The great palace is now in sight. The buildings to the right of the gates belong to the Palace and will be included in the next chapter. On the left there is a range of buildings in two parts. The larger block, although basically very old (it had to be reconstructed after the sack of Edinburgh in 1544), was restored in 1916 and is of no great interest except that it is used by officials of the Court when the Queen is at Holyrood. The two-storey block further east is substantially of the early seventeenth century. The unequal crowstepped gables are original,whereas the pend arch was built in 1935. Finally, just along the street to the left is an odd little building popularly known as **Queen Mary's Bath House**. It has a fat turret, a small turret, prominent chimneys and much corbelling out. There is no reason to suppose that the tragic queen ever bathed here, but the story that she did was in full circulation in the eighteenth century, with the addition of one very unconvincing detail:

> *That chamber where the queen, whose charms divine*
> *Made wand'ring nations own the power of love,*
> *Oft bathed her snowy limbs in sparkling wine*
> *Now proves a lonely refuge for the dove.*

It is not poetry and for the most part it is not true. The so-called bath house was evidently built in the late sixteenth century as a garden pavilion, when the gardens of the Palace were far more extensive than they are now. But the legend persists, and the doves sometimes return.

4

Holyroodhouse and the Abbey

HOLYROODHOUSE IS ONE of the most important buildings in Edinburgh, for it is the residence of the Queen during all her State visits to the Scottish capital. It is from the Palace that she goes, by limousine or coach, to whatever functions there are to attend, it is in the Palace that the royal receptions and dinner parties are held, and it is in the grounds of the Palace that the royal garden parties take place. Other members of the royal family live at Holyrood from time to time, and if you are lucky enough to be shown round just before or after one of these occasions you will see great vases of flowers in the rooms and on the stairways, as is only proper in a very grand house.

The origins of Holyrood – perhaps we should say, the fabulous origins of Holyrood – are in its name. David I, whose manners, if we are to believe an English chronicler, 'had been polished from the rust of Scots barbarity' at the court of Queen Matilda in London, was one day hunting in the woods near Edinburgh. The year was 1128. He had left the Castle and gone into the primeval forest of Drumsheugh, where the oak trees 'had shaken down their leaves and acorns upon the ground,' and in the ardour of the chase he became separated from his followers. Pausing for a moment, he was suddenly attacked by a white stag of gigantic size, maddened by the pursuit and by 'the noys and dyn of bugillis,' and his life was in the utmost danger. While he defended himself as best he could with his short huntingsword, there appeared a silver cloud from which a cross, or rood, slipped into the king's hand; and immediately the stag fled. That night, in a dream, St Andrew appeared before the king and instructed him to found, on the exact spot where he had been saved 'in the little valley between two mountains' (i.e. between Arthur's Seat and Calton Hill) a monastery for the Augustinians. Hence the abbey of the holy rood. It is a good story, told in the Middle Ages with much amplifying detail. Disconcertingly, however, medieval chroniclers tell the same story of other religious foundations in other countries. So the facts may be otherwise.

Holyroodhouse and the Abbey

But, as someone has said, perhaps there is more truth in the verisimilitudes of fiction than in the explanations of history. What cannot be doubted is that the Abbey was founded by David I in 1128. It quickly became important. The early twelfth century church was rebuilt and enlarged soon after 1300, and the guesthouse of the abbey was almost certainly used by the Scottish kings as early as the fourteenth century. By the fifteenth century Holyrood was pre-eminent as a royal residence; James II was born there in 1426, crowned there in 1437, married there in 1449 and buried there in 1460. But not until the days of James V was there a palace that we know about, quite distinct from the abbey. Some of this early or renaissance palace still stands, incorporated into the Carolingian palace which is the present Holyroodhouse. The ruined abbey is thus older than even the oldest parts of the palace. But because there is far more to see in the palace than in the abbey, and because you can inspect the abbey only after going through the palace, let us begin with the latter.

The best general view of the **Palace** is as you approach it through the main gates at the foot of the Royal Mile. This west façade is very handsome. Two massive towers with circular conical-capped angle turrets project forwards and are linked by a lower balustraded screen of two storeys with a central Doric portico. This portico has coupled columns, and above it there is an octagonal crowned cupola, with a clock dated 1680. Dolphins support the cupola and ladies recline upon it. Above the doorway there is a huge relief of the royal arms. This front is very long and almost perfectly symmetrical. It appears elegant and decorated, although the only decorations, apart from the central portico, are the balustrade, the string courses on the towers, their corbelled parapets and battlements, their gun loops, their pepper-pot turrets, and two panels on the left-hand or north-west tower carved with the arms of James V and Mary of Guise. The impression is of a uniform, relaxed design.

Yet there are really two buildings here. Most of what you see was built in the 1670s, but a large chunk of it dates from 1532. This chunk is the north-west tower, and here the gun-loops and battlements were intended not for elegance but for defence. James V built the tower, which is enormously massive, as an addition to a palace which had been built by his father. That palace has totally disappeared. The tower was originally free-standing, but now forms the north-west corner of a quadrangle. Towers and tower-houses of the same kind are to be found all over Scotland – for that matter, all over western

63

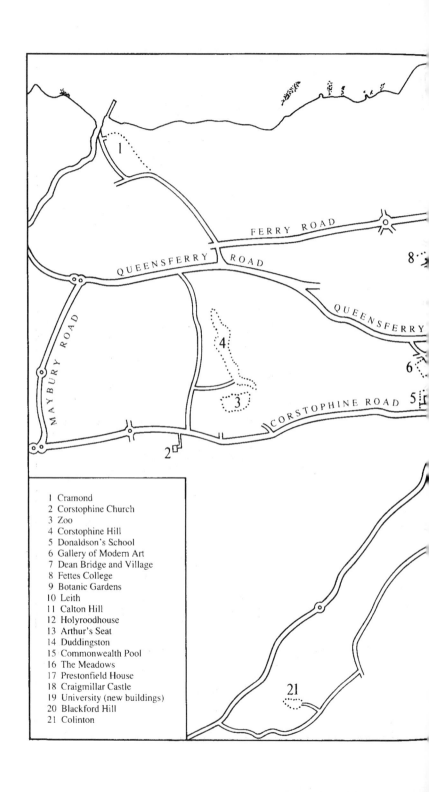

FERRY ROAD

QUEENSFERRY ROAD

QUEENSFERRY

MAYBURY ROAD

CORSTOPHINE ROAD

1
4
3
2
8
6
5
21

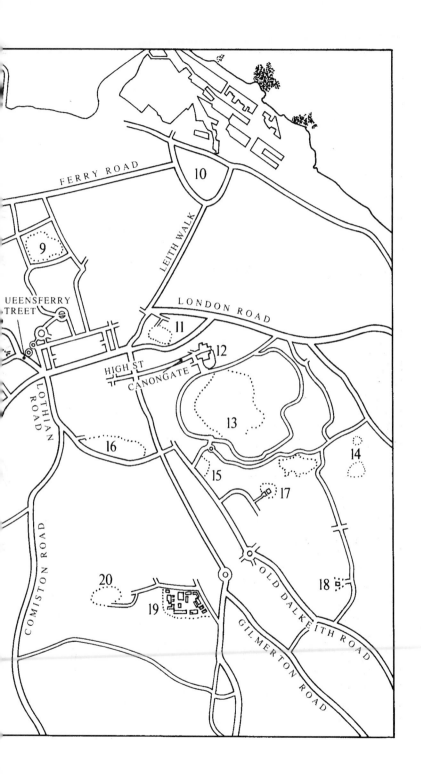

Europe. They were a popular design during several centuries, because in turbulent times they provided the needed balance between the claims of domestic comfort and those of defence. They could be very plain, or they could be very architectural, playing down the defence angle – Craigievar in Aberdeenshire is the ultimate fairy-tale tower-castle, wonderfully preserved. James V's tower was built to be imposing, with sets of apartments for the king and his queen on different floors; but it was also very defensible; there would have been no point in attacking it without cannon and scaling ladders.

Further building took place in the later 1530s, and it was then that the still-existing rectangular courtyard plan was established. In 1544, however, the forces of Henry VIII pillaged and burned both the abbey and the palace. Various repairs and rebuildings were carried out during the next hundred years, and we know from a drawing done in 1650 that at that time the west front extended a good distance south from the tower, having several tall bay windows, with other tall windows between the bays, and a round-arched entrance to the court. The palace was commandeered by Cromwell in 1650, and was then badly damaged by a fire started by his troops who were quartered there. When the Commonwealth collapsed in 1660, Holyroodhouse was pretty well a wreck.

What saved it was the Restoration – and Sir William Bruce. Bruce can be described with some justice as the first Scots architect; or more specifically, as a gentleman of moderate means, who was active in politics, and who knew a lot about architecture, and who from time to time advised important people about altering old buildings or designing new ones. He was a royalist, an active supporter of Charles II, and he counted among his patrons the Earl (later Duke) of Lauderdale, who virtually governed Scotland after the Restoration. (Don't miss the splendid portrait of him by Sir Peter Lely in the National Portrait Gallery). Bruce became the King's Surveyor and Master of Works in Scotland in 1671. There was work to do, for with a king again on the throne it made sense to have a palace in Edinburgh, fit to be used either by the King himself or by his Commissioner to the resurrected Scottish Parliament. So the Privy Council decided to repair and rebuild Holyroodhouse, and Bruce, in collaboration with Robert Mylne, the King's Master Mason, prepared the plans. Charles, who was destined never to visit Holyrood, took an active interest.

James V's tower was the starting point. Bruce decided to build a similar tower to the south, as we now have it, and these two formed the western corners of a quadrangular Classical design. The first plans had to be altered, because the internal arrangements were a muddle, and Charles himself proposed several extensive improvements. (He excised a chapel which was to have been in the new tower, and originated the idea of the Great Gallery). The quadrangle plan, however, remained. Building began in 1671, and the Palace was virtually complete by 1679.

Palace Yard, which is to the west of the frontage, is no visual help to the Palace, except that it is a large open space which enables the west front to be seen properly. In the Yard there are very large wrought-iron screens and gates made in the 1920s, modelled on ironwork by Tijou – one of the greatest craftsmen of the age of Baroque – at Hampton Court. There is an octagonal Victorian fountain in the centre, with small statues of historical figures which have been likened to garden gnomes. The buildings which face the Palace are almost wholly Victorian rebuilds. And worst of all, the surface of the Yard is unrelieved asphalt, grey and featureless, an abominable contrast to the trees and the solid stonework around it. When will those in authority learn that what is on the ground is visually almost as important as what is built above it? But even several acres of tarmacadam cannot spoil the Palace. The massive terminal towers give it authority, and the low balustraded range that connects them is elegant and correct.

The entrance leads directly into the quadrangle, which is of the utmost regularity. A loggia, cloister-like, runs round all four sides. The principal ranges are of three storeys, with large high windows above the loggia, and there are superimposed orders of pilasters on all four sides: Doric at ground level, Ionic on the first floor, and Corinthian at the top – again, all very correct. The range which faces the entrance has the centre bays slightly advanced and pedimented; the tympanum is carved with the monogram of Charles II and his coat of arms. Most of the quadrangle is grass, kept to much the same standard as a bowling green, and in the centre is a stone lamp standard, made in 1908 but a copy of a sundial of 1633 which stands in the Palace gardens. It is all very orderly and, except for the lamp standard, very Classical; an arcaded court in what was then the new Renaissance style. Nothing like this had ever previously been built in Scotland.

The door at the south-west corner of the quadrangle opens onto the state staircase, which is a remarkably easy three-sided well-stair with a ponderous stone balustrade. The ceiling, by John Houlbert, a Londoner, is the first of the Palace's many extremely elaborate ceilings. Some are by Houlbert and some by Houlbert and his partner

George Dunsterfield. Oak leaves and acanthus, borders of flowers in high relief and cherubs 'hung up whole' were their forte. Plasterwork richer than this is not to be found in Britain. The staircase ceiling is heavily enriched with high-relief foliage, and in the corners decorously clothed angels hold crowns and swords and blow trumpets. At the foot of the stairs is a set of seventeenth century carved chairs, and on the walls higher up hangs a set of four large tapestries which were woven in Brussels in the sixteenth century. The tapestry facing you as you go up is a boisterous bacchanalian scene, and on the opposite wall hangs that ever-popular subject, the toilet of Venus; what could be more appropriate for a house built for Charles II? Above the tapestries is a series of six paintings on plaster by the sixteenth century Brescian painter Lattanzio Gambara. They were acquired in 1856 by Prince Albert, who intended them as a guide for the fresco painters who were to decorate the Palace of Westminster.

At the top of the stairs, to the right, a door leads to what was originally the Council Chamber for the Privy Council of Scotland. This room, normally closed to visitors, has another Houlbert ceiling, and twentieth century oak panelling. It is the principal room in Bruce's 'replica' tower. A second door leads to a room in the west wing, which is open. This is the **Royal Dining Room**. It was created in the later eighteenth century out of a much larger room, and then was extensively modified around the time of King George V's visit in 1911. It is an architectural oddity in the Palace, but a very pleasant one, elegant and well-proportioned, Neo-Classical in style, with a screen of tall Ionic columns at the far end. There are several portraits, of which the most noteworthy is a full-length of Sir Mungo Murray, painted about 1680. What is so interesting about this picture is that it shows Sir Mungo in full highland dress, and is the earliest record we have of anyone thus attired. Very little is known about tartan and how it was worn before 1750, and paintings are our best source of information. There are also two portraits by Louis-Gabriel Blanchet, one of Prince Charles, the Young Pretender, and one of his younger brother Henry, who became a cardinal in the Roman Catholic Church.

You now leave the south-west corner of the Palace and enter the series of royal apartments that extends at this level along the whole of the south and east ranges. These rooms form a major part of a tour of Holyroodhouse. After seeing them, you walk the length of the Great Gallery in the north wing, and thus, going back in time, you finally arrive in James V's four hundred year old tower.

Holyroodhouse and the Abbey

Charles II's royal apartments were carefully planned, so that a visitor arriving at the head of the state staircase would proceed through rooms which were in ascending order of importance and grandeur. The most public rooms come first, and are not remarkably grand; then come those to which access was less easy, made more grand; finally, there are those apartments which only the King and his closest friends and advisers would enter, very grand. To modern eyes the gradation and its significance may not be obvious; but to the seventeenth century courtier, an expert on all questions of precedence and degree, it would have been perfectly clear.

The first room in the south range is now known as the **Throne Room**, because there is a pair of throne-chairs on the dais, made for King George V and Queen Mary in 1927. Originally this was the Guard Hall, very large, having been built, so to speak, for the multitude. It is now used occasionally for banquets and investitures; many a man has knelt here and risen a knight or a baronet. The panelling and the ceiling are twentieth century work. There are several portraits. Queen Victoria is above the chimneypiece, by Sir George Hayter (1838). Two paintings to the left are of James VII and II and his second wife, Mary of Modena; two to the right are of Charles II himself and his queen, Catherine of Braganza. All these four are the work of Sir Peter Lely, or are from his studio. But the most notable picture, which is by Sir David Wilkie, is a full-length portrait of George IV in highland dress as he appeared at his first levee at Holyrood in April, 1822. The picture is not a great masterpiece, but the occasion was a notable one, for at least two reasons. First, no reigning monarch had visited Edinburgh since James VI and I returned briefly in 1617. So the visit by George IV was remarkable enough in itself, and Edinburgh, by all accounts, went mad with loyal fervour. Still more remarkable was the King's attire for his levee at Holyrood. The House of Hanover in a kilt? Tartan was not only not fashionable, it was still generally regarded as the uniform of the rebels – which it had indeed been in 1745/6, inasfar as they had a uniform. So when the King donned his kilt he made a sharp and almost shocking break with tradition. (He was almost certainly guided by the romantic notions of Sir Walter Scott, who master-minded most of the ceremonials in 1822). It was a significant moment. From this time forward kilts and highlanders became, for the first time, readily acceptable in polite society, and the romanticizing of the once-dreaded clans proceeded apace.

Next comes the much smaller (although large) **Evening Drawing Room**. This was originally the **Presence Chamber**, where the king might come to greet important visitors. The oak panelling is twentieth century, the ceiling is original, again by John Houlbert; very fine, but not extravagant. The set of six French gilt chairs and a sofa are covered with Beauvais tapestry. Best of all are the four magnificent Brussels wall tapestries of about 1750. They were brought here from Buckingham Palace in 1851.

From the Presence Chamber pass into the Privy Chamber, now the **Morning Drawing Room**. This, being privy (private), is the most sumptuously decorated room in the Palace. Unlike the preceding rooms, it overlooks the garden to the east. The ceiling is superbly ornate – lavish and sumptuous are the words that spring to mind – and is regarded as Houlbert's masterpiece. There is an arabesque frieze and a large clear area in the middle, surrounded by deeply moulded plasterwork with much foliage decoration and, at the corners, cherubs who seem almost detached from the ceiling and who hold wreaths which surround the initials of Charles II and the regalia of Scotland. No doubt this ceiling was designed to impress; but it is also a triumph of artistic craftsmanship. Most of the wooden panelling was carried out by Alexander Eizat in 1677. The fireplace and surrounds are particularly fine: fluted Corinthian pilasters at the sides, and an over-mantel with big festoons of foliage (carved by Jan van Santvoort) beside a bay-leaved frame which holds a painting by Jacob de Witt. The painting is a study of Cupid and Psyche in appropriately amorous mood.

Some of the furniture in the room is known to have been in the Palace in the later eighteenth century, and the walls are hung with tapestries which were here at least a hundred years before that. They were mostly made in France, and they illustrate the story of Diana – Diana supplicating Jupiter, Actaeon being turned into a stag, Latona on the island of Delos, and so on. There is also a sixteenth century Flemish tapestry from a series illustrating the story of Tobit and Anna. Those who are not too familiar with the Old Testament, or with the amatory and other adventures of the gods, need not despair; these tapestries can be enjoyed without erudite explanations.

The next five rooms are much smaller, and can be thought of in present-day terms as the royal flat. First comes the **Antechamber** where the king could meet his closest advisers more privately and informally than in the larger rooms. The ceiling, once again by Houlbert and his partner George Dunsterfield, is moderately elaborate, with foliage, wreaths and cartouches. The chimneypiece has pilasters and a painting by de Witt, similar in spirit to the Cupid and Psyche in the Privy Chamber. The walls are covered with a series of seventeenth century tapestries, mostly French; Diana again appears, with her nymphs. The furniture includes a suite of eight carved and upholstered chairs of the late seventeenth century; the covers are modern.

Next comes the **King's Bedchamber**, at the centre of the east range; no trouble spared here to create a luxurious and yet intimate effect. The ceiling, again by Houlbert and Dunsterfield, is mostly filled with heavily moulded foliage decoration and the usual emblems of kingship. In the central oval is a painting by de Witt which shows Hercules being welcomed by the gods. The same hero, by the same painter, appears in the overmantel as an infant strangling snakes. The implication is obvious; Charles and Hercules have much in common. Strangely, Diana and Psyche are both absent. The tapestries are Flemish seventeenth century work, illustrating scenes from the lives of Diogenes and Alexander the Great. Much space is taken up by the bed, hung with red damask. This bed has been in the Palace since at least 1684. It was restored in the 1970s and rehung with material which matches the original fabric, a little of which had survived. The curtains are of the same material, and all the furnishings are of the period. Off the bedchamber is a small lobby. To the left of the lobby is the **Stool Room**, where was kept the royal close stool, or portable latrine; ceilings by Houlbert.

Straight ahead is the **Closet**, or what we would call the king's study. This is a very attractive room of relaxed grandeur. The ceiling, once more by Houlbert, has a circle of oak leaves, and centred on each wall are the royal arms and Charles's monogram, flanked by drapery which is pulled aside by cherubs. There is wood carving by Alexander Eizat and in the overmantel another painting by de Witt. This is the finding of Moses, a subject deemed appropriate because of a medieval legend that Pharaoh's daughter Scota was the ancestress of the kings of Scotland. The tapestries continue the life of Diogenes. The furniture is mostly in the chinese style, which was much in vogue towards the end of the seventeenth century. There are also a fine eighteenth century French harpsichord, two candlestands with climbing cherubs, and a most delicately carved looking glass, made of limewood.

Many visitors find it something of a relief to reach the end of the royal apartments. So much ornateness and magnificence is rather overwhelming. But then, it was meant to be. The majesty of monarchs must be supported, as the seventeenth century well understood. In our egalitarian age deep wood-carving and lavish plaster decoration seem extravagant, and may be found unsettling; our taste is for simplicity and smooth surfaces. But we should always be willing to try to appreciate what is not *à la mode*. And whatever our taste, we surely would not wish all the world to be the same. However that may be, you emerge from the royal apartments into something very different, although still of the 1670s. **The Gallery** occupies the whole of the inner side of the north range at first floor level. Charles II ordered that 'a little galerie for a passage' should be made to connect his own apartments in the east range with the queen's apartments which were to be fitted into the old tower; and this 'little galerie' somehow became the Great Gallery, its north (windowless) wall, the experts tell us, almost certainly being the north wall of the sixteenth century palace. Many long galleries were built in the late sixteenth and the seventeenth centuries – the long gallery at Hardwick Hall is very famous, and Wren had incorporated a long gallery into his design for Emmanuel College chapel only a few years before – but this one is wider than most. The ceiling was inserted in 1968 (with seventeenth century motifs) and the panelling, although original, is nothing out of the ordinary. What *is* out of the ordinary are the pictures, and the history.

The pictures, all eighty nine of them (there were once one hundred and eleven) purport to be portraits of Scottish kings from Fergus to James VII. This notion of a string of kings who, in the extreme version, stretched back to Moses, has aroused much derision. But although the portraits are absurd, the idea was not. The Scots were ever-anxious to establish the antiquity of their kingdom against English usurpers, and they could indeed trace their kings' lineage with some authenticity back to Fergus, son of Erc, who had come with his people from Ireland to Dalriada (Argyll) around the year 500. (In the high Middle Ages forty-five kings were claimed to have ruled *before* Fergus, a claim which 'was designed to give the Scottish dynasty a startling lead in any contest based on claims to antiquity'. The Irish, however, maintained that they had been ruled over by almost two hundred kings). In the seventeenth century the idea of an ages-old succession was no longer important, but in these portraits it persists.

De Witt was commissioned to paint the long-departed monarchs 'like unto the Originalls which are to be given to him', but it is not easy to imagine what these 'Originalls' were, or how an artist of de Witt's calibre could have sunk to turning out such sorry stuff. Probably some unfortunate assistant had to take on the job.

Holyroodhouse and the Abbey

With the history we are on firmer ground; the Gallery and Prince Charles Edward connect. The Prince came to Holyroodhouse on September 17th, 1745, eight weeks after his landing on Eriskay in the Outer Hebrides. He left Edinburgh briefly on the 20th to fight and win the battle of Prestonpans, a few miles to the east, and he left finally at the end of October on his long and unsuccessful march into England. For six weeks the Prince was in Holyrood, and the Palace enjoyed its 'crowded hour of glorious life'. There were councils of war in the morning, and in the evening Charles 'received the ladies who came to his drawing room: he then supped in public, and generally there was music at supper, and a ball afterwards'. These balls took place in the Gallery, which was obviously most suitable for the purpose. Prince Charles, who was a grand-nephew of Charles II, made a good impression on some Edinburgh citizens, but not on all. He was physically very fit and an excellent horseman; he looked every inch a prince; and he had the manner of a very distinguished and well-bred person. But impartial observers had their doubts about his ability to lead a successful rebellion on the grand scale: 'they acknowledged that he was a goodly person, but observed that the air of his countenance was languid and melancholy; that he looked like a gentleman and man of fashion, but not like a hero or conqueror... The ladies were much his friends'. So says John Home, who fought against Prince Charles at the battle of Prestonpans. But when the Prince rode away at the end of six weeks to overthrow George II, few if any Edinburgh citizens accompanied him. And in staying behind they judged their chances well; for he never came back.

From the Gallery pass into the most northerly room in the entrance range, and thence into James V's tower; from the misfortunes of Prince Charles back to the uneasy times of Charles II and his brother James, and to the tragedy of Mary, Queen of Scots.

The three rooms which you see at first floor level were originally the royal apartments of James V. But when the Palace was reconstructed by Sir William Bruce, these rooms were altered to become the Queen's Apartments. First there is the **Queen's Lobby**, which was the most public of the three rooms. The ceiling, which is the work of a Scottish craftsman, James Bayne, was completed in 1672, and is very much less grand than the ceilings by Houlbert. There are seventeenth century chairs and two seventeenth century Brussels tapestries, and a good fireplace with Dutch tin-glazed tiles.

The next room is the **Queen's Antechamber**, the Outer Chamber of James V before the Palace was reconstructed. You have moved into the sixteenth century tower, its walls immensely thick. The room is panelled, and the ceiling is again by Bayne. Here, too, there is an attractive fireplace. A group of early seventeenth century Mortlake tapestries on the walls provides an unusually charming background; naked but well-fed cherubs play and gambol in a sylvan setting; one of them is even doing a cart-wheel. There are chairs which were bought in the 1680s for the Council Chamber, and a painting of Prince Charles's father, the Old Pretender (a gloomy fellow who passed a despondent life in Rome), by Francesco Trevisani. There is also a table and a looking glass which are nineteenth century electro-type reproductions of the embossed silver originals which are in Windsor Castle. The originals were presented to Charles II by the City of London.

The **Queen's Bedchamber** contains two items of interest. The obvious one is the bed, which was bought in London in 1682 for the Duke of Hamilton. (The first Duke of Hamilton was appointed Hereditary Keeper of the Palace in 1646, and this gave the family some rights of occupancy). The canopy and bed-head retain the orig-inal red and yellow silk, and it is for the sake of these that the bed is in a glass case and the room kept dark. This museum-effect is an unfor-tunate intrusion in the Palace. The second item is the fireplace, which is the work of William Adam. It is flanked by superimposed pilasters, and has a basket-arched marble chimneypiece.

A narrow sixteenth century turnpike within the wall of the tower leads up and back in time to the most famous period of Scottish history. On this second floor are the rooms once occupied by Mary, Queen of Scots. Here, perhaps better than anywhere else in Scotland, the imagination is able to recreate the life of the sixteenth century – its turbulence, its passions, its intolerance, its heroisms and treach-eries, its faiths and dogmas, its savage cruelties and soaring ambitions. Kingship and religion dominated all.

Mary became Queen in 1542, when she was six days old. She was married to the Dauphin of France when she was fifteen and widowed less than three years later. She returned to Scotland in 1561 and was compelled to abdicate in 1567, at the age of twenty four.

On her return to Scotland the Queen took up residence in Holy-roodhouse. She was a Roman Catholic; but the Protestants were in control of the kingdom. To make matters still more difficult and dangerous, she was heir presumptive to the English throne, and many Roman Catholics, who believed that Henry VIII's marriage to Anne Boleyn was invalid and that Elizabeth was therefore illegitimate and not entitled to the throne, thought that Mary was the rightful queen of England. In 1565 she married (as already mentioned) Lord Darnley, her first cousin, whom she described as 'the best-proportionit lang [tall] man she had seen,' but who was described by a contemporary, with at least equal accuracy, as 'an agreeable nincompoop'. The ceremony was Roman Catholic. This marriage alienated Mary's Protestant subjects, enraged Queen Elizabeth,who saw it as a threat to her position, and turned Darnley's numerous enemies into Mary's enemies as well.

This is the background to the murder of David Riccio, a musician who had become Mary's French secretary. Riccio was widely disliked as an upstart favourite. Many nobles were envious of his influence, he was widely suspected of being a papal agent, and Darnley believed, or professed to believe, that Riccio's friendship with the Queen was not limited to the diplomatic and the platonic. One evening in March, 1566, a band of nobles, accompanied by Darnley, came up a stair which led to Queen Mary's Bedchamber (the room you are now in), burst into the northerly of the two closets leading off it where Mary was at supper, seized her wretched secretary, and stabbed him to death – whether in the Queen's presence or not is uncertain. He certainly died in the closet or the Bedchamber. The story, which in outline is unquestionably true, has been re-told hundreds of times, with all sorts of amplifying details; fifty-six wounds are often mentioned, 'and the king's [Darnley's] dagger driven to the hilt'. As a boy, the author used to be shown the red mark on the floor of the Outer Chamber which was said to be Riccio's blood. This mark was being shown in 1722, a fact which persuaded many people in the nineteenth century that it must be authentic. A brass plate now marks the spot where Riccio's body lay.

To follow the consequences of this savage murder (the barbarity of Scotland's history is probably unsurpassed anywhere else in Europe) would take us too far afield. Suffice to say that the Queen, who was six months pregnant at the time, survived the ordeal, and bore her son, as we have seen, in the Castle. As for Darnley, we shall meet him again in Edinburgh, murdered.

Mary Queen of Scots' Bedchamber has been significantly altered since her day. The wooden ceiling, geometrically divided into separate compartments, is the original, but the initials MR and IR at the centre almost certainly date from James VI's visit in 1617. The tempera-painted frieze of shells and flowers is of the same date. Painted initials and heraldic devices on the ceiling seem to have been added when Charles I visited the old palace in 1633. The tapestries are Flemish, of the late seventeenth century, and illustrate the story of Phaeton, who rashly drove the sun-chariot of his father, Phoebus Apollo, and came too close to the earth for the safety of mortals. Finally, the reconstruction work of the 1670s required the floor to be raised and the windows to be enlarged, and this has very much altered the character of the room.

The next apartment, **Queen Mary's Outer Chamber**, although it must strike the visitor as rather bleak and surprisingly large, has fared better. This is where she would have received visitors, such as John Knox, who, by his own account, admonished the Queen for her Roman Catholicism but graciously told her that he did not 'utterly condemn' dancing. He was no friend to the Queen, and when Riccio was murdered, he approved the deed. Round the walls there is another tempera-painted frieze probably of 1617, but the compartmented wooden ceiling belongs to the first half of the sixteenth century and has always been there. The compartments are decorated with roundels bearing initials and shields. These are thought to have been added in 1617, but they are older than that and are entirely appropriate. The arms of Mary of Guise, mother of Mary Queen of Scots, are at the centre; these were her apartments until her death in Edinburgh Castle in 1560. (She was a remarkable woman, a French heiress, who after James V's death could presumably have returned to live comfortably in France but who chose to remain in Scotland out of a sense of duty to her adopted country and her Church, and in order to protect her daughter's rights to the throne). Other shields carry the royal arms of James V, of Mary Queen of Scots, and of Henri II, also those of François II as Dauphin of France. (This fixes the date as 1558–9, after Mary's marriage to the Dauphin but before his accession. He died in 1560, six months after Mary's mother. What a background to her homecoming to Scotland!).

A number of items closely connected with Mary are on show. The Darnley Jewel is a jewel-locket of enamel and precious stones made in the 1570s for the Countess of Lennox, Darnley's mother. There is a portrait of Darnley with his brother Charles, and an extraordinary picture by Levinus Vogelarius painted in 1568 which shows the Earl and Countess of Lennox, with their little grandson James VI, kneeling at the tomb of Darnley. They pray for vengeance on his murderers. It is a dark and gloom-ridden canvas, which demonstrates that surrealism was not an invention of the twentieth century. There are also some pieces of needlework done by Mary when she was a prisoner in

England. One of these shows a luckless mouse in imminent danger of being eaten by a large ginger cat, and it has been suggested that Mary chose the subject as representing the relationship between herself and her red-haired cousin Queen Elizabeth.

It is now time to leave the royal apartments and head for the Abbey. On the way you may inspect the highland dress worn by George IV at Holyrood in 1822; but it looks much better in Wilkie's painting in the Throne Room. There are also several items connected with Prince Charles, and there is a display to illustrate the history of the Palace. And what a history it is! The tower built by James V; everything else reconstructed by Charles II; the whole place rediscovered by George IV, and subsequently lived in by Queen Victoria (who first came in 1842) and all her successors to the present day. Few places have such a living, continuous and dramatic history.

The **Abbey**, to which one seems to be led as an afterthought, is a sad ruin, gone the way of most Scots abbeys. It was founded, as we have seen, in 1128, but virtually nothing remains above ground of the modest-sized church which was then erected. Around 1195 work began on a far more ambitious scheme, completed some thirty years later, of which only the nave survives, and this is roofless. The dilapidations are easily explained. The Abbey, as well as the Palace, was pillaged and burned by Henry VIII's troops in 1544, and again looted in 1547. The church was patched up but the monastic buildings were left to decay (a process hastened on by the reformers), and in 1570 the choir and transepts were demolished. Major repairs and alterations were made prior to the coronation of Charles I at Holyrood in 1633. But a hundred years later the roof had become ruinous and was restored with flagstones which, being too heavy for the arches, fell and brought down a large part of the building in 1768. It then became an open quarry for the citizens, and remained nearly in that state until 1898.

It is difficult to imagine now what the Abbey once looked like. So much has gone, and the Palace slices into it in a manner that does no credit to Sir William Bruce. (Or to anyone else for that matter. But such was respect for old buildings in the seventeenth century). When it was built, the abbey was a remarkably elegant and in some ways original example of the Early English style. The nave was vaulted, and above the lavishly decorated west front rose twin towers, probably surmounted by wooden spires. Most unfortunately, the south tower and a large part of the front were destroyed in the 1670s to make way for the north east corner of the Palace. Details remain. On the north aisle wall there is a decorative arcade of intersecting round arches, and the piers and capitals have much finely carved stonework. The experts tell us that many features are reminiscent of Lincoln, which was building – in part rebuilding – at exactly the same time. The west front, although savagely mutilated by the intrusion of the Palace and the disappearance of much of the remaining tower, which now has no visible roof, is still impressive. There are two tiers of blind arcading, with large windows higher up, and a central arched doorway which has been described as 'almost French in its cavernous recession'. The arches are supported on multiple shafts, with beasts, foliage, dogtooth carving and some rather miserable-looking angels with overlapping wings. In the Abbey's great days this was the most elaborate entrance front to any ecclesiastical building in Scotland.

The **Palace gardens**, which are at the back of the Abbey and the Palace, are closed to the visitor. They are, to tell the truth, extensive but rather dull. To see them at their best you must secure an invitation to a royal garden party, when the band is playing, and the marquees are erected, and members of the Royal Company of Archers – that curious three hundred year old body of anciently-dressed prosperous citizens who constitute the Queen's Bodyguard for Scotland – hold the ring for royalty. Then you may wander as you please, and fancy that you enjoy 'the pleasure of the Pallace, secured ease and state; banquets abroad by torch-light, musics, sports ...'.

5

From the Cowgate to the Meadows

L EAVING HOLYROODHOUSE, AND the Abbey, turn towards the Park. Arthur's Seat is ahead, and on your right is a little-noticed area of Edinburgh – little-noticed, that is, until recently. It used to be the domain of abandoned breweries and defunct gasworks, and it was not much improved by a Victorian building with crow-stepped gables built in 1865 for 'the accommodation and reformation of females addicted to habits of drunkenness'. All around was densely populated, dark and dismal. But now all is changed, or changing.

On the lowest slopes of Arthur's Seat, overlooking the scene, stands – or perhaps crouches would be a better word – a very strange structure indeed – strange for Edinburgh, certainly: **Dynamic Earth**. Totally unlike the city's old historic set-pieces, Dynamic Earth is a brand new, calculated, up-to-the-minute attraction. There is a large concrete sub-structure which houses an underground car-park as well as the 'attraction' itself, and placed on top is a very large tent or marquee, long and low, glass-walled, oval in plan, one of those modern affairs which are taut, and curved, and canvas and full of light. And this means that Edinburgh at last has a spread-out café (with snacks) which provides views of the city; even if the foreground views are mostly of the backside of the Canongate.

And what of the 'attraction' itself, below ground? It is partly film, with 3D effect, partly mock-up, and more than an hour is needed just to walk through. It is, in the words of the organisers,

> *a thrilling journey through the history of our planet … a journey of discovery that spans over 4,500 million years and every environment known to humanity … everything from erupting volcanoes … to freezing icebergs and tropical rainstorms.*

We see, and hear, 'the forces that have shaped our planet, and the species that have lived here through the ages'. There is no shortage of movement, noise, and spectacle; Dynamic Earth is in the old fairground tradition. But there is one big difference. Dynamic Earth tells a true story: the world changes all the time, and everything connects with everything else. And this points a moral: man interferes with the environment at his peril: he must treat it with care.

From seismic tremors and warnings of doom return to Arthur's Seat, the Cowgate, and the present day. Undeniably, change is all around you. Next door to Dynamic Earth stands the new home (opened in 1999) of **The Scotsman** newspaper; three floors of shelved terracing with an atrium through the middle. Almost as close is a new large hotel. And on the other side of the road is a building site. Of these three, the building site is in a way the most interesting, because it is for this site that plans are afoot to build Scotland's new Parliament Building.

Scotland's latest tranch of political independence has come after decades (not to say centuries) of arguing, lobbying, speechifying, prophesying and, finally, voting. But it has now been found that even the quasi-independence which has been achieved requires visible grandeur; the new Parliament must be splendidly housed; the dignity of the nation is at stake (or so it is said). So all existing buildings in Scotland were declared to be inadequate, and the search began for a site and an architect. Arguing, lobbying etc. re-commenced, and this site at the foot of the Cowgate was finally chosen, and a Spanish architect, Enric Miralles, was appointed. What will emerge is anyone's guess. According to the First Minister, the site provides 'a dramatic setting', and the architect possesses 'imagination and flair'. According to the architect, his preliminary ideas were founded upon a landscape of upturned boats, simple clinker-built boats such as are used by fishermen all over Europe: 'We like these boats not only in their construction, but also in their delicate presence in a place. Something about their form floating in a landscape should be a part of our project'. The politicians were at once persuaded that something resembling a stack of upturned rowing boats would perfectly continue the style of High Street closes sliding down to the Cowgate, and it was declared that the scheme would be 'a vibrant addition to Edinburgh's famous architectural heritage … a people's building … a tangible symbol of our new democratic venture …' and so on and so forth. All this having been settled, the architects and the politicians set to work. Costs soon became the focus of attention. The first estimate was £40million, but after members of the legislature had voted to give themselves generous staff allowances in order to employ researchers, spin-doctors, PR personnel and others who would all require accommodation they rose to about £105million and then to something between £200m and £250million. To most citizens, five or six times the first estimate seemed rather steep, especially as few observers professed to know what the building would actually look like. The end is not yet in sight, but the latest statement is that costs will be held to £195million. Even if they are, the whole story suggests incompetent planning allied to self glorification regardless of expense. And the Scots used to be canny, thrifty people! (Incidentally, Queensberry House, adjacent to the site (*see* p 59), seems certain to be swallowed up in the great design, one way or another)

Next, turn up Holyrood Road, which in a few hundred yards becomes the Cowgate. In the Middle Ages the **Cowgate** (possibly meaning south gate i.e. south road) was a track running along the deepest part of a small valley, parallel to the High Street. Many wynds and closes descended into it from the old town, and the churchyard of St Giles was on the steep slope between the High Street and the possibly still more ancient track. It lay, to begin with, outside the city walls. In the course of time it became the most densely populated and poorest part of Edinburgh, and then the most derelict and squalid, teeming with life. Its old timber-fronted tenements began to be pulled down after 1850, and soon there was almost nothing left that was more than fifty years old.

Persevere, however, and at the first cross-roads and traffic-lights you will see one of the few remaining fragments of the **Flodden Wall**. (The other way to arrive is down St Mary's Street from the High Street). Edinburgh was a walled city from the twelfth century, but after the disastrous defeat inflicted by the forces of Henry VIII at Flodden in 1513 the walls were strengthened and extended, taking in the Cowgate. Of this new wall a short stretch is to be seen going south up the slope from the Cowgate and then turning into Drummond Street; the top has been removed, and also a bastion which was at this corner. It is not much to see, but is proof in masonry that the wall once existed. Go another hundred yards west, and the dismal congested old street has another surprise in store: St Cecilia's Hall, which announces itself as the Free Masons Hall 1812.

St Cecilia's Hall was designed by Robert Mylne for the Musical Society of Edinburgh and was completed in 1763. At that time its location was quite different from what it is now; an open scene, and only a step away from the houses of the most fashionable people in town. The great gloomy bridge which now stands beside it had not even been thought of, and neither had the buildings which abut the bridge and which raise their hideous rear elevations far overhead. Mean streets, general dereliction, and the back of the Crowne Plaza Hotel are now the setting for the Hall. It faces Niddry Street, but its blackened and dismal front elevation, two storeys high with a pedimented centre, can hardly be seen because it is only a few feet from the South Bridge buildings. To make matters worse, it has been crudely extended on two sides, partly in stone and partly in opaque glass, and it looks like nothing so much as a large public lavatory. But inside, it has been rescued. In the 1960s the University acquired and restored the building in order to house the superb Russel Collection of Harpsichords and Clavichords; and in the concert room music began to be heard again after a lapse of a hundred and fifty years.

The ground floor is divided into three nearly equal parts. The two furthest from the Cowgate open into one another through semi-elliptical arches, forming the Laigh (low) Hall; the third forms the foyer, with a Doric-columned screen and an Imperial stair with fluted balusters. The concert room is above, oval in shape and with a shallow oval ceiling, lit from above by a single lantern. The eighteenth century described this room as 'uncommonly elegant,' but in the nineteenth century it was made rectangular (mercifully, they left the ceiling alone) and was used at various times as a Baptist meeting place, a book bindery and a dance-hall. There was originally a gallery. The room was designed to accommodate five hundred people, and according to a contemporary was 'after the model of the opera at Parma'. It has been made oval again, pale green in colour, wonderfully restored. It provides a charming, intimate atmosphere; and the acoustics are first-class.

Even if you are not able to go to a concert, the collection of harpsichords and clavichords is well worth a visit. There are some fifty instruments, most of them made between 1585 and 1785, and most of them are maintained in playing condition. Even to the inexpert eye they are marvellous pieces of intricate craftsmanship: no one could fail to admire the two-manual harpsichord by Taskin (Paris, 1769), which has been frequently copied in the twentieth century 'because of its splendid sound and the simple elegance of its case decoration', or the English virginals of 1668, or the large and magnificent clavichord made in Hamburg in 1763. The decorations on the lids and the soundboards of many of the instruments are often colourful and superb – figures in a landscape with pale blue hills beyond, a woodland scene, boats on a lake, leaves and flowers – and there are veneers of rosewood and olive wood and much effective chinoiserie. This is one of the world's great collections of early keyboard instruments. Recordings of several of them are available.

The Hall being so attractive, it is all the more unfortunate that the **South Bridge** had to be built almost on top of it. But Edinburgh needed the South Bridge, and in the course of time it became a city of bridges. This is not at first obvious, because today we travel easily across them, not even noticing the little valleys and chasms below, up and down the sides of which, if there were no bridge, we would have painfully to struggle. The North Bridge, which is the most conspicuous, we have seen already (*see* p. 112). Here is the South Bridge, on the same line of road, taking the traveller from the ridge of the High Street not northward, like the North Bridge, but over the Cowgate to what is called Edinburgh's 'south side'. It is new Edinburgh built over the old. When the Cowgate was densely inhabited the contrast was extreme, as Robert Louis Stevenson observed: 'To look over the South Bridge and see the Cowgate below full of crying hawkers, is to view one rank of society from another in the twinkling of an eye'. Other bridges equally essential to the functioning of the city are the Waterloo Bridge (especially well concealed), the Dean bridge (the highest), and the George IV Bridge (how George IV keeps cropping up!).

There are two curious facts worth mentioning about the South Bridge. The first is that it has nineteen arches. This must seem surprising, because only one is visible; but the lie of the land down to and up from the Cowgate is such that a very long bridge, over a thousand feet, was needed if the gradients were not to be inconveniently steep for horse-drawn traffic. Secondly, Robert Adam was involved in the project. He did a design for an elaborate Italianate arch over the Cowgate, and proposed 'one connected design' of buildings, with a colonnade, along the bridge. These ideas came to nothing (the bridge buildings are a nondescript lot), but he had some influence on the scheme which was finally carried out. The bridge was opened in 1788.

From below the South Bridge to the Grassmarket, going west, is not very far – fortunately, because it is very dreary. You are now at the back of Parliament House and the Law Courts, and you squeeze along to the George IV Bridge, which carries the road southward from the head of the Mound. This bridge (1834) is also built up on both sides as an elevated street, and this time there are two open spans, one over the Cowgate and one over a small cul-de-sac called Merchant Street, entered from Candlemaker Row (*see* p. 86). For those who like to eat in unusual surroundings, it may still be possible to do so in Merchant Street. Doubt arises only because restaurants, like the flowers in the spring, come and go; the premises, in this case, are unlikely to change. They are formed within one of the huge concealed arches of the bridge, so you lunch or dine in a vast semi-elliptical stone vault. The masonry is first-class, a pleasure to look at, and the construction is so solid that there is not a hint of the traffic passing incessantly far overhead.

One last item, or relic, remains to be noticed in the Cowgate. The **Magdalen Chapel** on the south side, so narrow and black and locked up, so jammed between other black buildings that you can hardly find it, was first endowed in 1537 by Michael MacQueen to provide accommodation for a chaplain and seven bedesmen 'who should continuallie pour forth prayers to Almighty God'. It was completed in 1544 with help from MacQueen's widow, and miraculously escaped immediate destruction by English forces. There is a little square tower of the 1620s and a little lead-covered spire, dwarfed by everything around it. Inside, there are seventeenth century seats and panelling, and a barrel-vaulted ceiling. But what is very remarkable, there are four mid-sixteenth century heraldic roundels in the central south window which are said to be the only pieces of stained glass in Scotland to have survived the Reformation intact. They show the Royal Arms of Scotland encircled by a wreath of thistles, and those of the Queen Regent Mary of Guise within a wreath of laurel, and the arms of the founders. They are boldly designed, skilfully cut, and exhibit a wide range of brilliant colour. All this is lost in the Cowgate, scarcely noticed or remembered. How different the original setting of this little chapel with its heraldic roundels of marvellous colour, how forgotten the intentions of its founders! How much the world has changed!

The narrowness of the Cowgate at last gives way to the spaciousness of the **Grassmarket** – spacious but rather down-at-heel, in spite of one or two lively cafes and presentable shops. It is an historic area – in the Middle Ages the Greyfriars had a monastery here – but there is not much to see. During the nineteenth century dilapidation became the rule. By 1880 the whole of the south side had been demolished, and since then the north side has fared little better. The Grassmarket is now full of crow-stepped gables and ornamented by a few small trees. It is blessed, however, with a breath-taking view of the Castle, high overhead. Many artists have attempted this view but few have succeeded; they usually manage, somehow, to make it too pretty.

For several centuries the Grassmarket was the rendezvous of carriers and country people, and the market-place for a vast variety of goods; there were horse fairs and cattle markets, and in the eighteenth century highland drovers were sometimes to be seen at the White Hart Inn, which is on the north side. The White Hart claims to be the oldest inn in Edinburgh. Burns stayed there in 1791, and is said to have composed 'Ae fond kiss and then we sever' during his visit, and Wordsworth and his sister came a few years later, in 1803. Dorothy found it 'not noisy, and tolerably cheap'.

The Grassmarket is best remembered, however – or perhaps worst remembered – as the place of execution. Prior to about 1650, the grim spectacle was staged near the top of Castlehill, or near the Market Cross in the High Street; but then the east end of the Grassmarket was fixed on as the customary scene. From the Tollbooth prison to the Grassmarket became a well-known last journey:

> *Up the Lawn-market,*
> *Doon the West Bow*
> *Up the lang ladder –*
> *Doon the wee tow.*

The last public hanging here took place in 1784. Over the years, hundreds were executed at this spot. Murderers, petty criminals, so-called witches, religious martyrs – all went the same way, watched, almost always, by a large crowd of people. When the struggle against episcopacy was at its height in the seventeenth century, executions were almost daily.

The most famous hanging of all was part of a riot. The story of Captain Porteous and the Edinburgh mob has been told numberless times, and Scott's account in *The Heart of Midlothian* is a brilliant piece of imaginative reconstruction. It deserves to be read. But it would not be fair to leave the Grassmarket without recounting, however briefly and inadequately, this dramatic and revealing episode in the history of the city.

Early in 1736 two smugglers, Wilson and Robertson, robbed a customs officer in Fife. They were arrested and condemned to death. On the Sunday before the execution they were taken to St Giles to hear a sermon preached for their special benefit, and when the sermon was over Wilson, 'an active and powerful man', assaulted the guard and thus enabled Robertson to escape from the church. Once outside, the escaper had no trouble in getting clear of the city, for the population was as a matter of principle in favour of smugglers and opposed to customs officers. Wilson became a hero, and on the day of his execution a large crowd assembled in the Grassmarket, where the scaffold was defended by a detachment of the Welsh Fusiliers, and the City Guard. All was orderly until the body swung from the gibbet, when 'a howl of rage and execration burst from the people', and they assailed the City Guard with every missile they could find. The magistrates, who were present in their official capacity, took refuge in a nearby house, and Captain Porteous, in charge of the City Guard, began to retreat towards the High Street. The riot continued, and the Guard, with or without orders, fired on the crowd, killing several people. Porteous was arrested and in his turn sentenced to death. But while he lay in the Tolbooth awaiting execution, notice of a reprieve came from London, and a full pardon seemed likely. This was regarded as English interference in Scots affairs, and as showing how little the government in London cared whether Edinburgh citizens were shot in the street or not. On the night of 7th September a well-armed and well-organised body of men sealed off the Castle and the Canongate, disarmed the City Guard, broke into the Tolbooth, dragged Porteous down to the Grassmarket, and hanged him from a dyer's pole. The street, lit crimson by torches, was crowded with people, for a considerable mob had assembled. Spectators came to every window of the tall houses, and the Castle 'stood high above the tumult amidst the blue midnight and the stars'. When the deed was done the perpetrators of it melted into the night, and in the morning a pile of extinguished torches and a dead man hanging from a pole were the only proof of an extremely well-planned murder. The news reached London in due course and the Ministers of the Crown were, it is reported, beside themselves with rage. They took all possible steps to bring the murderers to justice. But nothing was ever discovered. How and by whom it was all arranged and carried out remains unknown to this day.

When Porteous and the City Guard retreated towards the High Street they went up the steep **West Bow**, which leaves the Grassmarket close to where the Cowgate enters it. The West Bow, its upper part now called **Victoria Street**, climbs in a steady curve to George IV Bridge; but in the old days it turned left half way up to reach the foot of Castle Hill. This line is now taken by a flight of steps.

In the eighteenth century the West Bow was a fashionable place to live, and Edinburgh's first Assembly Rooms were established here in 1710. But, like the rest of the Old Town, the West Bow went downhill rapidly after about 1780. Boswell records that after one drunken evening he 'roved the streets, and went and stayed above an hour with two whores at their lodging in a narrow dirty stair in the Bow'. By Victorian times it was thought of as picturesque rather than habitable. It was admired for its 'quaint old houses ... with stone gables and dovecote gablets, timber galleries, outshots and strange projections, dormer windows, patches and additions made in the succession of centuries ...'.

In the 1830s the George IV Bridge and its related 1830s 'improvements' altered much of this, but the West Bow itself still provides perhaps the best and longest series of pre-1750 houses to be found in Edinburgh, as well as a number of interesting shops.

On the south side only a few old houses remain; a pair of 1790s tenements where the Bow leaves the Grassmarket, an early eighteenth century building higher up; but mostly it is Victorian or later, with gablets. The north side is much more interesting. It begins at the Grassmarket with No. 105, gable-fronted and five storeys high plus an attic; the old door lintel is inscribed [BLESSED BE] GOD FOR AL HIS GIFTIS 1616, and the date seems likely enough. Next door is a three-storey building with a datestone high up which says 1561, but the seventeenth century seems more likely. Nos. 95–99 definitely date from 1729, which is on the pediment above the shop door, and next to them is a house and shop built still earlier in the eighteenth century. It is five storeys high, and provides accommodation for pigeons in the curvilinear gable. It has a four-bay front, although the windows of the left bay have unfortunately been blocked up. Inside, there is eighteenth century panelling in all the front rooms, plaster work on the stair ceilings, moulded wooden balusters, and pilasters framing the stone chimneypieces. No. 89 is late seventeenth century, four storeys plus an attic, with a shopfront at ground level inserted in 1863. It too is mindful of the pigeons, and inside there are late seventeenth century wooden chimneypieces and panelling of the same date. Above these, Victoria Street begins, and although the buildings are not especially interesting there is a line of round-arched shop-fronts at pavement level with a curving walkway (Victoria Terrace) above them. Towards the end of the walkway there are six storeys above you and three below and you have an excellent view of the old West Bow houses from roof-top level, as well as of Heriot's Hospital beyond. (*see* p. 93).

Return down the West Bow, cross the Grassmarket and enter **Candlemaker Row**. This is an ancient way that led out of the Old Town, named after the candlemakers whose smelly trade was so offensive that they were driven out here in the 1650s. The buildings on the left are not remarkable, but on the right side they improve as one climbs up. There are eighteenth century tenements, two of them with some seventeenth century stonework still in place, and above these **Candlemakers' Hall** (1722). This is a four-storey rubble building with three bays and a gabled stair-tower. The doorpiece was once elaborate, and there is still pine panelling in the old convening room on the top floor. Beyond the Hall is a very pleasantly proportioned pub, only two storeys with attics, built about 1828. Its projecting brown and black ground floor front, with plants on top, does no great damage to the rest, and gold lettering announces that it is Greyfriars Bobby's Bar. In this corner of town there is no getting away from Greyfriars Bobby. His story is one of those pathetic tales that were so popular in the nineteenth century; he is said to have kept vigil at the grave of his master, who died in 1858, until his own death in 1872. His fame was international even in his lifetime, and Queen Victoria is said to have enquired after his health. A life-size effigy of the little dog is perched on top of what used to be a small granite drinking fountain (1872) on the other side of the street; he is seated above the door of the pub; there is an announcement about him as you proceed towards the church; and the very first grave that you see on entering the famous churchyard is his.

Greyfriars Church, hidden behind the line of houses of which the pub is a part, is in many ways as historically interesting as St Giles. The building itself has had an unusually disastrous history. Work began in 1602, but the church was not formally opened until 1620. The plan was very simple: a six-bay nave (lined up east and west, in spite of the Reformation) with aisles north and south, and a square west tower of four storeys. Most windows had (and have) pointed arches and there was a curvilinear east gable. In 1650 the church was turned into a barracks by Cromwell, and wrecked internally. Three years later it was restored to ecclesiastical use, but in 1718 a quantity of gunpowder, stored in the church by order of the magistrates, blew up, wrecking the tower and the two west bays. So the tower was demolished, and a second church was ordered to be built. This church, to be called New Greyfriars, incorporated the two damaged bays of the old one, from the ruins of which it was separated by a dividing wall, and added two new bays. The new church was in fact the old one in reverse, except that it was given a Dutch gable against which a low semi-octagonal porch was built. In 1722 a two-storey pedimented Palladian porch was added on the north side, looking as if it had nothing whatever to do with the rest of the architecture, which remained very plain; and the gable of Old Greyfriars was altered. In 1845 Old Greyfriars was gutted by fire, and New Greyfriars was damaged. A so-called 'restoration' in the 1850s changed Old Greyfriars into an almost square box without aisles and with a very much altered roof. Finally, extensive reconstruction was undertaken in the 1930s, which brought back the 1722 external appearance, and also provided a dark timber ceiling over the six bays of the original church. So what we have now is a long, much altered, rather stark edifice, with two tolerably interesting gables. Greyfriars is no architectural masterpiece, either inside or out.

What matters about Greyfriars, however, is its history and its churchyard. As regards the first of these, it is the church of the National Covenant, a document of great importance in Scottish history. Charles I, unfortunately for him and for many other people, adopted the policy of forcing episcopacy on Scotland. Gentle persuasion would have won some converts, but the new Prayer Book of 1637, which many presbyterians considered to be popish in character, produced a violent reaction, and in February 1638 5,000 people signed the Covenant, which was a declaration of resistance against the King. This led to military operations – the two so-called Bishops' Wars – which the King's forces lost. Charles was obliged to accept the abolition of episcopacy in Scotland, and this confirmed and strengthened the dominant position of the Kirk and especially of its more fanatical elements. Later, these events led to the Scots supporting Cromwell in the Civil War, although the nation turned against the Puritans when Charles was beheaded.

Religious strife broke out once more under Charles II, when the liberty of the Scottish Church to conduct its own affairs was once again the issue. The Covenanters fought a guerilla war against the government, and conventicles and field preachers (the background for Scott's *Old Mortality*) were the order of the day. The best known figures of this bloody and convoluted phase of Scots history are the Marquis of Montrose, who fought a brilliant campaign for Charles I in 1644–5 but was ultimately defeated, captured and hanged in

Edinburgh in 1650 (*see* p. 53); and Viscount Claverhouse (Bonnie Dundee) who showed almost equal skill fighting against King William in 1689, but who was mortally wounded in the moment of victory at Killiecrankie. Peace was finally restored in 1690. It was during these prolonged 'troubles' in 1679, that at least five hundred – some say over a thousand – covenanters were rounded up and confined in a corner of Greyfriars churchyard, in the open, 'like a herd of cattle,' men women and children. After five months of starvation and almost full exposure to the Edinburgh weather, the 250 or so survivors were put on board a ship to be transported to Barbados. The vessel was wrecked on the Orkneys, and not more than fifty people got ashore. Not all of them survived. The Martyrs' Monument, 'that grim memorial of suffering, tears and blood,' stands in the north-east corner of the churchyard.

Grim it may be, and grim the whole churchyard, but what a feast for the lover of ancient, elaborate, time-defying, tempest-battered tombs and mausoleums! There is nothing else like it in Scotland. It is old, but not medieval. It was in 1562 that the Town Council requested Mary, Queen of Scots, to grant them the site and yards (i.e. gardens) of the newly dissolved Greyfriars Monastery in order to form a new burying-ground, 'being somewhat distant from the town'. St Giles churchyard was probably full up, and liable to be built upon, so the Queen agreed. In 1636 the new churchyard, already large, was extended to the south, beyond its present limits, and in 1798 to the west. Wall-monuments became the rule almost from the beginning, and for over a hundred years most of the central space was occupied solely by grass and trees. During the eighteenth century, however, interments must have proceeded at a great rate, and slum conditions began to appear. 'The graves,' declared an eminent author in 1779,

> *are so crowded on each other that the sextons frequently
> cannot avoid, in opening a ripe grave, encroaching on one
> not fit to be touched! The whole presents a scene equally
> nauseous and unwholesome ... soon this spot will be so
> surcharged with animal juices and oils, that, becoming one
> mass of corruption, its noxious steams will burst forth with
> the fury of a pestilence ... the effects of this burying ground
> would ere now have been severely felt, were it not that,
> besides the coldness of the climate, they have been checked
> by the acidity of the coal smoke and the height of the winds,*

which in the neighbourhood of Edinburgh blow with extraordinary violence.

Today, the churchyard presents, in detail, a somewhat neglected appearance. The paths are uneven, there is too much rough grass, and ivy threatens to engulf some tombs. But it is a strangely withdrawn place, very secluded in the middle of town. It is also large enough to be surrounded by buildings but not looked down upon, except by the Castle and the very high skyward-pointing spire of the one-time Tolbooth Church. Of both of these there are some striking views, especially when the churchyard trees are not in leaf.

The tombs and monuments defy description; but it is they that give the place its extraordinary character and atmosphere. Those that are free-standing, or lie flat on the grass, are much as usual. But all round the boundary there are wall-monuments of the seventeenth and eighteenth centuries, many of them large and elaborate, some ostentatious and of truly deathly magnificence, all crumbling and decaying more or less, quite a number supporting or being supported by the rear walls of the buildings in Candlemaker Row, so that the back windows of these buildings look onto and become an intimate part of the whole sepulchral scene. When many of those living in Edinburgh could hardly find a place to lay their heads, conspicuous expenditure on resting places for the dead reached epic proportions.

Even those visitors who are as a rule unsympathetic to urns and angels should do a quick tour, for the experience is unique. Start at the entrance gate, and go down the slope. Here is a series of a dozen or so monuments erected between 1613 and 1620. Near the gate lies James Harley, died 1617. There are baluster columns at the base, octagonal columns above, and Vitruvian scrollwork within the head of the arch; the frieze carries very delicately carved rosettes; and on top there is an inscribed panel with a skull and crossbones, an hourglass, and a hand which tolls a bell. Next to it is another early seventeenth century tomb, but altered over two hundred years later to accommodate the remains of Elizabeth Purves. Continue past many others to the tomb of Sir Robert Denniston of Mountjoy, dated 1626. This is not quite so Gothic as the Harley tomb, but it is imposing – well over twenty feet high – and is well carved. There are Corinthian columns, and a pediment, and Sir Robert's coat of arms. John Nasmyth of Posso is next to notice; he came here in 1613, monument dated 1614. He is sitting up in his tomb, but alas! headless. There are flying angels on the wall behind him, and decorated pilasters support the roof. After these and others like them the Martyrs' Monument comes as rather a disappointment. It was built in 1706 to commemorate the Covenanters who suffered there. The first two sentences of the inscription, which was added in 1771, are as follows:

> *Halt passenger, take heed what you do see,*
> *This tomb doth show, for what some men did die.*
> *Here lies interr'd the dust of those who stood*
> *'Gainst perjury, resisting unto blood,*
> *Adhering to the Covenants, and laws*
> *Establishing the same: which was the cause*
> *Their lives were sacrific'd unto the lust*
> *Of Prelatists abjur'd.*

Many martyrs have been remembered in much worse verse. Finally, for the quick tour, turn left and see the Bayne of Pitcarley enclosure (1685). It is large and blackened, and the outer walls enclose a mausoleum. There is a shallow dome with an urn, and round-arched openings with pilasters that look as if the weight of everything had been too much for them. It is dilapidated. But bend down to look through the moulded door and there, straight in front of you, in the midst of the dilapidations, in an arched recess, stands John Bayne himself. He is life-size, his hair comes to his shoulders, and he wears what looks in the semi-darkness like a voluminous cloak. He too is blackened, but he stands very upright, and he looks at you very directly.

Those who have now seen enough of tombs may omit the following paragraph and return to the church. But along the west and south walls there are many other remarkable structures. One of the grandest, near the foot of the west wall, is that built in 1635 for Thomas Bannatyne by his widow Janet McMath. It has twisted columns and a large aedicule which contains the following inscription:

> *If thou list that passest by*
> *Know who in this tombe doth ly*
> *Thomas Bannatyn abroad*
> *And at home who served God*
> *Though no children he possest*
> *Yet the Lord with meanes him blist*
> *He on them did well dispose*

From the Cowgate to the Meadows

Long ere death his eyes did close
For the poore his helping hand
And his friends his kyndnes fand
And on his deare bedfellow
Jennet Makmath he did bestow
Out of his lovelie affection
A fit and goodlie portion
Thankfull she herself to prove
For a signe of mutuall love
Did nor paines nor charges spair
To set up this fabrick fair
As artemise that noble frame
To her dear mausolus name.

It does not scan too easily, but even after three and a half centuries it sounds refreshingly sincere. Nor is this all. At the base of the monument lies a stone which was once on top, but can now be better seen. And it is worth seeing, for it is a curious picture in low relief: a not very attractive cherub in the foreground; a sheaf of corn; battlements, tall lands and a tree behind; and to one side a church in what looks like a picture frame. Is this Edinburgh or is it a recollection of some other place, perhaps the town where Thomas Bannatyn was born? Next to it are the Foulis of Ravelston and the Henryson monuments, both 1636, and both enormous. There are columns, caryatids, headless figures in shell-headed niches, a skull, a cherub, an hourglass and angels' wings. Both rise at least twenty five feet, and must be given an A for effort. They were outdone forty years later, however, by those who built the monument to Elizabeth Paton (1677). This has coupled columns, urns, a broken pediment, life-size figures of Adam and Eve wearing castles on their heads, drapery, and a skeleton between Father Time and a cherub with a skull. It is colossal, almost Vanbrughian in scale although not, unhappily, in design.

After these vast complications it is a relief to come to the dignified Roman mausoleum of William Adam (1753), by John and Robert Adam. It too is large, but excellently proportioned, with Classical motifs, round arches and a dome inside. There are large inscription panels, one with a portrait bust of William Adam, and a tomb-chest carved with a relief of Hopetoun House (*see* p. 237) and a ruined portico. You are now near the south-west corner of the churchyard and the Covenanters' Prison, entered via a broken pedimented gateway. It also contains many monuments, and there are many more along the south wall. The best is the mausoleum of Sir George Mackenzie (1691), which has been described as 'the most advanced architectural work of its period in Scotland,' and is said to derive from Bramante's Tempietto of San Pietro in Montorio. It is circular, with eight Corinthian columns and a domed roof with an urn on top. Between the columns there are tall shell-headed niches and a door between one pair of columns. This elegant temple, so different from almost all the others, commemorates a lawyer who successfully prosecuted many Covenanters and hence came to be known as 'Bloody Mackenzie'. He was regarded in Edinburgh as 'a species of ogre' and his tomb was believed to be haunted. It is said that the urchins of the city used to shout through the keyhole into the dark and echoing chamber –

> *Bluidy Mackenzie, come out if ye daur,*
> *lift the snek [snib] and draw the bar*

– and then run.

Back at the church, there is one last monument worth seeing, for it is more grisly than all the rest. It is on the east gable, and commemorates James Borthwick (1676), Deacon of the Surgeons. His portrait is the oldest hanging in the Royal College of Surgeons (*see* p. 100). In the centre of the monument is a remarkably realistic skeleton in low relief, and a scythe, and the border is decorated with nothing but surgical instruments. Eroded by time and blackened by fire, it is a singularly forceful and repellent reminder of mortality.

Leaving Greyfriars, turn right, and in a hundred yards or so you will see the start of Middle Meadow Walk, lined by trees. To the right of Middle Meadow Walk, and extending far along Lauriston Place, stretches the **Royal Infirmary**. Built in the late nineteenth century in a style that has been called – or rather mis-called – 'the old Scottish baronial of the days of James V,' this was in its time an exceptionally well designed hospital. It was laid out on the cottage or pavilion principle, which said, perfectly correctly, that hospital mortality would be reduced if patients were kept in a string of separate buildings instead of one large one, with as much fresh air around them as possible. Hence the four symmetrical pavilions with turreted towers on each, widely separated, and the spacious entrance, overlooked by a tall tower. Modern technology makes all this very wasteful of space, and a vast amount of ingenuity has been devoted to squeezing in extra storeys, wards, pavilions, radiography units, scanning machines and the rest. The whole complex reaches back to the Meadows. A replacement hospital is now under construction.

On the other side of the street, in its own spacious grounds, stands **Heriot's Hospital**, in reality and from its foundation a school. This is one of Edinburgh's most unusual buildings, erected between 1628 and 1700. George Heriot was a prosperous jeweller and money-lender whose prosperity increased still further when he was appointed goldsmith to Queen Anne in 1597 ('never had tradesman a better customer') and then to her husband King James VI in 1601. In 1603 he followed the King and Queen to London, where Anne's freespending life-style found greater scope – she is said at one point to have owed Jingling Geordie, as he was known in the Scottish capital, £18,000. When Heriot died childless in 1624 he assigned his fortune to the Town Council of Edinburgh for the erection and maintenance of a hospital (i.e. school) 'for the education, nursing and upbringing of youth, being puir orphans and fatherless children of decayet burgesses and freemen of the said burgh, destitute, and left without means'.

Heriot's is one of the finest of all Scots Renaissance buildings. It was not designed by Inigo Jones, as is sometimes said. The design seems to have been taken from a palace in Serlio's *L'Architettura* (1537–1551), but this was departed from in several respects, and what was finally built was decided, apparently, by a series of three Scots master masons. It is square in plan, with massive corner towers four storeys high, surmounted by turrets. The courtyard, arcaded on two sides, is also square, with stair turrets in the corners. The entrance, which faces the town and not Lauriston Place, is very elaborate, not unlike some of the tombs in Greyfriars Churchyard, which one would have thought might be depressing for the pupils. There are paired Doric columns beside a rusticated arch, and obelisks overhead and twisted columns, along with heraldry, heavily carved pediments, and the star and roses that are to be found all over the building. The tower above the entrance is topped by an octagonal dome and lantern, the chapel, facing north, has Gothic windows, and there are tall chimneys, sundials, domes, gargoyles and boldly carved monumental detail everywhere. Whatever its architectural origins, Heriot's is a splendid Gothic Renaissance palace. The interior was a good deal altered in 1908 when the school became a normal day-pupil establishment. The gatehouse on Lauriston Place, looking remarkably seventeenth century, was added by Playfair in 1829.

Heriot's can boast of no especially famous pupils, but it was the scene of an event that astounded all Edinburgh in 1785. On an October afternoon the famous aeronaut Lunardi, wearing a scarlet uniform, a powdered wig, and a three-cornered hat, ascended from the school grounds in his hot air balloon, 'passed over the lofty ridge of the old town at a vast height,' and disappeared from view. He nearly came down in the Forth. But he jettisoned some ballast and managed to reach Fife, where 'some reapers in a field near Ceres, when they heard the sound of Lunardi's trumpet, and saw his balloon, were filled with dreadful alarm, believing that the end of all things was at hand'.

A little beyond the gatehouse a narrow street called **Heriot Place** runs along the west side of the school grounds. This is where to see the best remaining stretch of the **old city walls**. They were extended several times and were never very formidable, being as much to control trade as to keep out invaders, but the 1514 extension, which took in both the Cowgate and the Grassmarket, was a response to the defeat by English forces at Flodden, and the walls were strengthened. Their military value remained very low, however; when the Earl of Hertford attacked Edinburgh in 1544 he simply demolished the gate of the Netherbow Port and then proceeded to demolish most of the city. Two hundred years later, as already mentioned (*see* p. 18), Prince Charles Edward arrived before the city and called upon it to surrender. He had no great wish to attack, because there was some doubt about the willingness and ability of ill-armed Highlanders to mount an assault on even feeble fortifications, to which they were quite unaccustomed; the Edinburgh citizens, for their part, had no great wish to fight from behind walls which were in places no more than high garden walls, and which were overlooked by many houses built outside the walls. The problem was solved this time, as we have seen, by outwitting the guard at the Netherbow Port. So the city walls seem to have had commercial and symbolic rather than military value. But this is not altogether how they appear if you walk along Heriot Place and then down **the Vennel**. The first stretch is part of Telfer's Wall, which is an extension built in 1620, not very high. Further down, however, the Flodden Wall still stands and has a distinctly warlike look. Built of large stones and several feet thick, it rises over twenty feet, and is battlemented. Where it now ends there is a substantial bastion, also battlemented, with gunloops on three sides. The wall is solid as a cliff. It looks on silence, for no traffic goes down the Vennel. Pause for a moment, and the centuries roll back, and you are standing just outside the Edinburgh of James V and Mary Queen of Scots. A flight of steps goes down to the Grassmarket, narrowing as it goes. And through the branches of a tall tree that overhangs these steps you see the Castle, a great vessel of stone riding high above the old city that it used to protect.

6

From the University to George Square

FROM THE EAST end of Princes Street going south over the North Bridge (sounds odd, but very simple) the street rises to cross the High Street at the Tron and then descends a little to pass over the Cowgate. A hundred yards or so beyond the Cowgate, Robert Adam's **University** building – his and Playfair's – stands on ground that used to be occupied by the dilapidated eighteenth century College (i.e. university), sited just inside the line of the Flodden Wall. Internationally famous, especially for medicine, the College was a wretched looking place. According to the Principal himself (appealing for money in 1768), it had 'a mean, irregular and contemptible appearance ... A stranger, on seeing such courts and buildings, might naturally enough imagine them to be alms-houses for the reception of the poor;' and an American visitor of the time dismissed them as 'a most miserable musty pile scarce fit for stables'. But they doubtless fitted in with their surroundings well enough. Horse Wynd and College Wynd came up to them from the Cowgate; these were ancient ways out of the city lined with ancient mansions, ramshackle timber-fronted tenements, and not a few dens and byres. Oliver Goldsmith took lodgings in College Wynd in 1752 when he was a medical student, and Sir Walter Scott's father removed his home from College Wynd twenty years later, fearful for the health of himself and his family. There were, however, some gardens in the vicinity, and other open spaces westwards towards Greyfriars.

Much of this is now covered by Chambers Street, buildings on the north side of Chambers Street, the Adam/Playfair University building (paradoxically called Old College), and the Royal Scottish (science) Museum and the new [1998] Museum of Scotland. These developments have obliterated not only the eighteenth century College and the house where Scott was born, but also the scene of one of the most famous of all murders, committed over two hundred years before the University was rebuilt.

From the University to George Square

Henry Lord Darnley was, as has already been mentioned, a thoroughly unlikeable young man. He seems to have had no brains, no sense, and no morals. He had dynastic and political ambitions, however, (what Scottish nobleman had not, in Queen Mary's days?), so he contrived to marry the Queen and he hoped for the best. After helping to murder Riccio, he naturally fell from favour, and it became clear to everyone that he and Mary would have to separate – somehow or other. At this stage Mary began to see a good deal of the Earl of Bothwell, 'a rash and glorious young man,' who was, however, married. Then she became pregnant. There were serious doubts as to who was the father, but in order to preserve appearances Mary effected some sort of reconciliation with her husband, brought him to Edinburgh from Glasgow, where he had been lying ill, and lodged him at **Kirk o' Field**, just inside the Flodden Wall, 'a place of good air, where he might best recover his health'. The site of Kirk o' Field is the south east corner of the present Old College buildings.

The house in which Darnley spent the last days of his life was a substantial stone building of two storeys. At two o'clock in the morning of 10th February, 1567, the house was totally destroyed when what must have been a very large amount of gunpowder exploded in a ground floor room. Immediately afterwards, the body of Darnley was found in the garden. He had been strangled. Who arranged this assassination is one of the puzzles of Scottish history. Mary must have known that Darnley's life was in danger, for he had many murderous enemies, and it was her business to be well-informed; nevertheless, she may not have known about the plot. Bothwell almost certainly did, and he may have been the chief conspirator. On the other hand, Mary frequently slept at Kirk o' Field, and was expected to be there on the night that the murder took place; and the scale of the explosion suggests that the target may have been Mary herself and all her companions, as well as her husband. No one knows. Three months later the unhappy Queen married the newly-divorced Bothwell. But she was unable to maintain her authority. A rebellion broke out and she was compelled to abdicate. After a year's imprisonment in Loch Leven Castle Mary escaped and fled to England, where, nineteen years later, she was beheaded. Bothwell, for his part, escaped to Norway, where he died after ten years in a Scandinavian gaol.

It is a relief to turn from these dramatic but dreadful events to something more constructive. When the South Bridge was completed in 1788 it provided a quite new entrance to Edinburgh from the south.

The deplorable old College buildings on the Kirk o' Field site were no ornament to the new street, and partly for this reason a great scheme was devised to extend the site and to erect on a much larger scale than before an entirely new university building.

The University of Edinburgh had received its charter from James VI in 1582. Governed by the Town Council, it was known as 'the Tounis College', and it remained a small affair for over a hundred years. But in the eighteenth century its fortunes rose. Its first great Principal (1702–15) (in Scotland university Vice-Chancellors are called Principals) was William Carstares, a presbyterian ecclesiastical politician who spent four years imprisoned in Edinburgh Castle for plotting against Charles II, subsequently sought safety in Holland, and later returned to Scotland with William of Orange. His influence in religious affairs then became so great that he was known as 'Cardinal Carstares'.

Later in the eighteenth century the University became a leading institution in the fields of history and medicine. One of its Principals (1762–1793) was William Robertson, who as a young man prepared to take part in the defence of Edinburgh against Prince Charles in 1745, and whose *History of the Reign of Charles V* and *History of America* led to his being called 'not the greatest British historian of his time, but only because he was a contemporary of Edward Gibbon'. In medicine the great eighteenth century names are those of Cullen and Monro. William Cullen became Professor of Chemistry in 1765 and subsequently Professor of the Theory of Physic. His *First Lines on the Practice of Physic* (1776–1784) were a revelation in medical circles throughout Europe, and as a result the long-unquestioned authority of Boerhaave began at last to decline. The name Monro requires more explanation. Alexander Monro became Professor of Anatomy in 1719, when he was twenty two. He was a great anatomist. More than any other man, he was the founder of the Edinburgh medical school. In 1769 he resigned and was succeeded by his son, Alexander *secundus*, who was a brilliant lecturer and whose research made him internationally famous. (Does not *Observations on the Structure and Functions of the Nervous System* sound up-to-date? Monro published it in 1783). Finally, Alexander *tertius* occupied the same chair from 1808 until 1846, with, alas! less distinction, but by no means uselessly.

In spite of its ramshackle buildings, therefore, the University was far from unimportant in the eighteenth century, and it was fitting that it should be re-housed in grander premises. Robert Adam (he had been a student at the University in the 1740s) prepared the plans, and the foundation stone was laid in 1789.

Old College is not a building that can be seen to advantage. It has been described as perhaps the noblest of all Robert Adam's works, but it has been blackened by accumulations of dirt from coal fires and railway trains, and is so surrounded and hemmed in by the pent-up pressure of adjacent streets and the rush of modern traffic that it is scarcely possible to get a good look at it. Even when you pass through the awe-inspiring entrance you find that the quadrangle is being used as a car park. Nevertheless, this is a great building. The entrance front is as Adam designed it, except for the dome, and so is the north front on Chambers Street; the south and west fronts are Adam modified by Playfair. The really big change to the original plans is the quadrangle. Adam intended that the entrance would lead to a transverse oblong first court, separated by a cross building from a square great court beyond. But in 1792 Adam suddenly died, and then the money ran out. When building began again in 1817, after Waterloo, funds were not sufficient to complete Adam's grand design, and Playfair was given the task of retaining the Adam style while spending less money. So the cross-building went, and the dome went, and some not-too-happy compromises and simplifications were effected in the quadrangle. The Old College is thus not what it might have been, but it is still very impressive. The interiors are Playfair's, and the large dome was designed and added in 1887 by Rowand Anderson.

The entrance front, which can hardly be seen properly because it is right on the street, is the glory of the whole: 'Nothing in Scotland is grander than Adam's entrance front'. It is very long, with a central archway flanked by two secondary archways. Each smaller archway is framed by a portico having two gigantic Doric columns, and two more of these columns flank the central archway. Overhead is a frieze, and then a balustrade and a huge semicircular framed window. Some idea of the Roman grandeur of it all is conveyed by the fact that each of these six columns is three feet in diameter and twenty-two feet high, each a single piece of Craigleith stone. Doubts were expressed at the time as to whether they could safely be taken over the North Bridge. The entry itself is beneath a high domed vault, and the quadrangle is distinguished by its balustraded terrace with wide stairways, added in 1831, and the curved corners, arcaded below and with Ionic columns above.

The interior of the building has been very much modified over the years, but the Upper Library remains as magnificent as when it was built; it looked better still when it had books in it. It is very nearly two hundred feet long and fifty feet wide, with a high decorated vaulted ceiling from end to end. Massive bookcases, terminating in broad and deep pilasters, divide the sides of the room into eleven bays, and leave a large open central space which, along with the bookcases, is lit from each side by high windows. A gallery runs all round, making the bookcases accessible on two levels, and the room is further dignified by two Ionic columns at each end. This is unquestionably one of the grandest Neo-Classical rooms in Britain, and, although in quite a different style, it can stand comparison with the justly famous Wren Library at Trinity College, Cambridge. The Old Senate Room in the south east corner, which was originally part of the librarian's 'house', contains four splendid Raeburns. At the back of the quadrangle, in the west range, is the **Talbot Rice Arts Centre**, originally the Upper Museum. It too is a very handsome room, with coupled pilasters, Ionic columns, a gallery all round, and the cornices and mouldings picked out in bright colours. Unlike the Upper Library, it is lit from above. There is a permanent collection of pictures here, and art exhibitions are frequently arranged.

After the Napoleonic wars the University gradually lost its pre-eminent position, partly because it ceased to be true that 'Oxford and Cambridge repose themselves under the shade of their laurels, while Edinburgh cultivates hers'. Nevertheless, many men who became famous during the nineteenth century were students at Edinburgh: Carlyle, Professor J Y Simpson, Darwin, Robert Louis Stevenson, Conan Doyle and Lord Haldane, to name only a few.

A little beyond the University, on the other side of the street, stands **Surgeons' Hall**, headquarters of the Royal College of Surgeons in Scotland. It is not accessible to the public, and, like the University, it suffers severely from accumulations of grime on the stonework and from being in a crowded built-up street. A beneficent providence would arrange its removal to happier surroundings; we should view it, as a nineteenth century traveller remarked, 'situated in a large park, particularly upon a rising ground; but situated as it is, it makes upon the mind of a stranger, in its exterior views at least, impressions chiefly of bewilderment and confusion'. Surgeons' Hall is yet another Playfair temple, Ionic and T-plan, completed in 1832. A screen wall with severe pedimented gates at each end conceals a good deal of the building itself. Six fluted columns rise from the wall and support a pedimented, honeysuckle-decorated portico. Smaller but still massive pedimented porticos project modestly on each side, and the bulk of the building runs back from these. It is really impossible to appreciate the proportions. Internally it has been a good deal altered, and tends to the severe and gloomy. The Museum, however, is as Playfair designed it, on a nave-and-aisle plan with pilastered piers, a compartmented ceiling, and a gallery.

Surgeons' Hall replaced **Old Surgeons' Hall**, still in Surgeons Square but not very recognisable. This is the building made famous by Burke and Hare. A medical school needs bodies, and Burke and Hare supplied them. They began with the body of an old man who had died naturally in their miserable lodgings near the Grassmarket, and from that they developed their business. They were not 'resurrectionists' i.e. grave-robbers, but relied on whisky and strangulation. They pursued their trade until 1828, when they were finally detected. Hare turned King's evidence and Burke was hanged. Robert Knox, the distinguished dissectionist to whom the bodies were sold, was obliged to leave Edinburgh for London; but once away from the Scottish capital he was able to continue his career.

Leave behind these gruesome recollections, retrace your steps to the University, and turn up Chambers Street. The University comes to an end in due course – after one hundred and twenty yards to be precise; it is a very large building – and you have reached the **Royal Scottish Museum**. There are two buildings here, conjoined but of different ages, different in purpose and totally different in style.

The Royal Scottish Museum is one of Edinburgh's most unusual and most successful buildings. It was designed by Captain Francis Fowke of the Royal Engineers, and the foundation stone was laid by Prince Albert (his last public act, it is said) in 1861. Externally, it is a large Lombardic Renaissance structure in pink sandstone, of two storeys (three storeys in the wings). There are long lines of pairs of arched windows, superimposed pilasters, and red sandstone shafts. A very broad flight of steps leads to the three-arched entrance, and overhead there are balustrades and urns. Portrait busts of Victoria and Albert are not omitted, along with (because the Museum began under the auspices of the short-lived Department of Science and Art) busts of Michelangelo, Newton, Watt, and Darwin. It is all very orderly and very handsome, but one feels that one has seen it all before, or something very like it. But a surprise is in store. Captain Fowke obviously knew about Renaissance architecture, but he also knew about the Crystal Palace. Step inside, and you are in a spacious, elegant, airy, excellently well-lit glass and cast-iron great hall. Curved at each end, it has a clear length of eighty-two metres; and a lofty glass roof, supported by semi-circular timber trusses carried on slender iron columns, soars overhead to a ridge height of twenty-one metres. Galleries at first and second floor level go all the way round, and there are other series of double arches which create bays and arcades at ground and first floor level. There are similar smaller halls off the main hall. No better enclosed space for a museum could be contrived, and none could in itself be more interesting. The exhibits range from asiatic sculpture to water wheels, from dinosaurs to tribal art.There is a particularly fine collection of ceramics, and the model ships, from eighteen inches to six feet, are first class. To encourage the visitor still further, there is a tea room, an up-to-date lecture theatre (in frequent use), and near the entrance a pool beside which the weary visitor may sit – and do nothing.

The **Museum of Scotland** is entirely different. Built in the late 1990s, it is dedicated to revealing the identity of Scotland through its arts, its crafts, and its manufactures, from earliest times to the present day.

Its form is markedly irregular. The circular flat-topped tower at the north-west corner (where Chambers Street joins the George IV Bridge) provides the entrance, but the curves of the tower do little to soften the straight-line severity of the rest of the building. The windows, having a general effect of the tall and narrow, appear in unexpected places. And these windows, along with the tower (which may have been intended to re-call the outline of the half-moon battery in the Castle) and various unusual large-scale projections and recesses, give to the new Museum the undoubted air of a fortification. Somewhere in its ancestry lurk the shapes and assurances of Scottish castles built long ago.

Internally, the effect is similar. It can scarcely be said that the light comes flooding in (although it is adequate), and spaces are decidedly enclosed. There is a central (although one can never be quite sure where the centre is) atrium, glazed overhead, and this main part of the building rises through five floors, including the basement. The surfaces are uniformly white concrete or white render, very well finished. (Externally, a sandstone cladding conceals the structural concrete). The interior plan is slightly baffling, and it is easy to get lost. But it is a very interesting building, original, challenging, uncompromisingly modern but subtly reminiscent of the past.

Over 10,000 objects are displayed on six levels. The story of Scotland begins in the basement with rocks and fossils and rises with the floor-levels and the centuries to the present day. No aspect of Scottish life is neglected. There are pieces of pottery from prehistoric chambered tombs; a drawing of a Viking ship scratched on a piece of slate; a leather-worker's tool box made before AD1,000; Celtic stone crosses, superb sixteenth century wooden carvings; weapons of all descriptions, including axes both decorative and meant for serious use; silver, ceramics, whisky stills, eighteenth century golf clubs, a beautiful silver and enamel vase made in 1989 – all are here, all made (or dug up) in Scotland.

Two dug-up items deserve special mention. The Lewis chessmen, squat wild-eyed twelfth century Scandinavian figures carved from walrus ivory were found in 1831 by a crofter in the outer Hebrides. And in 1919 the Traprain hoard was unearthed scarcely twenty miles from Edinburgh. This collection, mostly of table silver hacked up into pieces and flattened, ready for melting down, had lain for many centuries out of sight on Traprain Law. (Hilltop settlements and fortified refuges like Traprain were far more numerous in prehistoric Scotland than in England). The silver bowls, spoons, wine cups and other items had been made in various places on the Continent during the fourth century AD, and are thought to have been buried about 410–425. They were probably loot, from England or the Continent. A battered but much-decorated flask appears to depict an incident from the story of Ulysses. Here is history stretching from a Greek epic to a Celtic hill-fort, and buried for fifteen hundred years.

Two other items deserve special notice. One is a full-scale model of a Celtic two-wheeled chariot, commonly used in warfare up to the second century AD. Besides being military equipment, these chariots served as aristocratic status-symbols, and they could be very elaborate; we read of 'a chariot of fine wood with wicker-work, moving on wheels of white bronze'. This one is plain and surprisingly small (although the wheels are strong enough) and seems far too tame for Stuart Piggott's 'battle-drunk, screaming tribal chieftain in his chariot hung with the decapitated heads of his foes'. Children are apt to comment unfavourably on the fact that no knives are attached to the wheels. But they are sure to appreciate the other item, the Maiden, or guillotine, a massive affair which used to stand in the Grassmarket, and was worked by a lever and weighted with lead. It struck off numberless heads from around the middle of the sixteenth century until the days of Queen Anne. And if anyone asks how a sixteenth century guillotine which used to stand in the Grassmarket in Edinburgh (not to mention a main-line railway train) were got into place in the Museum, the answer is that they were put where they stand at a very early stage in the building's construction.

Across the street from the Museum Greyfriar's Bobby awaits you. Turn left, and in a couple of hundred yards you reach Middle Meadow walk, the Royal Infirmary (*see* p. 92) on one side and the Medical School on the other.

The **Medical School** was completed in 1886. It is Scots Italianate, with long lines of arched windows, but it lacks the campanile which was planned for it. Next to it is the McEwan Hall, used chiefly for university functions. It has been described, a little unkindly, as 'a magnificent petrified blancmange;' the head-on view, however, does a lot to justify the comment. Inside, the ribbed, gilded and decorated dome is rather splendid, as are the large circular lights above the two galleries. Decoration spreads from the dome all over the lofty proscenium arch, and the symbolic figures have been carefully chosen: Perseverance and Intelligence presumably for those who graduate for the first time, Fame Crowning Success for the veterans of half a dozen books, a hundred articles, or ten thousand meetings and especially for those who have reached the dizzy height of an honorary degree.

For a change from buildings and traffic, return to Middle Meadow Walk and stroll down to **the Meadows**. The Meadows are a very large open space, as large as Princes Street Gardens, and like the Gardens they too used to be mostly under water. The area was drained early in the eighteenth century, but seemingly with only partial success. Lime trees were planted, and cattle roamed about, but it was 'a damp and melancholy place'. Yet it cannot have been too melancholy, for this is where large numbers of Edinburgh citizens used to engage in that fashionable and popular activity, the promenade. 'Under these poor trees,' wrote one of them, 'walked and talked and meditated all our literary and scientific, and many of our legal worthies of the last and beginning of the present [nineteenth] century'. They have all gone now, along with the meditation; football is more likely. But it is a splendid open space, where idle walking is still a pleasure; and some visitors may rejoice to see, just beyond the main road, the higher ground of Bruntsfield Links, where golf was being played perhaps as early as the fifteenth century. Certainly there was a golf club on the links in 1535, and when Charles I visited Scotland in 1641 he was rebuked by the Moderator of the General Assembly of the Kirk for playing golf on Sunday. (He was, truth to tell, rebuked by the Kirk for almost everything).

From the University to George Square

Looking back towards the town, two groups of buildings dominate the scene. One is the Royal Infirmary, the rear view not very attractive. The other is the **University Library**, massively horizontal. This is one of the best 'modern' buildings in Edinburgh. It was built in the 1960s, and as those were the halcyon days when money for universities was readily available, it was built to meet not only existing requirements but also requirements well into what looked like an expansionary future; hence its enormous size. It was, and except for the new and hideous British Library in London, perhaps still is, the largest single library building in western Europe. There are six floors, with continuous glazing, and a balcony effect which is there to prevent the direct entry of sunlight. Being very large, and white concrete, it is very visible.

The book collection is also very large, in the region of 750,000 volumes. But, because the University dates back to 1582, the library is even more remarkable for its splendid and extensive collection of rare books and manuscripts. It possesses, for example, a first edition (once owned by Adam Smith) of Copernicus's *De Revolutionibus orbium coelestium* (1543); a copy of the Second Quarto of *Romeo and Juliet* (1599) (donated by Drummond of Hawthornden who bought it for fourpence), as well as several other Shakespeare quartos; two first editions of the *Principia Mathematica*; and a superb first edition of Audubon's *The Birds of America*, printed in London 1827–38, with the first ten plates engraved in Edinburgh. The collection of late medieval illuminated Books of Hours extends to several hundred, and includes some particularly fine examples from the early fifteenth century.

Perhaps the Library building looks best from a distance; there is nothing pleasant about a close-up view of concrete. But you must approach it, and enter **George Square**. Poor old George Square! In the 1960s, when conservation was not the force that it is now, the University, having a great appetite for more usable space, almost swallowed it whole; only one side was spared. It is a moderately large open space, with a moderately attractive garden in the middle, surrounded by a railing. The Library takes up most of the south side. It adjoins a nondescript collection of concrete university buildings which spread into the east side, plus a black tower. More nondescript buildings on the north side, but along the west side there still stands the original terrace of two-storey eighteenth century stone houses. It is not easy to imagine how this square looked when such terraced houses extended on all four sides, each side divided by a narrow lane.

Yet so it was until the 1870s, when the square began to be nibbled away.

George Square, although now it scarcely looks it, is a historic spot. It was laid out in the 1760s, and was the first piece of 'modern' town design in Edinburgh. It was the creation of a developer/architect called James Brown, who named it, he said, not after the king but after his elder brother George. The houses, as can still be seen, were not very grand, but they were all of two or three storeys and were unified in character. Most had Doric or Ionic columned doorpieces; a few remain. That one family should occupy a complete house was a most amazing innovation in a city of tenements and tenement stairs, and for a few decades this was far and away the most fashionable place to live in Edinburgh. Although not much given to snobbery in the eighteenth century, the citizens became snobbish about George Square:

> *It was formerly considered a great affair to go out to George's Square to dinner; and on such an occasion a gentleman would stand half an hour at the Cross, in his full dress, with powdered and bagged hair, sword and cane, in order to tell his friends with whom and where he was going to dine.*

So, at any rate, it was said in the 1820s.

Famous men once lived in George Square, and stirring events took place there. The most famous resident was Sir Walter Scott. When his father removed from College Wynd in 1774, he and his family went to 'a dwelling-house with cellars, coach-house etc., on the west side of the great square called George Square'. This was No. 25, which Scott's father built. It still stands, its back windows overlooking Middle Meadow Walk. Scott came to the house when he was two years old, and it remained his home, except for early years spent mostly with his grandfather at Sandyknowe near Kelso, until he married in 1797. It was in George Square that he contracted the illness which crippled him for life, and he later recalled its unhappy effect on his childhood:

> *Every step of the way [Middle Meadow Walk] has for me something of an early remembrance. There is the stile at which I recollect a cross child's maid upbraiding me with my infirmity as she lifted me coarsely and carelessly over the*

From the University to George Square

flinty steps which my brother traversed with a shout and
bound. I remember the suppressed bitterness of the moment,
and the envy with which I regarded the elastic steps of my
more happily-formed brethren.

He went to school at the High School in High School Yards, not far
from George Square (See p. 105) Later, he indulged what a friend
called 'his feudal taste for war' on nearby Bruntsfield Links. The threat
of Napoleonic invasion created many volunteer corps, and Scott was
an enthusiastic officer in one of them. Some derided his efforts – 'I
remember seeing Walter limping home in a cavalry uniform, the most
grotesque spectacle that can be imagined' – but he drilled and trained
his men as well as he was able. His troop used to practice with a sabre
at a turnip, stuck on top of a post and representing a Frenchman:

> *Every other trooper was far less concerned about the success*
> *of his aim at the turnip, than about how he was to tumble.*
> *But Walter pricked forward gallantly, saying to himself, 'Cut*
> *them down, the villains, cut them down!' and made his blow,*
> *which from his lameness was often an awkward one,*
> *cordially muttering curses all the while at the detested*
> *enemy.*

In case the reader does not know, or has not guessed it, Scott was an
ardent monarchist and Tory.

While he still lived in George Square, Scott had many distinguished neighbours. One of them was Henry Dundas, Lord Melville
'the absolute dictator of Scotland' for over twenty years, controlling
the elections in at least thirty-six of the forty-five Scottish constituencies. In 1792 his suppression of radical opinion led to what amounted
to a riot. A mob assembled, marched out to George Square, and
attacked Dundas's house. They broke the windows, and also those of
Lady Arniston and Admiral Duncan who lived nearby. All the residents sallied forth in defence of their property, armed with sticks, but
were pelted with stones and had to retreat back indoors. Another
neighbour was Lord Braxfield. Braxfield has been described as the
Jeffreys of Scotland; in all cases of sedition his formidable abilities
were directed, not to ensuring a fair trial, but to securing a conviction.
'Come awa', Maister Horner,' he is reported to have said to one
witness as he approached the witness box, 'come awa', and help us to
hang ane o' thae daamned scoondrels'. Best known is his response to

the luckless radical who observed that all great men had been reformers, 'even our Saviour himself'. 'Muckle he made o' that,' replied Braxfield, 'he was hanget'. Inevitably, he was widely hated. But when the law courts closed, often near midnight, he always walked home alone to his house in George Square, through the dark and unlighted streets.

Just south east of George Square, beside the University's slate-black tower of learning, is **Buccleuch Place**, most of it built between 1789 and 1800. This was laid out to complement and to be at least as grand as George Square, although it reverted to the traditional system of tenement stairs. Many of the original houses still stand, and there are columned doorpieces, Roman Doric columns, pilasters and pediments. Nos. 14–16 originally housed the 'George's Square Assembly Rooms,' which drove out of business the ancient dancing establishments in the West Bow and Assembly Close. The principal ball-room was ninety-two feet long and was 'lighted by eleven large crystal lustres,' and there were two card-rooms and a tea-room. All these were said to be 'most beautiful rooms,' and around them and around the entire neighbourhood there circulated, for two or three decades, 'the whole fashionable dancing, as indeed the fashionable everything'. Sedan chairs came and went continually, managed as a rule by highlanders in short tartan coats. Chairs were handier in the narrow wynds and closes of the Old Town than carriages, but by 1800 carriages were beginning to drive them out. (Boswell said that carriages provided 'the commodiousness of civilization"). Gentlemen in embroidered coats, and carrying Indian canes, strolled in the Meadows. Finely dressed ladies with powdered hair walked in George Square garden, which was neatly laid out, we are told, in shrubberies and flower borders. And in the double basements which were a feature of many of the houses hereabouts – depths below depths – scullery maids toiled at great stoneware sinks, equipped with mighty mangles.

It may seem strange that this part of town, which now appears to be of little historical interest, was for a time so very important and up-to-date. But for a few decades it was a main centre of Edinburgh life. The successful development of George Square and Buccleuch Place preceded the rise of the New Town to the north; the New Town really belongs to the nineteenth century, although it was begun in the 1760s. It was George Square rather than Princes Street which first drew wealthy families out of the wynds and closes, and thus began the slide of the Old Town towards dereliction:

From the University to George Square

*In 1763, people of quality and fashion lived in houses, which,
in 1783, are inhabited by tradesmen, or by people in humble
and ordinary life. The Lord Justice Clerk Tinwald's house
was lately possessed by a French teacher – Lord President
Craigie's house by a Rouping-wife or Saleswoman of old
furniture – and Lord Drummore's house was lately left by a
Chairman for want of accommodation.*

But the attractions of the new square and the grand street beyond the
University have themselves all, or almost all, gone now. Buccleuch
Place is still very spacious and shrubs and trees still grow in George
Square garden; but the charm has departed.

7

Princes Street

TAKING THE LONG view, the origins of Edinburgh's New Town lie in France. During the eighteenth century the philosophers of that country had the good fortune to observe a world that was entirely new – or, if not entirely new, one that could be entirely renewed, on better principles. This was because, they felt, that they were the pioneers, the enlightened ones, who had broken free of ignorance and superstition, and who now could, by taking thought, bring men's ideas and hence their behaviour and their institutions into harmony with a universal natural order. The perfectibility of all things, even of man himself, was not, after all, impossible.

This anti-traditional way of thinking spread out from France, and Scotland played a large part in its development, a part out of all proportion to the size of the country. David Hume, that superbly intelligent and uninvolved observer of the human scene, was the greatest philosopher of the age – perhaps of any age. Adam Smith wrote *The Wealth of Nations*, unquestionably the most important book on economics ever written. And in many other fields – science, medicine, architecture, mechanical engineering – Scotsmen made contributions of the highest importance.

This release of energy is partly explained by political changes. The Union with England in 1707 brought economic advantages, and in 1746 scheming to bring about a Jacobite revolution was finally and forever brought to an end by the gunfire at Culloden. Attention turned to commercial and cultural developments. Scotland became ambitious to catch up with richer countries like England, France and Holland, to develop a new agriculture, new industries, new lines of trade – and even to transform her ancient overcrowded capital.

A great national undertaking was proposed in 1752. The old town of 'one good street and many narrow lanes' was to be extended into the open fields, to acquire 'spacious streets and large buildings', and thus to become 'a centre of trade and commerce, of learning and the arts, of politeness, and of refinement of every kind'. If all went well Edinburgh would become as eligible a place to live as London. Subscriptions were called for. And George Drummond, the three times re-elected Lord Provost of the day, a man of remarkable foresight and resolve, pushed matters forward.

Around 1760, when the intention to build the new town began to take definite shape, the magistrates decided first that they needed a bridge, and then that they needed a plan.

The bridge was wanted because between the old town and 'the fields to the north' which were to be the site of the new town there lay, in a deep hollow, the North Loch, better described as a bog, scarcely passable. So part of the bog was drained and a bridge was built. That first bridge has long since disappeared (sheep used to graze between its arches, where the railway lines now run) but the North Bridge, leading straight from the High Street (at the Tron Kirk) to the east end of Princes Street, stands exactly where the first bridge stood. As for the plan, they could no doubt have done without one, and muddled along. But being anxious to build a city which would be the finest in Europe, they chose to follow the examples they saw set by Berlin and Turin and aim for a new town of a superior kind, which would consist 'of spacious streets and large buildings ... thinly inhabited, and that too by strangers [newcomers] chiefly, and persons of considerable rank'. Seeking 'order and regularity' in their new town, they organised a planning competition, which was won by a young man called James Craig.

Craig's 1766 plan (we have already seen a copy of it in Huntly House) has determined the street pattern of central Edinburgh to this day. Moreover, it set an example of wide streets and open spaces that was followed and developed in further plans for the surrounding areas during the next seventy or eighty years.

In all but one respect Craig's plan was good eighteenth century orthodoxy: three straight parallel streets, the central one connecting two large squares, one at the east end and the other at the west. Any other eighteenth century planner would probably have done very much the same. What was extraordinary about Craig's plan – the touch of genius that has raised central Edinburgh from the unusual to the remarkable – was that he left the two outer streets, Princes Street and Queen Street, built up on only one side, so that the houses in Queen Street would look clear across the street to the fields that sloped down towards the Forth, while those in Princes Street – and in later days the shoppers and the visitors – would look south across the little valley to the rock and the Castle and the spires and the rooftops of the Old Town. Both streets remain to this day open on one side, and in each case the effect is admirable. But Princes Street is the masterstroke. The visual conjunction of the old and the new is inescapable; the medieval – really post-medieval – looking down on the formal eighteenth century planned city, the Athens of the North. Craig might so easily have kept the two towns separate; but instead he united them, visually. As a result, in the very midst of Edinburgh there rises for everyone to see 'one of the most satisfactory crags in nature – a Bass Rock upon dry land rooted in a garden, shaken by passing trains [surely not!], carrying a crown of battlements and turrets, and describing its warlike shadow over the liveliest and brightest thoroughfare of the New Town'. No one has described it more picturesquely than Robert Louis Stevenson.

Nowadays there are too many vehicles in the New Town, too many road-signs, offices, shopkeepers and accountants. But Craig's town still resists transmogrification by the twentieth century. His plan was given scale and substance by architects such as Robert Adam, Sir William Chambers, W H Playfair, and their work still stands; the town was extended several times by new developments which again incorporated terraces and gardens and long handsome palace fronts; so that today an area of not less than one square mile is a Classical Georgian and early Victorian city of fine buildings and long vistas. There is nothing else like it in Europe. Bath is splendid and delightful, but it is quite small. Terraces and squares in London or Paris or Nancy are as good as any in Edinburgh, but they tend to be isolated, not parts of a large coherent scheme. In central Edinburgh, in the New Town, everything fits together. Here is the Classical city *par excellence*. And what is more, it is still largely occupied by private citizens living in their own homes, as it was meant to be. It is not a museum piece.

Start, then, at the present **North Bridge**, successor to the bridge which launched the great scheme of improvement. The old one was a handsome stone bridge of three arches, completed in 1772. It not only connected the Old Town with the New, but allowed the Fish Market, in the course of a few years, to be removed from the 'stinking ravine' which it occupied just off the High Street (*see* p. 29) and resited under the arches. There was invariably a wonderful supply of fish and shellfish and a wonderful amount of noise, for 'the Edinburgh fishwomen have an absurd custom of demanding, at first, about three times the price they expect and do accept for their fish. This gives rise to much cheapening on the part of the purchasers, and much noisy wheedling on the other side'. The bridge was widened in the 1870s, and then completely replaced twenty years later in order to accommodate the railway. It is very wide and very long and maintains an even gradient from the High Street to Princes Street, an arrangement which suited the old tramcars. There are three arches with arched iron girders, and the spandrels are filled with cast-iron arcading, so it looks like a bridge, not merely a continuation of the roadway on piers, as is the fashion nowadays. On the east side of the parapet is a large freestone memorial to the officers and men of the King's Own Scottish Borderers who were killed in the Boer War. It is well done. And from this point you can see down the Firth of Forth to Aberlady Bay, almost fifteen miles to the east; golf enthusiasts, with the help of a little imagination, can believe that they see Muirfield Golf Course, which is only a mile or two further on.

The line of the bridge descends straight to **Register House**, by Robert Adam. It sometimes seems that Robert Adam, when he is not being thought of as a firm of interior decorators, is considered to have been an architect who had the misfortune mostly to alter great buildings, very seldom to design them entire. This may be true of his work in England, but not in Scotland. Register House, the repository for Scotland's public records, is one of Adam's great buildings. His plan was ready in 1771, when the North Bridge was not yet completed. The form of the building (later extended to the rear) is a rotunda within a large square courtyard – the plan which he had proposed earlier for Syon House in Middlesex. The long frontage which faces the bridge contrives to be fairly simple and severe, and yet elegant at the same time, like a very good evening gown. The lower half is rusticated, with plain ashlar above. The centrepiece, pedimented and with four tall Corinthian columns, projects slightly; the projection and the columns are repeated at each end, with corner turrets. The overall severity is lightened by balustrades, three decorated panels between the central columns, and a roundel of the Royal Arms set simply but emphatically in the pediment.

Begun in 1774 and completed some twenty years later, this is the only one of Robert Adam's public buildings that he saw built as he had designed it. We, unhappily, do not have that good fortune. A large extension at the rear was built in the 1820s, which makes no great difference. What does make a difference is the series of alterations made to the area immediately in front of Register House. There used to be a curved flight of steps which led up to the entrance door. These steps rose from a wide elevated platform on which the whole building stood, or seemed to stand, like Santa Maria delle Salute floating on the lagoon in Venice. But in the interests of the flow of traffic – as usual – this elevated platform has mostly disappeared, and the public pavement and the roadway have been progressively pushed towards the frontage, while the steps to the entrance have been squared off. No doubt the perpetrators of these misdeeds congratulated themselves that they were not 'really' touching the building. But the result of their efforts is that Register House now has no foreground that belongs to it but stands uncomfortably on a slight and inadequate perch, just a few feet above street level, and just a few yards away from the traffic.

Three other developments have contributed to spoil the setting. It used to be possible to look along the North Bridge to Register House and enjoy an unimpeded view of Adam's imposing facade, with the dome of the rotunda above, carefully centred on the line of the bridge. That is how it was meant to be seen. But this view is no longer possible, because the General Post Office intrudes on the right and the Balmoral Hotel on the left, and the worst building complex in Scotland, the St James Centre and New St Andrews House, heaves itself up behind and above the dome.

Take these in turn. The **Post Office** is high renaissance Italian of the 1860s, replacing an ancient theatre of a hundred years before. It too has a rusticated ground floor and Corinthian orders, and it probably looked quite well when it rose to only two storeys, as was at first the case. But in the 1890s it doubled in size, and a few years later it doubled again, this time going up as well as sideways and reaching seven storeys, with the natural result that the poor thing entirely lost its shape and no one has looked at it since. The **Balmoral Hotel** is an even more formidable affair. It is a huge square block, completed in 1902, with much ornamentation which has been described as sixteenth century Franco-German. There are balusters and false balconies and bow windows and dormer windows and a massive tall tower with a very large clock and an open ironwork lantern on top. Inside, it has recently been 'done up'. The whole construction rises mysteriously from the dismal depths of the railway station, and until very recently it was black from the coaly hand of time. But now it has been cleaned, and emerges as a great decorated stone box, with a tower and a clock, and the obvious intention of dominating the east end of Princes Street. The Balmoral Hotel is not great architecture; but it has good intentions; it is not misshapen or dull, and familiarity has made it welcome. No doubt it derives additional importance from the acres of dreariness which prevail below.

What is not welcome and is never going to be welcome is the 1960s **St James Centre** behind Register House, a mix of shops and offices plus a hotel. It covers a very large area and is made of remarkably dismal grey concrete. As first proposed there were to be tall towers which would have dominated the entire city – towers were all the rage with architects in the 1960s. The scheme was severely criticised (although it was always hard to find out just what was going on) and the towers changed into slabs. The slabs broadened and widened, and the whole development grew into a massive ponderous lump, visible from all over town. A pedestrian bridge – a disgrace to the city and to the word 'bridge' which covers such structures as the nearby Waterloo Bridge as well as literally hundreds of modest but elegant little bridges all over Scotland – connects the eyesore to the Calton Hill, and shocks anyone entering Edinburgh from Leith or London Road. It must have been designed with the help of a twelve inch ruler and not much else. The St James Centre looks cheap and nasty and it is not even good to use. For its existence we are indebted to the developers who promoted it, the architects who designed it, the Government which hastened to occupy a large part of it, and the Town Council which sanctioned it and profited from it. All protests were unavailing. Too prosperous for a white elephant, it is not nearly handsome enough for a hippopotamus. It is truly a barbarous building, so please do not go there. Trade only encourages them. (It must be added, however, that the John Lewis Group have recently greatly improved the south-east corner by building across the frontage and hiding it. And the views from Lewis's restaurant on the top floor are outstanding).

Thus later building and more traffic have pressed round Register House and diminished it. The interior has fared better, and it is worth entering to see the rotunda alone, upon which Adam concentrated his efforts. It is a marvellous space, seventy feet high and fifty feet in diameter, the arcaded drum lined with bookcases which contain countless calf-bound folios; the dome far overhead is handsomely decorated and divided into eight compartments, each containing a roundel with figures. There are also two handsome staircases. The extension at the rear is more elaborately finished. Especially worth seeing is the Historical Search Room (i.e. reading room) to which access is easily obtained. This very attractive library room has two storeys of bookcases and a neat balcony running all the way round, below a very elaborate Neo-Greek ceiling. Probably no more agreeable place to carry out research into one's genealogy exists anywhere in the world. And the courtesy of the staff is unfailing.

Leaving Register House you have a splendid view of the rear quarters of the **Duke of Wellington's horse**, and of the back of the Duke himself. This vigorous equestrian statue (1848) is by Sir John Steell, the leading Scottish sculptor of the day; his work is to be seen as far afield as London, Calcutta, and New York. The Duke sat for the head and shoulders and must have been well pleased with the result, because he ordered two casts, one for Apsley House and the other for Eton. The horse rears up most convincingly. The attitude of the animal is extremely heroic and that of the Duke extremely upright, which is all as it ought to be. But a question must occur to the thoughtful spectator: How do the pair of them maintain their pose, when so much of the horse, and all of the Duke, are in front of the horse's rear hooves, and almost nothing behind? What is the strength in those rear legs that keeps so much up in the air? The answer, so it is said, is in the tail. That magnificent, spreading, well-combed tail is full of lead.

Exhausted by the sight of this energetic statue, the visitor may require refreshment; and only just round the corner, literally, is the Cafe Royal, artistically and gastronomically a worthwhile experience.

The **Cafe Royal** is Edinburgh's grandest pub, and the restaurant is among the most exclusive. The building (1861) was planned as a showroom for gas and sanitary fittings, became a hotel, and was brought to its present state in 1901. The pub section is notable for its solidly carved island bar with delicately fluted Corinthian brass columns, and its tiled faience murals by Doulton. These latter depict inventors: for example, 'Benjamin Franklin, Printer distinguished in Science and Politics'; 'William Caxton, Citizen of London, Mercer, brought printing into England 1476'; 'George Stephenson, 'There is no limit to the speed if the works can be made to stand'. The figures in all of them are almost life-size, and the colours are subdued but excellent. The panels seem to date from 1885 and are in tip-top condition. The restaurant is equally stylish, with more carved woodwork, eight stained-glass windows depicting British sportsmen, and three tile pictures, two of them of vessels on the Clyde and the Mersey. It all looks very Victorian-Edwardian, and very genuine.

Return to Princes Street and cross to the Balmoral Hotel. A long flight of steps goes down the side of the hotel to the railway station. The interest of these steps is that they are useful, and are believed to be the windiest place in Edinburgh. To the right of the steps is the **Waverley Market**, a shopping mall on several levels, with lots of escalators and lots of greenery. Its flat roof of pale grey granite looks out of place in a sandstone city, and the effect is not improved by the triangular fins (the fins of property sharks, it was said at the time) which poke up through the deck. It is not a good building; and according to James Craig's plan, it should not be here; and neither, for that matter, should the Balmoral Hotel. There was to be no building on the south side of Princes Street. So what happened? It is worth relating how the developers beat the plan, or at any rate dented it, for this is one of Edinburgh's most instructive stories.

When the New Town was just beginning 'to spread abroad its draughty parallelograms', an enterprising coachbuilder and a couple of his friends acquired land where the Balmoral Hotel now stands. The Town Council agreed that they might build on this land, provided that nothing rose above the level of Princes Street. Losing no time, the three developers began operations towards the end of 1770.

Fortunately, a small number of very influential people who had built, or were building, houses on the other side of the street took immediate legal action, and represented to the Courts that they had come to live in the New Town because it was understood that

> *no buildings were to be erected to the south of Princes Street, by which means the proprietors of houses on that street in particular, would enjoy advantages which they considered as of the greatest value, viz. free air, and an agreeable prospect. While, on the other hand, the fine opening of the city upon that street gave at once an idea of the beauty and elegance of the general design.*

The fact that even the chimney tops of the proposed houses would be below the level of Princes Street, they went on, was not a concession but the establishment of a deformity and a nuisance. The whole arrangement, they said, was 'a most gross violation of public faith, and a real injury to the town itself'. The Town Council's defence was that although Craig's plan showed the area south of Princes Street as laid out in gardens sloping down to a canal (the North Loch translated!), they were not legally bound by the details of a plan. The objectors lost their case in Edinburgh, but being rich as well as influential (one of them was the biggest banker in Edinburgh and another

was David Hume) they promptly took it to the House of Lords, where
Lord Mansfield decided the matter:

> *Let me earnestly recommend to this Corporation to call to*
> *their aid the same assistance they set out with – let them*
> *consult with their standing counsel what may be for their*
> *honour, what for their interest, neither of which they seem for*
> *some time to have understood. I give my opinion, therefore,*
> *my lords [in the plaintiff's favour], not only on the plain and*
> *open principles of justice, but from regard to the public, and*
> *from regard to this misguided Corporation itself.*

It looked like a victory. But the houses complained of were now more
than half built, so a compromise was reached: houses beside the
bridge to remain; only workshops to be allowed immediately west of
where the Waverley Steps now are; beyond that, all land to be 'kept
and preserved in perpetuity as pleasure ground'.

So we owe the open ground south of Princes Street and half the
charm of central Edinburgh to a banker, a philosopher, a handful of
other eighteenth century men of means, and Lord Mansfield; and, of
course, James Craig. The developers and the planning authority
battled for their own short-term interest, but not for the long-term
public interest. They, it seems, had no conception of Edinburgh as a
beautiful city. Today, in these more enlightened times, do we not all
strive for the public interest? Do we not all want beautiful cities? Of
course not. In the 1970s, the ground west of the Waverley Steps
having been long occupied by a large shed or hall with a roof garden
level with Princes Street, and this hall having become derelict, developers once more appeared on the scene. It would be advantageous,
they thought, if a shopping mall were built here, rising a mere fifteen
feet above the level of the pavement; why bother about the view? The
planning authority, like their eighteenth century predecessors, immediately agreed; and the battle for scenic advantage had to be fought
once again. Once again private citizens had to defend their city
against the planners, the developers and the Town Council, and once
again they won.

The Waverley Market and the Station are bounded on the west by
Waverley Bridge (1896), which affords good views looking towards
the Castle. Waverley Bridge leads to **Market Street**, where interesting exhibitions are often staged at the **City Art Centre**. Beyond
the Art Centre is the entrance to **Fleshmarket Close**. This Close

consists of a long (repeat long) flight of steps which climbs up virtually to the High Street and contains two pubs to assist those in transit between the Old Town and the New. These pubs are the Half Way House and Jinglin' Geordie, this latter the nickname of George Heriot (*see* p. 93).

Further east, adjacent to the North Bridge, rises an imposing building which used to be the offices of The Scotsman newspaper, an essay in late nineteenth century English Baroque. There are four floors below the level of the North Bridge and three floors above it; numerous arches, pediments, turrets and carved figures provide additional grandeur. The view from what used to be the editor's office, out across the Princes Street Gardens to the New Town, and north-east to the Calton Hill, must be one of the grandest views in Edinburgh.

On the north side of Princes Street, across from the station, you may shop in some unusual surroundings. At the corner of St Andrew Street there is a large building which dates from 1906, a well disguised steel-frame stone-clad building, the first of its kind in Scotland. It is easily identified, for the corner tower is topped by a gilded openwork sphere. Inside, there used to be lots of clear floor space, but that is now clogged up with escalators and clothes for sale, and the whole place is considerably smothered in blue paint. It may yet recover. The early renaissance-style marble staircase is intact, as easy to ascend as a staircase should be; the rises are so shallow that you just float up; obviously made for Edwardian ladies in ankle-length dresses. At the next corner, St David Street, stands **Jenners** (1895), said to be the largest privately-owned store in the world. It is an enormous pink stone building with renaissance undertones. There are paired caryatids and a great deal of strapwork, and the corner – some say architecturally related to the Bodleian Library at Oxford – rises six storeys to an octagon with flying buttresses. Inside, there is a most admirable galleried open space, some seventy feet by thirty, which rises through two floors from ground level to the glazed roof. From the upper gallery, safe behind a hefty Victorian wooden balustrade, you look down forty feet to the ground floor. Every Christmas a sixty foot high Christmas tree is brought in and erected in this very large open space, and of course suitably decorated. The tree always looks perfectly at home, and it is fun to walk round and admire it at tree-top level.

Not much else of note still stands among the Princes Street shops at this end. The original houses were not distinguished and only traces of a few of them remain. But deficiencies on the north side are

more than made up for by the **Scott Monument** and the Princes
Street Gardens. In any list of the seven wonders of Edinburgh the
Scott Monument would certainly have to be included.
Sir Walter Scott was an Edinburgh lawyer. His father was an Edin-
burgh lawyer (his great-grandfather, incidentally, fought for the Old
Pretender in 1715), and Walter was born in the family home in
College Wynd (*see* p. 106) in 1771. He was educated at the High
School (built in 1777, now part of the University in High School
Yards), and at Edinburgh University from 1783 (when he was twelve
years old) to 1786. He was then apprenticed to his father, and called
to the Bar in 1792. These facts are worth remembering, because Scott
is often thought of as a professional writer who lived at Abbotsford,
on the Tweed, and who rode about the countryside from time to time
in some vaguely official capacity. But behind Scott the poet and
novelist was Scott the lawyer, a practising advocate at the Bar in
Edinburgh, and sheriff of Selkirkshire. As Lord Cameron has
reminded us,

> *Scott was not like Robert Louis Stevenson, whose practice at
> the Scots Bar consisted of one petition and whose knowledge
> of the civic law of Rome just enabled him to know that stilli-
> cide was not a crime nor was emphyteusis a disease: he was
> a practising lawyer familiar with the world in which life and
> law made contact.*

Sir Walter Scott is still to be ranked among the most famous of all
Scotsmen, although his reputation does not stand as high today as it
did in the nineteenth century. When he died, romantic feelings about
chivalry and the Middle Ages and battles long ago (the blood and
horror of Waterloo were not for Sir Walter) and knights and maidens
and heroic highlanders were cultivated and enjoyed to the utmost, and
Scott was seen, not only by his own countrymen, as one of the great
creators of the welcome and uplifting anodyne myth of romance.
What his own contemporaries thought is clearly explained by the
words engraved on a plate which was laid beside the foundation stone
of the monument in 1840:

> *This Graven Plate, deposited in the base of a votive building
> on the fifteenth day of August, in the year of Christ 1840, and
> never likely to see the light again till all the surrounding
> structures have crumbled to dust by the decay of time, or by*

human or elemental violence, may then testify to a distant posterity that his countrymen began on that day to raise an effigy and architectural monument, TO THE MEMORY OF SIR WALTER SCOTT, BART., whose admirable writings were then allowed to have given more delight and suggested better feeling to a larger class of readers in every rank of society, than those of any other author, with the exception of Shakespeare alone, and which were therefore thought likely to be remembered long after their act of gratitude on the part of the first generation of his admirers should be forgotten. HE WAS BORN AT EDINBURGH, 15th AUGUST, 1771, AND DIED AT ABBOTSFORD, 21st SEPTEMBER, 1832

For an author so revered, and by persons so solemn and so sententious, could any lapidary tribute be too grand?

One hundred and fifty years later we may be somewhat out of sympathy with Sir Walter's nineteenth century admirers, but we have to admit that they could hardly have built a more appropriate monument. They took a good deal of time and a great deal of trouble. It was agreed from the start that it had to be Gothic (Gothic meant romance), and the site originally selected was Charlotte Square. A competition was held in 1836 which attracted no fewer than fifty five entrants, and after some argument and delay the winner was declared to be John Meikle Kemp. The story of Kemp is a strange one, and it has (of course) been romanticised. It is true that he was the son of a Border shepherd and was trained as a carpenter; but it is somewhat stretching the truth to say that he was 'an humble artist, not far removed from the position of an ordinary workman,' and to suggest that he was an uneducated but inspired young man with no training in architecture whatever. He had, in fact, worked in London, made a tour of France, and been employed in the office of William Burn, an Edinburgh architect who knew a good deal about Gothic as well as Classical architecture.

The Scott Monument is a Gothic steeple one hundred and eighty feet high, profusely decorated and ornamented. It would probably look absurd if the architectural detail were not so correct. Kemp knew his Gothic. The lowest stage, with its four tall arches and diagonal buttresses, forms an elaborate canopy for the statue, and has clear affinities with Melrose Abbey, which Scott greatly admired; and the experts tell us that other features have been borrowed or adapted from Rheims, Rouen, Antwerp and other continental sources. To most people it is a fantastic structure of pinnacles, pillars, arches, buttresses and niches soaring up into the sky, covered with skilfully cut detail. In the niches and on the capitals and pilasters there are dozens of statuettes and heads of persons famous in history or in the Waverley novels – Prince Charles Edward, Robert the Bruce and Richard Coeur de Lion belong in the first category, Dandie Dinmont, Meg Merrilies and Old Mortality in the second. Such a torrent of ornamentation might prove wearisome, but it is offset by two calming influences. First, there is the statue of Scott himself, seated, with his deerhound Maida beside him, cut by Sir John Steell in the 1840s from a 30 ton block of Carrara marble. It is very large, but simple and reposeful, a most effective piece of statuary. And there is also the soothing influence of the grass and trees of Princes Street Gardens, and of nearby Classical buildings. The Scott Monument is the right monument in the right place, a very unusual phenomenon. And it is also useful, for you may climb the staircase to the museum, where several items relate to Sir Walter and to the unfortunate John Kemp (he was accidentally drowned before the monument was completed), and then to the topmost tier, giving a splendid view of the gardens and the city.

The **Princes Street Gardens** run from a little east of the Scott Monument to the far end of Princes Street. They are interrupted only by two major art galleries on the line of the Mound, which is a street (*see* next chapter) connecting Princes Street and the Royal Mile. The whole garden area was originally 'a filthy and offensive bog' which was first drained, planned and planted by residents on the other side of the street. The proprietors kept the gardens for their own exclusive use, although the public was free to peer through the railings. Then in the 1830s came the first scheme to build a railway line through the gardens. No harm would result, the projectors explained; the trains would be out of sight and 'owing to the improved construction of the furnaces the smoke is now scarcely seen'. Permission was refused. But in the 1840s, as Princes Street became less and less residential and more and more filled with shops and hotels, resistance weakened, the railways came in, and a stone wall and embankment had to be built to conceal the nuisance. Thirty years later the gardens became public. They are unquestionably one of the delights of Edinburgh, a very large oasis in the very centre of town, often to be seen as Robert Louis Stevenson saw them, 'full of girls and idle men, steeping themselves in sunshine'. The flower clock at the foot of the Mound, begun in 1904 and replanted every spring to a new design, is unfailingly popular, as are the long grassy slopes for *al fresco* lunches on sunny days. But Sir Walter has the best of it: close to his monument a double line of trees (some of them old, alas, but replanting is in hand) provides a marvellous leafy screen behind which the Old Town is only half concealed, and beneath which beds of tall tulips, and lilies and ageratum in summertime, cry their wares of bright colours to all the passers-by.

Leaving until the next chapter the Royal Scottish Academy (which intrudes inconveniently into Princes Street) as well as the Mound and its other buildings, continue along Princes Street, keeping to the garden side. On the other side of the street, sad to say, there is almost no architecture worth noticing. The only modern building worth a glance is the New Club (1966) in a rather dark grey granite. It has large windows and projecting mullions and a general air of severity (and prosperity). What annoys older citizens is that it is not nearly as good as its handsome palace-fronted predecessor (the New Club being a venerable institution) which was by William Burn, completed in 1834; it had a singularly handsome skyline with massive urns, one of which is now inside the Club as a reminder of architecturally better days. Further along is the former Conservative Club (1884), a tall and carefully detailed palace front, asymmetrical, with fine balustrading. It now belongs to Debenham's who have devised a good entrance and have retained, at the rear of the new interior, the splendid original staircase in a two-storey open arcade. Also retained are the three stained glass lights which commemorate Disraeli – what other store can boast such a feature? Beyond Castle Street there is nothing much: a corner-tenement of 1786, mostly covered over; at No 128 a Graeco-Italian palace with superimposed orders and a strong cornice; and at nos 129–131 some residual evidence of the original eighteenth century houses. All in all, Princes Street is not and never was distinguished for its architecture.

Statues and memorials, however, are a strong feature of Edinburgh, and there are several good examples to be seen as you walk along beside the Gardens. First there is the **Allan Ramsay Monument**, a standing figure in Carrara marble by Sir John Steell (1865). Some have thought it 'rather grotesque' that the poet (he was a poet who made money, by the way) should be represented wearing a silk nightcap; but in his day this was a fashionable, although only occasional, substitute for a wig. The **Royal Scots Greys Monument** (1906, by Birnie Rhind) stands opposite Frederick Street. It is another fine equestrian statue (horses seem to appeal to sculptors), a bronze trooper on horseback on a rocky pedestal. The **Dr Thomas Guthrie Monument** (1910) is opposite Castle Street; it is in Portland stone. Few people now know about Guthrie, but in his day he was famous beyond Scotland. He was a minister who left the Church of Scotland with many others in 1843 to form the Free Church. His life's work was in Edinburgh, where he pioneered the establishment of non-sectarian schools for poor children; one child said of him, 'He was the only father I ever had'. His *Plea for Ragged Schools* (1847) was an influential book, and such was his reputation that when he wrote a volume with the unpromising title of *The Gospel in Ezekiel* it sold 50,000 copies. A true christian and great philanthropist, he is shown standing hand-in-hand with a child, and in his other hand he holds a bible. Now comes the last but not the least of the statues, the **Sir James Simpson Monument** (1876). Simpson, who began life as a poor boy, was a graduate of Edinburgh University. In 1847 he discovered chloroform anaesthesia, conferring one of the greatest possible blessings on mankind. (See p. 173). He too was a man of great humanity. Although not tall, his appearance was very striking, and this statue by William Brodie was 'admitted by all to be an excellent likeness'. Finally, for those whose appetite for sculpture is not sated, a stroll into the gardens at this west end will reveal the **Ross Fountain**. It is a colossal Second Empire piece of flamboyancy, crowded with voluptuous figures and cast in iron, in Paris, for the International Exhibition of 1862. When the Exhibition ended it was bought by an Edinburgh gunsmith named Daniel Ross and presented to the city. We do not know exactly what the city thought of it, but it was put in the gardens discreetly out of sight. What Dean Ramsay thought of it – he who ministered for many years in the nearby St John's Church, overlooking the fountain – is on record. It was, he said, 'Grossly indecent and disgusting; insulting and offensive to the moral feelings of the community and disgraceful to the City'. Yet the Dean was, we are told, 'a genial-hearted man'.

St John's church, at the end of the Gardens and of Princes Street, was completed in 1818 and cost £18,000. It was designed by William Burn in the Perpendicular style, and he did it extremely well (although a nineteenth century critic described it as exemplifying 'the somewhat feeble modern Gothic of that day'). It is a very beautiful little church, consisting of a nave and aisles. There are no transepts. The nave is divided into eight clearstoried bays with buttresses and pinnacles, and in the 1880s the chancel was extended by one aisleless bay and a three-sided apse. This extension was also very well done. The original west tower, surmounted by an octagonal lantern, fell through the roof during a tempest of wind before the church was consecrated. The vestry hall and chapel to the south are twentieth century additions. The interior is masterly. The tall arcades have clustered shafts, each surmounted by a projecting figure of Mary Magdalen. The slim clearstorey shafts rise and spread out into delicate fan-vaulting, each fan-vault being the same diameter as the central down-hanging fans. The effect is most delicate, and is supported by the ribbed aisle vaults. The later chancel is also vaulted, with an elaborate pattern of ribs. It is said that Burn's model was St George's Chapel at Windsor. The stained glass is not particularly notable, but the pews, pulpit and aisle panelling, all of the 1860s, harmonise with the architecture extremely well, while the canopied stalls and panelling in the chancel are equally good; these were inspired by the richly carved screen and stalls in King's College Chapel, Aberdeen, which are the finest surviving example of Scottish medieval ecclesiastical woodwork. There is a good reredos, a stone Gothic triptych with tile pictures, and in the aisles a series of nineteenth century marble wall-monuments, many of them commemorating officers killed in the Crimean war. Some are Gothic and some are Neo-Tudor. Perhaps the most interesting is a Gothic wall-tabernacle to Mrs Mary Arbuthnot, with two mourning figures, by John Flaxman. In the adjacent churchyard is the tomb of Sir Henry Raeburn, 'the prince of Scottish portrait painters'.

Just to the south of St John's, off Princes Street, stands a very different church, the church of **St Cuthbert.** It is best described as 'mixed Renaissance', and it is very large. It dates no further back than the 1890s, although it retains the steeple of its 1775 predecessor. And there were churches here before that, exactly on the present site. The medieval church, first mentioned in 1127, may have been founded by St Margaret. In the middle of the seventeenth century the church was a long narrow building with an offset square tower and one transept on the south side, and by 1772 it had become a strange assortment of barn-like buildings attached to a slim five-storey tower and a roofless ruin on the west. However odd architecturally, the church was of some importance, for its parish was the largest in Midlothian, nearly encircling the whole of Edinburgh. Being outside the city walls it suffered a good deal from war, especially after the invention of artillery, and it maintained a somewhat independent existence. Thus when Charles Edward occupied Edinburgh in 1745, most city ministers left their churches and 'sought refuge in the country' (for the Kirk was implacably opposed to the Jacobite rebellion). But the minister at St

Cuthbert's, the Rev Neil McVicar, was made of sterner stuff and – so the story goes – preached to a crowded congregation, many of whom were armed highlanders, and prayed for the King as follows:

> *Bless the King! Thou knowest what king I mean. May the crown sit long on his head. As for that young man who has come among us to seek an earthly crown, we beseech Thee to take him to Thyself and give him a crown of glory.*

It is further said that when this was reported to the Prince, he laughed. But students of his character may find that hard to believe.

A few years after these exciting events occurred, the church was discovered to be dangerous, and another took its place. This in its turn became unsafe, and in 1895 the present building, by Hippolyte Blanc, was erected. It is rectangular, with a domed apse flanked by two Baroque towers, which do not stand easily alongside the 1790 spire, which has been described as 'Gibbsian with Adamish detail'. Altogether it is bulky and odd; and, as was said in the nineteenth century, it 'looks so like a huge stone box, that some wags have described it as resembling a packing-case, out of which the neighbouring beautiful toy-like fabric of St John's church has been lifted'.

The interior is altogether another matter, and remarkable for a Scots presbyterian kirk. The body of the church is spacious but plain, with a u-shaped gallery on pseudo-Corinthian columns. There are wide transepts, and a wide gallery stairs leads to a wooden stair with Renaissance detail, cantilevered out, which gives access to the tower. So far, nothing very remarkable. But there is a mosaic floor, and the stalls are elaborately carved. The communion table is white marble, divided into three compartments by Corinthian pilasters; the centre compartment contains a cross of green Aventurine marble with a golden centre and porphyry infill, while the outer panels are of lapis lazuli and mother-of-pearl. The pulpit stands on four red marble columns from the San Ambrogio quarries near Verona, with verde antico panels, one of which bears a relief of the Angel of the Gospel. In the apse there is an alabaster wall frieze in high relief, which is a version of Leonardo's Last Supper, strangely divided in three by pilasters clad in orange-red Verona marble. The font is a hexagonal bowl of polished white marble based on the font by della Quercia in Siena Cathedral, and bearing a copy of Michaelangelo's Bruges Madonna. The stained glass is a good deal less surprising, but it is almost all one unified scheme of scriptural subjects decided upon in

1893. These windows are adequate, but they are boring in comparison with a David and Goliath by Tiffany of New York, which is bold and exciting in both composition and colour. Of the numerous memorials, the most notable are a panel to the children of Francis Redfern (Christ blessing the little children) by Flaxman (1802), and a wall tablet of 1842 in memory of John Napier of Merchiston, the inventor of logarithms; the title page of his book is reproduced. (For Napier's home, Merchiston Castle, *see* p. 215). It is a church of surprises. And the very large churchyard must contain several more, for there are literally hundreds of monuments and enclosures. Enthusiasts for De Quincey will find him buried here, within a few yards of King's Stables Road.

Finish, conveniently, at the **Caledonian Hotel**, opposite the west front of St John's. The long red sandstone façade of the hotel can scarcely be missed. Apart from its size, its most striking feature is the entrance front. An enormously lofty gable with a ziggurat-effect and a pile of little dormers soars into the sky, with three intermediate floors of no particular interest, and at ground level three tall arches with pairs of monolithic Corinthian columns. What is equally curious, the three arches were originally the monumental entrance to a railway station which occupied the ground now occupied by the hotel. Erected in 1893, they were incorporated into the new V-plan hotel ten years later. The east-facing ground floor has more pairs of Corinthian columns, and the roof rejoices in a long and cheerful procession of two-storey François I dormers. The interior ('re-done' several times) is pleasantly lit by the mezzanine windows, and has a spacious imperial staircase with rather solid bronze leafage, instead of balusters, supporting the handrail. After walking one mile from the other end of Princes Street, relax in Edwardian ease.

8

The Mound

WHAT USED TO be called 'the Earthen Mound' began as a private venture. In the early days of the New Town, when the North Loch was a swamp – 'the receptacle of many sewers, and seemingly of the worried cats, drowned dogs, and blackguardism of the city' – an increasing number of people found it inconvenient that there was no direct link between the Old Town and Princes Street; they had to walk all the way round by the North Bridge. So by the 1780s, when house-building had reached as far west from Register House as Hanover Street, a kind of track had been constructed, made of stones and planks, begun by a tailor called George Boyd whose shop was in the Old Town but who had many clients in the New; hence the original name, Geordie Boyd's Mud Brig. Interest rose with population, and it soon became the practice to deposit all the earth and rubbish from the construction of the New Town onto the line of the 'brig'. Thus, after some two million cartloads had been tipped out by contractors and private citizens, the Mound was created.

In its early days it was a place for caravans and wild beast shows, and until about 1850 there was a huge wooden rotunda, half way up the hill, which showed pictures of the battles of Trafalgar and Waterloo. But all this began to change in 1823, when at the junction of the Mound and Princes Street the foundation stone was laid of what was at first known as the Royal Institution, and is now known as the **Royal Scottish Academy**.

Designed by Playfair, the first stage completed in 1826, this building established the Mound as an appropriate site for great architecture. As first constructed, the Academy building was about half as long as it is now. But in 1831 the users asked Playfair to enlarge it, which he did by increasing its length, and at the same time reducing its severity. What we now see is a large and remarkably handsome Doric Temple. Above a uniform base of steps rise fifteen fluted columns along each side (originally there were only eight), with two-column projecting porticos at each corner, each portico surmounted by two sphinxes. The projecting porticos to north and south are each supported on eight columns, and the tympana are decorated with sinuous, foliage-like carving. A frieze with wreaths and triglyphs runs all the way round the building. The 1830s extension included advancing the north pediment by a second rank of columns (this is why it projects into the street), and in 1844 this north portico was surmounted by a large seated and robed figure of Queen Victoria (or it could be thought to be Britannia) by Sir John Steell. It is a most elegant building, decorated just sufficiently to relieve its essentially severe lines, and yet not so much as to make it in any way fussy or effeminate.

The interior has been completely altered since Playfair's day. The early occupants included the Royal Society of Edinburgh and the Society of Antiquaries of Scotland as well as the Scottish School of Design, the first such school to be established in Britain at public expense. But by the early years of the twentieth century these bodies had moved elsewhere, and the interior was altered to suit the Royal Scottish Academy. There are now six large rooms for exhibitions and a set of upper-level galleries in a simple Classical style, with coved concrete ceilings. Playfair would not have disapproved. (He would have been less happy about the foundations. Before building began in 1823 2,000 piles had to be driven in to make firm the travelled earth, but there has been occasional trouble). Every spring the Academy mounts a large exhibition of new paintings, sculptures, and architectural models and drawings.

Next to the Academy is the still larger **National Gallery of Scotland**, also designed by Playfair. The foundation stone was laid by Prince Albert in the summer of 1850, and the first visitors entered the Gallery in 1859. This building certainly has a claim to be one of the finest in Edinburgh. It is cruciform in plan (although not obviously so), with double Ionic porticos to north and south (reflecting the fact that it was originally shared by two users, the Gallery and the Academy), and on the face of each transept there is a six-column portico. The pilasters along each side are completely plain, and there are almost no windows, except by the north entrance. Balustrades surmount the outer wall, which is a decidedly odd arrangement in a Classical building. Except for these balustrades, there is virtually no ornamentation. The honey-coloured sandstone is the same throughout; the pillars are polished exceptionally smooth; the entablatures are plain. Everything depends on volume and proportion. 'I feel sure,' Playfair wrote, 'that the architecture of this building will be too simple and pure to captivate the multitude, but I am certain that I follow the right path in what I am doing and so am content'. It is certainly an austere design. And some of the austerity may be owing to Government reluctance to provide money – Playfair at one point proposed picturesque towers on the transverse porticos and a grand flight of steps down to Princes Street gardens. But probably he thought better of these extras. With the final result he had every right to be content. The Gallery is designed to fit into and enhance its marvellous setting, and to be seen from many directions. It divides Princes Street and the gardens into more comfortable halves, and can be seen equally well from the North Bridge as from St John's church; perhaps the best distant view is from near the Waverley Market, a view of which Playfair himself provided several preliminary drawings. And always the Academy's straight civilised lines, low profile and light colour provide an excellent contrast to the nearby trees and grassy slopes, and to the congregation of ramparts, battlements, bastions and other fortifications that tower overhead, rock-raised, perfectly detached, indifferent to everyone. As so often in Edinburgh, it is the combination and contrast, the old with the new, the natural with the man-made, that is so exceptionally fine.

The interior of the building consists of two parallel galleries running north and south. Each is divided into five octagons, the smallest at each end. The three central octagons are linked by 'railway tunnel' arches, large enough to permit a clear view through all three. The centre octagon on each side, gaining more space from the transepts, is particularly large. In the early 1970s an upper floor was inserted at the south end, which provided space for five new small galleries, and in 1978 a most ingenious solution to the problem of how to create still more accommodation without altering the appearance of the building was worked out; go underground. This subterranean extension, unlike the building above ground, is well supplied with windows, a paradox explained by the fact that they are part of the east-facing slope of the Mound. Probably few Edinburgh citizens have ever noticed them.

It is less easy to overlook the scheme of interior decoration, which embraces red, pink, blue, grey and green walls. Red predominates, and this is justified on the ground that red walls for pictures were common in the eighteenth and early nineteenth centuries. It is further argued that the practice may have stemmed from the red walls of the tribuna of the Uffizi in late sixteenth century Florence. It may be so.

The Mound

Whether these colourful walls do indeed give 'clearness to works of high art,' as a Victorian interior decorator claimed, or distract attention from them, must be left to the decision of each visitor. The close hanging of the pictures, incidentally, is supposed to bring us nearer to Playfair. Whether this is an advantage or not must also be a matter of opinion.

Works of high art: the Gallery is one itself, and it contains many more. Few collections of equal size anywhere in the world can boast the same quality with variety. There are numerous greater galleries, and there are galleries full of masterpieces by a single school or even a single painter; but such a bringing together as there is here, in a gallery of only modest size, of great works from many countries and many centuries is rare indeed.

The collection has been built up during more than a century and a half. One of the first tenants of the Royal Scottish Academy building was the Institution for the Encouragement of the Fine Arts, and the collection began to be formed when this Institution bought thirty eight paintings in Genoa and Florence in 1830–31. Among these were three van Dycks; one of these was 'the Lomellini Family', a magnificent work which shows van Dyck at the height of his powers. Thirty years later Allan Ramsay's collection was given; this included works not only by the painter himself but also by Watteau, Boucher and Greuze. In 1892 the Gallery was given its first Rembrandt, and during the next several decades it acquired or was given paintings by artists as diverse as Raeburn, Goya, Turner and Sargent. In 1960 it was given twenty two French Impressionist and Post-Impressionist paintings of the highest quality, and these have been supported by purchase. Most important, the Gallery has on loan from the Duke of Sutherland a group of paintings which once formed part of the Orleans collection. This is the most distinguished group of paintings privately owned in the United Kingdom and includes several very great works by Titian, Poussin and Rembrandt.

There are two ways to 'do' the National Gallery; quickly, or properly. For many visitors, unfortunately, time is of the essence, and therefore it may be helpful to begin by suggesting those works, or groups of works, which are of outstanding interest, and which no visitor ought on any account to miss. A process of ruthless (and inevitably personal) reduction has brought this list down to five (fifteen paintings plus a group of French Impressionists).

Enter the Gallery and keep a look out for four of the greatest Titians in the world. On the ground floor the two largest (they measure approximately seven feet by eight) are 'Diana and Actaeon' and 'Diana and Callisto'. They were painted for Philip II of Spain in the 1550s, and they show Titian, 'that epic poet of sensuality,' at the height of his powers. Pleasure in the sight of the naked female body has never been more frankly or fully expressed. The first is of the hunter Actaeon surprising Diana and her attendants at a grotto, an unlucky discovery which led to Actaeon being turned into a stag. later to be caught and killed by his own hounds. The figure left of centre was described by Lord Clark as 'one of the most seductive nudes in all painting'. The second shows how the pregnancy of Callisto, one of Diana's companions, was revealed when she was forced to undress to bathe. Banished by the goddess, her fate was to be turned into a bear (all this is in Ovid's *Metamorphoses*) and to be immortalized as the constellation Ursa Major. Both these pictures are great set pieces, evocations of the antique world, and each is filled with female nudes as a basket of fruit might be filled with ripe peaches. 'the Three Ages of Man' and 'Venus Anadyomene' are very different works. The former was painted about 1515 (Titian was born in the 1480s and lived until 1576) and depicts infancy, young love and old age. The girl wears a crown of myrtle, the plant of Venus, and the recorders which she holds suggest the harmony of music and of love. The lovers are in the foreground, she fully clothed, the young man almost naked; the cherubs are less important, and old age is almost forgotten. It is all in the open air, with a background of trees and meadows and a distant river winding through a remote, hazy-blue countryside. It is a picture of extraordinary calm, as atmospheric as Giorgione's 'La Tempesta' in the Gallerie del Academia in Venice. The last of these four Titians, 'Venus Anadyomene' , is again quite different. It was painted about 1525, and has unfortunately been much restored; Titian himself repainted her head, and it does not seem to belong properly to the rest of her body. Nevertheless, this is one of the great nudes of western art. She appears supported by nothing but a conch shell floating on an unfocussed sea beneath an unfocussed sky. She is splendidly substantial and splendidly rhythmical. Renoir had the same idea when he painted 'La Baigneuse Blonde' three hundred and fifty years later.

In another room there hangs a very different vision of the world. Poussin's 'the Seven Sacraments', from Baptism to Extreme Unction, were painted in the 1640s. The room in which they hang is intended to resemble the Poussin interiors – marble floor, drab walls, dimly glowing lamp, and a central seat which is very similar to the couch on which Christ reclines in the 'Penance'. It looks a little as if interior decoration had resolved to out-do art; but never mind that. These seven paintings form a set which makes it easier to understand why Bernini said that beside Poussin 'I am as nothing' – and also why, unlike Titian, Poussin has never been popular. He was an immensely serious painter, never more serious than in 'the Seven Sacraments'. In these dramatically lit and coloured scenes, every detail has been thought out, every figure counts. No one stands or sits idly by, for all are involved in actions that state or symbolise the moral seriousness of life. The colours, the gestures – and how many gestures there are! – are vivid against sombre or mysterious backgrounds.

In other Rooms are three magnificent Rembrandts, 'Young Woman with Flowers in her Hair' (1634), 'Woman in a Bed' (1645–6), and 'self-portrait aged 51' (1657). The supply of Rembrandts diminishes every year as the art experts pronounce one after another to be not by Rembrandt. To what extent this is a useful exercise it is hard to say, for what matters is the impact of the picture. 'Woman in a Bed' is an action-portrait, and a very fine one; it is possibly of Hendrickje Stoffels, who became the artist's loyal mistress after the death of his wife, Saskia. Rembrandt's women are seldom beautiful in a conventional sense, but they are unfailingly human. As for the self-portrait, it is one of that series of self-portraits before which criticism falls silent. Only the truth of the expression, the tenacity one sees in the eyes of some internal vision, is important.

The French Impressionists are on the upper floor. After Titian, Poussin and Rembrandt it is impossible for them to strike us as profound, or grand, for mostly they live on the surface of things, in the play of light. They are so enjoyable, these paintings by the children of the sun. Many art galleries have several and no doubt as good as any here. But opportunities to see in two rooms good examples of the work of every well-known French impressionist and post-impressionist painter do not occur very often, and these drawing-room size pictures show one another off to advantage. There are over two dozen of them, and the cumulative effect can only be described as delightful. Cezanne and van Gogh are of course more 'serious' than the others.. One of Cezanne's many paintings of Mont Ste Victoire is here, and there is a fearfully tortured 'Olive Trees' by van Gogh. But van Gogh has also a sparkling 'Orchard in Blossom', the very breath of spring, and Monet's 'Poplars on the Epte' is high summer in France, a shimmer of leaves and sunshine and blue water. And if you love colours, strong brilliant contrasting colours, see 'Martinique

Landscape' by Gaugin. The heat and harshness of the tropics have never been distilled into glittering colour as arrestingly as on this canvas. All these pictures were painted between 1888 and 1895. What wonderful years for art!

To complete this fast-art tour, give a few moments to the Scottish painters, especially Allan Ramsay and Sir Henry Raeburn. They do not rank with Rubens or Rembrandt, but they were very fine painters, and this is Scotland, and the visitor should not leave without seeing what could be done by Scottish artists, the range and quality of whose work is better seen in Edinburgh than anywhere else. Allan Ramsay's 'the Painter's Wife' is in his later, more delicate style. He was in Italy in the 1730s, then went to London where he became George III's favourite painter, and the rival of Sir Joshua Reynolds. His first wife died, and in 1752 Margaret, daughter of Sir Alexander Lindsay of Evelick, eloped with Ramsay; a few years later the couple went to Italy where this portrait was painted. Its soft colouring and the delicate treatment of the flowers and the fabrics have affinities with the work of Watteau and Boucher; but the face is the charm and the beauty of it. What a wonderful tribute to one's wife! Raeburn (See p 196) came later, his portraits broader in treatment, more dramatic and direct. There are several here, but the picture which attracts most attention, and which is certainly the most singular in its subject matter and composition, is 'The Reverend Robert Walker skating on Duddingston Loch'. It was painted in 1784 and appears to be an excellent portrait. But the background is remarkably woolly, and the handling is not at all characteristic of Raeburn. Indeed, it may not be by Raeburn at all. So spare a moment for two undoubted Raeburns, 'Mrs Scott Moncrieff' and 'Colonel Alastair Macdonell of Glengarry'. The latter can hardly be missed, for it is life-size. (Hard to believe that Raeburn began as a miniaturist!) The Colonel was Chief of the MacDonells of Glengarry, and a friend of Sir Walter Scott. The side-lighting is dramatic, and the full highland dress is supported by a rifle, basket-hilted swords and a claymore. It is a bold and romantic work. 'Mrs Scott Moncrieff' is also a romantic picture, done with extraordinary economy of means. One feels that Raeburn cannot have taken long over it; but the character of the sitter is fully and sympathetically caught.

Finally, look at McTaggart's 'spring', a painting of his daughters and a wonderful evocation of a cool northern spring day; and at Nasmyth's pictures of Edinburgh Castle and of Edinburgh in 1826, both good pictures as well as interesting topographical records.

The Mound

For those who have more time, there is much, much more to see. Portraits are mostly in the Scottish National Portrait Gallery in Queen Street and most twentieth century art is in the Scottish National Gallery of Modern Art in Bedford Road (*see* p. 205). But the Mound Gallery contains the nation's main collection of West European paintings from the Middle Ages to about 1914, including the best concentration of Scottish paintings anywhere, and there is a large assemblage of sculpture, watercolours, drawings, prints and photographs. The visitor must decide for himself or herself which items are the most interesting and enjoyable. But at the risk of offering unwanted advice, attention may be drawn to a few further items which are generally agreed to be of exceptional quality, or which have some particular connection with Edinburgh or Scotland.

Two paintings not by Scotsmen have strong and unusual Scottish connections. One of these is 'the Trinity Altarpiece' by Hugo van der Goes, which was originally in Trinity College Church, off the High Street. The panels were painted in the 1470s, and were probably commissioned by Edward Bonkil, who was the first Provost of the Church. He had a brother who was one of the leading Scottish merchants in Bruges, and van der Goes later worked near Brussels, in the Rode Klooster which was run by the Augustinians who were also in charge of Holyrood Abbey. Scots connections with the Low Countries were always close. The panels include figures of James III and his Queen, Margaret of Denmark, and a fine portrait of Edward Bonkil himself, kneeling beside a handsome auburn-haired angel who is playing the organ.

The second is a painting by Gainsborough, 'the Honourable Mrs Graham', full-length and life-size. The lady is gorgeously attired in silk and brocade. She wears a plumed hat, and leans elegantly on the base of a fluted column. She has a long slender neck, a tremendous eighteenth century hairstyle, a wonderful complexion, and is almost excessively good looking. Gainsborough thought so well of this picture that when he again exhibited at the Royal Academy in 1777 after a lapse of four years, and particularly wanted to make an impression, this is the picture he sent. And he judged well, for his technique is as assured as the lady's good looks. It is, in fact, a masterly and highly civilised version of the twentieth century pin-up. More remarkable still, we know some romantic facts about this picture. Mrs Graham was not yet twenty when she sat (or stood) to Gainsborough, and had recently married Thomas Graham, who commissioned the

135

picture. In 1792 she died in the south of France. Graham was destined to become Wellington's second-in-command during the Peninsular campaign, to defeat the French at Barossa, and to be created Baron Lynedoch of Balgowan. But at the death of his wife he was grief-stricken. He retrieved the body with much difficulty, and then ordered that the portrait should be removed from the walls of his house, crated, and stored in a London warehouse. No one set eyes on it for over forty years. But when Lynedoch died in 1834 his heir bequeathed it to the Scottish nation, on one condition; that it never leave Scotland. And there is one other curious fact. A head-and-shoulders study by Gainsborough of the same Mrs Graham hangs in the National Gallery of Art in Washington, D.C. She is easily recognisable, but is no longer the imperious society beauty, looking down on the rest of the world. Instead, we see a lively and unaffected young woman, full of good nature and happiness. It is the spontaneous portrait of a spontaneous sitter. That, surely, was the truth, and this is the show, both delightful in their different ways.

Constable, who learned so much from Gainsborough, is represented by one of his greatest masterpieces: 'the Vale of Dedham'. He once referred to it as 'a large upright landscape, perhaps my best'. It is a late painting (1828), in his most finished manner. Large trees bend a little before the wind, and the river Stour meanders towards Dedham and the Harwich estuary. There is the flicker of light in the morning air, and the movement of clouds across the sky. Reproductions of this painting cannot do it justice, for the details – a woman, a gypsy perhaps, with a baby, a tall foxglove, cattle by the distant river – are so many and so accurately observed that they cannot be scaled down. Yet all these smaller facts are brought together and unified in a great composition that is a careful and yet impassioned record of Constable's joy in what he often called 'the chiaroscuro of nature'. Constable was a great admirer of Claude, and the student of landscape painting should also see the latter's 'Landscape with Apollo, the Muses and a River God'. This too is a very large picture and a very good one. But while many elements of the composition are the same in both paintings, nature according to Claude is much more formalised and idealised. Here too the play of light is very fine; but it plays upon the Roman compagna at one or two removes. One sees how Constable was 'doing Claude over again from nature'.

Another great artist who comes brilliantly to life is Watteau. His 'Fêtes Vénitiennes' is one of his finest pictures, very frequently reproduced. A group of fashionable people are in a garden, overlooked by a large urn and a very curvaceous sculptured nymph. Two are about to begin a formal dance. The man, in oriental dress has been identified as a friend of Watteau who was later to become Director of the French Academy in Rome when Allan Ramsay was there in 1736; the girl dancer appears in several of Watteau's other pictures. The people are real, but the scene is decidedly not of the workaday world; it is of that 'impossible or forbidden world which the mason's boy (Watteau was the son of a humble Flemish workman) saw through the closed gateways of the enchanted garden'. It is easy to dismiss Watteau as trivial, a mere room decorator (so said Ruskin), a painter of butterflies. But he was a spirited and consummate artist, never more so than in 'Fetes Venitiennes'. And we should remember the tribute paid to him by no less an artist than Turner: 'I have learned more from Watteau than from any other painter'.

So what of Turner himself? The Gallery has three large oils by him, all in his Picturesque-Classical manner. They are excellent in their way, although perhaps they are not Turner at his most magical and original. In the Vaughan Bequest, however, the Gallery possesses thirty eight Turner watercolours of the highest quality, selected so as to show the development of his style and the variety of his techniques and subject matter. It is a wonderful progression, from 'Old Dover Harbour' (blue and grey washes over pencil) to 'the Sun of Venice' (watercolour) and then to 'Falls of the Rhine at Schaffhausen, Moonlight' (watercolour, body colour, and pen, with scraping out). And there are two scenes in the Borders and a view of Loch Coruisk in Skye, where Turner nearly ended his career by falling down a steep rock-strewn hillside. All these pictures are on display only during January; it is a condition of the bequest. But you may be lucky. More recently, the Gallery acquired twenty vignettes by Turner which were to be illustrations for an edition of the *Poetical Works of Thomas Campbell*, as well as an early watercolour, 'Snowdon; Afterglow'. (And still more recently it was able to show a work which attracted a great deal of attention: Canova's 'The Three Graces'. But those who are eager to see the ladies must meantime go to London, for they are shared with the V and A, and will not return to Edinburgh until 2006).

After so much art, try religion. Leave the Gallery and proceed up the Mound. It is quite a stiff climb, even although the road curves helpfully in a long S-bend. And this long S-bend is so unlike everything else in the Old Town and the New that one feels curiously 'out of town' on the Mound, belonging neither to one part of the city nor the other, suspended, like Mahomet's coffin, between heaven and earth. In this oddly detached frame of mind, half way up – or down – a hillside, it is good to pause, and admire the view, and enjoy the strangeness of one's urban – can it really be urban? – situation.

Starting from the foot of the Mound, directly in front of you is **New College**, originally called the Free Church College and Assembly Hall. This building was completed to Playfair's designs in 1850, the same year that work began on the National Gallery. It recalls the Disruption, one of the most singular events in Scottish history, when dissension within the Kirk reached such a pitch that Thomas Chalmers (*see* p. 158) led more than a third of the ministers out of the Church of Scotland to form the Free Church. The dispute, which came to a head in 1843, was about the freedom of congregations to choose their own minister. It is not easy now to feel the passions that then were felt; but to secede from the Kirk was a desperate thing to do, for those who left disrupted the life of the nation, were condemned by most of their countrymen, and they hazarded the well-being of themselves and their families. As Macaulay observed, the Scots have made sacrifices for the sake of religious opinion which find no parallel in the history of England. So the Free Church was set up, and the College was built in order to train its ministers. It is now partly owned by the University.

The College stands on the site of the sixteenth century palace of Mary of Guise. The twin towers of its gatehouse are lined up with Playfair's Royal Scottish Academy lower down the hill, and above them rises the spire of the Tolbooth Church (*see* p. 23). The towers and the rest of the façade are rather prim Tudor, very vertical and ecclesiastical; the verticality is further emphasised by the tall prominent chimneys. The effect is rather strange and almost toy-like – perhaps £21,000, which is what the College cost, would build nothing bigger, and yet equally good. On the other hand, it makes a successful link between the flat façades of the tall lands to the east and the romantic red-roofed absurdities of Ramsay Garden to the west. Once again, variety with harmony has been added to the ever-changing scene.

The vaulted arch of the gatehouse leads into the quadrangle, collegiate but very small. There is a bronze statue of John Knox (1895), which a few years ago looked down on the amicable meeting between the Moderator (leader) of the Kirk and the Pope. We do not know whether or not the great Calvinist turned in his grave. Behind the statue, within what used to be the church, and is now the library, there is a Jacobean roof with pendants at the tie-beams, painted grey, blue, red and gold. Opposite the entrance, a flight of steps flanked by tall ogee-roofed towers goes up to a pair of depressed-arch doors which are the entrance to the **Assembly Hall**. The Hall is large and almost square, with a deep gallery on three sides. Square timber columns support the roof, which is divided into only four compartments and looks remarkably dark and utilitarian. It is not an elegant hall, but it has a plain antique feel to it. During the Festival it is used for plays, with an open stage, and it does very well. In particular, it forms a marvellously appropriate setting for *Ane Pleasant Satyre of The Thrie Estates* by Sir David Lindsay, which has been put on several times. The first version of this play was written not later than 1540, the final version in 1554. Its hero is John the Commonweil, and it is a relentless attack on the un-Christian oppression of the poor, not least by the Roman Catholic clergy. It is forceful drama, and must have contributed to the unrest which preceded the Reformation in Scotland. It was written in broad Scots, as it should always be played, but is nevertheless easy to follow. If you have a chance, do not miss it. West of the Assembly Hall is the Rainy Hall. Unlike the other, the Rainy Hall (1900) is a cheerful place, with much wooden panelling and many painted shields, some at the corbels which support the hammerbeam roof, painted and gilded.

From New College, go up the Mound a little further, past the dark lofty gables and abutments of those towering edifices which terminate the northern closes of the High Street (shades of Hume and Boswell), and on towards the head office of the **Bank of Scotland**. You can hardly miss it, which was no doubt the idea of those who commissioned it. The original building (1806) was heavy and square, with a dome, and it pleased no one. But in the 1860s it was extensively re-modelled by David Bryce, and was made very grand. The entrance façade, facing south, remains as it was, rusticated at ground level and pilastered above. But wings were added, with coupled Corinthian half-columns, broken pediments, and circular attic windows. These wings extend half-way back along each side of the building, and are carried up as towers having open-arched top stages with clusters of Corinthian columns, and domes crowned with statues. The north front (at its base a massive retaining wall, added later) boasts a wide central bay with round-arched windows which rise through two storeys, more coupled Corinthian columns, two broken pediments one above the other, and a parapet emphatically adorned with sculpture. Bryce also removed the original central dome and substituted a larger one, topped by a lantern and crowned by a gilded statue of Fame, seven feet high. No wonder that the Victorians thought the bank impressive. 'It presents,' one of them wrote, 'a front of colossal proportions to Princes Street, from whence, and every other point of view, it forms a conspicuous mass'. It is a Baroque monument and rather a vulgar one; some Edinburgh citizens think that it would be better in Glasgow. Inside, a simple vestibule leads to a two-storey stair-hall. The stair rises to a cantilevered landing, and there is a Corinthian-pilastered doorpiece opposite the entrance. The telling room used to rise through two storeys, but has been mutilated.

Leave the bank, climb a little further, and you are back at Deacon Brodie's Tavern (*see* p. 29). Better to return to Princes Street, but go down by Playfair's Steps, past the National Gallery and with the gardens and the trains on your right. You have a very fine view of Playfair's masterpiece as you descend, and as you walk towards Princes Street the subterranean galleries of art, believe it or not, are beneath your feet.

For eleven months of the year the surroundings of the two Galleries are not much better than a wasteland, poor setting for fine architecture. But in Festival time all is changed. The wasteland has become a stage. A kaleidoscope of players, dancers, singers, jugglers assembles from nowhere to entertain a motley crowd. Children stare, and eat icecream, and adults peer over the shoulders of other adults. There are balloons and kilts a-plenty, and the youth of the Festival sit all along the mighty steps of the Royal Academy. Autolycus would have thought it as good as a sheep-shearing feast – 'songs for man, or woman, of all sizes;' 'a gallimaufry of gambols;' 'anything extempore;' and, of course, 'festival purses'. The area may not be as large as the Place Pompidou, but in August it is at least as lively.

9

Calton Hill

THERE ARE TWO advantages in walking along Princes Street from west to east; the wind is probably behind you; and ahead of you the steep grassy slopes of the Calton Hill gradually rise from insignificance and beckon you forward. They rise between twin porticos with fluted columns, one on each side of the street – a triumphal exit from the New Town – and they beckon you towards what looks like a region of rural felicity, so surprisingly different from Register House and the Balmoral Hotel that it might just possibly be inhabited by nymphs, shepherds and sheep. It is not, of course. But at least it is not much inhabited by vehicles, and there are no shops, no traffic lights, and very few municipal seats.

The Calton Hill used to be a treeless and lonely place, and it has some disagreeable associations with hangings. But that was a long time ago. In the 1540s Sir David Lindsay's *Ane Pleasant Satyre of the Thrie Estates* was played on the hill, and it was also a favourite scene for duels, secret assignations, and in the Middle Ages 'tilts and tournaments'. Although close to the Old Town and even closer to the New, it was not easily accessible because on the north and west it slopes sharply down to a deep ravine; and for this reason it could nowhere be built upon and made a part of the city until the ravine was bridged. Once again, as with the North Bridge and the South Bridge, Edinburgh had to leap over low ground in order to expand; and once again the bridge that does this can hardly be noticed.

The **Waterloo Bridge** was begun in 1815, and all along it, except over one arch, the buildings form palace fronts on each side of the street. There are porticos and columns and screen walls and tall façades, very vertical and very severe. Only if you walk, and pause to look through one of the triumphal arches which surmount the main arch of the bridge itself, do you realise that you are fifty feet above the road below. Waterloo Bridge was a major feat of civil engineering. Moreover, the triumphal arches were carefully planned so that users of the bridge would be able to look north towards the busy port of Leith or south to 'the curious City scene' then still unfolding. It is a sad commentary on urban progress that now, if anyone has the time to look, what they will see to the north is not Leith but a substantial chunk of the deplorable St James's Centre, and to the south nothing more curious than the shed-like roofs of the railway station and a glass-and-concrete box inhabited by civil servants.

So press on to the **Old Calton Burying Ground**, its entrance on the south side of Waterloo Place. (If you do not feel like pressing on, there are several bars and cafes nearby that present an attractive alternative). The Old Calton Burying Ground used to be much bigger, but a large part of it 'was decently carted away, covered with white palls,' when Waterloo Place was driven through the middle. In what remains there are three objects of interest. The most prominent is the Martyr's Monument, a tall obelisk which commemorates a number of would-be reformers and admirers of the French Revolution who fell foul of the authorities and were tried for sedition in the 1790s. Their leader was Thomas Muir, who had helped to found a society for parliamentary reform and had distributed copies of Paine's *Rights of Man*. This was rather like speaking up for peaceful co-existence under Ivan the Terrible, and Muir was sentenced to fourteen years transportation. Botany Bay was only the beginning of his troubles. He did tolerably well there, but was 'rescued' by an American ship in 1796, was shipwrecked, captured by American Indians, escaped to Mexico, was imprisoned in Havana, got back to sea and took part in an action against British warships, reached France where he received a hero's welcome and soon afterwards died at Chantilly. To such a thrilling life the monument is a very dull tribute. A few yards away is the David Hume Monument by Robert Adam; Scotland's greatest philosopher and her most famous architect are thus remembered together. (They had often dined together at the Adam family home in the Canongate). Hume's philosophical opinions were detested by almost all his countrymen; God-fearing men and women did not like to be told that their knowledge was no more than a series of impressions, like drops of dew on a blade of grass – except that the blade of grass did not exist. Yet Hume was a most charming and delightful companion, a man who had no enemies. What Adam Smith said of him is no more laudatory than what was said by scores of others: 'Upon the whole, I have always considered him, both in his lifetime and since his death, as approaching as nearly to the idea of a perfectly wise and virtuous man as perhaps the frailty of human nature will admit.' His tomb is a grand Roman cylinder with a fluted frieze, a Doric entablature, and a large urn in a niche over the door. Nearby is the Emancipation Monument of 1893 which commemorates Abraham Lincoln and the Scottish-American soldiers who took part in the Civil War. Lincoln stands erect, and a freed slave looks up at him. Lincoln is instantly recognisable. One feels that in our day he would be a compelling television personality.

The Burying Ground is overlooked by an edifice which is strange even by Edinburgh standards. Built with large blocks of stone, battlemented, towered and turreted, it looks too domestic to be a castle, and too castellated to be an ordinary house. It is, in fact, all that is left of a very large gaol (1815–1817) which spread for a considerable distance along this south side of the Calton Hill. The whole gaol was in the style of what remains – empty now, once the living quarters of the governor of the gaol – and its 'saxon style of architecture' was much admired when it was built. The fragment that still stands is perched on the verge of an abrupt little precipice above the main line railway. Running along the top of the precipice the builder of the gaol erected a bastioned retaining wall which runs east from the governor's house and appears to hold everything together.

The gaol, along with an earlier bridewell by Robert Adam, disappeared in the 1930s when **St Andrew's House** was built in its stead. Facing the upper slopes of the Calton Hill and looking south to the Canongate, this monumental building is the headquarters of central government administration in Scotland.

At this point the visitor may begin to ask whether he is or is not in a capital city. He has seen the Castle and the Palace – a genuine fortified castle and a genuine lived-in palace. He has seen the Scottish Law Courts, where Scots law is administered and from which there is no appeal to any English court. He has seen the National Gallery of Scotland, and in George Street he will find the headquarters of the Church of Scotland. He has seen the Bank of Scotland which, like the Bank of England, issues its own bank notes. And now here is the building where many of the decisions affecting the whole of Scotland are taken. With so many national institutions concentrated here, with so much history, with so much dignity and spectacle, surely this is a capital city? To many visitors it seems absurd that this metropolis should be ruled from London. Its seems absurd to a good many Scots too. But complete independence was surrendered almost three hundred years ago, and it is not easy to turn the clock back. Many Scots, however, are trying hard and some progress has been made.

The design of St Andrew's House caused a row which brought patriotic irritation – not for the first time – to the surface. Many angry words were exchanged before the design was settled, for the site is a very prominent one and it seemed at first that a choice made in Whitehall – orthodox Office of Works, something that would have sat tolerably well in a London street – would be foisted on the independent-minded citizens of Edinburgh. But after numerous protests and much wrangling agreement was reached, and a Scots architect was given the job. It is hard to know what to think of this very large, formidable, geometrical, Portland stone building. It has been called an assertive monumental mass; on the other hand, it has its admirers, for whom it is a good example of American Beaux Arts modern, and even possibly one of the finest British public buildings of the inter-war years. But its sheer size makes for difficulties.

It is strictly symmetrical, two long administering arms reaching out from a massive central block of seven bays. There are fine bronze entrance doors, an enormous stone-carved heraldic panel above them, glazed stairtowers, tall mullions, and half a dozen symbolic figures. It may be impressive, but it is impossible to like it; this is the stern not the caring face of government. Inside, there is a generous use of polished marble facings to columns and walls, along with some dis-spirited Art-Deco, and it feels empty. It is a 1930s building and looks it, but not a lively one. What would Charles Rennie Mackintosh have made of this opportunity, if he had been alive and been offered it?

A little further along (Waterloo Place has now become Regent Road) stands another large building, the one-time **Royal High School**. It was completed in 1829, one hundred and ten years before St Andrew's House; and one is tempted to say that it is one hundred and ten times better. It was designed by Thomas Hamilton, and is widely recognised as perhaps the noblest monument of the Scottish Greek Revival. It may be an exaggeration to say that no expense was spared in this building, but it is not much of an exaggeration; the city fathers had resolved to build a school that would out-do all other schools in Edinburgh, and the final cost was £24,000, which for those days was a very large sum indeed. The site slopes in two directions and was therefore a difficult one, but it lends itself to dramatic design. and Hamilton seized his opportunity. He went for a monumental composition; its centrepiece based on the Temple of Theseus in Athens. This centrepiece is of commanding proportions,

with tall fluted columns and an entablature all round. Low collon-
aded wings spread out on each side to pilastered pavilions, and
beyond each pavilion stands a smaller temple block with a portico
facing inwards.

All of this, except the outer temples, is mounted above a long
retaining wall which is interrupted at the centre by two massive pedimented gateways, with unpedimented gateways behind and above
them and which are part of the temple's base. Thus the building rises
well above the roadway and looks clear across to Arthur's Seat. It is a
splendid composition, all in Grecian Doric, splendidly sited, and
along with the National Gallery it is one of the two grandest pieces of
architecture in Edinburgh, and one of the finest Neo-Classical public
buildings in northern Europe.

The school continued as a school for almost one hundred and fifty
years. It was the replacement for the ancient High School in the Old
Town, 'notorious for its severity and riotousness,' which Walter Scott
had attended. When the new building opened, Scott was already a
sick man, but the ceremony was graced by another famous alumnus,
Henry, Lord Brougham. Brougham was an ardent Whig and a great
orator, and he sprang to fame when he appeared as Queen Caroline's
Attorney General at the so-called 'Queen's Trial' in 1820. (Caroline's
amatory adventures in Italy had become the scandal of Europe).
Later, Brougham became Lord Chancellor. He was well- informed on
many subjects, and it was said that if he had known a little more law
he would have been well-informed about everything.

When the school ceased to be a school in the late 1960s, the
problem arose of what to do with it. No permanent use has yet been
found, but at one time it was to become the home of the Scottish
Assembly. This idea has been given up, and a Parliament building is
to arise near Holyrood. (*see* p. 78); such, at any rate, is the plan. But
for so splendid a building as the Royal High School surely a good use
can be found? It offers a lot of accommodation. At at its centre the
School Hall is a pleasure to be in. It is semi-elliptical, with a shallow
plaster vaulted ceiling, decorated with rosettes in square panels. The
galleries are supported by iron columns with delicately designed capitals, and the seats are tiered down to the 'stage' end. Mercifully for all
future users, the original benches for the boys have been replaced by
something more comfortable.

It is now suggested that the School should become a Museum of
Photography. The association is a strong one, for it was on Calton Hill
that photography first spread its wings.

In 1843 a young engineer came to live nearby in Rock House, and he was joined in 1844 by a painter. The engineer was Robert Adamson and the painter was David Octavius Hill. Thus was born the famous partnership – it lasted for only four years – which established photography as an art form and also as a means for recording contemporary life. Adamson managed the primitive and unstable calotype process and Hill composed the subjects, including the lighting. The results, many of them of superb quality, are known all over the world – pictures of Newhaven fishermen and their families, of Greyfriars church-yard, of Bonaly Towers, and many other Scottish subjects. In three years Hill and Adamson produced over 3,000 images. Then Adamson's health deteriorated and he returned to his home toun of St Andrew's. But he and Hill had, in a very real sense, invented photography.

One other construction deserves notice before you finally set off for the top of the hill. The **Burns Monument**, almost opposite the school, is an enlarged and elaborated version of the Choragic Monument of Lysicrates. Designed by Thomas Hamilton and erected in 1830, it is a cylindrical temple with fluted columns, carried up to a second stage and then a finial supported by griffons. Within the angular base there used to be a statue of Burns by Flaxman, but it has been removed to the National Portrait Gallery. Thus the Greek temple remains without the poet, 'a barren home' and a curious one for a plowman.

Proceed to the top of the hill (as the guide books say). The best route is the steepest, up the steps from Regent Road and along the gravel path. Ahead of you, unavoidable, remarkable, and incomplete, stands the **National Monument of Scotland**. Or is it incomplete? These twelve great Doric columns and their architrave began as a monument to all those Scotsmen who had fallen in the Napoleonic Wars. To perpetuate their memory a National Church was at first thought appropriate. But because the Calton Hill was supposed to resemble the Acropolis, men of taste decided that it would be better to construct another Parthenon. The splendour of the design, they thought, would correspond to the grandeur of the purpose. Also, the new building would take over from the crumbling Athenian one, 'which time and barbarism will soon annihilate'. What foresight in 1825! So an appeal was launched 'to erect a facsimile of the Parthenon'. Sir Walter Scott and Lord Elgin were among the signatories, and the sum aimed for was no less than £42,000. This was an enormous figure, but the promoters believed that the scheme was not merely of Scottish but of international concern, and that the result would be 'a splendid addition to the architectural riches of the empire'. The empire, however, did not rise up as one man to subscribe, and money came in very slowly. It was resolved to go ahead nevertheless, and Playfair, along with the leading expert of the day on architectural antiquities, C R Cockerell, was put in charge. The foundation stone was laid in 1826, amid salutes of cannon from the Castle, Salisbury Crags and Leith Fort. A plate somewhat fulsomely inscribed was deposited with the stone:

> *to the glory of God, in honour of the King, for the good of the people, this monument, the tribute of a grateful country to her gallant and illustrious sons, as a memorial of the past and incentive to the future heroism of the men of Scotland, was ... founded ... in the third year of the glorious reign of George IV, under his immediate auspices, and in commemoration of his most gracious and welcome visit to his ancient capital, and the palace of his royal ancestors.*

Gratitude and royalism could hardly go further, along with a certain smarminess of expression. But what was needed was money, and there was never enough – never half enough. Costs were high – 'It takes twelve horses and 70 men to move some of the larger stones up the hill,' Playfair lamented – and the policy of using only the best materials and employing only the best workmen drove them higher. The design and workmanship are faultless. But in 1829 the money ran out, and building came to a 'dead halt'.

Proposals to continue have cropped up from time to time. In early days some people thought that it might be turned into a burial place for the famous and the great, a sort of Scots Westminster Abbey. In the later days of Queen Victoria there were proposals for it to become an alternative (or additional) national gallery, with a funicular railway running up from Waterloo Place. Another idea was that it should house a Scottish Parliament – that mirage that hovered for so long on the Scottish nationalist horizon. Fortunately, all these schemes for its completion came to nothing, for it is complete already. The entire Parthenon, seventy metres by thirty metres, would be too much for the site; and besides, would be merely a copy. A fragment is much better, mockingly, mysteriously, idiosyncratically 'incomplete'; a ruin, or at any rate a seeming ruin; and as a ruin imparting a Classical aspect to the entire city. Playfair, who was a man of sound judgment, does not seem to have been disappointed with the effect, for he wrote to Cockerell as follows: 'When the sun shines and there is a pure blue sky behind [the pillars] (a rare event, you will say) they look most beautiful, but surprisingly small'.

To reach the National Monument, which, for obvious reasons, is sometimes called 'the pride and poverty of Scotland', you pass the **Nelson Monument**, a hundred foot column on the very apex of the hill. This has a very different history. It was begun in 1807, soon after Nelson's death at Trafalgar, and was not completed until 1816. It rises in five stages to a corbelled and battlemented parapet with a cross-trees on top. The cross-trees supports a time-ball which, by falling from a raised to a lowered position, gives a visual signal every day at one o'clock. Because the monument stands so high, the signal can be seen by shipping in the Forth, a couple of miles away; and this was once useful; and besides, the Victorians were proud of the fact that the time-ball was 'in electric communication with the time-gun at the Castle,' and thus fell exactly when the gun was fired. The base is battlemented, with a sculpture representing the stem of the 'san Joseph' over the entrance. The two odd things about this odd monument are the following. First, many citizens in the nineteenth century thought that it was in such doubtful taste that it should be demolished; and demolition was more than once recommended. Presumably it did not accord well with Edinburgh's Athenian aspirations. Second, the base is divided into small compartments which were intended to provide 'accommodation for a few disabled seamen'. And when no disabled seamen willing to live on top of the Calton Hill appeared, the rooms were turned into a restaurant. They were 'leased to a vendor of soups and sweetmeats ... and the visitors to the monument have the opportunity of eating in them ... and drinking, under certain restrictions, to the memory of the great hero they commemorate'. What were these restrictions? We do not know, although it is not hard to imagine some. Perhaps it was their non-observance that led to closure of the restaurant. In any event, it is now a private dwelling; but the tower remains accessible.

Retracing your steps a little, you come to the **Dugald Stewart Monument**. (How many monuments are there in this town, one asks oneself, even without counting those in the churchyards?) Dugald Stewart was one of those learned men whose fate has been the fate of many other learned men; famous and admired in his day, he is now all but forgotten. He was a philosopher, a friend of Adam Smith, whose biography he wrote. He taught in Edinburgh University in the days when its corridors were crowded by the embryonic great, and his lectures were enormously admired; 'they were like the opening of the heavens,' one of his pupils declared; 'His noble views, unfolded in glorious sentences, elevated me into a higher world'. Those were the days when philosophy was about virtue and how to live rightly, and it would be difficult, to say the least of it, to fit Stewart's lectures into a modern University syllabus. We are told that they covered

> *the general constitution of moral and material nature, the*
> *duties and the ends of man, the uses and boundaries of*
> *philosophy, the connection between virtue and enjoyment,*
> *the obligations of affection and patriotism, the cultivation*
> *and the value of taste, the intellectual differences produced*
> *by particular habits, the evidences of the soul's immortality,*
> *the charms of literature and science,*

and that they were embellished 'by a judicious application of biographical and historical illustration'. No wonder he is almost forgotten! He made his mark as a didactic orator – 'there was eloquence in his very spitting' – and such fame does not last. His monument is by Playfair (1831), another and simpler version of the Choragic Monument of Lysicrates in Athens.

A few yards away is a strange construction, officially referred to as the **City Observatory**. It is better described as three buildings variously related to a retaining wall: the Old Observatory, the New Observatory, and yet another monument. The Old Observatory, at the south-west corner of the group, is a rough round tower, three storeys in height, from which extends a short rubble-built wing with buttresses and Gothic windows. It was begun in 1776 as a private venture by the brother of a Leith optician – unlikely as that may sound. But the basis of the scheme was the brother's reflecting telescope, which was said to be the best in Europe 'but for one in the possession of the King of Spain,' and the expectation was that ladies and gentlemen would be glad to pay for the privilege of looking through this exceptional instrument. In the days when astronomy was popular in the upper reaches of society this was not a bad idea, and the promoter obtained a lease of half an acre on the Calton Hill. The architect was James Craig, planner of the New Town, but he was unluckily advised by Robert Adam that on account of the elevated and abrupt nature of the site the whole edifice should be given the appearance of a fortification. Robert Adam did not believe, evidently, in form following function. More immediately serious, the Gothic style raised costs far above predictions, and before long the money ran out. As a result, the building was not completed until 1792, by which time the promoters seem to have lost interest, and the telescope seems to have disappeared. What was built was far inferior to what had been intended, and was of little use to astronomers.

A second effort was made when the Astronomical Institution urged the need for an up-to-date observatory. Its president was Professor Playfair, uncle of the architect, and one of his arguments was that the master of a foreign vessel lately compelled to take refuge in Leith had found 'that he had come to a large and learned metropolis, where nobody could tell him what o'clock it was'. This and some other arguments prevailed, and the new observatory was given the go-ahead. Young Playfair (he was only twenty eight at the time) got the job of designing it, and the foundation stone was laid in 1818. It is cruciform, with four projecting Doric porticos of six columns each, facing the four cardinal points of the compass. The central dome, which is only thirteen feet in diameter, contains a conical stone pillar for the telescope; other instruments, including the all-important clocks, are housed in the east and west arms. In 1895 the Astronomer Royal for Scotland abandoned the Calton Hill on account of the smoke from railway trains and domestic fires and took refuge on Blackford Hill (*see* p. 220) Many of his activities have again moved further out from the city centre – this time to Hawaii.

Finally, there is the **Playfair Monument**, by the nephew for the uncle. It also is Doric, square and solid on a high podium, reminiscent of the Lion Tomb at Cnidos but without the lion. It looks singularly indestructible. And it commemorates a singular man, for when he lay dying and a relative enquired what he would like to have read to him, his choice – so it is said – was Newton's *Principia Mathematica*.

Such is the extraordinary assemblage of objects which decorates the Calton Hill. Above the level of the road, where the old burying ground was, nothing had been built prior to 1792; except for a scattering of trees and bushes, it was a bare hillside. Then the Gothic observatory appeared; fifteen years later the Nelson Monument was begun; and everything else was added between 1817 and 1831. Thus in the space of a few years the townscape was radically altered, and the new emerging character of Edinburgh emphasised. Some thought at the time that the Calton Hill should have been left to nature; but others objected that nature meant waste ground 'occupied by blackguards and washerwomen'. Cockburn argued in favour of art and observatories, but he was against monuments 'except at a price implying a high order of merit ... if anything under £2000 be admitted, we shall have the tombs of Provosts. The air of the place ought to be kept pure, and its associations inspiring'. (For Provosts read Mayors in England). So different opinions were held, and the Calton Hill as it is 'just happened'. There was no overall plan. There was no consistent style. Two schemes never reached their intended completion because the money ran out. Three schemes designed to be useful are useful no longer, and the largest scheme of all is and has always been 'merely' decorative. But what a masterpiece the Calton Hill is! It is an echo of Greece and a reminder of the Regency, and after. Moreover, it has not altogether lost its wild character, has not altogether been tamed. The town laps around its feet, and third-rate buildings of the twentieth century multiply and come too close, approved by planners. But the sides of the hill are still very steep, and the grassy slopes above are mostly pathless. You cannot lose yourself here, but you can wander out of sight, and come on aspects of the hill and the buildings that are quite surprising.

The views, of course, are not to be missed. The best-known is from the path as you go up, looking down to Craig's New Town and across to the Castle. There are aquatints of this done in the 1820s which make much of the now vanished gaol, and of the length and straightness of Princes Street; in one of them washerwomen have laid out their cloths on the hillside to bleach in the sun. Turner drew this view more than once, dexterously distorted. Further up and looking south, the line of the Royal Mile can be discerned, the Canongate Church stands out clearly, and you have a good birdseye view of Holyroodhouse and the Abbey, with Arthur's Seat behind. To the north, streets and houses extend all the way to the cranes and docks and warehouses of Granton and Leith, and the waters of the Firth of Forth.

Around 1820, this north-eastern area below Calton Hill was planned to become a new town even more magnificent than Craig's. Although never more than partly realised, it was a first-rate scheme. Playfair was the author, incorporating Calton Hill as his starting point, and he accepted two planning principles put forward for the scheme by a young architect called William Stark who had recently died, 'too young to have done much'. Stark did not have a high opinion of straight lines and regularity, which meant that he did not have a high opinion of Craig's plan:

151

To a stranger occupied in the examination of the present New Town, it would import little to be informed, when looking along George's Street, that it is precisely parallel to Prince's Street and Queen's Street; or – if admiring Charlotte Square, to be told that it forms the exact counter–part upon the ground plan to St Andrew's Square.

Curves were better: 'in a bending alignment of street, much beauty, and perhaps the most striking effects'. And secondly, trees and architecture should not be separated, but kept together. They combine to advantage, as is proved by the fact that 'our best landscape painters, Claude and the Poussins, never tired of painting them, nor the world of admiring what they painted'. The attractions of Grosvenor Square, Stark wrote, are owing to its architecture and its trees. And, to take another example, what about Oxford? 'Would the view of the Colleges of Oxford excite the same sensations of pleasure, if the gardens and the trees were away?' So, following Stark's ideas, Playfair saved the fine double row of elms which extended along Leith Walk at the foot of the hill, placed his terraces at a moderate elevation and bent them round the hill, and then set off northwards with a crescent from which three streets radiate, 'the good effect of the diverging of several Streets from a central Point [having] been long felt and acknowledged particularly in the Piazza del Popolo at Rome'. This was the beginning of a vast radial layout which went as far as the outskirts of Leith.

Most of Playfair's grand new town was never built, and the crescent 'of great size', although it *was* built (Hillside Crescent), is unlikely to remind anyone of the Piazza del Popolo in Rome. On the hill itself, however, his plans were realised. **Regent Terrace** was begun in 1826. The houses are of only two storeys, the terrace very long but not monotonous, built upon only one side of the street, with continuous trellis balconies and a string of Doric porches. Enjoying splendid views to the Old Town and Arthur's Seat, it has always been an eligible place to live, and from the start it appealed to the 'fashionable and wealthy people' whom Playfair hoped to attract. At the east end, **Calton Terrace** curves round, following the sharp bend of the hill. It is on similar lines, with single-window balconies, porches, parapets and pavilions. The *pièce de resistance,* however, is **Royal Terrace**, which faces north. Royal Terrace is the largest single block of building in central Edinburgh. It is almost a quarter of a mile long, and comprises forty houses, most of them enormous. It was not so instantly popular as Regent Terrace, and it was not completely built until well into the reign of Queen Victoria; now it is mostly given over to hotels, and is spoilt by signs hung out, and tasteless alterations. But in its day, it was very grand, and some of the grandeur lingers. There are three sections, the middle one having three very high storeys, with giant Corinthian colonnades and balustrades; the outer two are not so high, with giant Ionic columns. The ground floor has semi-circular arched windows and doorways, and is rusticated from end to end. There is some excellent cast-ironwork including elegant bowed balconies to the first-floor windows, and lampholders integrated with the railings.

The interiors of Royal Terrace are enormous in scale, and often very grand in execution. There are Grecian columns in upstairs drawing rooms, and sometimes also in the entrance halls, which in several cases are vaulted. Many rooms have elaborately compartmented ceilings. All this is planned by a master-hand, probably Playfair's, and none of it is crude or merely ostentatious.

The space between the two great terraces is occupied by Regent Gardens, laid out in 1830. The gardens are in effect a private park, separated by a ha-ha from the public ground of Calton Hill. Playfair set much store by these gardens, which are remarkably pleasant. He foresaw some difficulty in attracting buyers to this ambitious new development, but the gardens, he believed, were 'the main-spring by which the whole may be set in motion'.

Perhaps the views were just as important. Regent Terrace looks south to the Old Town and Arthur's Seat. Royal Terrace looks north to Leith and the Firth of Forth. Many of the early residents in Royal Terrace found this view peculiarly attractive, for they were shipping magnates and traders overseas with offices in Leith, and they liked to sit comfortably in their drawing rooms in Royal Terrace and watch their laden argosies – belching out smoke by the time that Royal Terrace was completed – setting out or returning, most likely from Antwerp or Hamburg, Copenhagen or Bergen, or the Baltic ports beyond the North Sea. Leith was once a great place for distilleries and whisky was a major item of export. So it was not without reason that Royal Terrace was at one time known as Whisky Row.

10

From Charlotte Square to St Andrew Square

BUILDING HOUSES ROUND a garden square was almost a new idea in the eighteenth century. The Places des Vosges showed how it could be done, in 1612. But not until much later did squares of moderate size, with grass and shrubs and trees, begin to be laid out, most of them in London. The best of these eighteenth century squares give a feeling of harmonious enclosure and leisurely ease, and they are as much a product of civilization as Durham Cathedral or a painting by Canaletto. Charlotte Square is to be ranked among them, one of the finest squares in Europe.

Craig's plan showed two squares, and both were built; but he gave no indication of what the frontages should be like. In Charlotte Square that task fell to Robert Adam. The first twenty years of house-building in the New Town had produced very few houses worth looking at. Most were casually related to one another, of two or three storeys. Many of those in Princes Street relied on common stairs entered from the Mews Lane behind, and George Street, according to the artist Joseph Farington who visited the city in 1788, was 'so wide in proportion to the height of the buildings, that in the declining line of perspective they appear like Barracks'. So the Town Council resolved that **Charlotte Square** should set a new and better example.

Robert Adam had already designed Register House and the new University buildings, and in 1791 he was commissioned to produce elevations for Charlotte Square. The Town Council can hardly have been prepared for what they got: houses of the highest distinction, completely unified into one hundred metre long palace fronts; on the north and south sides of the Square pedimented centrepieces, pavilions slightly advanced, Venetian windows, and crowning sphinxes guarding pyramidal roofs. The whole composition is elegant and assured, but not at all assertive; not too big, not overwhelming. Many more palace fronts were to be built in Edinburgh in the course of the nineteenth century, some of them very fine, but none finer than those in Adam's Palladian square. He launched a new idea, and he set a standard that could not be surpassed.

From Charlotte Square to St Andrew Square

Sites for building in the Square were taken within a few days of Adam's death in March 1792, and building continued for over a quarter of a century. The result, even as we see it today, is almost as planned. The north side is the most elaborate and the best preserved, eleven houses in all, the centre section with four pairs of Corinthian columns and an acanthus frieze on the entablature. The south side is almost identical, without sphinxes at the ends. The east and west sides each consist of two short palace-fronts, separated by the entry of George Street on the east and by St George's Church on the west. The doors and windows of these frontages are not quite as Adam intended, and the Roxburgh Hotel has a mansard roof which should not be there; much worse, twentieth century attics have been added on each side of the church. Nevertheless, the total effect is admirable; elegant and yet vigorous, beautifully ornamented and proportioned, and without any of that pretentiousness which sometimes marred Adam's designs.

The best interiors are almost all on the north side, although many of the other houses (now converted to offices) have garlanded plaster ceilings, ornamental pine chimney-pieces, wrought-iron balustrades and sinuous handrails for the stairs. The two most interesting houses are Bute House (No. 6) and the Georgian House (No. 7). **Bute House** in the centre of the north side is the architectural climax of the domestic architecture of the square; it is now the headquarters of the First Minister for Scotland and his Cabinet. The entrance door is of polished oak, with a very fine semi-circular fanlight above the door, and the vestibule has a floor of polished Caithness flagstones in octagons and squares. There is a stone staircase offset to the right of the door; it is lit by a circular cupola, rising above a moulded frieze and cornice. The drawing room and library on the first floor are especially beautiful rooms, with panelled dadoes and doors and extremely elegant low-relief plasterwork ceilings. The white marble chimneypieces are meticulously detailed, that in the drawing room having a centre panel which shows, in low relief, a languorous reclining Galatea attended by dolphins.

No. 7, **the Georgian House**, which is open to the public, is similar, although plainer. The house was acquired by the National Trust in 1973, and has been very carefully restored to resemble a prosperous family home as it might have been around 1800. The furniture and decoration are entirely authentic. Thus the soft green on the walls reproduces what was originally there, and almost all the furniture – and there is a great deal of it – dates from about 1780–1820. Only a handful of items can be mentioned here. The dining table is set with a lovely blue and white dinner service by Wedgwood (c.1820) and Old

Sheffield Plate – silver was for the aristocracy. There is a magnificent portable water-closet made by Blades and Palmer of Piccadilly; a four-post bed with most of its hangings made in West Lothian during the last quarter of the eighteenth century; a Scottish square piano (c.1805); and a splendid array of contemporary pots, pans and other utensils in the kitchen. There are marble chimneypieces, chinese vases, and dozens of portraits and landscapes of the period. Spacious, comfortable and extremely elegant, it seems all ready to be lived in.

On the other side of the Square, the houses are equally well built but plainer. The National Trust for Scotland occupies Nos 26–31; No 28 is the central office of the Trust. Besides being an information point, it has a tea room, a restaurant and a shop. The large drawing room one floor up is a suitable setting for a collection of elegant early nineteenth century furniture, and also serves as an art gallery. The three handsome windows provide excellent views over the Square.

When the leaves are off the trees. **St George's Church** dominates the square. It is a church no longer, but its external appearance remains as planned by Robert Reid. There was a design by Robert Adam, with an eight-columned projecting portico and five maidens in long dresses above, but it was given up, probably on account of expense; it looked expensive, and was probably deemed too flamboyant for Edinburgh. Reid's design is relatively simple and severe. There are only four columns, no pediment and no maidens, but he heightened the drum, and produced a slim, Neo-Classical version of the dome of St Paul's, clad in copper and topped with a lantern. Hard things have been said about this building; 'heavy in appearance, meagre in detail, and hideous in conception', according to one critic. But it is not nearly as bad as that. It terminates with good effect the long vista looking west from George Street, and the dome, rising 150 feet above the square, makes an important contribution to Edinburgh's still marvellous skyline. The 'church' now serves as an annexe to Register House, and is used for storing documents.

The garden area was at first rather rough and ready; it supported a few low trees, and still lower bushes. Although the houses round the square were all occupied by 1820 – exclusively by the rich and the famous; its inhabitants included Lord Cockburn, several other judges, one or two earls, and Sir William Fettes, founder of Fettes College – the garden remained not much improved for fifty years. But in 1873 it was enlarged and enclosed, and in 1876 Sir John Steell's bronze equestrian **statue of Prince Albert** appeared in the middle. This statue, with four groups of statues round it and standing on a granite pedestal seventeen feet high, cost half as much as the church. Whether or not it contributes half as much to the square seems more than doubtful, but Queen Victoria must have liked it, for it was inaugurated by her in the summer of 1876, and the sculptor received his knighthood on the spot. Because there are now more trees and larger trees, Prince Albert is not very visible; you catch a glimpse of him, riding along. In the spring you are far more likely to notice the crocuses, thousands and thousands of them. And unfortunately you are bound to notice the traffic at all times of the year. The road used to be lower, but it was raised towards the pavements to suit fast-moving vehicles, to the detriment of everything else. We have half ruined Charlotte Square and seriously diminished the architecture solely in order to encourage the traffic.

George Street likewise is not helped by traffic. It was described early in this century as possessing 'the cool, elderly charm of a well-kept, old-fashioned, half-deserted library;' but no one would think so now. It is very wide, designed as the chief residential street and promenade of Craig's New Town; but today it is sub-divided down the middle by parked vehicles and clogged by moving ones. No residences remain, but there are some good shops and offices and several items of general interest. George Street is punctuated by cross streets, marked by statues, and it is best understood in four sections.

The first section is from Charlotte Square to Castle Street. Near the start are several older houses which appear just as they did in 1790, and they give a good idea of what George Street once looked like. The best of them – indeed, the best eighteenth century house front in the whole street – is No.125, part of a terrace of such houses built in the 1780s. It has three storeys plus a basement, and the four-pane windows are typically Georgian. Although the building is otherwise plain, the doorpiece is extremely handsome. It is framed by Doric pilasters with a shallow entablature, and the door itself is set off by slim lights on each side and a very large and delicate semi-circular fanlight above. It is a demonstration in one building of how to be simple and distinguished at the same time. Next door, Nos.127–129 used to be two houses, but was restored in 1975. The frontage is virtually original. The ornamental lanterns at each side of the entrance show how a good architect and a good craftsman can add a touch of distinction to a plain building, without using a great deal of money. No. 121 is the headquarters of the Church of Scotland. The Kirk is still a force in the land, and a very visible one when the General Assembly meets in Edinburgh every May. Then, for a week, there seem to be more clerics in Edinburgh than in Rome. Castle Street is signalled by the statue of Thomas Chalmers, yet another work by Steell (1878). Chalmers was an ecclesiastical politician, zealous for the preaching of the gospel and the independence of the church; it was he who led the minority party out of the Church of Scotland at the Disruption. He looks to the Castle, but what a splendid view there is behind him, one of those views of distant water and still more distant hills that add so much to the charm and variety of Edinburgh! The foreground to the view is **North Castle Street**, which is especially interesting for two reasons. First of all, it is perhaps the most handsome and best preserved run of late eighteenth century houses in the New Town. Most of them were built as tenements, i.e. divided into flats having a common stair. There are six spacious double bow fronts, and widely spaced balusters under first floor windows. There are arched doors and Doric doorpieces and pilasters (even a pub, located in one of the basements, has pilasters of a sort). Nos.39–43, built in 1793, have a pedimented Corinthian centrepiece between the bows. The second reason for noticing North Castle Street is that No. 39 was Sir Walter Scott's residence in Edinburgh for a quarter of a century. After a sad disappointment over a young lady in 1796 (is this why his heroines are always so unconvincing?), Scott married Charlotte Carpenter in 1797 ('we toasted her twenty times over – and sat together, he raving about her, until it was one in the morning'), and in 1798 the couple settled in North Castle Street. They also rented a cottage at Lasswade, just outside Edinburgh, and there and at No. 39 Scott wrote *The Lay of the Last Minstrel* which, however much it might be a pastiche of *Christabel*, set Scott on the road to becoming a popular author. In 1804 he made Ashestiel, on the River Tweed, his summer home, but he continued to live in North Castle Street whenever the Law Courts were in session. Much of his writing was done in the 'den' or study at the back of the house; of which his son-in-law left a careful description:

> *It had a single Venetian window, opening on a patch of turf not much larger than itself, and the aspect of the place was sombrous ... A dozen volumes or so, needful for immediate purposes of reference, were placed close by him on a small movable form. All the rest were in their proper niches, and wherever a volume had been lent its room was occupied by a wooden block of the same size, having a card with the name*

of the borrower and date of the lending tacked on its front ... The only table was a massive piece of furniture which he had constructed on the model of one at Rokeby, with a desk on either side ... The top displayed a goodly array of session papers, and on the desk below were, besides the MS at which he was working, proof sheets and so forth, all neatly done up with red tape ... The room had no space for pictures, except one, an original portrait of Claverhouse, which hung over the chimney-piece, with a Highland targe (shield) on either side, and broadswords and dirks ... A few green tin boxes, such as solicitors keep their deeds in, were piled over each other on one side of the window, and on the top of these lay a fox's tail, mounted on an antique silver handle, wherewith, as often as he had occasion to take down a book, he gently brushed the dust off the upper leaves before opening it.

Also usually present, often on top of a library ladder with oak rails, was Hinse, a venerable tom-cat, very dark and striped like a tiger, 'fat and sleek and no longer very locomotive,' and Maida, Scott's favourite deer-hound.

Scott's work at the Law Courts brought in a good income, but it was a fraction of what he made by his pen. He was a best-selling author anxious for money – not money for its own sake, but money to rebuild and decorate Abbotsford, support his children, entertain his friends, and live like a Border laird. In the full tide of success in the years after Waterloo four or five thousand pounds for a novel yet to be written was not out of the way; and Scott wrote at tremendous speed, rising at five o'clock in the morning in order to write before the law courts or other business required his attention. In the space of ten years, a good part of them spent at No. 39, he made what would today be the equivalent of millions. Then, late in 1825, came disaster. He had spent to the limit and beyond it, and when his partners in publishing failed for well over £100,000 he heroically undertook to shoulder the debt rather than leave creditors unpaid. His Edinburgh house had to go, and how strongly he felt the loss is indicated in his diary:

March 15, 1826. This morning I leave No. 39 Castle Street for the last time! 'the cabin was convenient', and habit made it agreeable to me ... So farewell poor No. 39! What a portion of my life has been spent there! It has sheltered me from the prime of life to its decline, and now I must bid good-bye to it.

He was only 57. When he died, on 21st September 1832, his unremitting industry had paid off £70,000 of debts and the rest was met by the sale of copyrights. But he had ruined his health by years of overwork. (For a fuller account of Scott's life *see* p. 329).

Between Castle Street and Frederick Street there are several Georgian houses, altered or restored in varying degrees. On the south side the Northern Lighthouse Board has two late eighteenth century houses made into one (Nos.82–84), and 'personalised' by a model lighthouse over the Ionic doorpiece, lit up at night; and almost opposite, at No. 87, is one of the best nineteenth century shop interiors (1835) in Edinburgh. A truly classical frontage is provided by the Bank of Scotland at No. 101. Built in the 1880s, it is a Victorian Italian palace, right to the last detail. The large hall is pure Neo-Classical, with Corinthian columns and a coffered ceiling. The next-door houses are now also part of the bank, No. 105 genuinely Georgian and Nos.97–99 a skilful replica built in the 1970s. The intersection with Frederick Street is presided over by a statue of William Pitt (1833), by Chantrey.

From Frederick Street to Hanover Street there are numerous original houses, all altered in one way or another. Many have shops stuck on to the front of them, which is unfortunate, but Nos.59a and 61 have good Victorian shop fronts, and the latter boasts an internal Ionic screen.

The most notable building in the block, however, is the **Assembly Rooms** on the south side, incorporating the Music Hall to the rear. These Assembly Rooms opened in 1787, almost simultaneously with the rival establishment in Buccleuch Place. For a time Buccleuch Place had more patronage, but George Street was architecturally much grander. It was at first a good deal less assertive in appearance than it is now, because the Doric portico and the arcade projecting into the street were added in 1818, and the wings which extend over the side lanes did not appear until almost a hundred years later. So to begin with the frontage was rather severe, and did not constitute 'an encroachment on the old monotonous amenity of George Street' as some Victorian citizens complained. But the interior was splendid from the start, and remains so. The ballroom, reached by twin stairs, is one hundred feet long and over forty feet wide. The ceiling, almost forty feet overhead, is concave with rounded ends, and has three large plaster roses for the three gigantic chandeliers. Huge mirrors at each end of the room reflect the chandeliers, and the dancers when there is a ball. There are also Corinthian pilasters and a shell-headed

From Charlotte Square to St Andrew Square

doorway. Small wonder that this 'dancing hall' was claimed at the time to be 'among the most elegant of any in Britain'. The music-hall (it cost £10,000) is almost equally impressive, a Greek cross in plan, with a shallow central dome, more rosettes, and a huge gas sunburner suspended from the middle of the ceiling. Dickens used to read from his *Christmas Carols* in this hall, and it was here that Thackeray was hissed down in 1856 for making disparaging remarks about Mary Queen of Scots. Curious how popular the Queen has been in Scotland, ever since she fled from it.

Nowadays the hall is a frequent scene of craft and antique fairs. In the ballroom balls still take place, with men in kilts and ladies in gowns and tartan sashes, and then is the time to see expertly-danced eightsome reels. During the Festival the whole building hums with the buzz of conversation in several languages, accompanied by the clink of coffee cups and glasses.

The Hanover Street crossing brings us back to George IV, in the form of a statue by Chantrey, erected in 1831. A guide book of nameless date, but definitely Victorian, informs us that the blocks of the granite pedestal were put in place by the cranes that served for the building of the National Monument; was this information recorded because it added to the dignity of the King or to that of the National Monument? Like the others in George Street, the monarch has his back to the mountains and the sea, but he enjoys an exceptionally fine view looking south: Playfair's Royal Scottish Academy in the foreground, the immensely tall spire of the Tolbooth Church directly behind it, and on the left the very tall late eighteenth century tenements at the head of the Mound; while to the right the sinuous line of Mound Place climbs up towards Castlehill.

As one approaches St Andrew Square, interest increases. The Commercial Union building at the corner of Hanover Street has an imposing air, with a large copper dome and a statue of Prudence, appropriately, on top; but what is most unusual about it is that it is white, built of Portland stone, a strange departure for George Street.

A few doors along is the **Royal Bank of Scotland** – its gigantic portico can hardly be missed. A hall for the Physicians once stood here, built by James Craig (his successes as an architect were few), but it was pulled down in the 1840s to make way for the bank, which was designed to impress. It is a large and elegant temple, almost flashy. The columns are Corinthian, the windows of the upper floor are arched, and the pedimental sculpture is a powerful composition of seven figures (Prudence appears again) in high relief. The side gates are original, with elaborate cast-iron work. The interior is also impressive, but less elegant. The central hall, or telling hall (bank clerks are tellers in Scotland) is entered via a much smaller top-lit square hall, from which twin staircases ascend by easy steps to the offices above. The telling hall itself is a Greek cross in plan, with arched ceilings and a circular dome roof. The floors are marble mosaic. There are numerous columns, which were once marbled wood but in 1885 became dark grey Devonshire marble, and these have black granite bases and bronze Corinthian capitals. The colours are subdued, and the general effect is handsome, spacious, and unassertive.

On the opposite side of the street is the **George Hotel**, which is rather fun. Improbable as it may appear, this large and almost over-comfortable hotel began as three plain houses built in the early 1780s. In 1840 No. 19 was given a Corinthian portico, and two more porticos arrived in 1879 for Nos.15 and 17, which then became a hotel on the upper floors only. Not until 1950 did the whole building become the George Hotel. Its glory is its dining room, a large square room on two levels, with columns and a high dome. People used to come here for insurance, not meals, for this was originally the business hall of Scotland's oldest insurance company, the Caledonian.

Next to the George Hotel is the **Church of St Andrew and St George**. (It began as St Andrew's, and so it is still commonly called). It is an unusual little church, and it has an unusual history. In Craig's plan a site for a church was designated in St Andrew Square, looking straight down George Street. But before the city got round to thinking about building a church there, one of the richest men in Edinburgh, Sir Laurence Dundas, who had risen from obscurity to fortune as Commissary-General of the army in Flanders, had secured the site for himself – probably by sharp practice; and had built a house on it, which every visitor should see. The magistrates baulked at trying to re-secure the site and then having to knock Sir Laurence's house down, so the church had to be built on the much less eligible site in George Street. A design competition took place, and the prize went to 'Mr Kay, Architect', who proposed a square church; but what was built was an oval church (1782–84) designed by an officer of the Royal Engineers, Major Andrew Frazer, who probably also designed the steeple, added in 1787. The four columns of the portico start almost at street level, which gives a simple and unassuming effect; but the steeple is much more complex, Gibbsian, in four stages, 51 metres high and one of the more prominent features of Edinburgh's fascinating skyline. The interior is plain, its ovalness (if there is such a word) prominent but pleasant. The curved gallery has the original pews, and the ceiling, with concentric ovals and garlands, is modestly decorative. There is a small chapel in the undercroft, created in the 1970s.

Between the church and St Andrew Square, more insurance. Standard Life has it all, a 1975 extension next to the church and then a large Neo-Palladian palace built at the end of the nineteenth century. The palace is vastly dignified, on three floors, with a Corinthian order rising through two of them. The frieze and the pediment above match very well, although the frieze was carved in 1900 and the pediment was taken from the company's earlier office building of 1839, which stood on the same site. The pediment sculpture, like so much else, is by Steell, and represents the wise and foolish virgins; the Bible does not mention insurance, but the implication is obvious. On the extension are more virgins, this time in bronze, by Gerald Laing. These are high up on the building and therefore not much noticed. Lower down and more noticeable, they might cause some scandal. It is worth crossing the road to have a look, for they are really rather charming.

Thus one reaches St Andrew Square. **St Andrew Square** is exactly the same size as Charlotte Square, in exactly the corresponding position, but its style and general appearance are quite different. Instead of being a completely unified design by one architect, it is all variety; the buildings which contain it were planned and erected over a period of two hundred years, not twenty; its centre is occupied not by Prince Albert on horseback but by a Scottish politician on top of a column one hundred and thirty three feet high; even the garden is different, for the trees are mostly cherries, not very large, and there is not the same woodland effect as in Charlotte Square.

Approaching from George Street, the column before you is inescapable, seeming to soar up to an immense height. It commemorates Henry Dundas, first Viscount Melville, and is usually referred to as the **Melville Monument**. Henry Dundas was a key member in the administrations of the Younger Pitt over a long period of years. Immensely able, he served successively as Treasurer of the Navy, Home Secretary, President of the Board of Control for India, Secretary for War, and First Lord of the Admiralty. Equally important, he 'managed' parliamentary elections in Scotland, selecting candidates and suitably rewarding those electors who voted in the Tory interest. It is said that at the height of his power he controlled the elections in at least thirty-six of the forty-five Scottish constituencies; and he was known as 'Harry the Ninth, uncrowned King of Scotland'. He resigned in 1805, not blameless but secure. His monument, designed by fellow-Tory William Burn, was erected 1820–23, and resembles the Trajan column in Rome, but is fluted instead of being ornamented with sculpture. The statue of the great man, from a model by Chantrey, is no less than fourteen feet high.

To walk round St Andrew Square is a lesson in comparative architecture. Leave George Street and turn right. The corner building is the **Guardian Royal Exchange** (1938–40), regarded by many as an outstandingly good example of 1930s architecture. It is not sandstone but black and white – almost-white granite above a black arcaded base. It makes no fuss about being not-Georgian, and not particularly modern either. It is tall and serene, with a proportion of window to wall that seems entirely reasonable, and the oriel on the corner, flanked by bronze figures, adds a touch of Art Deco that enlivens the whole. Cross St David Street (you are observed by Sir Walter Scott, still seated in East Princes Street Gardens) and reach the **Scottish Provident building** on the south side. Here is the architecture of the 1960s, one of Edinburgh's relatively few 'modern' buildings. It is of glass and polished granite, mostly glass with a separately expressed staircase tower. Its effect depends on proportion, on projections and recessions, on rigid angularity, and on the illusion of weightlessness. It has been called wilful, but some critics like it; and it is a test case for the proposition that a good 'modern' building can fit in comfortably with good older ones, for next door to it is an Edwardian Renaissance palazzo with tiers of carefully modulated windows and a carefully detailed frieze; beyond that another Italianate palace built in 1883, with consoled porches and arched windows, the central windows in groups of three; and beyond that a large 1890s structure in pink Dumfries-shire stone, with an arcaded ground floor and a corner turret surmounted by a spire. None of these is a nondescript building, neither the modern nor the Italianate nor the faintly baronial. And if the twentieth century style seems to some citizens to clash with the nineteenth and makes them raise their hands in horror, it does not seem so to all of us.

Before crossing to the east side of the square, observe it from a distance, for it is from a distance that one can best appreciate the **Bank of Scotland building**, a building which is a forcible reminder of the grandeur that was Rome. The building furthest to the right is of no special interest, but the Bank of Scotland (1846, originally the British Linen Bank) is in the grandest possible style. It makes everything else look plain. By modern standards it is not a large building, and the façade is almost square; but the scale is colossal. Three storeys occupy sixty feet. Above a rusticated ground floor, with a huge door and four large lamp standards, six fluted and projecting Corinthian columns and their entablatures rise to the roof line, each supporting an isolated statue eight feet high. The first floor windows, which are twelve feet in height, are pedimented, there is a richly decorated frieze with cupids and festoons of flowers, and a balustrade runs the whole width of the building well behind the statues. If it were not so well done it would be awful; but it is very well done indeed, a masterpiece of its kind, by David Bryce, true Victorian opulence. The interior, however, may not be to everyone's taste. There is first a plain square entrance hall and then a large stair-hall, which gives access to a stone stair with a heavily scrolled and gilded balustrade. Beyond is the telling hall, very large and very high. More than two dozen columns and pilasters of polished granite rise to large and elaborate gilt capitals. All round the room is a large and elaborate plaster frieze, with muscular plaster swags amid which erupt the busts of celebrated Scotsmen, more than life-size. The ceiling is coffered, and there is an ornate cupola of stained glass, thirty feet in diameter and rising almost fifty feet above the floor. To say that this hall is not restful would be putting it mildly. It reminds one of the physique of a professional weight-lifter.

The middle of this east side of the square is occupied by the (officially misplaced) house of Sir Laurence Dundas. Misplaced it may be, but it is a gem of architecture, free-standing and carefully positioned behind a fairly large forecourt. On each side of the forecourt, flanking the bank, is a handsome town house. That to the north was built in 1769 (and was thus probably the first grand house to be built in the New Town) with a giant Ionic order and a fluted frieze; the corresponding house to the south was built twelve years later, almost to the same design.

The centrepiece of the group, Sir Laurence's one-time house, was designed by Sir William Chambers in 1771. It is not a large or particularly ornate structure, but everything about it is just right. It is rusticated on the ground floor, and has a Corinthian order of four pilasters supporting the pediment. The Royal Arms within the pediment (a rare example with the French fleur-de-lys quartering which was discontinued in 1801) was added in 1794, the Excise Office having acquired the building after Dundas's death in 1781. In 1825 the **Royal Bank of Scotland** bought it, and added the porch. Perhaps it is the porch, allied to the modest scale and perfect proportions of the whole, that make one feel, as one approaches the front-door even today, that one is about to enter a private house. The interior has been altered, although one first-floor room – now the board room – remains as it was, with an Adam-style ceiling which features in the *Book of Ceilings* of 1776, and a pilastered chimneypiece. The vestibule has a first-floor landing and screens of coupled columns, very elegant, and the two-storey stair-hall has an 1850s stair and an 1850s Rococo ceiling. These hardly prepare one for the telling-hall, which can only be described as breath-taking. It was added by John Dick Peddie in 1857. 'Oh, look at this! Oh, my goodness me!' is a typical comment. It is almost sixty feet square, enclosed by four almost semi-circular arches which spring from low down in the corners. Large medallions contain groups of sizeable but decorative cherubs. The arches support a splendid dome, forty-five feet in diameter, which is pierced all over by 120 windows in the shape of six-pointed stars, arranged to diminish in size from the base of the dome to its apex, with a clear light at centre-top. There is much fairly simple plaster-work and no end of gilt, and the colours have been laid on with a vengeance: blue for the ceiling, maroon for the arches, elsewhere biscuit, white and gold. This is not a room for those who dislike colour. It is at once magnificent and pretty, and it demonstrates to perfection the confidence and high spirits of mid-Victorian times.

In front of the Bank stands the **Hopetoun Monument** (1834), a dismounted equestrian statue by Thomas Campbell of the fourth Earl of Hopetoun, in Roman guise, who was once Governor of the Bank. He was also a soldier. (It was he who assumed command of the army at Corunna, after the death of Sir John Moore). The lamp standards by the door were specially cast for the Bank in 1828, and the enclosed garden is always immaculate.

As for the other buildings on the east side, try not to notice them; it is no excuse that they conceal the bus station; But there are plans for the bus station ... Edinburgh, nowadays, is awash with plans. The north side, however, is well worth looking at, because by and large it is made up of the original houses, although a good deal altered. The oldest are the four central houses, put up simultaneously with Sir Lawrence Dundas's house in the early 1770s. All were of three storeys and were rubble-built. Nos.21 and 22 are also of the 1770s, and were built as flats. The porches, pedimented and otherwise, have all been added at later dates, as have the ashlar fronts. No. 23 is outstanding, remodelled by Bryce in 1846 as a bank; it is a beautiful

Italian Renaissance façade, with a pedimented Ionic porch and pedimented windows. This side of the square looked plainer to begin with than it does now. But it still gives an idea of the fashionable New Town of the eighteenth century. Judges, generals, and knights of the realm were once commonplace in St Andrew Square. The Earl of Northesk, who was third in command at Trafalgar, lived in No. 2, Lord Brougham was born in No. 21, and at No. 22 there dwelt a physician who continued to wear a three-cornered hat and knee breeches well into the nineteenth century: the bell-ringer of the Tron church is said to have had the reversion of his left-off cocked hats. Gradually the square became invaded by banks, offices and hotels, and now it is purely the abode of business. Executive suites and computers have taken the place of drawing rooms and tea services. Cars replace carriages. And business deals are arranged where pitched battles at whist were once a nightly occurrence.

11

Queen Street and the Moray Estate

QUEEN STREET IS worth a visit, for at least three reasons: because it is by far the longest continuous sequence of late eighteenth and early nineteenth century house fronts in Edinburgh; because it duplicates the Princes Street plan of leaving one side of the street quite open and unbuilt on, with excellent effect; and because at the east end, just north of St Andrew Square, there stands the **Scottish National Portrait Gallery**, which contains many remarkable pictures, and is itself a most singular piece of architecture. It looks, in fact, as if it would be more at home in Venice than in Edinburgh.

Reach the Gallery from St Andrew Square, going down North St David Street. (There is a story – apocryphal, no doubt, but yet a good story – concerning the name of this street. David Hume lived in the other section, South St David Street, south of the square, when he removed from James's Court in the Old Town in 1771. No street names had been put up in the New Town, but one morning the neighbourhood awoke to find 'St David Street' chalked on the wall. Hume was sometimes called by his few enemies 'the atheist,' and the allusion was obvious. His servant took it as a personal affront. But Hume consoled her. 'Never mind, lassie,' he said. 'Many a better man than me has been called a saint.' Boswell visited him in South St David Street a few years later when he lay dying, and found that 'Mr Hume's pleasantry was such that Death for the time did not seem dismal'. The house has long since disappeared). As you leave the Square for Queen Street, and especially if there is sunshine, one of those wonderful views looking out of the heart of the city lies before you: the fields and hills of Fife and the blue or silver waters of the Firth of Forth stretch out beyond extensive suburbs mantled and for the most part hidden by ascending trees.

The Gallery is at the foot of North St David Street. The long line of Queen Street is to your left, the gardens are opposite, while to your right the street continues as York Place, where Raeburn built a large house in 1795 (it still stands, No. 32) to use as his studio and gallery. Broad and stately, York Place leads to the foot of the Calton Hill, and contains a very handsome Neo-Perpendicular church, St Paul and St George (1818). Its lofty octagonal angle-turrets can be seen from afar. The Scottish National Portrait Gallery is an astonishing building, almost as romantic as the Scott Monument and as eccentric as the Brighton Pavilion. First of all, it is built of red Dumfries-shire sandstone, like the Caledonian Hotel; very unusual in the New Town. Then, in its general appearance, it recalls the Doges' Palace in Venice, massive in its almost windowless upper storeys (which provide top-lit galleries) but the façade pierced by wide Gothic windows on the ground floor and having on the first floor a continuous succession of paired traceried windows and much sculptural decoration. There are octagonal corner turrets, corbelled out, with statues, and surmounted by tall corner pinnacles. The central doorway is highly decorated, with numerous tableaux and figures, and is flanked by tall pinnacled buttresses. The style has been called Franco-Italian Gothic, but to most people it looks Venetian, made sterner for the northern hemisphere. It is an exuberant building, but not excessively so, and it certainly does not look cheap. The architect, J Rowand Anderson, must have had a wonderful time, and one hopes that his patron, J R Findlay, the proprietor of *The Scotsman* newspaper, who footed the bill, enjoyed himself too. He paid £50,000 for the entire building, which was a lot of money in 1890. But what value!

Inside, the exuberance is confined to the central hall, square and arcaded, which rises through the full height of the building. Red sandstone columns with gilded foliage capitals support the gallery which goes right round the hall on the first floor. This gallery, thirty feet above the floor of the hall, is decorated with a painted and gilded frieze showing almost one hundred and fifty figures from Scottish history. All are full length, although some have to peep over the shoulders of their neighbours. They range from stone age man (and woman and child) to celebrities living in the later nineteenth century such as Carlyle and Livingstone. Much trouble was taken by the artist, William Hole, to ensure accuracy in the features and the costumes, and the effect is very striking – 'one of the most notable examples of mural decoration ever accomplished in this country,' according to one critic. It succeeds because it is so decorative, and because it fits in so well. The walls of the gallery are covered with huge murals by the same artist, mostly of fighting scenes. The ceiling above has timber beams, and on a dull green background the stars in their constellations are picked out in gold. From the ceiling hang four dramatic cylindrical wrought-iron lanterns, in black and red. It is a strange place, at once exciting and soothing, lofty, penumbral, Victorian-medieval.

With notable exceptions, the pictures in the Portrait Gallery have historic rather than exceptional artistic interest; here you see what many of the men and women referred to in other chapters actually looked like. Almost all the best existing portraits of the kings and queens of Scotland are on the ground floor, which is devoted to the Stewart dynasty. There is a very fine portrait of Mary of Guise, full of character, and one of Darnley, without any; but he was only nine years old when it was painted. There is a portrait of Mary Queen of Scots, by an unknown artist. It was painted more than a quarter of a century after her death and is based upon a miniature by Nicholas Hilliard, done when Mary was a captive. No portrait of Mary painted while she was Queen is known to exist, which may tell us something about her relations with her turbulent subjects. Also, several of the best-known portraits of Prince Charles Edward are here, as well as an excellent portrait of Flora Macdonald by Richard Wilson, painted soon after her release from the Tower of London in 1747. (Flora Macdonald had an exceptionally adventurous life. Orphaned early, she was brought up by the Clan Ranald family. In 1746, when she was twenty-four, her courage and loyalty were indispensable in helping Prince Charles to escape his pursuers in the Highlands after Culloden. Arrested and imprisoned, she was released in 1747. Three years later she married Allan Macdonald of Kingsburgh in Skye, and accompanied him on service in the American War of Independence. She returned to Scotland and died in Skye in 1790).

Artistic quality is not wanting in these pictures, but there are numerous others which, while historically interesting, are also outstanding works of art. There is the well-known portrait of Hume by Allan Ramsay, that of Burns by Alexander Nasmyth, and a fanciful depiction of 'George IV's Entry into the Palace of Holyroodhouse' by Sir David Wilkie. Two of the most magnificent pictures in the Gallery are the Duke of Lauderdale by Lely, a commanding portrait of a domineering man, and the 4th Duke of Argyll by Gainsborough, where the subject's age is sympathetically seen 'as a lusty winter' and the whole canvas is painted with dazzling technical skill. What is on no account to be missed is the room on the top floor devoted largely to Raeburn. If more of Raeburn's portraits were in

England, or France or America, he would be more widely recognised than he is as a very able portrait painter. He eschewed the elaboration of Reynolds and the charm of Gainsborough, but, like Rembrandt, concentrated on the force and truthfulness of character and expression. This room contains no fewer than twenty six portraits by Raeburn, and none of them fails to suggest the temperament and faculties of mind of the sitter. Perhaps he was too facile, and his work lacks depth. But his depiction of each individual is masterly, and his canvases are a pleasure to behold.

Besides the portraits as such, a few other items deserve mention. 'the Execution of Charles I' is especially popular with children; they stare at it goggle-eyed. The scaffold is in the background, with five black-attired figures, one of whom holds up the severed head. For good measure, the head appears again in one of the insets. Someone in the colourful crowd has fainted, and there is blood everywhere. It is a nasty scene. Tartan enthusiasts should see 'the Macdonald Boys', who between the two of them wear four different patterns of tartan (in 1755) which shows how people in the eighteenth century wore whatever tartan they fancied. Golfers should see the picture of William Inglis, an Edinburgh surgeon, wearing the coat of the Honourable Company of Edinburgh Golfers, of which he was twice captain in the 1780s. He holds a strangely shaped club in his right hand, and his youthful curly-haired caddie stands behind him with three more clubs. No golf bag, no trolley. The game was simpler in those days.

Finally, for those who demand neither great art nor important historical reference, there are two delightful and very large family groups by David Allan, painted in the 1780s. Eighteenth century art is usually elaborate, formal, carefully arranged, like eighteenth century life in the upper reaches of society. But here are two families at play, painted with an almost primitive simplicity and ingenuousness – indeed, with here and there an almost primitive lack of skill. Both canvases are pleasantly, even excitingly composed. In one, the 7th Earl of Mar is shown with his wife, his aunt, his six children, and a nanny. Alloa House, burned down in 1800, is in the background. James, aged 10, aims an arrow at a respectable-looking hat lodged in a tree, watched by a not so respectable-looking dog. The grown-ups are convincing enough, and so is James; the other children are dolls. The Earl is seated on a fallen tree, but his feet mysteriously fail to make contact with the ground. In the other, Sir William Erskine, his wife and his seven children are arranged before a long, low Gothicky building, with grooms, horses and several dogs in attendance. Father and two boys have been hunting, successfully; one boy has the fox's tail fixed to his hat, while the other one carries the head. Three little girls are pushed into the lower right hand corner with a rabbit and reduced to total insignificance. Again, the grown-ups look convincing – the eldest daughter is even attractive. It is not great art, and some may say that it is not art at all. But these pictures provide a true glimpse of eighteenth century life.

Not far from the Gallery (which, incidentally, has a convenient cafe) stands the **Royal College of Physicians of Edinburgh**, designed by Thomas Hamilton, who also designed the Royal High School (*see* p. 144). The College was founded in 1681, and did much to make Edinburgh one of the three or four greatest centres of medical education in the world in the eighteenth century. The Fellows used to meet in a hall in Surgeons' Square, not far from the University, but they moved to Queen Street in 1844. It is a strange building, rather squeezed into the domestic architecture of the street. Set a little forward from its neighbours, it consists of three storeys, the third without windows. The central doorway is framed by a four-column portico, surmounted by a pedimented portico which frames the centre window on the first floor. The lower portico supports very large statues of Hippocrates and Aesculapius, while on top of the pediment stands Hygeia, her head just below cornice level. It is all severely Neo-Classical, and rather too square to be satisfactory – Hamilton had more room to spread himself on Calton Hill. The interior (into which visitors and ordinary citizens do not penetrate) is very grand. An imperial stair with heavy gilt scrolls to support the handrails leads up to the hall, which is lined by marbled Corinthian columns with gilt capitals. The hall was originally five bays across and three deep, but in 1866 the physicians decided that it was not large enough, so the three bays were increased to seven, making the hall very large as well as very grand. There are many roundel portraits of famous physicians, and much plaster work. The College has a superb collection of books, happily accommodated in a delightful Upper Library.

Not content with all this, the physicians also own No. 8 next door, built by Robert Adam for an English judge, Baron Orde, in 1771. The façade is simple but beautifully proportioned, and it provides an example, along with other buildings in the street, of the superb quality of workmanship which was achieved by many of the masons who built the New Town. No. 8 is five windows wide, wider than the College, and oddly there is a mansard roof. Although rearranged internally, the building contains several fine Adam ceilings and chimneypieces, and there is original woodwork in the two drawing-rooms, which are located, as was the custom, on the first floor. The kitchen was originally at the bottom of the garden, reached by a passage at basement level; it now serves as a library. There are other fine domestic houses – or what were once domestic houses – further down the street: there are astragals, balustrades, pedimented porches and fanlights a-plenty, all facing the lime-trees and the sycamores in the gardens opposite, and when the leaves have gone, looking across the water to the green fields and hills of Fife. One of the finest is No. 64, built for the Earl of Wemyss in 1790, possibly the grandest house built in the New Town after the completion of the Dundas mansion in the 1770s. From a history point of view, however, No. 52 is the one to notice. Here lived Sir James Young Simpson from 1845 until his death in 1870. Simpson is famous as the discoverer of chloroform anaesthesia. His life like his great discovery is an extraordinary story. He was the seventh child in a poor family in Bathgate, outside Edinburgh; but by the time he was 28 he was professor of midwifery in the University. During the 1840s many doctors were searching for a serviceable anaesthetic, and the use of ether was pioneered in Boston late in 1846. But there were difficulties, and the hunt for an alternative continued. Simpson was not an experimental scientist, and he proceeded by the hazardous method of trying different volatile fluids on himself. The crucial discovery was made on 4th November 1847, at No. 52, Queen Street. Late one evening (the account is that given by the professor who lived next door) Simpson and two colleagues 'sat down to their work in Dr Simpson's dining room'. They tried 'several substances, but without much effect' and then turned to chloroform.

> *Immediately an unwonted hilarity seized the party: they became bright-eyed, very happy and very loquacious ... The conversation was of unusual intelligence ... But suddenly there was talk of sounds being heard like those of a cotton mill, louder and louder; a moment more, then all was quiet, and then – a crash. On awakening, Dr Simpson's first perception was mental – 'This is far stronger and better than ether,' said he to himself. His second was to note that he was prostrate on the floor.*

This was a great discovery. And although chloroform had disadvantages of its own, Simpson's work helped enormously to eliminate pain and danger from both surgical operations and childbirth, and to make possible further advances in medicine.

Before leaving Craig's New Town, a visit to a couple of side streets will tell us a little more about eighteenth century ideas of urban living. **Rose Street** and **Thistle Street** (the latter confusingly called Hill Street and Young Street in its eastern half) run parallel between the main thoroughfares. They are narrow streets, intended for 'the better class of artisans,' i.e. skilled workmen and shopkeepers, although from the beginning Thistle Street was infiltrated by merchants and a few professional people. The scale and style of the houses in both streets is modest. At the east end of Thistle Street, Thistle Court on the south side boasts what is almost certainly the earliest New Town buildings that remain, possibly the very first that were put up; two pairs of well-composed little houses, reputedly built in 1768. Both pairs have pediments, and Nos.1 and 2 have fanlights as well; Nos.3 and 4 look very grave; they have been turned into an electricity transformer station. Many other original houses are in this street, some more workaday than others and some with a touch of distinction – here and there an arched doorway or a doorpiece with columns or pilasters. A number of late Georgian and early Victorian

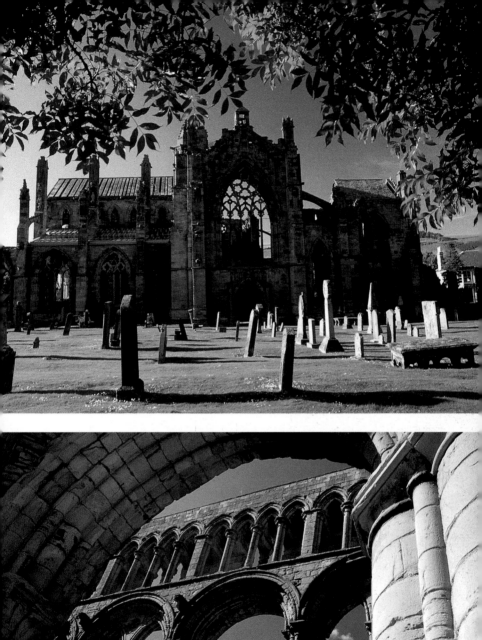

shopfronts have been inserted, and No. 21 has the Bourbon coat of arms in the middle of the wall recording the residence of Louis Philippe's grandsons from 1859 to 1873. Rose Street, where it has not been spoiled by later building, is similar. It is pedestrianised towards its west end (Edinburgh is remarkably niggardly with its pedestrian precincts) and is particularly well known for its pubs. Not far from St Andrew Square stands the Abbotsford Bar (1902), dignified with a good Jacobean interior, while west of Frederick Street there is the Kenilworth Bar, created in the 1890s out of the two lower storeys of the original building. It is very lofty, with good tiles and once again Jacobean-style woodwork.

The western part of Queen Street, beyond where the Queen Street gardens end, is the north-west edge of Craig's New Town. There is no view, because tall and partly Doric buildings take the place of the Gardens, but the Water of Leith is not far away, running in a deep wooded ravine, and just beyond it is the Queensferry Road carrying all the traffic into Edinburgh from the north. The area adjacent to Queen Street and Charlotte Square and stretching as far as the river was once the estate and abode of the **Earl of Moray**. It was described by Lord Cockburn as being, at the start of the eighteenth century,

> *an open field of as green turf as Scotland could boast of, with a few respectable trees on the flat, and thickly wooded on the bank along the Water of Leith.... That well-kept and almost evergreen field was the most beautiful piece of ground in immediate connection with the town, and led the eye agreeably over to our distant northern scenery ... I have stood in Queen Street, or the opening at the north-west corner of Charlotte Square, and listened to the ceaseless rural corncraiks, nestling happily in the dewy grass.*

This prospect began to disappear in 1822, the Earl having decided to develop his property.

He resolved, moreover, to do it in a handsome manner, and to shoulder as little of the cost as possible. His planning rules, which covered the whole thirteen acres, were extraordinarily detailed. Apart from the ground-plan (mainly a crescent, an oval and a polygon) and the principal elevations, there were rules about the stone to be used, the design of the stables, the width of the pavements, the construction of the sewers, the appearance of the iron railings that were to enclose the gardens (they were to be 'in a suitable and handsome manner'), and many other matters too numerous to mention. The result of the Earl's care and enterprise, of the public's willingness to build as they were told and to pay for the roads as well as everything else, and of the architect's knowledge and ability (he was James Gillespie Graham, who was later to collaborate with Pugin in building the Tolbooth Church) is the grandest and most unified housing development on a large scale in Britain.

True, Graham's elevations are almost too grand, and **Moray Place**, the polygonal showpiece of it all, is almost too big; but not quite. Graham aimed at something 'totally different from the monotony of our present streets and squares,' and this he contrived to produce on an awkwardly shaped and inconveniently sloping site. Perhaps the best approach is from the north-west corner of Charlotte Square, down Glenfinlas Street and into Ainslie Place. Ainslie Place (the oval) is only moderately grand – a few Doric pilasters give a mere hint of what is to come. Moray Place is directly connected, a huge twelve-sided circus almost two hundred yards across. Every house has four storeys, the ground and first floor being of no small height, with mostly arched openings on the ground floor, which is rusticated throughout. Placed regularly round the twelve sides are six pedimented centrepieces having four tall columns each, and there are pilasters on all the corner blocks. It is a noble style on a noble scale, and one cannot be surprised that the earl himself condescended to build and to live at No. 28. Moray Place is still lived in, although there are offices too, and its appearance very fortunately remains much as it was, in spite of the removal of astragals from numerous windows and the building of attics on top of many of the linking houses.

The architecture, however, as is so often the case in Edinburgh (and perhaps should more often be the case elsewhere), is only part of the effect. Apart from the mature trees in the centre, which shed their leaves and colour the pavements gold in the autumn, there are the steeply sloping banks of the Water of Leith not far away. These were made a part of the scheme, and so they remain. The Earl 'resolved to preserve the beauty of the bank on the south side of the river ... and to reserve the same as pleasure ground, for the benefit of himself and his feuars' [i.e. those who built], and therefore rules were laid down about 'laying out the pleasure grounds ... and keeping them in proper order'. The result is exceedingly agreeable, for these pleasure grounds slope steeply to the river, covered with rhododendron and hazel and tall trees. Carefully laid paths wind through them, some of them flagged, and massive arched retaining walls add to the grandeur of the scene. These gardens are overlooked by some rear elevations, but the Earl was careful that on his estate the rear elevations, like the front ones, should be 'in a regular and uniform order,' and be built according to the designs supplied by the architect. These cliff-like backs are very imposing, seen from the Dean valley or from the other side of the Water of Leith.

The interiors on the Moray estate vary enormously. Many houses have become offices and others have been converted into flats – No. 28 in particular has been much sub-divided, but its ground floor rooms are intact and very grand. Almost all houses have large rooms with very high ceilings, and big windows almost to floor level. Entrance halls are often a feature, designed to make a good first impression; elaborate friezes and coffered ceilings are to be expected, with here and there a pair of columns, Doric or Ionic. Into all this grandeur lifts have sometimes been inserted, for it is a long way up to the top floor, even to the second top floor. And of course the wide streets with their granite setts serve admirably for parking cars.

Although a little commercialised, this area has at least not been desecrated or vulgarised. When the traffic has gone, it is not too difficult to imagine how once it was; when Playfair had his office in a back room at No. 17 Great Stuart Street, and Francis Jeffrey, editor of the famous *Edinburgh Review* (which, when independent thought was almost treason, dared in the first decade of the nineteenth century to question every established practice and institution) lived at No. 24 Moray Place; when Baron Hume, nephew of the philosopher and friend of Walter Scott, lived at No. 34; and carriages rolled up in the evenings to dinner parties where the bill of fare might be oysters (very plentiful in the Forth in those days), cold beef, two hens, a bottle or two of whisky, and very large quantities of punch.

12

The Northern New Town

CRAIG'S NEW TOWN was a successful speculation. Begun at the St Andrew Square end in 1768, building spread westward and Charlotte Square, a mile to the west, was half built by 1800. So, as Edinburgh continued prosperous and 'in want of accommodation,' a second New Town was planned, going down the slope from the Queen Street gardens in the direction of the Firth of Forth. When the plans were drawn up in 1802, most people thought that the entire scheme was as ridiculous as the erection of the first few houses in and near St Andrew Square had seemed to be over thirty years before. But the first house in the new development, No. 13 Heriot Row, was ready for occupation within a year, and by 1823 almost everything was built.

The Northern New Town, as this second major development is often called, is comparable in size to the first. It is also comparable in the senses that it is regular in lay-out and unified in execution, and that it has a central axis, Great King Street, which, instead of connecting two squares as George Street does, connects a large circus on the west (Royal Circus) to a large U-shaped space further east (Drummond Place). Why is this second New Town so much less visited and admired than the first? Partly because it has no view to rival the view from Princes Street – but what town has? Then, it is on a fairly steep slope, which makes going down the hill not a little dangerous in icy weather, and walking up not a little bothersome in hot. Moreover, it suffers to some extent from that monotony which Gillespie Graham sought so successfully to avoid in the Moray development. There are fewer distinguished buildings in the Northern New Town, and the private buildings are on the whole less grand; indeed, as one goes down the slope the standards of elegance and accommodation fall steadily, from the prolonged dignity of Heriot Row to the unpretentious decency of Cumberland Street. In fact, what is at the bottom was built 'in a style of less elegance, for the accommodation of shopkeepers and others,' like Rose Street and Thistle Street. Yet there are fine things in this part of Edinburgh, and it recalls at least one famous name.

The best approach is down Frederick Street and straight on into Howe Street. This way you bisect **Heriot Row**, which has a particularly fine situation, facing south to the Queen Street gardens; and makes good use of it. The whole Row was designed by Robert Reid in two very long palace fronts, the houses of only two storeys, except for the centrepieces and the end pavilions, which have three. This Corbusier-like uniformity (there are sixty nine door and window openings, on the same level, exactly symmetrical, in the west section alone) has been much modified by private unco-ordinated action; most of the two-storey houses have been raised by one storey, and the centrepieces have also been altered. The long low symmetry has thus disappeared, but Heriot Row remains impressive, with its three-storey centrepieces, three-storey end pavilions, and continuous rustication at ground level. The tall first floor windows come down almost to floor level, making the rooms exceptionally light and airy, and there are elegant standard lamps along the pavement at regular intervals. Heriot Row is very calm and dignified.

From the start it was seen as a desirable place to live; wealthy people built in Heriot Row, and wealthy people still live there; for some reason it is especially popular with lawyers. The interiors vary a great deal, but many of them are extremely elegant, especially in the eastern section. Spacious entrance halls are the rule, some with screens of columns; No. 14 has a double entrance hall with two screens of columns, and at No. 10 there is a stairwell with an arcaded first floor landing; there are several large L-plan drawing rooms, and numerous very fine ceilings, some with an oval pattern, garlanded. Arches, cupolas, columns, wrought-iron balusters and sinuous handrails, lofty Adamesque ceilings – all promote in these houses a sense of solidity, dignity, prosperity and space.

It was at No. 17, commodious but not as grand as many, that Robert Louis Stevenson lived from 1857, when he was seven years old, until 1879 when he set off on his travels. He died, as everyone knows, fifteen years later, on one of the Samoan islands, on a large estate that he had bought overlooking the blue Pacific. His last novel lay unfinished beside him. How did a boy brought up in the decorous atmosphere of Heriot Row in Victorian Edinburgh, 'known and pointed out,' as he himself wrote, 'for the pattern of an idler,' become one of the best-loved literary figures of the nineteenth century, with a universal appeal, and come to die in a tropical paradise? His was certainly a romantic life. And it struck all his contemporaries that it was so. As a friend wrote to him, 'Since Byron was in Greece, nothing has appealed to the ordinary literary man so much as that you should be living in the South Seas.' And in that notion of the romantic lies some part of the secret. He was one of the great writers of romances, because he believed in romance, and he believed that romance brought beauty and sparkle to life; but at the same time he steadily kept his imagination in check, for he observed people and their affairs critically as well as sympathetically, always optimistic, but always aware of life's sadnesses and contrasts.

It might be supposed that his life and his writings were an escape from his native city; but that is not the case. He was from his youth a close observer of Edinburgh, 'this profusion of eccentricities,' he called it, 'this dream in masonry and living rock'. He knew about 'the gay people sunning themselves along Princes Street,' but almost equally as much about the half-starved families herded together in the slums of the Royal Mile. He knew about them because he wandered, often at night, through the closes and into the tall lands: 'In the first room there is a birth, in another a death, in a third a sordid drinking bout, and the detective and the Bible-reader cross upon the stairs.' Edinburgh was essential to him. *Dr Jekyll and Mr Hyde* is a vivid story of a dual personality, brought home to our imaginations with masterly skill; but its author must have been familiar with the history of Deacon Brodie. *Treasure Island* is full of exotic scenes and dramatic adventures; but Long John Silver, far from being yet another pasteboard villain, is a treacherous cripple the like of whom the young Stevenson had doubtless encountered more than once during his expeditions into the wynds and closes of the Old Town. The sheltered dignity of Heriot Row did not contain him. He was a free spirit, audacious and enthusiastic, a consummate artist who never seemed to be apart from or above the rest of humanity, but who was as other men were, or felt that they might be.

The continuation of Heriot Row to the east is Abercromby Place. The architectural style is much the same, but instead of being straight Abercromby Place is a shallow crescent, and this is noteworthy, for it was the first curved street to be built in Edinburgh since Craig laid down his rectilinear plan. The slight curve to the north is a welcome relief from so much straightness, and it moreover allows the **Queen Street gardens** to widen and be seen to best advantage. They are a wonderful foil to the architecture, for the mature and fairly dense planting, and the undulations of the ground, give them mystery and enchantment. There are lime trees and sycamores, yews and hollies, enormous hawthorn trees and horse-chestnuts in flower in the spring. What an arcadia for the grave householders of Heriot Row and Abercromby Place to frolic on a dewy May morning, or, more probably, for their offspring to play hide-and-seek! These and other gardens like them are an essential part of the charm of Edinburgh, a city so severe and yet also so natural. But it was not always thus. Until a few years after the completion of Abercromby Place in 1819 the gardens were a neglected wasteland. Not until 1823 were they enclosed, and laid out 'in pleasure walks and shrubberies for the inhabitants of these localities'.

Resume your descent of Howe Street, and North East Circus Place forks off to the left. (Madam Doubtfire and her old clothes shop used to be here, but she and her shop, alas! have not survived into the computer age). **Royal Circus** (early 1820s) is an unusual piece of town design, a tree-filled circus cut diagonally by a sinuous road going downhill to Stockbridge, and also entered by two other streets. This produces two large and two small crescents on opposite arcs of a large circle, one pair of them, because of the slope of the hill, considerably lower than the other. The streets are broad and stately, the hill is steep, and the result has fairly been described as singular and picturesque. The buildings on the crescents, by Playfair, are three storeys high, fairly severe, with small iron balconies at first floor level. Each crescent maintains a strictly horizontal line, which emphasises the fall of the ground. The interiors are not especially distinguished, but they reach the usual New Town standard – large entrance halls, spacious drawing rooms at first floor level, the occasional plastered ceiling and at least one Doric screen (No. 28). Several of these buildings are now hotels. Just beyond Royal Circus, on the left hand side, is another notable piece of town design and building. A stone wall, beautifully built, rises twenty feet above the pavement; it holds up the termination of India Street, a broad and handsome thoroughfare which comes to an abrupt stop because of the steepness of the hill. The last house in India Street rises six storeys above North West Circus Place, which curves down to Stockbridge. But there is a way up to India Street. Look closely, and you will find that an opening in the wall gives access to a dog-legged stairway which climbs to India Street, a mere thirty steps. Pedestrians were catered for in those days. But they had to be fit.

Returning to Howe Street, the continuing descent appears to lead straight into the cavernous portal of a very large church; and in a way it does, for **St Stephen's** terminates the view with remarkable finality. Designed by Playfair and completed in 1828, this church has been described as 'of vast scale, Baroque power and Grecian severity'. It is square in plan, set diagonally to suit the site, but is octagonal within. The porch and the tower dominate the neighbourhood. The tower, which is also square, is over one hundred and sixty feet high, in three stages, with corner turrets and a balustrade. The porch, which attracts at least as much attention, turns out, when you finally reach the church, to be raised well above street level. The consequence of this arrangement was, in the old days, that parishioners who had come all the way down Howe Street and then St Vincent Street, next had to ascend a huge flight of steps in order to get into the church, and then, unless they sat in the gallery where they had arrived, had to go downstairs to their pews. It seems a rather perverse piece of planning, and now it is altered. Once through the porch, you are standing on a reinforced concrete deck at the original gallery level. When the church was found to be too large in the 1950s, (it was designed for a congregation of 1,600!), the deck was inserted and the main part of the church thus became a lower hall. It was a drastic solution to a now familiar problem, but it saved the church from demolition (nothing was safe in those days) or from being turned into a bingo hall, and it remains in religious use, one of Edinburgh's minor landmarks.

In this part of the Northern New Town – Stockbridge to the left of you, Canonmills ahead – there is a most godly concentration of churches: St Vincent (episcopal, 1857), curvy English Gothic, adjacent to St Stephens; St Bernard's (Free, 1856), Decorated, now disused; Davidson Church (1881), more Gothic, now a warehouse; and Bellevue Chapel(also 1881), still more Gothic, built for a small congregation of immigrant God-fearing Germans. But architecturally and historically religion hereabouts is eclipsed by education. The **Edinburgh Academy** stands one street down from St Stephen's Church. It is not an architectural masterpiece, but its cheese-paring severity of style may be a significant indication of what was once thought 'right' for education; and its founders' principles were downright revolutionary in Scotland, for they proposed to restrict admission to those who could afford to pay. The school was set up in 1824 as a better alternative to the almost-non-fee-paying general education-for-all Royal High School on Calton Hill. The objection to the latter, according to Cockburn, was that its standards were 'lowered, perhaps necessarily, so as to suit the wants of a class of boys to more than two thirds of whom classical accomplishment is foreseen to be useless'. So the new school was ostensibly designed *inter alia* to arrest the decline of Latin and Greek in Edinburgh, and to help boys to acquire 'a pure English accent'. Cockburn, by his own account, resolved to promote the new school while walking one day on the Pentlands. He may have been influenced by the fact that the High School was run by the Tory Town Council – he was himself an ardent Whig; on the other hand, he was actively supported by Sir Walter Scott, who was an equally ardent Tory; so a genuine concern for the classics, and unconcern for continuing the old Scots tradition of educational equality for all (male) children may have been the whole cause. The establishment of this 'elitist' school was fiercely opposed by the Tory Town Council and rejoiced in by all Liberal reformers. Thus do political sympathies revolve.

The building was designed by William Burn and has been described as 'Basic Greek'. Its foundation was a private venture and money was none too plentiful, which accounts to some extent for its spartan appearance. The columns of the portico are unfluted, the pediment undecorated and the whole façade is two or three feet too low for its height. Above the columns, however, are inscriptions appropriately in Latin and Greek. One announces that the Academy was dedicated to the education of youth, and the other affirms that Education is the Mother of Wisdom and Virtue. Inside, the best feature is the long oval hall, with a long high lantern which peeps mysteriously above the façade. The Academy boasts among its former pupils Robert Louis Stevenson (for eighteen months), an Archbishop of Canterbury, numerous judges, and a torrent of other lawyers and doctors. Latin and Greek are still taught, and rugby has been added to the curriculum with much success.

The other notable building in this part of Edinburgh is **St Mary's Church**. It is several streets distant, further east, so the best plan is to walk along Great King Street to Drummond Place. This main axis of the Northern New Town, mostly built in the 1820s, is decidedly severe; from end to end there is not much variation, and it is saved from monotony only by the prospect of the trees in Royal Circus at one end and in Drummond Place at the other. It is, of course, wide and handsome, and along with Drummond Place it benefits from its roadway being still surfaced with granite setts – how much better to look at than asphalt! The great and the famous have lived here too. But greatness and fame have a way of soon disappearing. Who now remembers Dr Christison, or reads his once-celebrated *Treatise on Poisons*? He lived at No. 3. Or Sir William Hamilton and his *Course* *of Metaphysics*, at No. 16? Perhaps Sir William Allan (d.1850), at No. 72, has fared better. He began with an atelier in Parliament Close but rose to be Queen's Limner in Scotland, an Office which carried a knighthood. (The Office still exists although the duties are obscure. The same may be said of the position of Queen's Sculptor in Ordinary in Scotland). Sir William's paintings are now out of fashion, but what titles some of them have! Who could resist 'Jewish Family in Poland making merry before a Wedding' or 'Murder of Archbishop Sharp' or – most irresistible of all – 'sale of Circassian Captives to a Turkish Bashaw'? He had a swarthy complexion and a profusion of black hair, and his day, one feels, may come again.

From Drummond Place walk along London Street and turn left. You emerge into **Bellevue Crescent**, and the contrast is not favourable to the grander streets and terraces left behind. Not that Bellevue Crescent is anything very wonderful in itself. It is a simple curve of three storey houses with some Ionic pilasters and rustication, with the church near the centre of the curve. But, because it faces the gardens which separate it from the main road, it is light and airy, and the slope of the ground, combined with the curve of the street, give a feeling of movement and liveliness which is conspicuously absent from Great King Street and the other streets nearby. **St Mary's** helps too. It was designed in 1824, not by a famous architect but by the City Superintendent of Works, Thomas Brown. There is an imposing six-columned Corinthian portico surmounted by a shallow pediment, and then a very tall and rather splendid steeple. The first stage of the steeple is square, with Doric columns at each corner and a clock, then there are two upper stages, circular, with more columns, and finally a slim dome and lantern. It is really rather uplifting, as good as St Andrews in George Street. The interior is also very well planned. It is U-shaped, with a deep U-plan gallery supported by fluted Corinthian columns, a compartmented ceiling with a large central rose, and a highly unusual drum-shaped pulpit entered from a double stair on either side. The stained glass, some of it belonging to the twentieth century, is also of a high standard. St Mary's is a spacious church (it was built to meet the needs of 'the rapidly expanding population of the New Town' and was planned to seat 1800) and inside and out it is a complete piece of architecture. That it was designed by a local architect/official is a tribute not only to his ability but also to the educated taste of the age.

From Bellevue Crescent it is best to retreat to the New Town, aiming for the Calton Hill and the east end of Princes Street. At the top of Broughton Street you encounter the fruits of demolition on a fairly large scale, i.e. modern town planning: a huge traffic roundabout (many acres) which pedestrians must work their way round as best they can. The site was described in 1783 as 'remarkably pleasant', and so it must have been. This unhappy spot used to be known as Picardy (the north side is still **Picardy Place**) because a colony of French silk-weavers settled here in 1730, encouraged to come and teach their skills to the backward Scots. They must have had a hard time of it (they are referred to as 'these poor people') for they endeavoured to improve their lot by cultivating mulberry trees on the slopes of Calton Hill, but without success; this was owing, as a later historian put it 'to the variable nature of the climate'. Recently, a few less exotic trees have appeared beside the desolation of traffic, along with a pensive figure in a deerstalker hat. Can this be Sherlock Holmes, so far from Baker Street? If it is, why is he here, looking a little lost? The explanation is that Conan Doyle (1859–1930) was born at No. 11 Picardy Place, now demolished, and studied medicine at Edinburgh University. How many cases his great detective solved north of the Border is a question for the experts.

The still-existing Picardy Place houses were built in the very early years of the nineteenth century. Avoiding, if you can, the awful spectacle of the back of the St James's Centre (it all seems to be back) which looks down on you, go west along York Place, leading to Queen Street.

York Place is not exactly a part of Craig's plan, but it was suggested in it. The buildings mostly date from just before and just after 1800, and the north side is one of the best unaltered stretches of Classical architecture in Edinburgh. None of the houses is of exceptional architectural interest, but No. 32 contained for some years Sir Henry Raeburn's studio and exhibition rooms, although he continued to live at Stockbridge. The façade has a Roman Doric doorpiece, and is admirably detailed. The interior is relatively plain, but the studio has multi-leaved shutters for the windows which give fairly close control over the amount of light admitted. The other noteworthy building in York Place is **St Paul's and St George's** episcopal church, at the east end. It was designed by Archibald Elliot with consummate and scholarly skill, and was completed in 1818. In 1892 it was a little enlarged and altered; one bay was added, and the galleries were removed from the aisles. But it remains a handsome church before that, and it says something about the novel splendour of the New Town that the congregation moved to this rather grand building from a church in the Cowgate. St Paul's has been likened to a first-rate late medieval English parish church. It is very lofty and spacious, with a timber ceiling and tall aisles and a clearstorey buttressed and pinnacled. The furnishings are almost all late nineteenth century, but when St Paul's (from the Cowgate) united with St George's (also in York Place, now a store and unrecognisable; it was, according to one critic, 'in every way hideous in conception and detail') the latter church supplied the eighteenth century white marble font, as well as the box pew that had been used by Sir Walter Scott and his family.

13

Dean Bridge, Dean Village and the Western New Town

BRIDGES AGAIN; EDINBURGH is held together by bridges. Having seen the North Bridge, the South Bridge, Waterloo Bridge, the George IV Bridge and Waverley Bridge, come now to the Dean Bridge, just a few hundred yards from the West End, along Queensferry Street. If you approach the Dean Bridge from this direction, you have the Moray development on your right, and what is sometimes called the Western New Town on your left.

The Western New Town is not the equal of Craig's New Town or the Moray development either in scale or in interest, but it contains two of Edinburgh's most conspicuous landmarks, has many elegant, well-planned middling streets, and is full of accountants and similar important people. It therefore requires to be noticed, and is worth a small detour.

This so-called New Town, unlike the others, was never a single coherent plan, but is a fusion of several plans, the first of them devised before 1810, and the last in 1872. These plans were implemented at varying speeds, and only one or two streets were completely built before 1840. It is therefore fair to describe this part of Edinburgh as Georgian-Victorian.

Leave the West End via Shandwick Place, which heads for Glasgow, and now for the airport as well, and almost immediately you encounter one of the above-mentioned conspicuous landmarks, the church of **St George's West**. As originally completed in 1869 this church was not nearly as prominent as it is now. It had, as it still has, Corinthian columns and pediments and a corner tower base, heavily rusticated, surmounted by a clock; but no tower. There was a plan for one, but it was not built. In 1879, however, Rowand Anderson, Edinburgh's most distinguished Victorian architect, produced the design of the 56-metre high Venetian campanile which competes with the

Caledonian Hotel for domination of this part of Edinburgh. It is a fine campanile, as it should be, for it closely resembles that of San Giorgio Maggiore; and it is a handsome addition to a not very interesting street. Inside the church there is a spectacular vaulted ceiling and much fine woodwork, and a general feeling of Gibbsian Baroque.

Once past the church, **Shandwick Place** opens out with crescents on each side, one divided and one in a single unbroken arc, each with its garden separating it from the main road – very civilized. These crescents, with their Ionic pilasters and well-designed balconies are pre-Victorian, and look it; so it is a little disconcerting to find Mr Gladstone, in bronze, standing in one of the gardens, surrounded by several admiring and deferential figures. Turn north from the divided crescent (Coates Crescent) into Walker Street, and you at once begin to see the style of this part of town. Walker street is wide and handsome, but William Street, which crosses it, is another example of the street built for artisans and small shopkeepers, and it retains its original character remarkably well; here and nearby is a locality of basement areas and boutiques and slightly 'left-bank' cafes, the shopfronts still much as they were in the 1820s.

But next comes **Melville Street**, the main axis of the main development, and dating from 1820. Like many other streets in the New Town, Melville Street has long Classical frontages and a vast amount of dignity. Wide enough to be a considerable car park, and therefore partly so used, it nevertheless retains its confident air, helped, perhaps, by its iron balconies and protective railings and long sequence of iron arched lamp-holders which covers the front steps that lead to the wide, solid doors. Heads of finance houses love Melville Street, for it has a great air of prosperous security. And at the junction with Walker Street it aspires to grandeur, for the end buildings are cut back to create a huge hexagonal space looked down upon by columns and pediments and tall wide windows, and graced in the centre by the statue of a viscount – the first Viscount Melville, as it happens, by Steell, on a stone pedestal. This is Georgian/Victorian urban building at its most decisive.

What gives additional interest and dignity to Melville Street is that it terminates with a cathedral. Not many streets do that. **St Mary's Cathedral** arose because two sisters, the Misses Walker, heirs of the chief developer of this part of Edinburgh, left their considerable fortune for the erection of a cathedral for the Scottish Episcopal Church, to be built on this site. Six architects submitted plans in 1872, and the trustees accepted a design by Sir George Gilbert Scott ('the great restorer') which, however, had only one spire; two years later they persuaded him to add two more. The foundation stone was laid in 1874 by the Duke of Buccleuch, the first service took place in 1879, and the building was finally completed in 1917.

Two opinions are possible about this large and late-in-the-day version of early ecclesiastical Gothic. For connoisseurs of the style, St Mary's is a must. Scott was a scholarly as well as an able architect, and the details of his cathedral are genuinely Gothic. Thus the experts tell us that the western door is a variant of that at Holyrood, that the three gablets above it are to be seen in Elgin Cathedral, that the rose window in the south transept is a reminiscence of Lincoln, the wheel window in the north transept a reminiscence of Chartres, and so on. Also, the central tower (275 feet high) is no ordinary affair, with its flying buttresses, octagonal belfry, and lucarned spire; it and the two west towers make one of the finest features of the Edinburgh skyline; the *tout ensemble*, seen from Princes Street, is a not inadequate response to the Calton Hill at the other end. Inside, the rib-vaulted nave, with its long-drawn aisles and interlacing arches, is grand and impressive, in the style of the twelfth century. Clustered columns rise to stiff-leaf capitals, there is much elaboration in the clearstorey, and the lancet windows show to good effect. That is one view. But for the rest of us, St Mary's may tend to bring to mind the words of Dr Johnson: worth seeing, but not worth *going* to see. It is, of course, a nineteenth century structure pretending to belong to the Middle Ages, and that makes some people uncomfortable; almost everything, one feels, is a studied imitation, not genuine. Then, perhaps, the building is an unfortunate size, too large to be intimate and too small to be grand; the central tower is a good height, but the whole church is no longer than the tower is high. And finally, the interior is dismally dark in spite of all the windows; one has to take it on trust that somewhere overhead there is a timber tunnel-roof. So a visit may prove to be disappointing. In the grounds, however, there stands a small two-storey L-plan house built in 1615. It was enlarged in the eighteenth century and altered in the nineteenth, acquiring a number of odds and ends retrieved from the Cowgate – demolitions were frequent in those days – and it is now the cathedral's Music School. The cathedral towers over the old house, but the latter is not to be looked down upon, seemingly conscious of superior antiquity.

The Western New Town spreads west and north from here by tall wide streets and magisterial crescents, but it is best now to make your way to Queensferry Street. This is the modern road to the Forth

Bridge and the north. The Water of Leith flows here, in a deep ravine, and until a high-level bridge was built this was where the expansion of Edinburgh had to stop.

Private enterprise spanned the river. The owner of the ground on the far side – he was Lord Provost at the time – came to an agreement with the owners of more ground farther out, and Thomas Telford was called in. Telford was dubbed by Southey 'the Colossus of Roads,' but he was also a colossus of bridges and canals. The **Dean Bridge** (1832) is one of his finest achievements; four arches spanning a distance of just over 400 feet carry the road 100 feet above the river bed. Slim piers attached to the main ones support flatter arches which carry the footpaths, an ingenious arrangement which gives the bridge lightness and style, and helps to make it so unlike the dreary utilitarian affairs that are produced nowadays.

Telford's bridge at once superseded the old Dean Bridge, a narrow single-arch stone bridge a hundred yards upstream, which had stood for perhaps a century. Inevitably, the old bridge and the old Dean Village around it, almost out of sight, began to be forgotten. Both were out of the way of progress; and so they were preserved, gradually decaying, for about a hundred and fifty years. Now they are restored and revived, a surprising little enclave, rural and remote, not unfashionable, almost in the centre of Edinburgh.

To see the **Dean Village** it is best to begin on Telford's Dean Bridge. Looking over the west parapet, you at once appreciate how much it *is* a village, and not an ordinary one; the houses cheek by jowl and not a straight street anywhere; oddly shaped and larger buildings dotted here and there; grey slate roofs and red tiled roofs falling down the steep slope and rising up the other side; the river flowing through, wide on a rocky bed; all surrounded and sheltered from the rest of the world by as many trees as, gathered close together, would make a fair-sized wood. You see, too, into the well-looked-after private gardens (hard work on these steep slopes), and you have a long view of the backdrop of trees that stretches up the river. No houses are to be seen immediately beyond the village, but a couple of towers and a church spire peep mysteriously over the horizon.

At the city end of the bridge, before you descend to the village, stands a very strange building. It was a tavern once, perhaps as early as 1700, and it no doubt served the inhabitants below. But in the 1890s it was expanded into a Scottish baronial house, and given a slightly unconvincing air of dignified antiquity by the incorporation into it of two sculptured stones brought up from the village, one dated 1619. This odd house is bigger than it looks, for although only two storeys show above the bridge there are three lower down, clinging to the precipice. Bell's Brae descends from this house, an iron handrail helpfully provided all the way down. (The village itself was once known as Bell's Mills, from the name of the owner of the flour mills by the water). Nothing remarkable to begin with, except the ever-rising Dean Bridge overhead, but at the foot of the brae stands a four-storey block built in 1675 as a granary for the Baxters' (i.e. bakers) Incorporation. It has two rectangular stair turrets with carved door-ways, and an inscription which reads

> *God bless the Baxters of Edin*
> *brugh who built this hous 1675.*

A panel over one door shows a wheatsheaf, cherubs' heads, two crossed shovels (used for thrusting loaves into the oven), a pie, three cakes, and a pair of scales. The building was converted some years ago into flats. You have now almost reached the bridge, and at this point you suddenly realise that the sound of traffic has blessedly disappeared and has been replaced by the sound of running water; it is pouring over a broad weir just below the bridge. Cars and buses pass overhead, but they belong to a different world.

Before crossing the old bridge, squeeze along Hawthornbank Lane on the south bank, past an eighteenth century L-plan house at the corner and some old cottages decently modernised, and look across the river. This is the best view of Well Court, another of Edinburgh's astonishing buildings. If it belongs anywhere, it might just possibly belong to the Bavaria of Ludvig II, or more likely to Hollywood, except that it is too substantial, too real for the latter. It was put up in the 1880s, paid for by the same philanthropist who paid for the National Portrait Gallery. Partly he aimed to provide housing, partly he wished to have something unusual to look at from his house in the Western New Town, high above the village, and partly he saw it as a means of helping the villagers, who were falling on hard times as the mills closed down, one after the other. Built entirely of red sandstone, with red tiled roofs, Well Court is madly picturesque. It has very steep high roofs, crow-stepped gables, tall chimneys, corner oriels, and a five-storey clock-tower topped by an ornamental spire which closely resembles the original (1671) spire of the Tron Church. It is a large building, full of surprising angles and openings and projections, and all seems to be fantastic disorder. You cannot quite make it out. Yet in its own way it is harmonious. And the last surprise in store is that it is rationally organised, all arranged round a good-sized courtyard.

After Well Court, the Hawthorn Buildings behind you (more red roofs) seem tame. Half-timbered from half way up, they were built in 1895 and fit into this eccentric village not badly. Beyond them is an iron footbridge across the river, and beyond that is new housing, of the usual modern artistically impoverished character. Better go back to the old bridge, and listen once more to the water splashing over the weir, and take a look at one of the very few mill buildings to survive, **West Mill**, just over the bridge, built in 1805. It is a very large building, two ranges together, four storeys high to the road and five storeys over the twin sluice arches to the Water of Leith. There was a mill here in the sixteenth century, but the present building dates from 1805, when the Baxters' Incorporation built or rebuilt it. It ceased to exist as a mill in 1891, when – how times do not change! – the city became concerned about pollution in the river. For years it lay neglected, like much else in the village, until it was converted into flats in the 1970s.

From the bridge Dean Path climbs up the west slope. At the foot there is the late nineteenth century Gothic school, not very interesting and a school no longer, and a number of small houses, some of them dating back to the eighteenth century, but altered. More houses of a like kind rise beyond them, only on the river side of the road, and then give up, to be succeeded by a wall. An opening in the wall announces 'Water of Leith Walkway', and if the ground is dry, try it. You are on a steep, thickly wooded bank, so thickly wooded that the river, and the village, and the whole city of Edinburgh are nowhere to be seen. It is a world entirely of leaves and tree trunks and branches, filled with the sound of running water somewhere below, and perhaps a few squirrels are scampering about. There are steps, of a kind, and a handrail for the zig-zag path that will take you back to the village, if you are sufficiently agile and adventurous to attempt it. It should be attempted, for one of the great attractions of the Dean Village is its seeming rural isolation, and here is a walk through the woods that could hardly be improved upon if you were in the depths of the country.

If the Walkway proves to be too steep or too wet or both, best return down Dean Path. Higher up, the tower of Dean Parish Church (1903) looks down on you, and before you know it you are on Queensferry Road, full of speeding vehicles. That is the modern way to Fife and the north, but where you are, on Dean Path, is the old way. Those who had time and wanted to play safe could go due west out of Edinburgh and cross the Forth at Stirling; but the shortest way was via the Dean to Queensferry, and risk an hour or two's voyage to Fife. The voyage could be delayed or even disastrous; and sometimes it was difficult enough to get beyond the Dean Village. In 1764 the *Edinburgh Advertiser* reported as follows:

> *On Thursday night the high wall at Bells Brae, near the Water of Leith Bridge, fell down, by which accident the footpath and part of the turnpike road are carried away, which makes it hazardous for carriages. This notice may be of use to those who have occasion to pass that road.*

Such was travelling in the eighteenth century, before the days of motorway repairs. Small wonder that many travellers (but not Boswell and Johnson) chose the route through Stirling.

Re-cross the bridge and turn left into **Miller Row**. The name tells all; this side of the river was once lined with mills – Marr's Mill, Lindsay's Mill and many others. Their operations came to an end in the later days of Queen Victoria; they had certainly been going on during the reign of David I, who died in 1153. There was also once a blacksmith's forge – the blacksmith found himself in trouble in 1792 for making pikes for revolutionaries – as well as a farmhouse and steading, a tannery (which can't have been pleasant for the neighbours), and a public house called 'speed the Plow', all gone. But do not suppose that the village is now merely a dormitory for Edinburgh, silent and deserted from nine till five. Not at all; it was discovered several years ago by the architects, who inhabit it largely.

Miller Row is the start of the walk along the Water of Leith to Stockbridge, and it is a walk well worth taking. It begins with a curiosity, a squash court sited just below the Dean Bridge, crenellated and with a pepper-pot tower; probably the only squash court with so much style in the world. The wonder of this is a little spoiled by the fact that it is a squash court no longer and has become an industrial establishment; but even as an industrial establishment it is a minor marvel. Once past the Dean Bridge, which towers overhead, the path winds along beside the water, flowing over a stoney bed. Again it is a woodland walk, but quite different from the one west of the village, for it is smooth and level, with railings on each side. This was clearly made for ladies with long skirts and parasols, and gentlemen in top hats.

Wild nature is under control, so much so that here and there lawns and shrubs reach down to the path from the remoter heights above; and through the trees the enormous arched retaining walls of Ainslie Place and Moray Place can be seen, looking like the discrete ramparts of a half-concealed city; for these are the pleasure grounds of the Earl of Moray. One feels privileged to be so close. After a few minutes walk, an odd little windowless structure appears, dated 1810, perched on the bank. This is St George's Well, little regarded. But a hundred yards further on a genuine temple appears (how many temples are there in Edinburgh?), an elegant structure calculated to re-locate this sylvan scene in ancient Greece, or at least in eighteenth century Britain.

And so, in a way, it does. This is **St Bernard's Well**, built in 1789. It celebrates the presence of a mineral spring which was declared in 1760 'to be equal in quality to any of the most famous in Britain' and which soon became so famous as to set up a pressure of visitors resembling the annual stampede to the Edinburgh Festival today:

> *As many people have got benefit from using of the water of St Bernard's Well, there has been such demand for lodgings this season that there is not so much as one room to be had either at the Water of Leith or its neighbourhood.*

Among the patrons was Lord Gardenstone (he had been taken prisoner by Charles's forces during the '45, and was later a man who 'increased the mirth of the company') and he was so well pleased with his visits that he erected this temple to advertise his appreciation of the 'sulphurous waters', and no doubt to demonstrate his good taste as well. It consists of ten Doric columns on a solid circular base, surmounted by a carefully carved entablature, and beneath the dome a statue of Hygeia. This is the second statue to occupy the temple. During thirty years the first statue remained 'untouched by the hand of mischief'; but manners and morals changed, the statue was made of poor stuff, and in the 1870s it was reported to be 'so battered by stones as to be a perfect wreck'. So another was carved in 1888, the building renovated, a terrace added, and stability restored.

Soon after the temple – only five minutes from the Dean Bridge – the walk ends at St Bernard's Bridge (1824). This is a small bridge, one arch over the Water of Leith and a smaller arch over the land, and in itself it is quite simple. But a hundred years ago two flights of steps were skilfully added, one facing north and one south, leading up from the riverbank to the road, and they make the whole structure look a little puzzling, and rather fun. Which way to go? Either flight of steps will do, and you are in Stockbridge.

14

Stockbridge and the Botanic Gardens

A HUNDRED YEARS AGO Stockbridge was described as 'a curious mixture of grandeur and romance, with something of classic beauty, and, in more than one quarter, houses of rather a mean and humble character'. To a large extent this is still the picture, although the numerous straw-thatched cottages which once stood round Virgins' Square (so-called because the inhabitants were mostly washerwomen; there seems to be a probable non sequitur here) have all gone, and so, at the opposite extreme, has the great house where Raeburn died and which was the centre of the whole Stockbridge estate. But Stockbridge retains its variety. There are Georgian houses and Victorian tenements, properties with delightful outlooks and properties without any, shops a-plenty, pubs and small restaurants, and always the river, the Water of Leith. Stockbridge is an independent place ('why go to town? You can get it in Stockbridge'). Above all, it is up and coming.

The development of this part of town was largely due to Raeburn. He was born in the village in 1756, in a little slated cottage that stood by the side of the mill-lade. During his childhood luck was against him, for before he was ten years old he found himself an orphan, a penniless inmate of George Heriot's School. But his rise was meteoric. At the age of sixteen he was apprenticed to a goldsmith in Parliament Close; at twenty two he married a wealthy widow, who brought him her estate in Stockbridge; and by the time he was twenty eight he was the best-known painter in Scotland. Having added over the years to his property, he began in 1813 to develop it as a new housing area on the outskirts of Edinburgh.

If you arrive in Stockbridge from the Dean Village you are on St Bernard's Bridge; if you come down from Royal Circus you reach the Stock Bridge itself (1773, since altered), which is only a couple of hundred yards further downstream. In either case, cross the bridge to the north side of the Water of Leith and turn left. It was on this north side of the river that development began, and Dean Terrace, where you are standing, was one of the earliest streets to be built.

The houses in **Dean Terrace** (once called Mineral Street, because of the healing well on the opposite side of the river) are modest, simple two-storey houses with iron balconies. They look over their small front gardens to the trees on the river bank, and to the mansions of the Moray estate raised up beyond the trees. Modest housing could not look more attractive, nor be more pleasantly set. But there is better to come. Dean Terrace becomes Upper Dean Terrace and turns right into **Ann Street**, and Ann Street is the jewel in the Stockbridge crown. It is not a long nor a wide street, and it is built on both sides. But when you enter it the houses are not conspicuous because they are set back behind fairly deep, well-planted gardens; lilacs and laburnums overhang the pavement. Then, as you walk along, you realise that behind the gardens each side of the street is a palace front. There are pedimented centrepieces with giant Ionic pilasters, three storeys; then two storey houses set back a little; then a row of smaller houses set back once again, followed by the end houses stepped forward. It is all very Classical, with fluted columns here and there, iron balconies, tall windows, fanlights, and very elegant – one feels very *special* – lamp standards. The detail is excellent. But the appeal of Ann Street lies not in the detail but in the overall effect. Ann Street is not so much a street as a composition, Classical architecture in a garden setting. Wisteria climbs up to the balconies, and a Gloire de Dijon rose half hides a column.

This stylish street was built soon after the battle of Waterloo. It was thought at the time to be 'quite out of town', far removed from the fashionable parts of Edinburgh. But its secluded character seems soon to have made it popular with writers and artists. John Wilson, who was professor of philosophy in the University and who wrote for the once famous *Blackwood's Magazine* (as Christopher North) lived here, and de Quincey made a lengthy stay in 1829. De Quincey's style of living led to unusual social arrangements which were described by Wilson's daughter:

> *An ounce of laudanum* per diem *prostrated animal life in the early part of the day. It was no infrequent sight to find him in his room lying upon the rug in front of the fire, his head resting upon a book, with his arms crossed over his breast, in profound slumber. For several hours he would lie in this state, till the torpor passed away. The time when he was most*

brilliant was generally towards the early morning hours;
more than once, in order to show him off, my father arranged
his supper parties, so that, sitting till three or four in the
morning, he brought Mr de Quincey to that point at which, in
charm and power of conversation, he was so truly wonderful.

He suffered at this time, we are also told, from perpetual dyspepsia (which is not surprising) and had to have a daily audience with the cook.

Descend to the north end of Ann Street (being on the gentle curve of a hill it is higher in the middle than at either end, which adds significantly to its slight mystery and charm), and turn down Dean Park Crescent, which leads straight into **St Bernard's Crescent**. This double crescent is almost the opposite of Ann Street, for it is bold and grand; according to a nineteenth century author it is 'adorned with the grandest Grecian Doric pillars that are to be found in any edifice not a public one'. Certainly the north side (the south side was completed later, and not done so well) is an imposing piece of architecture, three storeys in the centre with giant columns, two storeys stretching away on each side with smaller columns supporting a continuous first floor balcony. No hiding behind foliage for St Bernard's Crescent; it announces itself with assurance, almost, perhaps, a little loudly. Two streets open off it to the south, parallel with Ann Street, which they were once intended to resemble. But the front gardens were never made and the architecture is less ambitious, so they seem more like an extension of the New Town, well proportioned and correct; one of them, Danube Street, has even been called 'the most attractive of Edinburgh's Neo-Greek streets'. (Raeburn's house, demolished in 1826, stood near here). Just beyond Danube Street the pair of crescents comes to a sudden and sad end in Leslie Place, confined and not a little grim. But go down it, and you are in the very heart of Stockbridge.

Not that there is a great deal to see in this lively heart, except its liveliness. On your right is the bridge and a strange bank with balustrades and a corbelled-out clock tower (1900), and on your left is all that remains of an 1840s church, re-erected here in the 1860s and demolished, all but the tower, in 1980; what you now see is housing. Beyond the church is the start of Raeburn Place, built soon after 1814 as a mix of tenements and villas. It is now Stockbridge's main shopping street, and shops have all but obliterated what was originally built, although a number of attractive small houses remain. There is some history, too. Sir James Simpson (*see* p. 124), when he was a medical student in the 1820s, and was in his own words 'very very young and very solitary, very poor and almost friendless,' lodged on the top floor of No. 1; and further west, where Raeburn Place has become Comely Bank, is the house to which Carlyle and Jane Welsh came in 1825 after their marriage, and in which they lived for over a year; so it was here, as Carlyle put it, that his 'first experience in the difficulties of housekeeping began' – difficulties, one may add, which he did little to diminish.

Before leaving Stockbridge to go farther north to the Royal Botanic Gardens and Fettes College, it is necessary to decide about antiques. Do you like poking about in antique shops? If you do, a great opportunity awaits you on the other side of the Water of Leith. Cross the bridge, go fifty yards, and turn left into St Stephen Street. St Stephen Street, also built in the 1820s, is nothing much to look at. Its most remarkable feature is the entry to Stockbridge Market, an arched gateway which once led to stalls selling meat and poultry, fish and vegetables, in the manner of a country town; but it was never a great success, and closed in 1906. The buildings in the street, however, remain. They were designed in the early 1820s as shops with housing above, and so they are still. Most of them have two storeys of accommodation above pilastered shop windows, and below street level there are more shops, workshops or cafes. In some cases stone steps go up to the upper shops and down to the basements; a plentiful supply of iron railings keeps the shoppers safe. Whatever the plan, the maximum number of little shops is provided per given length of pavement. The whole arrangement is as antique as the antiques themselves – much more so in most cases – and probably makes the goods for sale seem, by association, older than they are. To the connoisseur from the salerooms of London or New York St Stephen Street may not make much appeal. But to the middlebrow or occasional collector it is as a sunken Spanish galleon to an underwater archaeologist; there is no saying what may be found, in one hold or another. A tile from the Persia of Shah Abbas; a wine glass that might have glinted in the firelight of the '45; a Spode dish, a Victorian table, a pair of bagpipes in need of repair – it is a very mixed cargo, but the visitor with time to spare and an eye for these things is almost sure to be tempted. And in any case he or she is in Edinburgh as it used to be, little changed except for the cars in the street.

These, then, are the highlights of Stockbridge. Time now to press on to 'the Botanics' – as the Royal Botanic Garden is usually called –

following, for a short distance, the Water of Leith. At the start of Raeburn Place find St Bernard's Row (not particularly inviting) and after a few yards fork left into Arboretum Avenue which runs along the side of the water. From here you have a good view of an interesting group of houses on the other bank, **the Colonies**. This small development consists of eleven parallel terraces laid out in 1861 by an organisation called the Edinburgh Co-operative Building Association. Home ownership for respectable artisans – that was the idea; so they were kept simple. The design, however, is ingenious, for each terrace consists of two storeys, one 'cottage' on the ground floor and one above; the ground floor is entered from one side of the building, and the upper cottage by means of outside stairs on the opposite side. Coupled with front gardens on either side and the original iron clothes poles, this arrangement looks decidedly attractive. And there are some imaginative touches – the tools of various trades carved on the keystones of the ground-floor windows, and obelisk piers at the entries to the intermediate streets. How different all this is from a typical twentieth century housing development! No wonder that the Colonies were an immediate success, or that similar schemes were later carried out in other parts of the town. No wonder, either, that these smart-looking little dwellings with their unpretentious charm have been 'gentrified' (to use the popular, emotion-laden word) for better or for worse, and have thus played their part in helping Stockbridge to regain its place in the sun.

Arboretum Avenue now rises from the river level, swings left and becomes Arboretum Road, running straight ahead with Inverleith Park on one side and the Botanic Garden on the other. There is much well-heeled Victorian housing in this neighbourhood, in a variety of styles. Renaissance, Jacobean, Georgian, baronial, even François I – no style came amiss to the versatile Victorian architect. The common characteristic is an air of opulence, enhanced by the fact that the nearby areas are mostly parks and playing fields. Many of these houses have the good fortune to look over the Garden, and some of them also look south over the whole New Town to the ridge of the Old Town more than a mile away.

The **Royal Botanic Garden** is one the glories of Edinburgh, for it both contains a superb collection of plants and is one of the most agreeable places in the kingdom in which to wander. It is an old institution, almost exactly as old as Kew (1759), and is recognised as one of the great botanic gardens of the world. Its antecedent history dates back to 1661, when Sir Robert Sibbald, one of the founders of the

Stockbridge and the Botanic Gardens

Royal College of Physicians of Edinburgh and the University's first Professor of Medicine, started the Physic Garden on a small piece of ground near Holyrood, growing medicinal herbs. A few years later this garden was moved to a site now obliterated by Waverley Station (in the station a plaque on the south side of the Booking Office marks the spot), and in 1766 to Leith Walk. It already attracted the attention of visitors, and was commented on as follows in 1771:

> *At a small walk's distance from Calton Hill, lies the new botanic garden, consisting of five acres of ground; a greenhouse fifty feet long: two temperate rooms, each twelve feet, and two stoves, each twenty-eight: the ground rises to the north, and defends the plants from the cold winds: the soil a light sand, with a black earth on the surface. It is finely stocked with plants ... and was founded by the munificence of his present Majesty, who granted fifteen hundred pounds for that purpose.*

The garden was moved to its present site in the 1820s (in effect, into the country), without, it is said, 'eventual injury to a single plant'. Since this final move the garden has been successively enlarged, and now extends to over eighty acres.

To an amateur gardener, the outstanding features of the Garden are its collections of heaths and rhododendrons. The heaths have something to show all the year round; the rhododendrons are at their most splendid from April until June, from small rock plants to magnificent tree rhododendrons, protected from the winds by banks of pine and other conifers. But there is something for everyone: a herbaceous border almost two hundred yards long, backed by a twenty foot high beech hedge; an extensive rock garden to climb into and over (the gentians are a lovely sight in September); a pool with ducks and water lilies. Every feature pleases. And what adds so much to the quality of this garden is the rolling, up and down terrain. You can walk round almost on the level; but from the highest walk you have one of the best views of the city's skyline, and look down on many of the Garden's finest trees. Indulge in a little gentle mountaineering, and understand why Kew is left far behind.

The buildings are interesting, too. In the centre of the Garden stands **Inverleith House**, a Georgian country house built in 1774, facing south over the city (what a view!) but with the entrance, so to speak, at the back. The porch is an addition, and projects from the large bowed stair-tower, which overlooks the approach drive and a small round pool where there used to stand the bronze figure of a modern nymph, now replaced, sad to say, by a rather strange, evil-looking bird. This house used to be the residence of the Curator, until, so it is said, a new appointee declared that he would not live in a house that had no garden. Thus the house became, for a time, the Gallery of Modern Art, and gathered to it several Henry Moores and Barbara Hepworths. For a few years the combination of the skyline, the trees, the eighteenth century house and the twentieth century statuary (set out on the south lawn) was superb. But the art collection grew too big and was carried off to Belford Road, statues and all, and now the house, like many other fine old buildings, is used for exhibitions. No change of use is ever likely to trouble the **Large Palm House** and the new glass houses (1967). The former was completed in 1858 and is adjacent to the Old Palm Stove (i.e. House) of 1834. The solid walling of the Palm House is relieved with Roman Doric pilasters, and the arch-headed windows have very fine Georgian-style glazing bars. Inside, cast-iron columns support the second tier of glazing. In the Old Palm House there are two cast-iron spiral staircases, the balusters with rose motifs. The new glasshouses are entirely different, an admirable exercise in modern technology. Their external tubular steel frame leans outwards and holds the glazed frame by means of tension cables. This design permits a very wide span, and an elevated internal walkway enables the visitor to stroll along at tree-top level and survey the entire scene. Just north of the glasshouses a secluded patio provides an ideal site for the Linnaeus Monument. This was commissioned by Professor John Hope, who for a quarter of a century taught Materia Medica in the University in summer and Botany in the winter. Linnaeus was the first systematic botanist, the first master of genera and species, orders and sub-kingdoms; and Hope was one of the first to follow his lead. The design is by Robert Adam and the monument was dedicated in 1779, the year after Linnaeus's death. It takes the form of a decorated urn on a pedestal with an inset marble panel inscribed 'Linnaeo Posuit J.Hope 1779'.

From the Botanics it is not far to the Firth of Forth. But Edinburgh has not made a great deal of its estuarine setting hereabouts, so instead of going north go west along Inverleith Place (or, directly from the Garden gates, go straight through Inverleith Park). Long before you reach it you will see **Fettes College**, another of Edinburgh's extraordinary buildings.

Stockbridge and the Botanic Gardens

William Fettes began business as a tea and wine merchant in the High Street, went into underwriting, became a contractor for military stores during the Napoleonic wars, was elected Lord Provost of Edinburgh, was knighted, and in 1800 retired at the age of fifty to live in Charlotte Square. He was now the possessor of several estates in Scotland, and when he died in 1836 he left most of his considerable fortune to the creation of a school in the grounds of Comely Bank, which was one of his properties.

It is almost as hard to find words to describe Fettes College as it is to find words to describe the Scott Monument; to say that it 'forms a conspicuous object from almost every point of view' is to say the least of it. Built between 1863 and 1870, it was designed by David Bryce and has been described as an exceptionally florid example of Scottish baronial; alternatively, it may be seen as a slightly – but only slightly – severer version of Chambord or Chenonceaux. It is certainly large, confident and complicated, and it makes an outstanding contribution to Edinburgh's skyline. The frontal approach is best; a wide stairway ascends the terrace to the towering, monumental entrance. A very high arch over the doorway is carried up through four storeys, and after two more storeys a very steep roof, surrounded by four turrets, leads up to a slender Gothic spire which in its turn sets off for the sky. The wings on each side of the central tower are three storeys plus Gothic dormers, and arcaded loggias (perhaps a recollection of Blois) stretch out at ground level. The pavilions project boldly, with crowstepped gables and oriel windows and two turrets each; these, like the turrets on the central tower, are corbelled out. To complete the effect, each end of the front terminates in a large tower with a steep ornamented roof, and massive ornamental chimneys punctuate the long roofline. Scottish baronial and French Gothic are a heady combination. And, because this is an H-plan building, additional turrets and chimneys rise mysteriously behind.

Fettes College has fairly been described as an exhilarating composition. It has height and breadth and endless diversity of detail; there are pinnacles and buttresses, hood-moulds on windows and Gothic doors, and a seemingly endless supply of griffins contending in unexpected places. It is studiously romantic. Yet there is a curious feature. For all its extravagance of ornament, it is most carefully symmetrical. One wing is the mirror-image of the other wing. Fettes does not throw symmetry to the winds like Villandry or Blois, but maintains a strict balance like a pair of scales. Yet this posture is not un-chateau-like, for Chambord, which Fettes a little resembles, is almost exactly symmetrical, like many other French chateaux.

Inside, the lay-out is various and commodious. There is an imperial stair with Gothic ironwork leading to a spacious landing; wide corridors and outsize classrooms; and a fine chapel, ornamented externally with statues on corbels and in canopied niches, and well worth entering (if that can be arranged) to see the hammerbeam roof.

Edinburgh has four schools of most striking appearance, each very different from the others: Heriot's (Jacobean), Royal High (Greek Doric), Daniel Stewart's (Victorian Jacobean) and Fettes (French Gothic). They are all splendid, but old. Some day, one hopes, new ones in a new style will be built, as interesting as their predecessors, planned spaces of lightness and elegance, flexible designs of simple shapes and precise forms, not palaces of stone and learning admirable as these are, but pavilions of exploration for another century.

15

Outer Edinburgh: West

B EYOND THE DEAN Village several items of interest can be composed into a little tour, starting with the **Scottish National Gallery of Modern Art**. The Gallery is pleasantly, albeit and paradoxically, accommodated in a Doric temple that is getting on for two hundred years old. The best approach from the West End is via Queensferry Street and fork left down Belford Road just before the Dean Bridge. Once over the Water of Leith the road turns and rises, and there on your left is the Gallery, in its own park with its own parking spaces behind, and screened by handsome trees. Statues diversify the landscape, including two reclining figures by Henry Moore.

Built as a school 'for the Maintenance and Education of Destitute Children', it was completed in 1828. The architect was William Burn, who designed the Edinburgh Academy (a much less costly building) at almost exactly the same time. Victorian critics called it 'a very plain design' and they were right; but it is handsome; a long run of two storeys with rectangular windows, and a very large strongly projecting six-column central portico. Given the elements of the design, it would not be easy to find fault with the proportions. Internally, there are long central corridors, flagged with dark stone, a main hall with a compartmented ceiling to the rear, and a new spacious stair. The upstairs rooms were originally dormitories. As few changes as possible were made when the building was converted, yet it seems remarkably well adapted to its new use. The collection of modern art was moved here from Inverleith House in the Royal Botanic Gardens (*see* p. 200) in 1984. There is an excellent cafe in the basement.

Although the collection was not begun until 1960, strenuous efforts were made to build it up reasonably quickly, with the result that good examples of twentieth century art from several countries were acquired before rising prices made additional purchases extremely difficult. The Gallery has also benefitted from numerous gifts, including a 'blue period' Picasso, a 'Head' by Rouault, and Matisse's 'the Painting Lesson' (1919).

The contents of the Gallery have a wide appeal, for they come from many countries and cover many decades. The Trustees have interpreted modern art to mean, roughly speaking, twentieth century art, and there are therefore numerous canvases that were painted long before 1960; there are, for example, pictures by Sickert and Orpen, by Vuillard and Bonnard; and these are on show alongside works done in the 1980s. Secondly, the collection is by no means insular. Indeed, the Gallery claims that its greatest strength is in German Expressionism, Surrealism and 'French art generally'. Leger is especially well represented by a number of late works and also by 'Woman and Still Life' (1921), a marvellous composition of soft colours in a marvellous golden frame. Another memorable picture is Picabia's 'Fille née sans mère' (not what you would expect), and in yet another style altogether is 'Der erste tag' (1989) by the German artist Bernard Schultze, a large diptych strongly reminiscent of the apocalyptic landscapes of Altdorfer, painted in the early sixteenth century. Many English artists are represented, including Lucien Freud, Barbara Hepworth, and Paul Nash, whose 'Landscape of the Vernal Equinox No 3' (1944) is so much in the English landscape tradition. Modern Scottish art is not forgotten, but some may think that it is stronger here in quantity than quality. There are good examples of the Scottish Colourists – notably a cheerful Peploe ('Roses') and a strong Cadell ('Lady in Black') – and a very fine and assured Ann Redpath ('In Corsica'); but other distinguished Scottish artists such as William McTaggart and Charles Rennie Macintosh are either poorly represented or are not here at all. In general, however, this is a collection worth seeing, wide enough in scope and good enough in quality to enable you to have an opinion about where 'modern art' is going – if, indeed, there is such a thing as 'modern art', and if it is going anywhere.

Returning to Belford Road down the tree-lined avenue, the highly unusual towers of the **Dean Gallery** (1833) are visible on the other side of the road. This building began as the Dean Orphanage, a foundation which was created in 1733 and which was originally located near Leith Street. The Belford Road site is a fine one, high above the Water of Leith, and the building stands out boldly amid the lofty trees that surround it. It is by Thomas Hamilton, architect of the grandly Classical Royal High School on Calton Hill; but for the Orphanage he produced an unusual, eclectic design. It is of two storeys, with a four-column Tuscan portico, pedimented; above the pediment there is a substantial attic, which is surmounted by – of all things – the clock that used to be on the Netherbow Port (*see* p. 51). The prominent pavilions at each end of the main block have pairs of arched windows at the upper floor level. Dominating everything, two idiosyncratic quadrangular towers rise from the rear of the building. The lower stage of each is solid, but above the scrolls and tall urns there rise in each case four octagonal columns, united by arches. What could be more fanciful, one wonders; here is an architect given a free hand, amusing himself by spending his client's money on ornamental frivolities. But no. The octagonal columns are chimneys, and the spaces that they surround are glazed, and light the twin stair-cases. How ingenious the Victorians were! The Dean Gallery is commonly described as Baroque, and the bulky attic with its clock and the two open-work towers are certainly reminiscent of Vanbrugh. But imagine these away, and behold! the lower and plainer building that remains is almost purely Classical, not so very different from the Gallery of Modern Art across the road. Inside, the square stair-halls are the most noticeable feature, for they are very high, and are made to seem higher still by narrowing towards the top.

The task of converting Hamilton's school into an art gallery began soon after the Edinburgh-born sculptor Sir Eduardo Paolozzi offered to donate a substantial body of his work to the National Galleries of Scotland. The conversion has been well done; doubtless the job was made easier by the large windows on both ground and upper floors, and by the twin stone staircases (their steps well worn) which make circulation easy. Besides works by Paolozzi, the Dean Gallery has an exceptionally fine collection of Dada and Surrealist art; there are works by Magritte, Miro, Delvaux, and Man Ray; also, there are three Picassos. And perhaps the coffee shop deserves a mention.

Another school building, in appearance still stranger than the Dean Gallery, is just to the north, beyond the crossroads and on the right: **Daniel Stewart's and Melville College** (originally just Daniel Stewart's), completed in 1853. It is best seen from Queensferry Road, where its commanding position and energetic style take full effect. It was described in Victorian times as 'a mixture of the latest domestic Gothic with something of the old castellated Scottish style;' more recently as 'blending the influence of George Heriot's and the Scots Renaissance with English Jacobean'. Significantly, the architect, David Rhind, produced three variants of the same basic plan: Italianate, Gothic, and what was built. It is an affair predominantly of towers, turrets, bartizans, arches, hood-moulds and bay windows. The fundamental design, hard to detect beneath and behind all the icing, is a U-plan; the central doorway, flanked by lodges, is part of an arcaded screen in front of the court. The two staircase towers have ogee lead roofs, and there is so much on the roof line that the substantial chimneys seem insignificant. It looks best from a distance; close to, the eye becomes tired, and credulity strained. But it is an interesting exercise in architecture. The progression from John Watson's through the Dean Gallery to Daniel Stewart's is an education in design. And there are two more schools to come.

So from Daniel Stewart's go west along Queensferry Road; there is a fine view of Fettes College to the north. In a little over half a mile you see the entrance to a Sainsbury supermarket on your right, built almost on the site of Craigleith Quarry. There is almost nothing old to see now, but at one time Craigleith was the largest quarry in Scotland, and it supplied the stone for several of Edinburgh's grandest buildings, for example, Old College, the north side of Charlotte Square, West Register House (St George's) and Parliament Square. After a few hundred yards turn left and go up Craigleith Crescent to Ravelston Dykes, turn right, and almost at once Ravelston Park is on your right. The Park contains two sharply contrasting buildings. One is Ravelston House (1791), not by Adam but in the late Adam manner, a Palladian villa with Venetian-windowed pavilions and a three-storey castellated bow which is a reminder of Culzean Castle in Ayrshire, one of Robert Adam's boldest designs, built between 1771 and 1792. Adjacent is **Mary Erskine School**, completed in 1967. Mary Erskine is a spread-out cubist design, very rectangular and uniformly white. The critics have never been quite sure about this building. 'Strong composition,' says one author; 'clean-cut geometric shapes,' says another. Then they pass on. Perhaps they are wise, for there is no understanding the school by looking at it. Where is the front door? or the hall? or the library? or the labs? And why is it all white? Must 'modern' buildings always be white? Are they white because Le Corbusier liked them that way ('all houses should be white by law')? or is it to claim kinship with the Parthenon? The pupils must know the answers to some of these questions, but the onlooker does not. By comparison with the three schools seen already, this one seems angular, puzzling and even disorderly.

You are now on the eastern slopes of **Corstorphine Hill**, a hill covered by trees, golf courses, two hospitals, acres and acres of anonymous suburbs and the Zoo. Reserving the Zoo for later, go back to

Queensferry Road and after about a mile turn left into Clermiston Road (signposted to the Zoo) as the route south over the hill. This has two advantages. First, the road climbs sufficiently high to afford some distant views, south to the Pentland Hills and west towards Glasgow. The prospects were extensive before the suburbs came, and they were one reason why Corstorphine appealed to wealthy families in the nineteenth century who wanted a country villa not too far from town. Some of these villas remain, solid and imposing in their own grounds. The second advantage of Clermiston Road is that if you want some exercise, and a change from urban scenery, there is a path to **Clermiston Tower** at the top of the hill. It is not much of a climb, but the path winds most pleasantly through the trees, oak and beech and pine, past outcrops of rock and stretches of bracken, the abode of blackbirds, tomtits and rooks. The Tower, built in 1871 to commemorate the centenary of the birth of Sir Walter Scott, is of no great interest, and the walk to it, if you start from the parking area near the Fox Covert Hotel, takes nearly twenty minutes; but take a short stroll if it suits you – this is a hill not to conquer but to enjoy.

Continue down to the Glasgow Road, turn right and about a mile further west you reach the Royal Scot Hotel and a highly confusing double roundabout. The hotel is best ignored, architecturally speaking – everyone agrees about that. But what of the roadhouse, or restaurant, on the west side of the roundabout? Here is a memento of the 1930s. Its metal windows, curves and sharp angles and emphatic horizontals proclaim the days of 'streamlining' in architecture, of Hollywood musicals and bright young things, of 'cocktails and laughter but what comes after?' There are better mementos of the 1930s than this, but now not many are left; and the **Maybury roadhouse** should not be passed over in silence, for it arouses strong passions. Is it to be classed as one of those 'offensive modernistic atrocities' so detested by dear old Sir Nicholas Pevsner, its interior in the words of another critic, 'a ghastly memorial to inter-war taste'? or is it an example of a genuine style, not without merit, a style that lived briefly, like a dragon-fly for a few weeks in summer? Surely it is worth seeing, and keeping, partly as a reminder of times past, and partly – in the words of a third critic – for its 'considerable vulgar flair'. It is designed with conviction, and that is more than can be said of many buildings. Moreover, the original interior fittings are still in place. Art Deco designers believed that every detail was important, from keyholes to decorative panels, so a building as complete as this one is especially valuable.

Now head for home, and something very different. Beyond the first big cross-roads, on the right and just off the main road, is **Corstorphine Church**, an exceptionally good example of a medieval Scots kirk. It looks solid and venerable (quite out of place in suburbia), and very Scots, and its plan is strange to the point of unintelligibility; it seems to consist of a number of separate items oddly stuck together. The explanation is that some time before his death in 1405 the king's hereditary forester, Sir Adam Forrester, built a chapel alongside the parish church. During the fifteenth century a chancel and a tower were added to the chapel, and in the middle of the seventeenth century a porch was added to the tower. At about the same time the parish church itself was pulled down, and replaced. In 1828 it was replaced again, and enlarged. The chapel was now part of the church – in fact, most of the nave of the present building was once the chapel, but it is not easy to see this because modern doors and windows have been inserted into the medieval structure, and because of the 1828 extensions on the north side of it. Yet the character of the building remains strongly medieval. This is chiefly due to the square tower with pinnacles at the corners, the stocky stone octagonal spire decorated with bands and lucarnes, and the slabbed roofs of the chancel, the nave, and the south-projecting chapel. The interior was much renovated a hundred years ago, but the work was well done. The three-light window of the south chapel is typically early fifteenth century, and the arched and recessed tombs are particularly good: Sir Adam Forrester, his feet on a complaisant dog; his son (d.1440) with his wife holding a book; and his grandson (d.1454), with angels and figures in cloaks the best of the three. There are other monuments, both within the church and in the churchyard. All is small-scale, a little pool of dignity and quietness, left behind by the retreating seas of the Middle Ages. The only neighbour that the old church might recognise is the sixteenth century dovecote in Dovecote Road, a flat-topped beehive design with over 1,000 pigeon holes, once an appurtenance of Corstorphine Castle, which has vanished without other trace.

Continue towards town and reach the **Zoo**, next door to the Post House Hotel (concrete, good view from). The lay-out of the zoo was begun in 1913 (Patrick Geddes had a hand in this too) but there had been an earlier zoo, at Canonmills. A nineteenth century guide book describes this earlier version as 'a small imitation of the old Vauxhall Gardens in London,' and it seems to have been an odd sort of zoo, for within it 'the storming of Lucknow and other such scenes of the Indian mutiny used to be nightly represented'. It proved a failure –

unfortunately or otherwise, as the same guide book cryptically remarks. The 1913 zoo (since extended) was planned on very up-to-date lines, for it was modelled on the Stellingen Zoo near Hamburg, where the animals were seen in surroundings that bore at least some relation to their natural habitat. The Zoo extends over 80 acres on the south slope of Corstorphine Hill, and the visitor can climb up above the trees and enjoy extensive views to Arthur's Seat and the Pentlands. There is thus room for a wide variety of birds and animals – pink flamingoes, brown bears, white sulphur-crested cockatoos, monkeys, penguins, elephants and a genuine Scottish wild cat. Most of them are in fairly spacious enclosures – the night-herons are even free-flying, and depart at dusk (weather permitting) to investigate a number of lochs in the vicinity. The big cats, however, seem sensibly confined, pacing up and down behind the wire. They are so muscular. They look at you so coldly, and – is it enviously? hungrily? who can tell? Somehow, one does not feel that they can enjoy captivity. Yet they are in splendid condition, as are the beautifully coloured parrots, not a feather out of place. No matter how well artists paint these birds and animals – and they are often painted very well indeed – one is still surprised to see how beautiful they look in real life. Parking is not difficult, and there is a cafe in the grounds.

From the Zoo to the West End it is a story of ever-increasing traffic, with not much visual relief. Rugby enthusiasts may respond to the nearness of the **Murrayfield Rugby Ground**, which is on the right, but cheerfulness is soon diminished by a singularly nasty railway bridge over the road, which no longer carries a railway. A few hundred yards further on, however, on the left side of the road, the last school of the day comes in sight, set back in its own spacious grounds behind long railings; **Donaldson's School**, by Playfair, built between 1842 and 1854. Originally for poor children, Donaldson's has concentrated for many years on working with the deaf, and has always been recognised as an admirable institution. In style it is far more genuinely Elizabethan than Daniel Stewart's, which is a hotch-potch by comparison. Limited, like the other two schools already noticed, to two floors, it forms a quadrangle, with four octagonal five-storey towers in the centre of the main façade, and four square towers of four storeys each at the corners. All have turret roofs. The central towers, which rise to over 100 feet, are derived, so the experts tell us, from Burghley House (begun 1552) near Stamford, and the sixteen corner towers are said to be derived from Audley End (begun 1603), near Cambridge. Tall windows and buttresses line the front and sides, and handsome bay windows are piled on top of one another on or between the towers. Chimneys punctuate the roofline, and a long balustraded terrace provides a foundation for this correct and grand composition. It was much admired by Queen Victoria in 1850, even before it was finished. The interior is plain, but the ceiling of the chapel must once have been painted, for in a letter Playfair likens it to 'a Baronial Hall fit to receive Henry VIII, Anna Bullen and Wolsey. Excuse your poor friend's vanity'. But in 1916 the chapel was damaged by a bomb dropped from a zeppelin. The painting on the ceiling did not survive, nor did any of the original stained glass windows.

We are now at the western edge of central Edinburgh, what is sometimes called the Western New Town, developed after 1825; St Mary's Cathedral (*see* p. 188) is in the heart of this area. **Haymarket Station** does not formally belong to it, being on the other side of the road, but it is worth a glance, or more, being one of the few remaining well-proportioned unaltered Classical railway station buildings in Britain. It went up in 1840, the terminus of the Edinburgh and Glasgow Railway. It is in no way ambitious, neither is it dull, and its modest four-column porch is nicely set off by the modest clock which projects from the shallow roof above. What is especially agreeable is that the station still works. Trains still go from here to Glasgow. And if you are seeing Edinburgh on foot and are feeling tired, there is better news still; go down the steps, catch a train for Waverley Station, and see the Castle Rock and Princes Street gardens from a new angle.

16

Outer Edinburgh: South

FROM THE WEST end of Princes Street **Lothian Road** leads south, up the slope from the Caledonian Hotel to Tollcross. Robert Louis Stevenson thought the world of it – 'the ever glorious Lothian Road,' he called it – but that was when he was far away, looking back on the escapades of his youth. It may once have been, or seemed to be, disreputable in a romantic sort of way; but there is nothing of that left now. At its mid-point it has recently grown a square, or what is called a square; Festival Square. It is an odd sort of square, open on one side to Lothian Road and on another to the Western Approach Road, which resembles an unattractive race-track that leads towards Glasgow. To have Festival Square (late twentieth century) and Charlotte Square (late eighteenth century) within a few hundred yards of one another invites comment, not favourable to modern planners. At the back of Festival Square the Sheraton Hotel is also likely to raise a few eyebrows, so obviously does it lack the right hand third of itself. The architect *must* have intended that pediment to be in the middle; and so he did; but it was one third of the hotel or the race-track, and the hotel lost. The square is an open space with greenery, and that is something.

North of the race-track and adjacent to the Caledonian Hotel there were until recently nine acres of waste-land where once had stood the Caledonian Railway Station and goods yard. Tansy and thistles grew well there. But in 1997 the Exchange, also known as The Financial and Conference Centre, took over. It was built 'to meet commercial needs' and clearly it intends to be noticed. The entrance is wide and high and is marked by towers surmounted by copper-clad domes – landmark towers which give nothing away to the mighty Caledonian Hotel – and there is a strong cornice which aligns with the eaves of the hotel. When it was at the design stage, much was made of the fact that it would be connected by a walkway to nearby Rutland Square, which was presumably seen as a humanising influence. The walkway

213

was built, but was soon closed and remains closed. Two features worth mentioning are not visible to the outsider. First, the complex is built over the main line railway tunnels, which caused some anxieties. And second, there is one large auditorium and two revolving sub-auditoriums, seating, respectively, 900, 600 and 300 people. They fit together or can be moved apart. Thus conferences from the modest to the spectacular can be smoothly and tidily accommodated. Such are the feats of modern architectural engineering.

Facing the so-called square from the other side of Lothian Road is the **Usher Hall**, focus of the musical life of Edinburgh. Completed just before the 1914–18 war, it is an ingenious building on an awkward site. In plan it is octagonal, with two entrances facing Lothian Road; internally, the auditorium is horseshoe-shape; and overhead there is a circular, copper-domed roof. Each entrance is flanked by pairs of Doric columns, and each has a projecting bronze-work canopy; above the principal entrance the city arms are carved in stone, and above each of the other four archways are heroic figures, one of them representing (oddly enough) Municipal Benevolence. (Why Municipal Benevolence? The money for the Hall was left by Mr Andrew Usher, brewer). Inside, the style is cheerful, almost festive. The foyer is spacious, colour is used discreetly, and there are 'period' gilt light fittings. The auditorium, although it seats 2,900, is a pleasant place to be in. It does not feel enormous, and the gilding is not overdone; best of all, before the conductor approaches the rostrum one can admire the woodcarving on the organcase, and observe the trumpeting angels above, *comme on écoute une mélodie de Fauré.*

Throughout the winter, concerts are given here by the Scottish National Orchestra, and are well supported; and there is other music as well. During the Festival the Usher Hall is the scene of intense musical activity. It is no exaggeration to say that over the past forty years most of the great orchestras of the world have performed within its walls. As a centre for music Edinburgh is not to be despised.

At the back of the Usher Hall is the **Royal Lyceum Theatre**, home of Edinburgh's repertory company. The building went up in 1883. A large enclosed portico has just been added, which is a considerable amenity. The auditorium, designed to seat almost 2,000 people, has three tiers of galleries and a circular ceiling with Adamesque ornamentation. Some think that the interior is unduly gaudy; others are more surprised by the two carved wooden monkeys, dressed as mendicants, last sighted in one of the bars.

What is important is, that the theatre prospers as the home of Edinburgh's repertory company.

Behind the Hall and the Theatre, in Castle Terrace, stands a very large office block (it also houses the lively Traverse Theatre) completed in 1991. Office blocks seldom deserve to be noticed, but this one is an exception. Dignified, non-eccentric, modern, it proves that good architecture does not have to resemble a palace in Verona, or an oil-rig in the North Sea.

Continuing south, negotiate the tangle of Tollcross, where five roads meet but it feels more like a dozen, and then go up the slope past the King's Theatre (1906). Red sandstone outside, the interior is generous Edwardian Baroque – bevelled glass, gilded figures, elaborate plasterwork, red seating, all beneath a sky-blue saucer-dome. This style was once out of fashion; but now it is back and the King's is one of the best examples anywhere.

Soon after the theatre you come in sight of Bruntsfield Links (*see* p 104). The **Barclay Church** (1864) – its spire the finger of faith pointing to heaven – is dominant in front of them. Perhaps domineering would be a better word. The style has been described as Ruskinian Gothic, but to those without special knowledge its ancestry must be uncertain. In any case, it clearly scorns classification. The spire is enormous, over 200 feet high, heavily corbelled and lucarned; it is visible for miles. The roof system, incorporating all varieties of slopes and angles, is vastly complicated, and along with the numerous arches and stair-towers quite conceals the fact that the plan of the building includes transepts and a chancel. The north gable, if you can find it, has a large rose window. There are two tiers of galleries inside, massive piers and columns to support the roof, and a great variety of trusses, rafters and rib-vaults. The architect, F.T. Pilkington, must be given full marks for confidence.

Continue up the slope to the traffic lights where Colinton Road turns off to the right. Those who make maps do not mark this as Holy Corner, but so it is known, for it is straddled by four churches (one disused). None of them is of especial interest, but the concentration is noteworthy. A short distance along Colinton Road, on the right stands Napier College. The College consists mostly of dreary modern buildings, long lines of windows and flat roofs, but it is a brick-and slab oyster which encloses a pearl, for here in the very middle of the complex is **Merchiston Castle**, a late medieval L-plan tower-house which was probably standing before 1500. It is not exactly as once it was, for wartime firemen sixty years ago practised their skills by playing hoses against its crumbling walls (it was then empty, and going fast to ruin); and the concrete stair to the second floor entrance, along with the elevated glass corridor which attaches the tower to the main block are post-war additions which constitute a disgrace to those who designed them, and to those who authorised them. But Merchiston Castle remains a historic building in the full sense of the phrase.

The lands of Merchiston came into the possession of Alexander Napier around the year 1440. One of his descendants, John Napier, was born in Merchiston Castle in 1550. John Napier went to St Andrews University, and then spent several years abroad, where 'he applied himself closely to the study of mathematics'. In 1572 he was imprisoned for a time in Edinburgh Castle because Kirkaldy of Grange (*see* p. 4) found him unenthusiastic in the exiled Queen's interest. Also during that year, **Merchiston Castle** was involved in fighting between Mary's supporters and those of King James. When the fighting ended Napier returned to Merchiston, resumed his studies, and in 1593 published *A Plaine Discovery of the Whole Revelation of St John*. This book surprises in two ways: first, it is not what would be expected of a student of mathematics; and secondly, it went into five editions in English and was translated into French, Dutch and German. It is now forgotten, just another piece of protestant propaganda. But in 1619 Napier published something quite different: *Mirifi Logarithmorum Canonis Constructio*, which is decidedly not forgotten. Napier was the inventor – or is it the discoverer? – of logarithms, and *The Construction of the Wonderful Canon of Logarithms* was a great step forward in applied mathematics. It did nothing, however, to dissuade the local population from regarding Napier as a magician – he dabbled in the occult, and a jet-black cock which lived with him in the tower was believed to be his 'familiar'.

Merchiston Castle is an excellent example of the L-plan tower house, none the worse for being still in use. Externally it is plain enough – small windows, a corbelled parapet, and crow-stepped caphouses (the dormers were added later); the recessed entrance, the Napier arms and the drawbridge slots are restoration improvements. The entrance is at second floor level – the lower floors of tower-houses were invariably for storage – and leads to a lobby and then to the original hall, which now has a plaster ceiling with the monogram of Charles II. The fireplace in the south wall incorporates some fifteenth century work. A turnpike stair in one corner of the tower – as was customary in tower-houses – connects with the different floors. Going up to the third floor, one finds a room which has been a good deal enlarged since Napier's day, the room above it having disappeared altogether. This room is the glory of the building, for it shows off to perfection a painted beamed ceiling dated 1581 which was rescued from a house in East Lothian and installed here in 1964. The fit was found to be marvellous – only a few inches shortening was required. Ceiling paintings of the late sixteenth or early seventeenth centuries are to be seen in various places in Scotland, but none is as good as this, either in design or execution. The artist, it seems, must have been French or Flemish. The colours are unusual, and the designs are extraordinarily inventive; if you can gain access to the little gallery which leads from the turnpike to the wing of the tower you will be close enough to observe above your head some remarkable little figures – remarkably indecent.

Colinton Road is not one of Edinburgh's major attractions. Soon after Napier College there appears on the left **George Watson's College** (1930, dull), and in a short while, on the same side of the road, elevated above almost all else, looms the grandeur of **Craighouse** (1894). This is another of the city's magnificent chateaux, its complicated skyline dominated by a huge square tower. Inside, there is a grand panelled hall, and a very grand marble stair. But do not seek admission. This was built as the Royal Edinburgh Asylum, planned by a Doctor Clouston who believed that the surroundings of mental patients 'should be made as bright and pleasant as possible'; and now, renamed the Thomas Clouston Clinic, it serves the same purposes as before. Pass another golf course, fork right by the 1915 Redford Barracks (cavalry officers' mess much superior to the infantry officers' mess), get clear of the barracks, and at last you are in **Colinton**.

> '*The picturesque little parish village of Colinton,*' says a nineteenth century writer, '*is romantically situated in a deep and wooded dell, through which the Water of Leith winds on its way to the Firth of Forth, and around it are many beautiful walks and bits of sweet sylvan scenery. The lands here are in the highest state of cultivation, enclosed by ancient hedgerows tufted with green coppice.*

Like almost everywhere else, Colinton has changed since the 1870s. The coming of the Caledonian Railway started the process, the motor car intensified it, and for many decades the lands have been more cultivated by developers than farmers. It is now a part of Edinburgh. But something of the old character remains, several distinguished late Victorian and Edwardian villas have been added, and twentieth century Colinton has even been described as 'the perfect suburb – or nearly so'.

Perhaps significantly, there is no singular attraction, no remarkable focus of historical interest in Colinton. Cockburn (*see* p. 533), when the law courts were not sitting, lived at Bonaly Tower, south of the village and now south of the Edinburgh by-pass. Bonaly is a tower-house, built by Playfair in 1836, and it adjoins the original farmhouse which Cockburn found 'scarcely habitable'. The tower is tall and square, not elaborate, with a five-storey circular turret topped by a conical roof. Cockburn loved his tower, along with the two burns that ran nearby, a few old surrounding trees, and the mountains. 'Human nature,' he wrote, 'is incapable of enjoying more happiness than has been my lot here'. He died in 1854. The farmhouse was baronialized and extended after his death.

Robert Louis Stevenson likewise knew Colinton; his maternal grandfather was the minister here. Years later he remembered it as it had been in the 1850s – 'the church and the terrace of the churchyard, where the tombstones were thick ... the smell of water rising from all round, and an added tang of papermills; the sound of water every-where, and the sound of mills ...'.

The paper mills and the grain mills have all gone. Even the **parish church** has been much altered, but perhaps it has been improved. The 1771 church was enlarged in 1837 and a campanile was added. Seventy years later the exterior was livened-up, a porch added to the campanile, and the interior made Neo-Byzantine. For a Scots kirk the colours and general cheerfulness are positively startling; pink sand-stone columns in the nave with angel capitals, more angels in the spandrels of the nave roof, and the apse framed in dove grey marble. Even so, is this Colinton's most cheerful church, or is it eclipsed by **St Cuthbert's** (episcopal) just across the road? This latter was built in 1889, extended in 1934. It is in two colours of stone, has a red-tiled roof and a lead-covered belfry with a lantern which bears a family resemblance to the 1675 spire of St Ninian's kirk in Leith. (*see* Ch. 19)] The roof of the nave is green and red, with sacred monograms in black lettering, and there are angels and foliage patterns on the roof of the chancel. All in all, a good example of lively late Victorian work.

The attractions of Colinton, in fact, apart from its setting, are Victorian and Edwardian. Many of the prosperous families who came here between eighty and a hundred years ago chose good architects, and built well. Their houses give the place much of its atmosphere. The best of the architects was Sir Robert Lorimer (Scottish National War Memorial, *see* p. 134) and his work in Colinton can readily be admired. He was a friend of Lutyens. A 'traditional' architect who thoroughly understood Scottish styles and techniques of building, he had no need merely to copy them. He was a master of craftsmanship and design. It was Sir John Sterling Maxwell who said of Lorimer:

He recognised that the character of a building is not deter-mined by form alone, that it lies even more, though less obviously, in texture, scale and silhouette, in the relation of part to part, the pitch of the roof, the subtle battering [sloping] of walls, the pleasant irregularity which enlivens work done by hand and eye without mechanical guides.

Dominant roofs and a great variety of windows are characteristic features of Lorimer's Colinton houses. The best-known of them are Laverockdale House (1914) in Dreghorn Loan, tall and stone-slated, and Colinton Cottage (1893) in Pentland Avenue, and the attractive Rustic Cottages close to the episcopal church.

Lorimer and Stevenson both reappear at Swanston, less than a couple of miles to the south-east, on the southern side of the city by-pass. Swanston scarcely seems to deserve its fame, for it is little more than a miniscule ill-related clutch of buildings on the lowest slopes of the Pentland Hills. Stevenson loved the place. He spent his summers from 1867 to 1879 at Swanston Cottage, which dates back to 1761. It does not much resemble a cottage, having been much altered and enlarged, last time by Lorimer in 1908. Close beside it there are eight cottages built for farmworkers in the mid-nineteenth century, and restored in 1964. They form a half-square, keeping close together on a windy hillside. It is the setting that gives Swanston such charm as it possesses. Stevenson was enthusiastic about it even in winter, when the rooks pass continually, he wrote, 'between the wintry leaden sky and the wintry cold-looking hills'.

From Swanston go back towards town (by car you have no choice, because Swanston is on the edge of two golf courses; on foot you can follow a right-of-way along the hillside) and reach the cross-roads where Oxgangs Road meets Comiston Road. A little further ahead but out of sight is the **Princess Margaret Rose Hospital**, where black blocks of reflective glass step up the slope, to the admiration of some. See it, if hospitals are your interest. If not, go north down Comiston Road and branch off it into Braid Road (skirting two more golf courses on the right) and then turn sharp right into Braid Hills Road.

Braid Hills Road provides some panoramic views of the city. Immediately to the north is Blackford Hill, and tucked in below the top of the hill is the **Royal Observatory** (1892); there are two telescope towers, each crowned with a green copper cylinder. A golf course separates the Observatory from the science campus of the University, known as **King's Buildings**, built at various times and in all sorts of styles by a dozen or more architectural firms between 1920 and the present day. The general clutter cannot be described as pleasing, and must offend, one would suppose, orderly scientific minds; nor are any of the individual buildings of much aesthetic merit. One of them, however, the James Clerk Maxwell Building, commemorates one of the greatest physicists of the nineteenth century, whose work on electricity and magnetism was an essential step towards wireless transmission and ultimately towards Einstein's special theory of relativity. Clerk Maxwell was born in the New Town in 1831, educated at Edinburgh University, and at the age of forty became the first professor of experimental physics at Cambridge.

After less than a mile **Liberton Tower** appears on the left, another late medieval tower-house. It is a grim-looking place, not much relieved by its slab roof peeping over the battlements. The inside is almost as forbidding as the outside, the few visible concessions to convenience and comfort being three plain fireplaces, and an aumbrey (cupboard) and a garderobe in the hall. It suggests, correctly, that life in Scotland around 1500 could be more than a little bleak. A short distance further on, **Liberton House**, on the other side of the road, is an L-plan mansion built a hundred years later than the tower and a good deal altered. Its design is that of a Scottish town house of the period, and it indicates how much more civilized the country had become by 1600. The kitchen, however, is provided with a gun loop covering the approach. Is this significant, or was a gun loop in the seventeenth century no more a symbol of conflict than a burglar-alarm is today?

Finally, take one more step towards civilization, although it is a longish step (say, three miles) and not everyone may agree that William Adam, father of Robert Adam, and the eighteenth century are an acceptable proxy for civilization.

Drum House, once known as Somerville House, stands in an isolated situation between Gilmerton Road and Old Dalkeith Road, and can be reached from either. It was built between 1726 and 1734 for Lord Somerville, whose family had owned land here since the days of David I. William Adam was Scotland's foremost architect, a follower of Palladio, but with a difference; his classicism is peculiarly Scottish, and robust. His chief aim, he said, was 'to ensure that Architecture be expressed at first view,' and one glance at the Drum shows what he meant. The façade of the main block (there were to be two pavilions, but only one was ever built) is crowded with Classical activity. Rusticated from top to bottom, it flaunts Gibbs-surround windows, Ionic pilasters, numerous pediments, widely spaced balusters, and an extremely large Venetian window squeezed in above the front door. The double stair is a late eighteenth century addition, and possibly an improvement. Even Vanbrugh could hardly be more dramatic. The whole is an arresting composition, not one of the most elegant examples of eighteenth century Scottish architecture, but certainly one of the most striking and memorable. (It has to be added that Duff House in Banffshire, along the same lines but much bigger, and also by William Adam, is even more striking and memorable. It is, in fact, one of the most remarkable eighteenth century houses in Britain).

The thrust and exuberance of the outside of the Drum is more than matched by the interior decoration. There is white marble, grey marble and pale brown marble. In the hall, an almost riotous display of military emblems surmounts the mantelpiece. Elsewhere, foliage, flowers and rosettes burst from the walls and hang suspended from the ceilings. An elegant stair, turning without interruption through 180°, leads to the upper floor, where the decoration, although still profuse, is more delicate and refined. The Drum is not for all tastes; but no one could say that it is boring.

From the Drum the direct roads to town have no particular attraction. The nineteenth century complained about 'unsightly cottages' in the neighbourhood, and now it is different but no better. An early nineteenth century traveller was disappointed that on this part of his journey 'continual showers of rain involved the whole surrounding country in such a density of vapour as totally to preclude all perception of distant objects'. He could have expressed himself more briefly. And in any case, he did not miss much.

17

From Holyroodhouse to Craigmillar Castle

HOLYROODHOUSE HAS A mountain for a neighbour. Going south from the palace, there is level grassy ground for a couple of hundred yards and then the slopes of **Arthur's Seat** begin, rising suddenly and steeply to a height of over eight hundred feet; so abrupt is the ascent that in some places the hill seems, as an eighteenth century traveller put it, 'to over-hang the lower parts of the city'. The old volcanic core, for such it is, like the Castle rock, is part of Holyrood Park, which extends to some 650 acres. This area is one of the grandest open spaces within a city anywhere in the world.

Many explanations have been put forward regarding the name of Arthur's Seat. It does not look particularly like a seat – from some points of view it looks a little like a crouching lion, or a chaise longue – and it can be connected with King Arthur only in the realms of speculation. One suggestion is that the name is a corruption of the Gaelic *Ard-na-Saith* meaning Height of Arrows; 'than which nothing can be more probable,' says one author, 'for no spot of ground is fitter for the exercise of archery'. Perhaps; but no one can be sure. At least Arthur's Seat is a name of respectable antiquity, for it appears in a poem which was published in 1508.

Arthur's Seat once formed part of the ancient Sanctuary of Holyrood Abbey. Within the sanctuary, debtors were safe from their creditors for twenty four hours, and longer if granted the protection of the Bailie of the abbey; which protection was probably not too hard to obtain if they had had the foresight to bring with them a little ready cash. James V 'enclosed' the park (it was probably never fenced) in the 1540s and extended it; he may also have cleared some trees.

Arthur's Seat itself is a large and extensive hill, visible for miles around, with several high points and small valleys between them, a loch, a ruined chapel, and the abrupt face of Salisbury Crags on the western side. Its outline changes unpredictably from every successive direction. There are so many different contours and so many different slopes, planes and angles, rock surfaces and grass surfaces, all of which catch or deny the sunlight and alter their appearance every hour of the day. The size and variations of Arthur's Seat make it a little mysterious, not altogether easy to get to know. The best way to appreciate the hill is to walk round it and climb over it, which is quite a lot of walking and climbing. The second best is to drive round it. There are two roads for most of the way, one a little elevated and the other following a lower and more extended circuit. This latter allows the traveller to see the nearby works of man, as well as to appreciate the shape and slopes of the hill from a little distance.

Leave the palace, and there, set into the hill almost opposite Holyrood, is **St Margaret's Well**, named after the same St Margaret whose chapel is the most ancient building within the Castle walls. The Well is a late medieval conduit removed in 1859 from its original site north-east of the Park, where the march of progress had all but buried it under the newly constructed workshops of the North British Railway. The modern entrance arrangements are repellant, but the well itself is a piece of genuine architecture, a small hexagonal room with a rib-vault supported by a single central column. The water flows into its ancient basin through a grotesque mask, now considerably the worse for wear. How much skill and art there usually is in even minor medieval structures! Go east, along Queen's Drive, past Haggis Knowe (meaning knoll; were haggis in the old days ever this shape?) and higher up the slopes you see a small broken-down ruin perched on a crag. This is **St Anthony's Chapel**, the only human habitation ever built on Arthur's Seat. Why it is there is a bit of a mystery. It is medieval, and seems to have consisted of a vaulted chapel with a room above at the west end, where the priest probably lived. Near to the chapel is **St Margaret's Loch**, formed in 1856 as part of Prince Albert's plans to 'beautify' (anglify?) the park. It is the haunt of noisy ducks and noisier seagulls, and often of greylag geese as well. Facing it is Queen's Park, a smooth grassy stretch of ground where hundreds of cars are parked during royal garden parties.

Queen's Park has twice appeared in history. The first and much the greatest occasion was in 1745, after Prince Charles's forces had taken Edinburgh. That very September morning he

> *stood some time in the park to shew himself to the people; and then, though he was very near the palace, mounted his horse, either to render himself more conspicuous, or because he rode well, and looked graceful on horseback.*

He was twenty five years old, tall and handsome, wearing highland dress with a blue bonnet on his head, and on his breast the star of the order of St Andrew. Charles remained in Edinburgh for six weeks before he began his ill-fated march on London. During this time the main body of his army was camped in or near the park. A young man who went to see the rebels reported that they were

> *strong, active and hardy men, many of them of a very ordinary size ... but the Highland garb favoured them much, as it shewed their naked limbs, which were strong and muscular; their stern countenances, and bushy uncombed hair, gave them a fierce, barbarous, and imposing aspect.*

The second occasion was one hundred and thirty six years later, when Queen Victoria reviewed a force of 40,000 Scottish Volunteers. 'So many men under arms,' a Victorian commentator proudly but perhaps incorrectly announced, 'had not been assembled together in Scotland since James IV marched to Flodden'. The spectacle was sublime; the rain, however, fell in a continuous torrent, and caused the vast slopes of Arthur's Seat to be denuded of spectators before the proceedings were half way through. Only the Queen, her retinue, and the luckless Volunteers remained to the last.

Just beyond St Margaret's Loch a road turns up the hill. It is a winding one-way road with views far along the coast and out to the entrance of the Firth of Forth. On this stretch, above and below the road, there are cultivation terraces, strips of ground which were once narrow cultivated areas, cropped in the Dark Ages or possibly in early medieval times. They are most clearly seen from a distance, and when the sun casts shadows along their irregular ridges. The road levels out at **Dunsapie Loch**, almost four hundred feet above sea level. There are parking spaces here, and more seagulls and ducks and often a pair of swans which, indifferent to the public gaze, have built a nest on the small island carefully provided for them by the authorities. Children scamper up and down the slopes, and those persons who are fit enough set off for the top of the hill, four hundred and fifty feet higher up. It is not really a climb, more in the nature of a steep walk, grass all the way, The distance is about half a mile. From the summit the views are unimpeded, and the remote horizon is visible in every direction. Arthur's Seat is less than a thousand feet high, but there is nothing higher to the north until half way across Fife, and to the south the Pentlands, the Moorfoots and the Lammermuirs, extending in a long shallow arc, are below the one thousand foot contour until more than ten miles from Edinburgh; the eastern tip of the arc is forty miles away. Having seen the view and tested the strength of the wind, you may decide, if you have no car, to head for Holyroodhouse, or to go west towards the Meadows. But remember that Arthur's Seat is an extensive hill. Holyrood is a mile from the summit, up hill and down dale, and it is not possible to follow a direct line going west. There is plenty scope for taking wrong directions and for consequent solitary meditations on Arthur's Seat.

From Dunsapie Loch the road swings south and then west. Duddingston Village (reserved for the extended circuit) is tucked down almost out of sight, but Duddingston Loch is plainly to be seen, and also Prestonfield House (likewise reserved for later), and three of Edinburgh's innumerable golf courses. (In the Middle Ages the city was hemmed in by bogs, now it is golf courses). Here the road narrows and is cut into the rock ('Beware of falling stones' is never a very helpful notice) but after half a mile or so you come over a rise and have one of the finest of all views of Edinburgh, looking north-west. Almost every well-known feature of the skyline is to be seen; the three spires of the Episcopal Cathedral west of the McEwan Hall and the Castle; the immensely tall spire of the Tolbooth Church and the dome of the University; the crown of St Giles and the Melville Monument column further east. The Calton Hill is out of sight, hidden by the escarpment of **Salisbury Crags**; but the Crags close the view dramatically. Salisbury Crags appealed strongly to the eighteenth century admirers of the picturesque. Pennant found in them 'a romantic and wild scene of broken rocks and vast precipices. Great columns of stone, from forty to fifty feet in length, hang down almost perpendicularly, or with a very slight dip, and form a strange appearance'. Being nearly unscaleable, the Crags in very early times provided a means of defence, and there are still traces above them of an extensive stone-faced rampart which was probably constructed during the final centuries of the first millennium BC.

The road turns away from the Crags as it reaches them, but there is a path along their base, known as the Radical Road. Cockburn records that when he first visited the Crags in the 1780s the path was not six feet wide, and in many places there was no path at all; but by 1816 'the cliff had been so quarried away that what used to be the footpath was, in many places, at least 100 feet wide'. This quarrying was at first hardly noticed. But unemployment and severe distress after the Napoleonic wars led to the creation of a fund to employ out-of-work shawl-weavers and others to clear the ground and make a new foot-path at the bottom of the Crags; and as most of the destitute were, or were believed to be, supporters of the principles of the French Revolution, the new path was christened 'the Radical Road'. No doubt the men who built it were peaceable enough. But its creation spelled trouble for one aristocrat, Lord Haddington, hereditary Keeper of the King's Park. He it was who had quarried and sold the stone for his own profit (most of the stone was sold to the Town Council), and when the citizens began to use the new 'promenade' and found out how the Keeper had been 'keeping' the Park they were very wrath, and an action was commenced against Lord Haddington. In 1831, after twelve years of wrangling, the House of Lords decreed that no more stone was to be quarried, and the Crags were saved.

From the high point beside the Crags the road continues on a sweeping downhill line to Holyrood. University halls of residence are on the left, completed in 1952; they are distinguished by their shallow copper-clad roofs and Swedish-style lantern towers. But as the road descends it enters a splendid unbuilt-on area, a broad stretch of grass on the right and beyond it the ground rising steeply, first to the foot of the Crags and then to the start of the main ascending hill. Sheep used to graze here, until sheep-stealing got the better of old familiar ways; but football, mountain-climbing and courting continue as popular activities. It is or should be a leisurely place, so try not to exceed the thirty mile an hour speed limit as you go down; thirty miles an hour is too fast anyway.

Pass the palace and this time go straight past St Margaret's Loch as well, to the end of the Park. You reach London Road close to the **Meadowbank Sports Centre**, built in 1970 for the Commonwealth Games, an event which returned in 1986. The dominating feature is the 15,000 seat stadium which has a cantilevered steel roof to protect rather more than half the spectators from the weather – a wise precaution. Turn right into London Road, and at the first traffic lights turn right into Willowbrae Road. At the first major cross-roads turn right into Duddingston Road West and after a few hundred yards fork right into Old Church Lane, which is the main street of Duddingston Village.

Duddingston Village is a curiously individual little place, a village certainly and not a suburb, quite out of sight of the town. It has a kirk beside the loch and a big house, Duddingston House, in the park (now separated from the village by a main road, unfortunately). There is also a respectably ancient pub called The Sheep's Heid Inn (not far from the church). The best plan is to see the village first (there is a small car park beyond the church) and then, if you wish, back-track to Duddingston House.

Near the start of **Old Church Lane**, to the right, is a modest plain two-storey house which has a little niche in history. It was here that Prince Charles spent one night, the 20th of September 1745, and held a Council of War before he and his small army marched eastward to fight their first battle, the battle of Prestonpans. He told the chiefs of the clans that on the next day he would lead them himself and charge at their head. But the chiefs replied that in that event 'they were ruined and undone; for if any accident befel him, a defeat or a victory was the same to them; that if he persisted in his resolution, they would go home, and make the best terms they could for themselves'. So Charles gave way, and attended the battle, as he attended the subsequent battles, as a spectator and not, as he longed to be, a man of action. As things turned out, Prestonpans was a remarkable victory for the highlanders. The battle lasted for only a few minutes, and because the government forces were unexpectedly and utterly defeated the rebellion dragged on for a further seven months before the final disaster at Culloden.

Warfare and Old Church Lane, however, cannot be much connected; it is a peaceful place (except for the traffic), a short street with a wall on one side and mainly Georgian houses standing behind carefully tended gardens on the other. It leads directly to the gateway of **Duddingston Parish Church**, where there is a loupin-on-stone (to help departing parishioners mount their horses) and the jougs (an iron collar and chain fastened securely to the wall) which were used to expose transgressors to public ridicule and abuse. The church itself is much older than it looks; the basic structure and some of the stone-work belong to the twelfth century. But many alterations and additions were made in the seventeenth. The prominent stocky tower was built then, crowsteps and pinnacles were added to the east gable, and additional buttresses were provided for the south wall. An ancient semi-circular arch divides the choir from the chancel, and in the west bay there is a Romanesque doorway. This doorway is much damaged by time, but the familiar lozenge and herring-bone patterns can still be seen, and on one of the shafts there is a tiny group of figures, one of them a soldier holding an axe and sword, and another who wears a tunic and an overmantle. The church stands on a rocky peninsula that juts into **Duddingston Loch** which is now a bird sanctuary, popular with both birds and visitors; coot, duck, geese and teal frequent it. A

227

hundred years ago it was much larger than it is now; skating parties took place in the winter, and in the summer reeds were cut, and otters used to swim in the cool water. Moreover, it too has its place in history. Lister, one of the greatest pioneers in the development of medicine, was working in Edinburgh in the 1850s on the process of inflammation. His fundamental research, of vast consequences for surgery, was on frogs – 'having got a frog from Duddingston Loch ... I proceeded last evening to the investigation'.

From Duddingston Loch there is a choice of route. You may continue the circuit of the hill and go back towards town, turning left at the first roundabout; or you may make a small detour to see two fine eighteenth century houses, one of them now a hotel, and Craigmillar Castle, not far away, a favourite retreat of Mary Queen of Scots.

The first of the country houses, **Duddingston House**, has now been converted into flats. It is on the other side of Duddingston Road West, not far from the village. Designed by Sir William Chambers and completed in 1768, it has been described as one of the finest eighteenth century houses in Britain. It is of two storeys plus a balustrade, and has a pedimented Corinthian portico with four fluted columns; the overall appearance is slightly austere, but the carving and the proportions are absolutely correct. There is no basement, but the house is connected by a covered passage to a very extensive range of stables and kitchens which face each other across a piazza bounded on the west side by a Roman Doric colonnade, and having a pedimented central block with a cupola belfry. Inside the house there is a spacious two-storey hall with a hexagonal coffered ceiling. A stair leads straight up to a tall mirror which reflects the pillars of the portico through the windows; the stair then divides. The principal rooms contain some good ceilings and elaborate chimneypieces. The park was laid out when the house was built, and survives as a golf course.

Return to Duddingston Road West and go south into **Craigmillar Castle Road**. The castle is soon visible, for it stands high, the strongest fortress within easy reach of Edinburgh. Although roofless, it is remarkably complete, and few castles in Scotland do more to conjure up the military life of the fifteenth and sixteenth centuries.

Built and rebuilt during a period of at least two hundred and fifty years, the castle illustrates the progress of both fortification and domestic comfort. To begin with – that is to say, some time after 1374, when the barony was acquired by the Preston family, who later presented St Giles Kirk with an armbone of the Saint (*see* p. 35) – Craigmillar was a tower-house, a simple fortified residence of a type which was widely built in every country in western Europe during the Middle Ages; there are some splendid examples in the Borders. This tower-house, built in the latter part of the fifteenth century, is the core of what was expanded into a courtyard castle, probably very soon after 1500. The tower-house is L-plan, with a not easily accessible ground-floor entrance. There is a tunnel-vaulted lobby and a turnpike stair which leads to the great hall. The hall is extremely lofty, rising to a great barrel-vault which is above the third floor level and carries the roof. But originally the hall had its own beamed-ceiling – the corbels for the ceiling-joists are still in place. There is also a splendid fireplace eleven feet wide, where traces of painting could once be seen. The door to the right of the fireplace leads to later building, but must originally have led to a privy. There are embrasures with seats, and so thick are the walls that there are rooms within them – one of them is supposed to have been used by Mary when she came here after the murder of Riccio. The space which once existed above the hall probably served as the principal bedroom.

When first built, the tower may have stood within a palisaded enclosure. But this was a poor defence, so the rectangular curtain wall took its place (1508 is the preferred date). This curtain wall is the castle's most interesting feature, because it is joined to the tower and has built onto it a whole range of domestic buildings. The wall is a fortification, no doubt: there are four corner towers, plenty of gunports, and machicolations (projecting parapets) which were convenient for pouring boiling oil and suchlike on the heads of attackers. But the three-storeyed east range, added during the sixteenth century, provided kitchens below and living quarters above, while the west range, reconstructed in 1661, contained further domestic accommodation and even has dormers, chimneys, large windows which look out on a walled garden, and a spacious room (perhaps the 1508 Great Chamber) which has a fireplace and an oriel window next to the tower. Thus the castle was gradually made more agreeable to live in; and it is not surprising that Mary often stayed in it, for by the 1560s it provided that combination of security and ease which she must often have longed for.

But in becoming more comfortable the tower gradually lost its strength. Openings were made in its walls to give convenient access to the better services and the extended accommodation, and this may help to explain why Craigmillar was seized, sacked and burned by the

English army in 1544. Rebuilding ensued, and included the formation of the outer court, within which there is a second garden and the ruins of a small early sixteenth century chapel. The castle was inhabited throughout the eighteenth century, but fell into ruin and decay soon after 1800.

From Craigmillar go back to Peffermill Road, turn left and then right into Priestfield Road for **Prestonfield House Hotel**. This mansion, built in the 1680s, replaces an earlier one which was destroyed by fire in 1681 – possibly arson, the owner 'a merchant of great eminence and wealth,' being suspected of popish sympathies. The new house was designed either by Robert Mylne or by Sir William Bruce, who had just finished working at Holyrood; no one seems to be sure. There is also uncertainty about which features of the old house, if any, were incorporated into the new one; it looks as if some have been, for it is an odd design.

The west front is both attractive and unusual, combining two Dutch gables of three storeys with a two-storey central section between them, flat-roofed, and topped by a balustrade; to make matters still stranger, a large classical balustraded *porte-cochère* has been added, which looks too big for the house, too severe for the gables, and hopelessly out of keeping with the Jacobean quoins. The east front has three gables, but in 1830 it too was altered, by the addition of a large single-storey extension with bowed ends, to contain a drawing room and a dining room. It is all an agreeable muddle, or, if you prefer, a happy blending of the old and the up-to-date.

The interior is another matter, for it shows what it was to have money and bad taste after the Glorious Revolution, and plenty of both. Never mind the ground floor, which is where the family apartments were. Go upstairs (the original staircase has been removed) to the Tapestry Room. Here is a perfect extravaganza of mindless dust-collecting over-decoration. There is a marble chimney piece set in an exhaustively carved surround; the consoles carry realistic male heads with pots of lilies above. Most of the walls are panelled, but there are also tapestries. The doorcases have convex friezes. The ceiling is deeply modelled with a foliaged centrepiece, circles with animals, and a pot of lilies in a grotesque cartouche. Try the Leather Room, once a bedchamber. The panelling here is enhanced by the addition of red leather, embossed in high relief with flowers, shells, insects, snakes and cupids, brought from Cordova. The fireplace has squares of roses. In the Cupid Room, on the top floor, a cupid dangles from the ceiling. It is a relief to return to the ground floor and find in the

Italian Room little more than a few classical landscapes in the panelling and a seventeenth century fireplace with an Ionic pilastered overmantel. The stables are simpler, circular in plan and roofless; but the doocot is pedimented. There used to be extensive grounds, likewise elaborately developed, with parterres, fountains, carved stone seats, sun dials, statues and the rest. Cockburn knew the estate as a boy, and loved it. 'How we used to make the statues spout! There was a leaden Bacchus in particular, of whose various ejections it was impossible to tire. A very curious place.' Agreed.

Time now to make your way to Dalkeith Road, and turn right for town. This is a very old approach to Edinburgh, but nothing very old remains along it. There are, however, two modern buildings of some interest. The **Royal Commonwealth Pool**, completed for the Commonwealth Games in 1970, is said to have been Edinburgh's first introduction to modern architecture. Long and low, it is not as simple as it looks – the diving pool, for example, is at the low end of a sloping site, and what one sees is all above the water, alternating layers of concrete, glass and aluminium. Across the road stands the headquarters of the **Scottish Widows Life Assurance Society** (1975), all dark glass and hexagons. It is not too easy to decide what the shape of the building really is, but its colour and angularity go well with the Crags behind it. Look closely, and you will find that the entrance is across a shallow pool; all of a sudden, moats and drawbridges and medieval castles float before one's eyes. Enter, and you see a cranked staircase ascending upwards, as if not quite sure which way to go. These reflections in the water, these unexpected planes and angles – what do they tell us? that life is fleeting, full of surprises? but that life assurance is well secured?

18

Cramond, the Forth Bridge, and Hopetoun House

ONCE MORE LEAVE the West End and cross the Dean Bridge on the road to Queensferry. Three miles further on turn right into Quality Street, which is in Davidson's Mains. (This suburb, when it was an insignificant village in the eighteenth century, was known as Muttonhole; but no village could become genteel and rise in the world with a name like that). Quality Street becomes Cramond Road South, and in a few hundred yards Lauriston Castle is on the right.

Lauriston Castle began as a T-plan tower-house, built about 1600 for the father of John Napier of Merchiston (*see* p. 216). It replaced an older castle burned by the Earl of Hertford in 1544, and in later years has been greatly altered and added to. Rising to four storeys, it has two two-storey turrets with gun-loops and a very large chimney, all facing south. A tablet above the door, inserted by the then proprietor c 1650, is in Latin and is to the effect that the stars do not govern life; possessions, he says, are a gift from God. Some twenty years after the tablet was inserted John Law, the so-called 'great financier', was born in the tower. Reckless but plausible, he was much given to gambling; killed a man in a duel in London; was pardoned, and went to France. He rose to be Controller-General of the French finances, but his scheme to promote economic development by issuing large amounts of paper money was, as Adam Smith later remarked, 'the most extravagant project both of banking and stock-jobbing that, perhaps, the world ever saw'. (Adam Smith would not have been surprised by the events of 1929, or those of 1987). The crash came in 1720, ruin in France was widespread, and Law fled to Venice, where he died in 1729, a poor man. Almost one hundred years later the old tower was added to by the provision of pseudo-Jacobean extensions designed by William Burn, and there have been further additions and alterations since then. In 1926 the Castle became public property, and it is now open as an Edwardian home, kept as it was in the days of its last private owners. It is a good interior, and handsomely furnished.

Cramond, the Forth Bridge, and Hopetoun House

There is a seventeenth century tapestry from Brussels, several Adamesque chimneypieces, and a magnificent Edwardian bathroom. The well-kept grounds overlook the waters of the Forth, and there is a free carpark.

From the high ground of Lauriston Castle the road descends in a gentle incline to Cramond: a golf course on the left and another on the right, and a superb view of Cramond Island and the Forth beyond shelving park-land and handsome trees.

Cramond used to be an industrial village, 'embosomed among fine wood,' where the river Almond enters the Firth of Forth and where the Carron Iron Company established the nail trade in the eighteenth century; there are still the remains of two late eighteenth century iron-mills beside the river, as well as a few cottages that were once connected with the mills. The nail trade in due course declined, and so did Cramond. The Victorians were scarcely aware of its existence. But in modern times its fortunes revived, for it was and still is very picturesque. The river flows quietly, broadening out into a little tidal harbour edged by a substantial stone quay where iron ore once came in and nails, spades and axles went out. White-washed houses, mostly late eighteenth century, descend the steep slopes and line the quay, which is kept mercifully free of traffic. (There is a car park not far away). The Cramond Inn, half-way up the hill, was there in 1670, but was without its Scoto-Queen Anne extension (obviously) which was added in 1887; as Cramond grew popular, another extension was added not long ago. The inn used to possess a table on which Robert Louis Stevenson carved his initials during one of his frequent visits; but it has mysteriously disappeared. A short distance off-shore lies Cramond Island, accessible by a causeway at low water. Small sailing boats, and sailing people, add interest to the scene. On a summer evening Cramond is hard to beat, for the 'fine wood' is still its backdrop, the sailing boats add colour and sparkle (how Dufy would have enjoyed painting Cramond!), and the silver waters of the Forth spread invitingly forward to the shores of Fife.

Besides all this, Cramond is very old. The bridge, a mile upstream and out of sight of the harbour, was standing in 1500; it has three pointed arches and heavily buttressed piers. The Tower, near the church, is of much the same date, a four-storey tower-house with a stair-turret all the way up and a round-arched doorway. It may once have formed part of a castle or palace – the property belonged originally to the bishops of Dunkeld – and a hundred years ago it was in a dangerous condition. Now it has been turned into a private residence;

very interesting, but could it be described as convenient? The church is a relative latecomer, basically 1656, built on the site of a medieval church, and retaining the old plain fifteenth century tower. It is cruciform, and has been enlarged several times. The Victorians disliked its appearance; it was built, one of them said, 'in the plain and tasteless style of the period,' and to modern eyes it may not look very interesting. But the interior, virtually all twentieth century, is spacious and pleasant; all four limbs of the cross are galleried and have hammerbeam roofs. The monuments in the churchyard date back to 1608, and the whole setting is attractive.

The tower-house, the church and the bridge, however, came late to Cramond; the Romans were here long before them. The Antonine Wall was built from Forth to Clyde in the middle of the second century AD, and one of the 'anchor' stations on the Forth was known to have been at Cramond. Coins and pottery have been discovered over a long period. But the exact site of the station was not found until the 1950s, when excavation revealed it to be in the churchyard; part of it lies beneath the church itself. The outlines of what was found are marked in the grass. The station appears to have consisted of several principal buildings protected by a clay-and-stone rampart several metres wide, and double ditches. Two bath-houses have been found outside the rampart, and an official's residence. Antonine's Wall was the Romans' first line of defence against the northern tribes from about 140 AD until 212, although by that date Hadrian's Wall existed further south. During this period Cramond must have been occupied fairly continuously; although no trace of a Roman harbour has been found. It may have been used again later, but by then it was a perilous outpost, for it was a hundred miles north of Hadrian's Wall, which had become the frontier. Hadrian's Wall is to this day in unpopulated and remote country, easy to associate with barbarian attacks; but nothing could seem more peaceful than Cramond and Cramond churchyard.

Pressing on further west, there are two ways to cross the river. The orthodox and less interesting one is by car, either over the old bridge or over the 'new' main road bridge, built by Rennie but later widened out of recognition; the better way is to take the ferry across the harbour, twenty or thirty yards in a small boat (daily except Friday), and then up the bank and into the trees. Once over the ferry you have the prospect of a very agreeable walk along the shore, wooded for much of the way and giving marvellous views across the Forth and west to the road and rail bridges which link the Lothians to Fife.

The path is in the grounds of **Dalmeny House** (1815), a Gothic extravaganza by William Wilkins. The house is the home of the Primrose family, Earls of Rosebery, who have lived here since the seventeenth century. It is chiefly notable for its collection of portraits by Reynolds, Gainsborough and Raeburn; its Napoleon Room which contains paintings of the Emperor and furniture which once belonged to him; and the superb Rothschild collection of eighteenth century furniture, porcelain and other items, which came from Mentmore in Buckinghamshire. The house has to be approached from the A90.

It is possible to walk from Cramond to Queensferry, which is several miles. But to do so is to miss Dalmeny Kirk, which is of great interest.

Dalmeny Kirk is an outstandingly well-preserved parish church of the mid-twelfth century; it is perhaps the best example of its kind in Scotland. Romanesque in form, it consists of a nave without aisles or vaulting, a small square-vaulted chancel and a semi-circular vaulted apse. The arches between the nave and the chancel and between the chancel and the apse are elaborately carved, and the south doorway is a splendid example of Romanesque carving and grotesque decoration; above it is an arcade of interlaced arches on pairs of columns. The round-headed windows, several of them with decorative surrounds, are few and narrow, so the interior of the church is dark. Sir Robert Lorimer added a small but massive-looking Normanesque tower at the west end, where one had probably always been intended. What is remarkable about Dalmeny, apart from its age, is its overall quality: the stonework is first class, the carving is good, and the whole building has the appearance of having been arranged by a master hand. It is, as one critic observed, 'a model of consistent design and ornament perfectly applied'.

From Dalmeny to the two great bridges over the Forth is less than two miles. They are built near one another, to take advantage of the unusual narrowness of the Firth at this point. The rail bridge – still sometimes referred to as *the* Forth Bridge – was completed in 1890, its companion in 1964. There are three ways to appreciate the size and design of these two very different structures: to cross them, which includes seeing one from the other (train services are very frequent); to view them from Queensferry, which the rail bridge virtually passes over; and to see them from look-out points near the south end of the road bridge.

Queensferry was of some importance in the Middle Ages; there have been ferries here since the eleventh century. The name associates the place with Queen Margaret, for in her day Dunfermline as much as Edinburgh was the capital of Scotland, and the court frequently moved from one place to the other; when she died in 1093 her body was taken across the Forth from Edinburgh for burial in Dunfermline. Sailing vessels were succeeded by steam ferries in the nineteenth century, and numberless travellers experienced lengthy delays at both sides of the crossing until 1964, when the road bridge opened.

In spite of being important and once well-known – Queensferry appears in both Scott's *The Antiquary* and Stevenson's *Kidnapped* – there is not much in the village to see. The Hawes Inn, where Stevenson stayed in 1886, is an old and agreeable inn; and the main part dating from the late seventeenth century. And the Tolbooth, a tower-like structure with a slated spire, which was remodelled in 1720. Plewlands House in the main street was built in 1643 and converted into flats some years ago. There is a Visitors Centre near the pier.

The **Forth Rail Bridge** is the grandest and most monumental of all the bridges in Britain; more than any other, it conveys a powerful impression of the force of human endeavour. Including the viaducts, it runs in a straight line for a mile and a half, and the highest points of the three cantilever spans are 360 feet above high water. Its main members are tubes twelve feet in diameter. 54,000 tons of steel were used in its construction. 57 men were killed building it. But these are mere statistics. This bridge is too grand to be described in figures. Had it been built to impress it could not be more impressive. It looks as durable as a land form. The massive platform for the double line rail system is secured by an intricate web of girders and tubes that cross and criss-cross at countless angles. It stands astride huge foundations, caissons sunk deep into the riverbed. Its superstructure soars into the sky like a steel cathedral. When it was built it was reckoned to be the eighth wonder of the world

The world now has far too many wonders – real wonders – for them ever to be reduced to eight, but on any reasonable count the Forth Rail Bridge would have to be included. It is a gigantic structure. It does not look light and elegant and self-effacing as many fine twentieth century bridges do – as its neighbour the Forth Road Bridge does, for example. It looks what it is, a triumph of Victorian engineering. How much of a triumph is best understood when one remembers what happened to the rail bridge over the Tay, on the same line fifty miles north. That was a suspension bridge, so great a work that the designer was knighted by Queen Victoria on its completion in

1878, and was forthwith commissioned to design a similar bridge over the Forth. But three days after Christmas 1879 the Tay Bridge collapsed into the river on a driving night of wind and rain, taking with it the 4.15 pm train from Edinburgh and all the known seventy five passengers and crew. Plans for a suspension bridge were hastily abandoned. To reassure everyone, the new Forth Bridge was massively over-designed; it was planned to be strong enough to withstand two separate hurricanes, one at each end of the bridge, blowing from opposite directions. To see it properly, wait until a train is crossing; a big modern diesel-electric locomotive looks, quite literally, like a toy.

It would be absurd to say that the **Forth Road Bridge** is a comparatively modest affair, for it is one of the two or three longest suspension bridges in the world. (It was the longest when it was built; but in the modern world records are broken every day – that is part of our way of life). It took six years to build. It is a little shorter than the rail bridge, only one and a quarter miles, but the main towers are much higher, 512 feet over the water. The central span is over 1,000 yards long. That 39,000 tons of metal could be turned into such a graceful structure is a real tribute to modern engineering. This bridge looks well from every point of view, not least at night when the lighting emphasises the long arch of the carriageway.

Less than four miles west of Queensferry lies another very grand structure, but of a different kind and coming from a different age. **Hopetoun House**, designed and begun in the early 1720s, but not finished until the late 1760s, is a country-house of a size and grandeur not previously known in Scotland, rivalling Holyroodhouse itself. Seat of the Hopes, Marquesses of Linlithgow, it is generally regarded as William Adam's masterpiece; but it is really a family effort, because after William Adam's death in 1748 Robert Adam completed the work to a somewhat altered design, and it was he who was responsible for the decoration of the principal rooms.

Lord Hopetoun inherited a mansion built for his father by Sir William Bruce between 1699 and 1707. It was, apparently, a distinguished example of the Classical revival in Scotland. But Lord Hopetoun was not satisfied. He wanted something more Palladian and more up-to-date, closer to the styles of Gibbs and Vanbrugh. So he instructed William Adam along these lines, architect and patron agreeing that the whole of the rear part of Bruce's house should be left as it was, but that the remainder should be replanned and much extended so as to form the central feature of a very splendid design

237

consisting of the house itself linked by colonnaded quadrants to two pedimented Classical pavilions.

The great central section of Hopetoun House is as William Adam intended; and the eighteenth century called it 'a house worth looking at'. It is of three storeys plus a lofty attic storey, topped by a continuous balustrade surmounted by eighteen enormous urns. A broad and too plain flight of steps (William Adam had intended to have two flights) leads up to the front door (no portico; William had also intended a giant portico). The centre and ends of this main elevation project slightly, and across the whole façade there marches a continuous giant order of fourteen deeply-cut Corinthian pilasters. The round-headed windows on the wings have grotesque heads carved on the key-stones, after the manner of the garden front at Castle Howard. The whole effect, indeed, is subdued Vanbrughian.

The rectangular pavilions, however, which are advanced in front of the main house, are by Robert Adam, and perfectly offset it. They are elegant and restrained, with pedimented windows, unemphatic pedimented entrances, and tall octagonal lanterns. The Adam style – the Robert Adam style – has here emerged. He must have designed these pavilions before he was thirty. (The south pavilion, incidentally, now contains the ballroom. Once used as an indoor riding school, it was converted in 1881, and was provided with eight newly-purchased Aubusson tapestries depicting the story of Dido and Aeneas. Don't miss it).

The interior of the house makes clear, as the exterior does not, that more than one architect had a hand in it. In the older section the most striking feature is the central stone staircase, which turns through 180° in an octagonal panelled stairwell. It is lit from above, as well as ornamented with restored and twentieth century wall paintings and with long descending wood carvings of fruit and flowers by Alexander Eizat, who had worked at Holyrood (*see* pp. 68–9). Most of the rooms are not very large, and, after the manner of the seventeenth century, they open into one another. They are panelled, and there are good Dutch tapestries.

To pass from these rooms into the State Apartments created by Robert and John Adam between 1752 and 1767 is to move forward, one would think, by a hundred years; from the sturdy rustic grandeur of the seventeenth century ('Ah Rustick! ruder than Gothick!') to the elegance of the later eighteenth century.

Robert Adam's interiors have a refinement, a lightness of touch which neither Bruce nor Adam senior could ever approach. From the entrance hall (heightened by Robert Adam, and with a good deal of marble, to link the new with the old) one enters the spacious Yellow Drawing Room; silk damask on the walls (1850, admittedly), pedimented doorcases, large gilded rococo cartouches in the angles of the coved ceiling, a handsome marble chimneypiece, and paintings which include a huge 'Adoration of the Shepherds' from the studio of Rubens; then the spacious Red Drawing Room, on the walls red damask purchased in 1766, a florid rococo plasterwork ceiling, a very large marble chimneypiece carved by Rysbrack (1756), eighteenth century chairs in red damask, and fine paintings which include a view of Venice by Canaletto; and finally the State Dining Room. This is quite different, not by Adam but by Gillespie Graham, who created the room – a large one – out of a bedchamber and a closet. It is all 1820 or thereabout – mahogany chairs, sideboard and table, French dessert plates, Meissen and Dresden vases, as well as numerous portraits by Gainsborough, Raeburn, David Allan and others. Best of all, it is just as it was (or as near as makes no difference) when George IV sat down to lunch (turtle soup and three glasses of wine) at this very table on August 29th, 1822.

These do not exhaust the pleasures of Hopetoun. An enormous building – the total frontage is about 170 yards – it is surrounded by very large and beautiful grounds, full of rare specimen trees, and laid out in the grand manner. From many of the windows there are splendid vistas of rolling grassland and noble trees, and the views from the roof (92 steps, but shallow ones) are extensive, both of the Firth of Forth and of the surrounding countryside. There is a garden centre, and nature trails wind through 100 acres of magnificent parkland. Finally, there is a restaurant. But in how many restaurants do you sit with huge tapestries on the walls, delightful woodland scenes woven in Antwerp and London some three hundred years ago? From first to last, Hopetoun is a great house, excellently well presented.

19

Leith

LEITH IS TO Edinburgh as Horatio is to Hamlet; a useful prop, but seldom given much consideration. Yet Leith is a very old town, and has seen stirring times. It is the port for Edinburgh, which made it a place of some consequence even in the Middle Ages; and in 1548, during the bitter civil war between Mary of Guise and the protestant reformers, the Queen Regent transferred her government to Leith, fortified the town, and for twelve years carried on operations with direct military support from France. Her daughter, Mary Queen of Scots, landed at Leith in 1561. 'The cheers of the people,' according to one writer, 'mingled with the boom of cannon,' and 'serried thousands' lined the route from Leith to Holyrood, dazzled by 'the delicacy of her beauty and the liveliness of her wit'. Knox's version is rather different. The face of heaven, he says, 'did manifestlie speak what comfort was brought to this country with hir – to wit, sorrow, dolour, darkness, and all impiety ... the myst was so thick that skairse mycht anie man espy another; and the sun was not seyn to shyne two days befoir nor two days after'. The young queen landed in August, which may make Knox's account a little suspect; but the Scots climate is admittedly capricious.

The 1548 fortifications have long since disappeared, along with the pier where Mary landed. It was Leith's destiny to concentrate on commerce, not war. (Once, however, the port was threatened from the sea, by Paul Jones the American privateer. Born in Scotland, Jones obtained a command in the American navy during the War of American Independence, and waged war on British trade. In 1779 he beat up the Firth until almost near enough to open fire on Leith, while the citizens prepared to defend themselves with 'three ancient pieces of cannon' and a few brass field pieces. Luckily for Leith, the wind strengthened from the west, and no shots were exchanged). The old character of the place is indicated by many unusual street names: Baltic Street, Salamander Street, Madeira Street, Carpet Lane, Cables

Wynd, Vinegar Close, Sugar House Close, Coal Hill, Timber Bush (a corruption of bourse; the timber trade with Danzig and other Baltic ports was always important), Rotten Row (said to be so named from the houses in it being built of rattins, a Scots word for rough timber; Rotten Row in London is supposed to derive from Route du Roi). The old trades and occupations have mostly disappeared, however, and along with them many of the old wynds and closes, and everywhere the busy streets of modern Leith are overlooked by gaunt and largely unused buildings of strange and curious shape, and of indeterminate age.

Yet the character of a seaport, and an old one at that, is still strong in Leith. The docks have been progressively modernised, and ships are sailing every day between Leith and Iceland, Scandinavia, the Low Countries and ports in England as they have done for hundreds of years. The Forth Ports Authority operates from Leith, administering the ports and the oil terminals all the way up the Forth. There is industrial and commercial activity as well in Bangor Road – a woollen mill, a Clan Tartan Centre (computerised) and a large distillers group responsible for what it calls 'a strategic portfolio of brands' which includes such distinctively highland names as Bruichladdich and Cluny. Best of all, from the visitor's point of view, there are some interesting pubs and restaurants, both old and new. Among the oldest is the Ship Inn on the Shore, mentioned by Robert Fergusson in his poem with a title that would not have appealed to the Romantic School: 'Good Eating'. The frontage is mid-Victorian, distinguished by a superbly detailed model ship, a three-master, mounted on a bracket above the door. The interior of the building has been successfully modernised, retaining its old walls of remarkable thickness. Within the last ten years many new restaurants have opened hereabouts, for Leith, like Stockbridge, is rising in the world. Most of them occupy old premises, but the Waterfront Wine Bar is a conspicuous exception. It presents itself as a modern brick shed, with a door in the middle and no windows; but in spite of its studiously dull appearance it is on the very edge of the docks, and provides its customers, once inside, with a sight, as well as a taste, of the sea.

Leith's principal focus of interest, however, is not on dry land but afloat; the **Royal Yacht Britannia**. She was built in Glasgow in the early 1950s, was commissioned for service in 1954, and after steaming for over one million miles she tied up in Leith in 1997. She at once became one of the biggest tourist attractions in Scotland.

It is quite easy to get there, for the Visitor Centre is well sign-posted. From the bottom of Leith Walk (or Ferry Road) turn left; or take advantage of the dedicated bus service from Waverley Bridge, beside the main line railway station. There is an enormous car park. The price of entry includes an audio handset to serve as a guide during the tour of the ship.

At first glance **Britannia** appears to be nothing extraordinary except that she has three masts and her dark hull and white upper works are spotlessly clean. The tour (you are not left free to roam at will) starts on the bridge, which nowadays looks rather old-fashioned. From the bridge you go below and start moving towards the stern. Interests picks up when you reach the wardroom, where the ship's nineteen officers took their meals; it is roomy and handsomely fitted-out, and opens onto an ante-room which houses the bar. But of course the royal apartments are the thing – you walk through the wardroom but you do not walk through the royal apartments, except for the dining room which occupies the full width of the ship, and thus has portholes on two sides. In this handsome room fifty six people could comfortably sit down to dinner, which is possibly a larger number than some ducal residences could manage ashore.

The royal drawing room and ante-room, two royal sitting rooms (one each), two royal bedrooms (again one each) and the sun-lounge (one deck up) are all on view. All these rooms have windows, not portholes, and the sitting rooms are large enough for two people to sit comfortably – a requirement, because they were often used as offices, and space was therefore needed for a private secretary to do his work. The bedrooms too are a good size, and the furnishings are simple and uncluttered; well furnished but by no means ornate. The Queen's bedroom has its original 1950s furniture; also a very fine embroidered silk panel above the bedhead. The drawing room is the *piece de resistance*. It is a large space – the baby grand fits in quite easily – and is divided from the ante-room – not quite so large – by folding mahogany doors; when the doors are open, an eighteen-metre-long room becomes available; and if one includes the dining room as well, we are told that 250 guests could be accommodated; perhaps it was sometimes a bit of a squash. Here too the furnishings are mostly nothing out of the ordinary, although a mahogany bookcase and side-board came from a previous Royal Yacht **Victoria and Albert III**; and the whole room is given an air of restrained opulence by two large and luxurious Persian rugs, given during a visit to the Arabian Gulf. Sir Hugh Casson was the adviser on interior decoration, and most people would agree that he (and the Queen, of course), did a good job. 'Britannia' Sir Hugh Casson thought, had been given an attractively old-fashioned air, something of the atmosphere of a country house at sea.

The sun-lounge, which looks out astern over the extremely large and quite uncluttered verandah deck (glorified quarter-deck; the real quarter-deck is out of sight, one deck lower down) is a pleasant room. It is timber lined and sparingly but comfortably furnished. There is a solitary porthole, perhaps to remind you that you are at sea. But reminder cannot have been needed, the picture windows providing superb views over the open sea, and the ever-receding wake of the ship.

Most of Leith, and most of the best of Leith, is south of the Water of Leith. So travel down to the foot of Leith Walk (which is a continuation of Leith Street, which starts at Register House) and make your way to the Shore. The Shore is not the shore, but a curving street along the riverside, leading to the docks. It starts from Coalhill, which sets the tone with a small eighteenth century warehouse, rubble-built and pantiled. From the foot of Coalhill you can see The Vaults, another but larger warehouse built in 1682, and given a fourth storey in 1785. The vaulted cellars are said to be sixteenth century, and the building is now a restaurant, well worth a visit.

If you are not that way inclined, go up the Shore a little way, and just behind the buildings that face the river, in Water Street (no water in sight), you find **Andrew Lamb's House**, built in the early years of the seventeenth century. This is as good an example of a wealthy merchant's house of the period as is to be found within fifty miles. It is four storeys plus an attic in height and seven bays across, tall rectangular and large, with a projecting staircase tower, corbelled out. Although standing in a wasteland of abandoned and half-abandoned buildings, it is really rather splendid, white harled, and its three asymmetrical crow-stepped gables and irregular fenestration give it an unmistakably Scottish air. It has been skilfully restored; the windows, for example, are now the original size and design, with fixed leaded lights above and shutters below. The interior is less interesting; not much to see, except two slop-recesses on the stair and some stone fireplaces. Mary Queen of Scots is supposed to have come here when she landed in 1561; but the house was not standing then. For several decades it has served as an old people's day centre.

Water Street leads into Bernard Street, which concentrates on banks, not warehouses, and provides a good setting for a 1898 statue of Robert Burns. As an open space, Bernard Street is a great success; it broadens to one end, the proportions are good, and the architecture is varied – but not too much so – and civilized. The centrepiece on the south side is the former Leith Bank, now the **Royal Bank of Scotland**, completed in 1806. It is of only two storeys, and looks more like an elegant little villa than a bank. It has a central bow with Ionic columns and a shallow dome, flanked by pilastered bays. Inside, a circular vestibule leads into the oval banking hall, which boasts an Adamesque frieze – griffons, winged damsels and scrolls – and a gilded clock with cornucopias down its sides. Above, there are two rooms with a handsome domestic air, one of them bow-ended. The other banks in the street are mid-Victorian, except for one built in the twentieth century, which is not in the same class. But there is a good mid-Victorian palazzo on the north side, along with a series of fine late-Georgian buildings. For industrial archaeology, turn into Carpet Lane and see an enormous flour mill built in 1828. The main block, six storeys high plus an attic, is Z-plan, with an arcaded ground floor and five-storey brick-filled arcades facing Broad Wynd.

Beyond the bridge which crosses the river at this point are several more warehouses, all in Timber Bush, an 1802 tenement, and the circular **signal tower** which is, if any one thing is, the sign and symbol of Leith. It was built by Robert Mylne in 1686, and was originally a windmill for making rape-seed oil. During the Napoleonic Wars, however, more was required of it, and the original roof, which resembled a Chinese coolie's hat, was replaced and a battlemented parapet added. It is shown as it used to be in many eighteenth century engravings of Leith, when its base was almost washed by the waves beating against old Leith Pier.

Old Leith Pier was demolished long ago. It stretched northwards from the Tower for a good distance, in an easy curve, continuing the curve of the Shore. Where it stood is now dry land, for Leith Docks have been extended and reconstructed several times. But its place in history is secure, for this is where George IV landed when he visited Edinburgh in August 1822. The story of that visit has been told a thousand times, but always from Edinburgh's point of view. Leith, as usual, is neglected. But the style of his arrival belonged to Leith, and deserves at least a mention.

The king embarked on the royal yacht – appropriately named 'the Royal George' – at Greenwich on 10th August. Accompanied, and towed for most of the way, by two steam-boats, the 'Comet' and the 'James Watt', 'the Royal George' dropped anchor two miles off Leith on the 14th. (The trouble about Leith was and had always been that there was no deep water anywhere near the pier). That day it rained, so the king decided to stay on board for twenty four hours. At twelve o'clock the next day, however, a gun announced that His Majesty had disembarked. All manner of important people were awaiting his arrival on a floating platform at the foot of Bernard Street, covered with scarlet cloth, and as the royal barge progressed up the harbour the king was 'loudly and enthusiastically cheered' by 'the immense multitude' assembled on the pier, the shore, the specially erected scaffolding, at the windows, perched in the rigging of ships in the harbour and covering – so it is said – the roofs of the houses. His Majesty, seated in the stern of the barge, 'repeatedly bowed to the spectators,' and on landing 'shook cordially by the hand' all the members of the reception party. He then took his seat in an open carriage, drawn by eight horses, which drove off 'at a slow pace,' preceded by a host of cavalry, knights of the realm, clansmen, trumpeters, pipers, judges in carriages, and sixteen Yeomen of the Guard. A similar retinue followed behind, also a band. The cavalcade went along Bernard Street and turned into Constitution Street, taking the route to Leith Walk which in a short time we shall follow.

But first there are two buildings to see on the other side of the river. **Leith Custom House**, just by the bridge, was completed in 1812. It is a heavy-handed design by Robert Reid (compare his efforts in Parliament Square, p. 32). Originally a square block of two storeys plus attics, the single storey wings were added later, as well as the balustraded stone steps in front of the portico. The royal arms of George III are in the central pediment. Inside, the best feature is an oval room on the first floor, with a fine cornice. The attics, reached by an iron spiral stair, have two dormers with loading doors and hoists, used to raise contraband for secure storage; that is to say, out of sight and out of reach of the public. The confiscated goods would later be sold. The detached buildings to the north were erected as stables for the horses of the customs officers, whose work included visiting harbours along the coasts; the stables were thus the exact equivalent of modern car parks attached to offices.

The second building to see is **St Ninian's church**, or what is left of it, half a mile to the west, starting down Sandport Street. This is one of those picturesque little fragments which make some people deplore the march of time. What you see now is the Quayside Mills, which incorporate St Ninian's (also called North Leith Church and Manse). The original chapel was erected by an Abbot of Holyrood towards the close of the fifteenth century, but virtually nothing remains. It was rebuilt in 1595 and again in 1736, but was abandoned to secular uses in 1826, becoming 'the unhallowed repository of peas and barley'. The four-storey block at the east end of the premises is in part the church, and in part the manse. An elliptical arch rises non-functionally from below street level, and there are crowstepped gables. But the attraction is the old stair-tower, surmounted by a wooden belfry with a lead-covered ogee spire, added in 1675. Seen, as it once was, above numberless red-tiled roofs, wooden wharves and slipways, this tower must have perfectly fitted the scene. North Leith was still an old-fashioned picturesque place when George IV landed, as well as a little dilapidated; had he seen more of it than he did, he would not have liked it.

Retrace your steps to Bernard Street (unless you want to go back to Edinburgh, straight on down Ferry Road) and go to its farther end, where it meets Constitution Street. Facing you are the **Exchange Buildings**, completed in 1810, a long three-storey frontage, rusticated on the ground floor. The three centre bays project slightly, and giant Ionic columns support the pediment. A casual observer might be forgiven for thinking himself back in Charlotte Square. The building is now in commercial use, but originally contained, *inter alia,* a coffee room, a sale room, a reading room and a subscription library. At the rear are the old Assembly Rooms of the 1780s; the ballroom is of generous proportions, rising through two storeys. Along Constitution Street there are numerous Georgian houses, the finest of them being No. 92, 'the grandest late eighteenth century house in Leith'. It has giant Corinthianesque pilasters topped with urns at the corners, and a pediment across the entire five-bay front. The frieze is decorated with rosettes, and at second-floor level there are portraits in roundels. Leith was rising in the world in the 1790s. No. 44 is also interesting, a pub-front of the 1890s. It has a parapet with swags, and doors with pedimented transoms – not the way they do pubs nowadays. Inside it is equally good: a bar-counter which looks tolerably Jacobean, a ribbed ceiling, and a frieze with sailing ships.

Before you reach the end of Constitution Street it is worth turning right at South Leith Church, not to see the church, which is a messy restoration of what was once a fifteenth century chapel (although it does contain two sixteenth century stone panels in the north-west vestibule, one bearing the arms of Mary of Guise and the other the arms of Mary Queen of Scots), nor even the monuments in the churchyard, which at least have not been restored, but to have a look at **Trinity House**, in the Kirkgate. Trinity House has been described, with much injustice, as parochial, and dismissed as a local sacred cow. Certainly it has no great claim to antiquity. It stands on the site of the old Trinity House, which was a hospice as early as 1530; a stone taken from the old building is inserted in the south wall of the present one, inscribed

> *In the name of the*
> *Lord ye Masteris*
> *And Mareners bylis*
> *This hous to ye pour*
> *Anno domini 1555.*

Built for the Corporation of the Shipmasters of Leith, the present Trinity House is a well-balanced Classical building, completed in 1817. It is now a charitable foundation and is open to the public only by special arrangement. In the Master's Room on the ground floor there is a black marble chimneypiece with an elaborate cast-iron surround. The first floor, reached *via* the oval stair-hall, is a single long room, with a black marble chimneypiece at each end and the central window framed in Ionic pilasters. The ceiling is elaborate plasterwork, painted in several colours. A central octagon encloses a foliaged pendant; rectangular end panels display nautical figures – Neptune, dolphins, ships and other emblems; and the frieze is a cheerful procession of figures, ships and flying fish. There is a large collection of pictures, a number of nautical instruments some of which go back to the eighteenth century, a dozen or more model ships, and a curious wooden container (1809) for charts and maps of a kind installed in nineteenth century sailing ships.

Not far from Trinity House, Constitution Street joins the foot of Leith Walk, where a bronze statue of Queen Victoria (god-daughter and niece of George IV) looks fixedly at Leith Central Station, a pretend-Renaissance steel-framed train-shed. In 1822 this area was sufficiently unbuilt on for the king to be able to see Leith Links, immediately to the east. The Links used to be the scene of military parades, religious meetings, occasional executions, but especially golf. Duncan Forbes (*see* p. 34) frequently played here in the 1740s, and players before him included the Duke of York, later James VII and II, and Charles I, in 1641.

But if Leith Links remains much as it was, Leith Walk decidedly does not. When George IV and his cavalcade left Leith, they set off through open country. Fields and nursery grounds bordered Leith Walk, and the few blocks of houses that had been erected had long open intervals between them. One of the best of these is Smith's Place, not far up on the left-hand side, a cul-de-sac laid out in 1814. At its end is Smith's Villa, an excellent example of Georgian design, two storeys with Venetian windows in over-arches, and a very handsome doorway with a good fanlight; three urns surmount the central pediment.

From here to Edinburgh [administratively, it is all Edinburgh) there was not much to see in 1822, except countryside. The King must have noticed the old Botanic Gardens which were near here, but which were soon to be moved to Inverleith. He may also have noticed Gayfield Place, begun in 1790, which still remains. It is a large and dignified development, with Gayfield Square adjacent. Gayfield was once a fashionable area, with stately trees as well as handsome houses and it was occupied by influential people – Prince Leopold, afterwards King of the Belgians, was once entertained to dinner in Gayfield Square. But now there is too much traffic negotiating a huge automobile merry-go-round or roundabout, in the disapproving shadow of Calton Hill, and you are moreover unpleasantly close to the monstrous St James development.

Things were better ordered in 1822. Here or hereabouts, in fairly rural surroundings, the Lord Provost, accompanied by the Magistrates, 'presented His Majesty with the silver keys of the city, amidst the applause of thousands; for every house and every part of the streets was crowded with spectators,' and Calton Hill 'was terraced with human beings'. The king remained in Edinburgh for a little over two weeks. During this time, we are told, Edinburgh presented 'a general expression of gaiety'. And if this is true, it was something perhaps not repeated until the Edinburgh Festival first took place one hundred and twenty five years later.

EAST LOTHIAN

20

East Lothian

THE LAND EAST of Edinburgh shelves gently to the sea. Over many miles it descends from the rough grass and heather of the Pentlands, the Moorfoots and the Lammermuir Hills to the cliffs and beaches of the coast. It is easy undulating country, not calculated to seize the attention or to stir the imagination of the visitor. Until modern times, the only people who appraised and took much notice of East Lothian were the landowners who 'improved' and farmed it and the leaders of the armies and the raiding parties that fought over it. Early travellers usually avoided this route into Scotland. They came either by sea, or *via* Coldstream or Carlisle, and so knew nothing of it. It was not deemed to be picturesque like the Highlands, or romantic like the Borders, and so it was not 'written up'. Even today it is one of the lesser-known parts of Scotland. But an eighteenth century engineer, no less a person than James Watt, described it well. 'The high Mountains', he wrote in 1785, 'are several Miles distant from the Sea Coast, the intermediate Space consists of Arable Lands intermixed with Hills of moderate Size and Height. In many Places, great Tracts of level Ground are in a very advanced State of Cultivation ... Although the Sea Ports are in general inconvenient, and the Coast no Way sheltered, yet it is lined with Towns ...'.

The last two hundred years have not greatly changed the scene. Edinburgh has spread out and East Lothian has grown closer to the city. Agriculture has intensified, great houses have been built or re-built, old castles have fallen further into ruin. But the hills are still half the landscape, and the sea is rarely out of sight.

Until recently, the road from the city to what used to be called Haddingtonshire – the London Road – lay along the coast. It wound its way through a string of small towns and fishing villages with curious names – Portobello, Musselburgh, Prestonpans, Cockenzie, Port Seton – each separated from the other by open country. Now all that is changed. The eastbound traveller, in the ordinary way of

249

things, joins a two-lane highway well away from the coast, and is far beyond Port Seton in no time. No fishing villages for him, and hardly even a glimpse of the sea. Perhaps he has not missed very much, for the little coastal communities have expanded and been overtaken by the full dreariness of council housing and other modern developments; indeed, the twentieth century has almost swallowed them up. But, as the poet says (often with truth), though much is taken much abides; and a drive along the old road, now heavily built up, reveals a few nuggets of gold amid the modern desolation.

Portobello derives its name from that of a thatched cottage built about 1740 for a veteran of Admiral Vernon's victory over the Spanish at Puerto Bello in 1739. In due course the starveling village acquired a brickworks and a soapworks, and then – it is hard to believe, looking at it now – it became a fashionable mid-Victorian bathing-place where mansions and villas were built to be 'the homes of capitalists and annuitants, who have adopted Portobello as their constant retreat, and who give it a tone of selectness and elegance'. Some of these nineteenth century villas remain, most of them on side streets, in motley congregations. They came later to be inhabited by seaside landladies, and on a summer day the beach was peopled by energetic children and bulbous figures in bathing suits. But that phase too has gone, and Portobello has become merely a drab extension of Edinburgh. It is saved from obscurity by its name, by its being the birthplace of Harry Lauder, and by the fact that when the sands were used as a military training ground during the Napoleonic Wars Walter Scott (of the Edinburgh Light Horse) 'used to delight in walking his powerful black horse up and down by himself, within the beating of the surge; and now and then you would see him plunge in his spurs and go off as if at the charge, with the spray dashing about him'. During these intervals of relaxation Scott was composing, so we are told, parts of that fantastic romance *The Lay of the Last Minstrel* which proved to be a great and immediate success.

Musselburgh comes next, deserving more serious attention. Its name proclaims what was once its trade; mussels (and oysters also) used to be very plentiful in the Forth. It is a unified market town, an independent little place and an old one, as its citizens have declared:

> *Musselburgh was a burgh*
> *When Edinburgh was nane,*
> *And Musselburgh'll be a burgh*
> *When Edinburgh's gane.*

Standing where a main road to the capital crosses the River Esk, Musselburgh was important from an early date; it was frequently burned, for example by the Earl of Hertford in 1544, and the crossing was fought for on several occasions. The five-arched bridge now in use was designed by John Rennie in 1806. It was very much widened in 1924, but the work was so well managed as to leave the appearance of the bridge almost unaltered. Coming from Edinburgh, the best plan is to cross the bridge and turn immediately right, where an inconspicuous car-park has been arranged beside the river.

Rennie's bridge made all but useless the old bridge, which is just by the car park. Probably dating from early in the sixteenth century, this narrow stone-built foot-bridge of three shallow arches is supposed to rest upon Roman foundations. This is a dubious claim, and the bridge, approached by steps at each end and rising high over the central arch, is interesting enough not to require it. Further downstream there are two more bridges, one of them a remarkably elegant structure of reinforced concrete (1968). Musselburgh has done well for bridges.

The centre of town, where the High Street widens out just as it does in Edinburgh, is dominated by the tower and belfry of the Tolbooth, usually dated to 1590. It is reputed to have been built with stone taken from the chapel and hermitage of Our Lady of Loretto, which stood near Loretto School (*see* below), and which was destroyed by the religious reformers in the mid-sixteenth century. The tower of the Tolbooth may not date so far back as 1590, the Classical wing at the east end was added in the 1730s, the hall to the rear was added in 1900, the outside stair is modern, and the interior has been adapted to new uses. Nevertheless, the Tolbooth, looking a little like a Dutch windmill with its corbelled parapet and its belfry, gives Musselburgh a strong central focus and identity. It provides that note of emphasis and distinction to the market-place – for such the street is, or was – which a true town-centre requires. The buildings round about are a mixed lot, varying from an ice-cream parlour of local renown through a series of Georgian frontages to what is called the French Ambassador's House at the east end, a lowish building with triangular dormers, built early in the seventeenth century. The Mercat Cross near the Tolbooth holds aloft a dejected worn-out lion. Musselburgh has seen grander days; but the town centre is still an example to others.

Like any well organised small town, Musselburgh also has its great house, **Pinkie House**, just off the High Street at the east end. Pinkie

House is now a part of Loretto School, a public school on the English model, most of which is painted a memorable – indeed unforgettable – orange colour. It stands in its own grounds on the north side of the street. Pinkie House, on the south side, is not open to the visitor, but it may be glimpsed from the gateway, which is flanked by tall impressive columns.

The oldest part of the house is the tower, some part of which may have been standing as early as 1390. At the end of the sixteenth century the property was acquired by Alexander Seton, first Earl of Dunfermline, who by extensive additions and alterations converted a fortification into 'ane noble house', one of the most splendid mansions in seventeenth century Scotland. It is L-plan, with the old tower near the centre of the north wing, which extends towards the gateway. Seton seems to have raised the tower, and he added the two turrets, making a feature also of two square pepperpot turrets on the new north gable. At the opposite end of this wing there is – or was before ground floor alterations were effected – 'the most nearly perfect ascending series of oriel windows in Scotland'. The south front of the other range is dominated by a long row of remarkably imposing chimney stacks. In the centre of the uncompleted courtyard there is a fine well-canopy with columns, arches, and an open lantern, all profusely decorated with carving, monograms, and heraldic devices. The grand feature of the interior is the second-floor gallery – 'the Blue Room' – some 85 feet long and 19 feet across. It has a shallow curved timber ceiling, elaborately painted with mythical and allegorical figures within panels which are within painted arches, coats of arms, and other devices. It has been described as 'the finest of the Scottish pictorial ceilings' – and was probably painted by an Italian.

Before leaving Musselburgh, enthusiastic golfers may insist on visiting the Links, where James IV, Scotland's go-ahead renaissance king, is said to have played golf in 1504. The Musselburgh Golf Club was founded in 1774, and the Honourable Company of Edinburgh Golfers moved here from Leith in 1836. The Open was played over these links six times between 1874 and 1889, but the nine-hole course is now in a poor state, ground down by neglect and a horse-racing circuit. There are hopes of restoration.

The Links are by the sea; but the next objective lies in the other direction, just south of Musselburgh, on the high ground that overlooks the town; the ancient village of **Inveresk**.

So many tourist attractions are nowadays called ancient that the word must be used with care. But Inveresk really is ancient, for it is in part built on the site of a Roman fort and civil settlement; little of this remains, although numerous finds have been made in the neighbourhood. Why it should be called Inveresk is also a question, for 'inver' means 'at the mouth of' and Inveresk is well away from the mouth of the Esk; the explanation is that the name was given to the whole parish, village and river-mouth included. Another difficulty is that Inveresk is not much of a village; it is rather a series of mansions along the side of a road, some of them seventeenth and some of them eighteenth century, standing amid tall trees behind high walls. There were more cottages once, but the owners of the mansions caused most of the cottages to disappear, and Inveresk became 'a scene of gracious and sequestered tranquillity', situated – as the Victorians saw it – a convenient distance from town. Now, it gives an impression of being a little lost, of grandeur misplaced and in decline. The tall spire of St Michael's church (1805) can be seen a long way off; being at the end of a cul-de-sac, the church and its churchyard are left in peace. Elsewhere, the tranquillity is a little stand-offish. The Manor House (1748) is enormous, domineering even, with a pedimented doorway and another pediment far overhead, with vases and a monogram. Halkerston is late seventeenth century, and odd; there seems to be no order in the placing of its windows or the angles of its gables, besides which it has a pyramidal roof with a chimney popping out of the top. Inveresk Lodge is an L-plan house of much the same date, with a very well laid-out and lovely garden which is open to the public. The whole street is all very pleasant, dignified, withdrawn, somehow scarcely in touch with the twenty-first century. The wrought-iron gates, the stately façades, the quoins, the pediments, the attendant doocots and the high stone walls in this strange village all combine to provide a setting in which George IV, say, or Sir Walter Scott would have felt entirely at home.

Return to the coast road, and two miles east of Musselburgh the **Scottish Mining Museum** is on the right. It stands on the site of Prestongrange mine, and its great attraction is its magnificent beam-engine, made in Cornwall and set up here in 1874 to pump water from the mine. The massive cylinder is in a tall rubble-and-wood engine house, and the beam is arranged to pivot on the front wall. The engine was still working when the mine closed in 1952.

Next down the road comes **Prestonpans**, one of those places that have been washed up on the shores of history, an almost total wreck. Its fortunes were founded on coal mines and salt pans, but its fame today rests chiefly on the battle of Prestonpans (1745), the site now covered over by the railway line and houses. The battle was a crucial encounter. Prince Charles's forces, having eluded the government troops in the Highlands and captured Edinburgh, marched out from the city and totally defeated the government forces, led by General Cope, in less than five minutes. It was the only battle that the Prince ever won, but it opened the road to London. The sole memento of the battle is the house of Colonel Gardiner, an officer who was cut down within sight of his home. For many years the house lay roofless and derelict amid trees just south of the railway line;; but now it is rehabilitated and lived in. It is a handsome eighteenth century building of five bays, with a few steps leading up to the front door, prominent chimney stacks, and two pavilions connected to the house by a high wall. Its colour, not far off burnt sienna, makes it easy to spot, but it is not open to the public.

Hamilton House (1626) adjoins the main street. It encloses three sides of a small courtyard, has crowstepped gables and a stair-turret, but is in a sad state. Close to it is Preston Tower, a fifteenth century tower-house which also belonged to the Hamiltons. It was burned in 1544 by Hertford, in 1650 by Cromwell, and in 1663 by accident. It was enlarged in the seventeenth century and now looks rather absurd within its own tidy enclosure and beside its own tiny car-park. Northfield House, nearby, was built around 1600, but was soon afterwards enlarged. It has angle turrets and tall chimneys but is otherwise plain, except for the south doorway (1611) with arms on the lintel and the pious inscription 'Except the Lord buld in vane bulds man'. Inside, there are wooden ceilings and partitions decorated in the early seventeenth century with birds and fruit, leaves, flowers and animals. The colours are red oxide and pale blue. Finally, there is the mercat cross at the roadside, one of the few remaining examples in Scotland of the seventeenth century style. It is circular in plan, with shell-headed niches for seats, waterspouts, and a corbelled-out platform above. The shaft rises twenty feet above the platform, with a unicorn on top; the unicorn holds a cartouche carved with a lion rampant. Only Aberdeen has a finer old mercat cross, for the Edinburgh cross has been much re-built.

Enthusiasts for Late Gothic and devotees of the work of Robert Adam may wish to see nearby **Seton Collegiate Church** and **Seton House**, close together on the Musselburgh-Longniddry road. The house need not detain us, for it is private property and only a corner of it can be glimpsed beyond the trees. It was built in 1790, and has been described as 'the most perfectly executed' of Robert Adam's castle-style houses, of which Culzean is the best known. There is a forecourt behind a low screen, and then tall towers – square towers and round towers – sail up and dominate the three-storey façade. There are Venetian windows and a very large fanlight over the front entrance, and the total effect is as successful as building a house in the manner of a castle can possibly be.

The Collegiate Church was built between 1470 and 1545. The nave, if it was ever built, has disappeared, and the spire was never finished. The church stands on a knoll amid trees, and has a rather forlorn – and obviously uncompleted – appearance. There are numerous buttresses and much stone-slab roofing and blank wall. Internally, it is tunnel-vaulted, wide, lofty and almost empty. The principal items of interest are the effigies of a knight in plate armour and a lady, probably of the fifteenth century, and an elaborate Renaissance monument to James, Earl of Perth (d. 1611) which takes the form of a large wall-tablet between marble columns. A few yards away are bare outlines of Seton Palace, where Mary and Darnley came shortly after Riccio's murder, and where the Queen came again with Bothwell not long after Darnley had been strangled. The whole place has an air of detached antiquity and quiet gloom.

Once beyond Prestonpans and Port Seton you are well and truly out of Edinburgh. At Longniddry the road turns sharply to the coast, and suddenly the Firth of Forth is in front of you, a pencil line of silver water – for the road hereabouts is only a few feet above high tide level – that stretches across to the shores of Fife twelve or more miles away. On the right are a series of bays and headlands, but westward the view is uninterrupted to Edinburgh; Arthur's Seat is long and low and the Castle stands out perfectly distinctly. All the way from here to North Berwick there are wonderful views looking back to Edinburgh.

To begin with, the road stays very close to the rocky shore. It winds along with a seven foot wall on the inland side, the low trees behind the wall unable to grow any higher but pushing always eastward, their topmost twigs and branches laid flat by the strong salt-laden winds which prevail, blowing down the Forth. The high wall suggests a great house; and sure enough, within a mile you are at the gates of **Gosford House**, home of the Earl of Wemyss.

For several reasons Gosford House is truly remarkable. First of all, it is extremely handsome. But, secondly, although it looks intact, four fifths of it are no more than an empty shell, burnt out when occupied by the Army in 1940. And finally, the remaining section, the undamaged south pavilion, although little more than an entrance hall, is an entrance hall of the most captivating style and proportions.

Gosford House is yet another mansion partly by Robert Adam, begun in 1790 and completed in 1800. It was considerably altered by William Young around the 1890s. The site when building began was a rabbit warren; but the high surrounding wall and the shelterbelt, to the west, which both date from early in the nineteenth century, have helped to turn the grounds into parkland. The trees in the shelter-belt, to the west, so stunted near the road, are over fifty feet high where they are farthest from the sea, and the whole is reckoned 'one of the arboricultural curiosities of Europe'.

Facing the bleak and all but abandoned Italian garden, the west front is strikingly handsome, dominated by three huge Venetian windows flanked by tall pillars and pilasters. Above the central window is a pediment; a parapet runs across, with snarling lions at each end; and overhead is a graceful central dome. All this is by Adam, and it is not diminished by Young's addition of a rusticated arcade at ground level and wide branching staircases leading down to the garden.

Adam also designed flanking pavilions, linked to the main block, but these have been replaced by Young's 1890 pavilions, which are perhaps a shade over-assertive. The east front, which was Adam's entrance front, is dominated by a very large porch with columns and urns and couchant lions at the foot of a remarkably wide flight of steps, a decorated entablature with a swan on top, and sphinxes on the parapet above. Young, acting on instructions, turned the original front hall into a billiard room, and the entrance to the house is now *via* a forecourt (more lions) on the south side.

As Adam designed the building, the rooms behind the west front were each fifty feet long, each lighted by one huge Venetian window, and were not well related to the rest of the house. These rooms did not survive Young's reconstruction, and the fire of 1940 totally destroyed what succeeded them.

All that is left of the interior is in Young's south pavilion, which owes nothing to Robert Adam. Apart from a small entrance hall and a few side rooms, this interior consists of the Marble Hall, an astonishing Victorian/Renaissance tour de force.

The Hall is rectangular, with a white marble floor. Twin staircases rise over a very large, recessed and highly decorated marble fireplace which faces the entrance. At first floor level a gallery goes round all four sides. Three Venetian windows are at gallery level above the entrance, and colonnades in fawn and white alabaster repeat this Venetian theme round the remaining three sides of the gallery. The walls are mostly polished Caen stone, with large insets of fawn and white alabaster, and the generous balustrades of the twin staircases are likewise alabaster and Caen stone. The lighting is excellent, due to the three large Venetian windows and a glazed dome overhead. With so many arches and columns the effect is perhaps a little theatrical, reminding one, in a far less grand (or pompous) way of the Great Hall at Holkham; but the columns and the arches and the openness of it all give a wonderful sense of space, of simultaneous enclosure and liberation.

On the ground floor decoration is limited to busts and alabaster urns, along with an attractive copy above the fireplace of a plaque by Donatello. At first floor level, pictures and *objets d'art* are numerous; but it must be confessed that they are a mixed lot. There is a Virgin and Child by Botticelli, and another Virgin and Child by Montegna. There is a small Rubens and a somewhat larger Canaletto, a second-rate Richard Wilson, a dark and dismal-looking Ruisdael, and numerous paintings by Lely, Raeburn, Reynolds, Murillo, and lesser names. These attributions may or they may not be correct. One item, however, has a detailed history, a Graeco-Roman marble eagle and altar. This piece was dug up at Rome in 1742, acquired by Horace Walpole, and bought at the famous Strawberry Hill sale by the 9th Earl of Wemyss. What could be more interesting! Those who expect Old Masters of the highest quality may not find much at Gosford House. But for a trifling entrance charge you can enjoy one of the minor – or perhaps not so minor – architectural thrills of a lifetime.

Not far away there are the stables, possibly by Robert Adam. They are showy, with a pedimented centrepiece, vases, griffon reliefs, and stone panels of Classical scenes. To complete the estate, there is a pyramidal mausoleum in the woods.

From the gates of Gosford House the road runs through a tunnel of trees to emerge at **Aberlady**. This little village, most of it single-storey cottages and small houses along the sides of the road, many of them set behind tiny gardens, is notable for its church and its nature reserve. The church is almost the first building you see on entering the village, set back from the road and standing free in its open churchyard; admirably displayed. It is a most attractive structure of honey-brown sandstone, with a rubble-built square tower and a slated pyramidal spire on top. There is a loupin-on stone at the gate. Without making any marvellous claims to antiquity, the church is not exactly new; the lower part of the tower went up in the fifteenth century, and some walls belong to the eighteenth. But in 1886 the church was considerably recast and enlarged, and its stylish appearance is owing to what was done then.

Nor is all the style on the outside. Within the church there is a wall monument to Margaretta, Lady Elibank, wife of Lord Elibank, who expresses his regret at having taken so long to erect this memorial. But the delay is easily forgiven, for his lordship commissioned Canova to do the work. Beneath a Doric pediment an angel in flowing marble bends over an urn, a wreath in her right hand, her hair falling forward in an artless expression of grief. It is a lovely thing. Nothing by Canova, it is said, is to be found farther north in the United Kingdom. There are also some lines composed by her husband, supposed to have been put into Latin by Dr Johnson, but not quite comprehensibly. (Lord Elibank, incidentally, was known to the minister at Inveresk, 'Jupiter' Carlyle – his portrait by Raeburn is in the National Portrait Gallery in Queen Street – who informs us that Lady Elibank was ten years older than her husband, who was 'turned sixty' when she died. She had been, Carlyle says, 'a beauty in her youth ... and had no uneasiness about his infidelities, except as they affected his prospects in a future world'. When Lady Elibank died (in June, 1762) his lordship 'lamented his wife very much', but soon after her death he went to Newcastle, where he met 'a very handsome young lady, Miss Maria Fielding', by whose charms he was completely bowled over. He then went to Harrogate, where 'there was plenty of gay company, and play, and every sort of amusement for an afflicted widower, so that his lordship soon forgot his lady, and Maria Fielding, and all his cares and sorrow, and became the gayest man in the whole house before the month of July elapsed').

The nature reserve is at the far end of the village, and consists of the whole of **Aberlady Bay**. The Forth on this stretch of the coast has a very gently shelving shore, so that whereas Aberlady Bay is full of water at high tide – but not at all deep – an enormous extent of mud, grass and sand is exposed at low tide. This habitat is ideal for a great variety of waders, and observation is not difficult, because the road runs right by the shore, and there are sand dunes further east. Besides gulls, dunlin and redshank, there are the superbly decorative oyster-catchers (looking for sea-worms and crustacea, not oysters) and curlews when they are not on the moors and high ground in summer; many species of duck, the eider-duck especially noticeable, partly because of their plumage (*not* the females) and partly because of their size; and smelly, voracious, sociable cormorants, most likely to be seen on exposed rocks at low tide. Depending on the season, the range of bird-life is enormous. There is no best season or best time of day to be there. For some people, the bay is at its most magical in the autumn, early or late, when the tide is in and the silver water shines more brightly under the grey light of the sky, ducks exchange their clanking non-commital monosyllables, and perhaps a flight of oyster-catchers skims with fast wing beats over the surface of the sea.

Beyond the sand dunes that border Aberlady Bay lies the first of **Gullane's** several golf courses – Gullane has four, so far. The turf-covered springy slopes around the village have made it famous, and the landscape all around is alive in every daylight hour with devotees of the game. The village itself is of no particular interest, although it has a fine mile-long beach, the ruins of a small medieval church, and a hotel, Greywalls (1901), by Lutyens, the extensive walled garden by Gertrude Jekyll. The golf course that matters – that matters internationally, that is – is Muirfield, where the ancient and Honourable Company of Edinburgh Golfers came in 1892, thus putting Gullane on the map, and where the Open is played every fourth year. This is well-nigh sacred ground, not to be seen from the road, for it lies east of the village and almost against the sea.

No sooner is Gullane left behind than **Direlton Castle** comes in sight. It is as well that the distance between the two villages is only a couple of miles, because when the kirk at Gullane began to be 'continewallie overblawin' with sand early in the seventeenth century the parishioners were told to walk to the services at Direlton. They may have felt that both man and God were against them. But shortly afterwards they received their due reward, when a new kirk was built at Direlton, and a very attractive one too. It is on the north side of the village, with round-headed windows and a west tower and a stone roof. Hidden away down a lane, it is seldom noticed, because visitors come to see the castle, and the village round the village green. And so they should, because Direlton can justly claim to be one of the most picturesque villages in Scotland. It is on the English plan – so many Scots villages are simply strung out along the sides of a road – its triangular village green enclosed by the well-designed school (1910), the Castle Inn (by no less a person than William Burn, c 1820), a number of eighteenth and nineteenth century cottages, the early nine-teenth century wall of the castle grounds, ornamented with a small pavilion, and a suitable number of ancestral trees, carefully looked after. Direlton is one those villages that look almost too good to be true. Yet it is true, and no part of it is truer – or at any rate older – than the castle itself, which is in part one of the oldest in Scotland.

During the thirteenth century military engineers began to build what are now called 'great castles of enclosure', fortresses strong enough to withstand attack by the latest military technology – movable assault-towers, stone-throwing catapults and so forth. These castles are great monuments of military architecture, and Direlton is one of the best examples in Scotland, closely resembling both in design and workmanship the more splendid contemporary fortresses in England and Wales. There was a castle on the present rocky site about the year 1225. It was taken by Edward I in 1298 and partially destroyed, but the thirteenth century keep (or donjon, or tower) remains almost as it was, and the fourteenth/fifteenth century additions, like those made here in the sixteenth century by the Ruthvens, largely repeat the ground-plan of the old castle, because the rock which forms the site naturally defines the shape and extent of the building.

A short flight of steps leads to the present-day entrance, and you are in the close, or courtyard. On the right is the inner close, which is very small, hemmed in by the great round tower, its walls three metres thick, a square tower adjoining it, and a smaller round tower, all of the thirteenth century. What is built on the north side of this close is a sixteenth century rebuild on the original plan. The apartments in these towers are angular and vaulted, and may originally have been lighted only by narrow loopholes. The lord's chamber has seats in three of the window openings and a fireplace enriched with dogtooth and other decoration. The drawbridge entrance to the south, built around 1400, is the castle's most striking feature. It is high and narrow, with a pointed arch, and was once surmounted by twin turrets, one on each side. In the old days the drawbridge let down to a removable wooden bridge across the moat. The sill of the gateway inclines so steeply that no one could stand on it; entry here when the drawbridge was up was virtually impossible. The east range also dates from about 1400. (The thirteenth century towers at each end of this range have disappeared). The outer wall is enormously thick, and the floor of the continuously tunnel-vaulted basement is in part cut out of the solid rock. There is a chapel at the north end, aligned approximately east-west, with a prison below it and a dungeon below that. Little remains of the late medieval hall, which was on the level of the close, but the kitchen can be identified by its arched fireplaces and the circular vent in its high vaulted roof. Much of this east wing was originally built higher, and would have contained living accommodation for the lord and his family.

Direlton Castle has been a ruin since it was taken by General Monck in 1650, during Cromwell's subjugation of Scotland. Today, there is a mellow peacefulness about both Direlton and its castle. No village green can seem warlike. The garden inside the castle wall is simple but well tended. The beehive doocot in the castle grounds was built in the sixteenth century, solid and reassuring, a beautifully preserved example of the type. The seventeenth century bowling green has been remade, and the yew trees beside it are reminders, if not survivors, of an earlier, formal garden scheme. The sanguinary past has disappeared, and been replaced by horticulture and conservation.

Drive another mile or two along the coast, with the blue waters of the Firth not far away, and you come to **North Berwick** (not to be confused with Berwick-on-Tweed, forty miles further on). As a small town, North Berwick is not of compelling interest. It is crowded down by the harbour, now given over to week-end sailors and their boats, and in recent decades it has spread, in varying forms of orthodox respectability, up and out from where it began. It is a holiday resort, full of cars and people in summer, offering breezy prospects of a widening sea. There are two beaches, and it is worth going to the east beach and then up the slope beyond it to the rocky headland which overlooks the town. The view is outstanding; north to the shores of Fife, west to Edinburgh and the Forth bridges twenty-five miles away, north east to the Isle of May, low and shadowy in the North Sea, and, best of all, the **Bass Rock**, little more than a mile off shore. The Bass is one of three prominent volcanic plugs in this area. About a mile in circumference, it rises suddenly from the sea to a height of over three hundred and fifty feet, solitary, massive and inhospitable but adding to the scene. There is only one landing place, for the cliffs are sheer, and it is inhabited only by sea-birds. There are many thousands of them – guillemots, kittiwakes, puffins, and above all gannets, for this is by far the biggest colony of gannets in British waters. The gannet, still sometimes called the Solan goose, is the largest British sea-bird, with a wing-span of six feet, and the whitest; it is, moreover, a spectacular diver. The birds have sometimes had human company. St Baldred was on the Rock fourteen hundred years ago, living a life 'of solitary contemplation', and there are the remains of a castle where some covenanters were imprisoned in the later seventeenth century. But people and history are irrelevant to the Bass.

It stamps its character upon the coast, an isolated tower rising through the surface of the sea. It is possible to circumnavigate it, by boat from North Berwick.

On the southern edge of the town there is another volcanic plug called **Berwick Law**. (A law in these high latitudes is a hill). Berwick Law is a prominent grass-covered pyramid, almost geometrical in outline, 600 feet high, not too steep to be climbed but steep enough for a careless pedestrian to roll down it, with unhappy consequences. It is visible for miles around, an unfailing landmark, with the ruins of a watch-tower on top and a rude archway formed from the jaw-bones of a whale. Stevenson as a boy climbed to the top 'in the buzzing wind', and recalled many years later how he saw 'the face of many counties, and the smoke and spires of many towns, and the sails of distant ships'.

Eastward once more, this time to **Tantallon Castle**, only a couple of miles away further along the coast. This is another great castle of enclosure, probably begun later than Dirleton, for there is no mention of it before 1374. But it is one of the half dozen most spectacular medieval castles in Scotland. Its situation is superb, a high grassy headland projecting north-eastwards into the Firth, the waves breaking on three sides of it at the foot of perpendicular cliffs. The Bass Rock is just over a mile away. The cliffs are one hundred feet high and virtually unscalable, so what was needed was to construct defences across the landward neck of the promontory. These consisted of a massive curtain-wall approximately twelve feet thick and fifty feet high, with a central projecting tower-gateway and flanking towers at each end. To make doubly sure, a wide deep ditch was cut into the rock in front of the curtain-wall. Further out, another ditch crosses the promontory.

The grandeur of the castle matches the grandeur of its site. Although it has decayed and been knocked about (finally by General Monck in 1651) it is by no means an abject ruin. The massive wall still stretches entire across the neck of land, barring all further progress. The flanking towers are much damaged, but the centre tower still rises to its full height, thrusts confidently forward from the curtain-wall. The entrance, originally reached *via* a drawbridge over the ditch, is a lofty gateway, ten feet wide, with mouldings and a pointed arch. From the courtyard there is access to the two stair-cases built within the immensely thick curtain-wall. They are lit only by slits in the wall, but the climb to the wall-walk on top is amply rewarded. The view of sea, farm-land and hills is immense; but the predominant sensation is of rugged, primitive height; fifty feet straight down to the grassy platform on which the castle stands, and a further hundred feet from that to the white waves breaking on the rocks below. And if the wind is blowing, the top of the tower and the bulky crenellations of the wall give little enough protection. Fresh air and a hint of danger are the essence of Tantallon.

The details of the castle are not of great interest. War and the passage of time have made the internal arrangements hard to understand. James V attacked it – stronghold of the Douglases – in 1528, and after its negotiated surrender, he enlarged the entry-tower, stopped up some openings and passages, and made new gun-embrasures.The doocot in the grassy area before the curtain-wall dates from the seventeenth century. The hall, kitchen and other domestic rooms were built along the north-west side of the court, over a vaulted basement, probably in the fifteenth century. There are some vaulted garderobes, and there is a dungeon under the north-west tower. The remains of a sea-gate and of what was probably a landing-stage are to be seen in the bay north-west of the castle. The well in the courtyard is over one hundred feet deep.

Tantallon Castle is built of a strongly pink sandstone, common in East Lothian. Inevitably, it is sometimes referred to as the rose-red castle, which equally inevitably reminds one of Petra – the 'rose-red city, half as old as time'. They could hardly be more different. Petra is far older, a very quiet place, baked by the desert sun for two thousand years. Tantallon belongs to relatively modern times, to the clash of battle and the ever-moving sea.

The road from Tantallon turns south, following the line of the coast, but a little inland. After passing a few farms and negotiating not a few sharp corners, you reach the hamlet of Whitekirk. There is only a handful of houses, a rose-pink church and a barn; but the church and the barn are worth looking at. They date back to the Middle Ages, when there was a well nearby which possessed miraculous healing powers. Because of this, Whitekirk became a place of pilgrimage; in 1435 it was visited by the future Pope Pius II, who walked barefoot to Whitekirk from Dunbar, a feat which so impressed James I that he took the well and chapel under his protection. Another pilgrim was James IV – whose piety did not prevent him from having five illegitimate children. The well and the pilgrims' hostels disappeared before the Reformation, but the church remained, and it continued quietly for another four hundred years, when a most extraordinary fate befell it; it was set on fire by suffragettes, and gutted. Restoration was completed in 1917, but nothing old remains in the spacious interior. Externally, it is much as it was: a simple unassuming late-medieval church, extremely expressive of a confident faith. Perfectly proportioned, it stands slightly above the village on a green hillside, square-towered, cruciform and aisleless, its short spire rising above a heavily corbelled parapet.

The barn stands just north of the church, a teind or tithe barn, one of two first-class examples in East Lothian. (The other is at Foulden, a few miles east of Berwick-on-Tweed. See p. 302). It dates from the seventeenth century but the west end is part of a sixteenth century tower-house built with stone which was taken from the old pilgrims' hostels. It has crowstepped gables and an outside stone stair, but is otherwise unadorned. Like the church, it shows how much attraction there can be in age, good materials, and good proportions.

From Whitekirk wend your way south for a couple of miles to where a road branches off to Tyninghame and East Linton. Tyninghame House is out of sight, nearer the coast, converted into flats. It was once a plain old seventeenth century mansion, but was enlarged and quite transmogrified by William Burn in 1829. It is very high, and very spreading, and very pepper-potted. There are features that are Grecian, others that are Jacobean, and still others that are French Rococo; there is even a Venetian well-head dated 1586, complete with the winged lion of St Mark. In brief, it is revived Scottish Baronial at its most pretentious, and with minimum character. It cannot be visited and therefore does not need to be noticed, except that it stands in such utter contrast to the village, which is simple and delightful.

Unlike most estate villages, **Tyninghame** is not over-orderly. Its houses were mostly built in the 1830s and 1840s, and are scattered along the main street, some nearer the roadway and some further off, in what seems a quite arbitrary manner. No two are alike, except for the cottages, and almost all are pink sandstone. The oldest house is on the corner – it was once an inn – and a little further down, by the bridge, is the crowstepped sawmill with its undershot water-wheel. The whole village is planned development without a hint of planning, the inborn art that conceals art. Not many villages so unspoiled, and of equal charm, are left in Britain.

The road through Tyninghame leads westward to Preston Mill, which (confusingly) has nothing to do with Prestonpans but is tucked away on the edge of East Linton, just off the A1. **Preston Mill** is of no great architectural or historic importance, but it is one of the most photographed objects in Scotland, because it is so 'quaint and picturesque' and therefore falls an easy prey to the camera. But this is to speak rather slightingly of an old and still functioning mill. There used to be scores of mills in East Lothian, for it is grain country; in the middle of last century there were fourteen on the River Tyne alone, the river which drives Preston Mill. They have all gone now, except this one. The complex – for it consists of the mill itself, the drying kiln, the mill lade and related buildings – looks curiously un-Scots, probably because of the large ventilator on top of the polygonal kiln, which makes it resemble an oast house in Kent. The mill itself is on two levels, with the grinding stones and hoppers on the upper floor. The process, which involves cleaning and separating the grain from the husks, is surprisingly complex – no linear flow of operations here – and the machinery, which is almost all wooden, is powered by an undershot water-wheel and wooden cogs and gearing. Once set in motion, the clanking and rumbling noises are considerable. The mill was probably built in the eighteenth century, the kiln perhaps earlier. The walls are roughly-laid orange-red sandstone, and traditional east-coast pantiles are used for the extensive roofing. With its alder trees and mill pond beside it, well off the road, Preston Mill is a genuine glimpse into the peaceful hard-working countryside of two hundred years ago.

A path from the mill leads to Phantassie farm, where John Rennie, famous builder of canals and bridges, including the old Waterloo Bridge in London, was born in 1761. Along the path there is the Phantassie doocot, which once contained nearly six hundred nesting boxes. It is of the beehive type, possibly seventeenth century. But it has been patched up and conserved without mercy. The twentieth century has seen fit to seal it and cover it in mouse-coloured harling, with the result that it resembles nothing so much as a rotund and meaningless pillar of concrete; no self-respecting pigeon would look at it, and neither should the visitor.

It is now worth taking to the hills. Across the A1 a small road leads up through trees and farm land that is increasingly occupied by sheep as you climb higher to the village of Stenton. Unlike Tyninghame, **Stenton** is a hill village, three hundred feet up in the foothills of the Lammermuirs; a mile to the south-west there is a forest trail and a splendid viewpoint looking over the entire low country to North Berwick and the coast of Fife beyond. Stenton (i.e. stanetoun) is built of local stone, deep pink or grey shot with red, taken from a quarry at the end of the village; as a rose-pink village with pantile roofs it is not remarkable in East Lothian. What is remarkable is its lay-out, for it is neither centred round a village green nor strung out along the road; its basic plan probably goes back to medieval times.

The village begins with a little Victorian school and West Green, which is no more than a triangular patch of grass. From this point a narrow curving street sets off past the eighteenth century School House and other buildings to Mid Green, which has an octagonal horse-mill, and then past the Joiner's House (1692) to East Green, where there is an outside-stair cottage known as the Church Officer's House. Each of these spaces is defined and bounded by a variety of cottages and small houses, but none is enclosed and shut in; and the slope of the ground adds enormously to the variety of the scene. Beyond East Green is the parish church (1829), Gothic revival with a good tower; within the churchyard are the remains of the previous parish church, built in the sixteenth century, its two-stage tower converted to a doocot. Just east of the village there is a medieval well at the roadside, a small cylindrical affair with a conical stone roof and a leafy finial, half-buried in summertime grass. Like the rest of the village, the well is in good shape. In East Lothian, to be stentonised means to be carefully but sensitively conserved.

From Stenton go to Traprain, which is marked on most maps as a village although it is little more than a farm steading and a couple of houses. Just before the houses are reached, take the road west to Haddington, and you are driving along the south side of **Traprain Law**, where a remarkable hoard of Roman silver was discovered in 1919 (*see* p. 103). Traprain Law, accessible from the south-west over a stile, is a volcanic plug, long, low, and scantily covered with soil; rising suddenly above the surrounding fields, it looks rather like a partially submerged but enormous whale. Two thousand years ago it was a good site for a fortress, and in the first century AD it seems to have been the capital of the Votadini. The Votadini were collaborators with the Romans – there are almost no Roman military sites east of Dere Street (the Roman road from South Britain to North Britain, crossing the Cheviots near Carter Bar) because they were not needed – but the Votadini had to protect themselves from the Picts north of the Forth and other raiders, and the defences that they built on Traprain Law are still to be seen, although not easily. The original enclosure, perhaps dating from about 50 AD (therefore pre-Roman), extends along the west and north sides of the hill, ending abruptly at the quarry; late in the fourth century the higher rampart was built, turf faced with stone and some ten feet across at the base. It is believed that some time about the middle of the fifth century the Votadini left

Traprain and established themselves in the much more powerful fortress of Din Eidyn, now Edinburgh. Here they emerge, no longer romanised, as the Gododdin. And there were earlier, shadowy occupants of Traprain; bronze socketed axe heads have been found and dated to the sixth – seventh century BC., as well as pottery urns for cremation burials, which suggest occupation as far back as 1500 BC.

Just north of the hill (a road goes all the way round), a narrow side-road leads to a fortification of a different kind; **Hailes Castle**, seat of the Earls of Bothwell. Hailes Castle is one of the few castles in Scotland where masonry is still to be seen that is over seven hundred years old. The site is a strange one, a rocky outcrop low down on the very banks of the River Tyne, overlooked by higher ground but protected by water on two sides. There are two towers and a long curtain wall above the river; only part of the curtain wall on the south side remains, containing the main gateway. The original tower, which was standing before 1300, is in the centre of the riverside curtain wall, the upper parts rebuilt. A little to the east, the curtain wall is pierced by a stone stair, vaulted and ribbed, which once led down to a well, and possibly over a drawbridge and, by a ladder, to the river itself. This is all thirteenth century work. In the fourteenth century the square western tower was built, and in the fifteenth century the range between the towers. Both towers have pit prisons, and the range bas a tunnel-vaulted basement which is said to be a bakehouse, which seems strange. The room above may have been a chapel. Although much ruined, Hailes Castle is an historic and an attractive place. It was attacked several times during the Wars of Independence, and it was here that Bothwell came one night in April, 1567, with his bride, Mary, Queen of Scots, on their way to Dunbar. Cromwell destroyed the castle, as he destroyed so much else, in 1650. But now, buried in the countryside (although just visible from the A1), it is a most peaceful spot. Black and white cows graze quietly in the fields nearby; rock and ruin seem fused together by the jarring complexities and then the silence of time; and the little river, smooth and tranquil, flows quietly past in a long slow curve, reflecting the light of the sky.

Five miles nearer Edinburgh, along narrow country roads, lies Haddington, county town and market town of what is probably the richest agricultural area in Scotland; Cobbett said of the country hereabouts, 'The land is the finest that I ever saw in my life'. This is where 'high farming' began in Scotland in the second half of the eighteenth century. But even before then – before the planned villages and the solid elegant farm steadings and the planted woodlands appeared – there was enough prosperity and even security for wealthy noblemen and landlords to improve their property and build something more comfortable and convenient than a tower-house with gun-loops, small windows, and no entrance at ground-floor level. Fighting was over, more or less, and elegance and refinement at last began to get the upper hand. This progress, from habitual war to habitual peace, from walls eight feet thick to drawing rooms in the manner of Robert Adam, is nowhere better to be seen than at **Lennoxlove**, just south of Haddington, which since 1946 has been the home of the Dukes of Hamilton.

The approach to the house is clear evidence of the age of improvement. For over half a mile the drive leads straight on beneath magnificent oak trees, interspersed with beech and lime, planted irregularly on each side, with parkland or fields behind them. Then it curves down to a gate and a cattle-grid, and Lennoxlove comes into sight just beyond a turning-circle for vehicles, rimmed with cherry trees. The tower-house is nearest, huge, unexpected, abrupt; the later additions lie beyond it.

No one could call Lennoxlove a beautiful building, but an air of authentic history pervades it. Originally known as Lethington, it probably began as a simple tower-house, which, along with the estate, was acquired by the Maitland family in 1345. It was the Maitlands who built the existing massive L-plan tower some time around 1400, three storeys high, austere and of immense solidity, looking to the Lammermuir Hills. In 1626 John Maitland, Earl of Lauderdale, made the tower more pleasant to live in by enlarging the windows and providing a second entrance door and an easier stairway; but he had already made a more extensive change by adding the east wing, where the entrance to the house now is; and in 1644 the scheme of modernisation was carried further when the tower at the east end was added. The range to the north (where the cafe is located) and the twin-arcaded coach house are eighteenth century additions.

Lethington became Lennoxlove because of a woman, and there are three different versions of the story. One begins by telling how John Maitland, first Duke of Lauderdale, used to meet and dine with other landowners in East Lothian. These dinners were attended by Lord Blantyre, who had no land in the county, and the Duke resented this intrusion. To express his annoyance, he made a practice of offering to sell Lethington to Blantyre, who he knew was too poor to buy it. But Blantyre had a cousin, Frances Teresa Stewart, Duchess of Lennox and Richmond, who was very beautiful and also very rich, and she advised him to accept the offer next time it was made. He did so. And soon afterwards the Duchess sent to her cousin the purchase money in a casket, 'with the Duchess of Lennox's love'. So Lethington became the property of Lord Blantyre, who promptly changed the name to Lennoxlove. The second version is rather different, and brings the Duchess more prominently into the picture. Frances Teresa was 15 in 1662 when she became Maid of Honour to Charles II's Queen, Catherine of Braganza. No woman was safe at Charles's court, especially one as beautiful and vivacious as Frances, and Charles became very anxious to add her to his list of mistresses. He wrote her a poem with the refrain

> *Oh, then 'tis I think that no joys are above*
> *The pleasures of love,*

commissioned the great medallist John Roettiers to use her as the model for Britannia on the nation's coinage, and showered her with gifts. The court took bets on the result. But Frances – 'La Belle Stewart' – refused the royal advances. She married her cousin, the Duke of Lennox, and the couple went to Copenhagen, where the Duke very soon afterwards died. (He is said to have fallen off a ship in the harbour during a party). Grief-stricken, the Duchess returned to London, and although now disfigured by smallpox was appointed Lady of the Bedchamber. She lived a life of the utmost respectability until her death in 1702, when her Trustees, acting under her instructions, bought Lethington and settled it on her cousin, the Master of Blantyre, with the injunction that its name be changed to Lennoxlove in memory of the Duchess's love for her husband. The third version closely resembles the second, but declares that once Frances Teresa had achieved the status of a married woman she found it natural and agreeable to fall in with the King's wishes, and the change of name from Lethington to Lennoxlove was made in order to commemorate her love not for Lord Lennox but for Charles II. This version is not approved in the great house itself.

Lennoxlove is no masterpiece of architecture, but it is an unusually interesting house to walk through. The entrance hall is both intimate and elegant, with an attractively carved eighteenth century chimneypiece, several portraits (three of them by Mytens), and a wide flattened arch which replaces an original dividing wall and thus makes the entrance hall much more handsome. Upstairs, the principal room is the drawing room. It has yellow walls, yellow and white doors, a cream and ochre oriental carpet with an elaborate floral design, and a chimneypiece of white marble having a frieze of cherubs in low relief. The walls are hung with numerous portraits by Van Dyck, Janssens and Lely. These include the well-known double portrait by Janssens of the 2nd Duke of Hamilton and the Duke of Lauderdale; and the even better-known full length of Frances Teresa herself by Lely. Anyone who thinks that a yellow drawing room must be a mistake should see this one. It is an overwhelming success. But of course not everyone can clothe their walls with pictures like these. Nearby is a small apartment of a very different style. It contains three pieces of furniture which belonged to the celebrated Duchess: a large inlaid tortoiseshell writing cabinet given to her by Charles II; an ebony and pewter inlaid work table; and an escritoire, painted with cherubs but later japanned. The walls are extraordinary. They are lined with a buff-coloured seventeenth century damask, onto which have been sewn motifs taken from older – probably sixteenth century – embroideries. These motifs, about the size of a man's hand, but mostly smaller, are of flowers, birds, animals, men on horseback, all in soft colours, arranged in an almost random fashion across the fabric. It is a wall-covering rare, ancient, and delightful.

After one or two other rooms and passages, and many portraits, the visitor passes through the thickness of the tower wall into the fifteenth century tower-house. The show-piece here is the great hall, at first floor level, filling the whole of the main block. It has a vaulted roof, and when Sir Robert Lorimer rescued it from serving as a kitchen he stripped it down to the bare stone and exposed the old openings in the roof which were there to let out the baronial smoke. Unfortunately, he also removed the gallery at the south end and devised a far too smooth and affected stone fireplace across the whole length of the north wall, making rather a mockery of the ancient dignity of the room. The ante-room contains two remarkable objects relating to Mary, Queen of Scots. One is her death mask. The other is a fifteenth century French silver casket given to her by her first husband, King Francois II. This is the casket in which Mary's enemies found, or planted, the famous 'casket letters' which implicated her in the plot to murder Darnley. The connection with Lennoxlove is that Sir William Maitland of Lethington was one of Mary's principal advisers in the early 1560s. He was almost certainly involved in the murder of Darnley, and he was with Kirkaldy of Grange when Edinburgh Castle was held for Mary against the supporters of her son King James, and was overwhelmed in 1573. Maitland died immediately afterwards, possibly by taking poison.

A turnpike stair leads down past the guard-room to a small room which contains a striking bust by Epstein of Admiral Lord 'Jackie' Fisher (the 13th Duke of Hamilton served under him before the 1914–18 war) and several items relating to the flight made by Rudolph Hess in 1941 to Scotland, in the hope of contacting the 15th Duke of Hamilton who was then on active service with the RAF. There are also photographs taken before and during the first flight over Everest in 1933, when the 14th Duke was the leading pilot.

Finally, do not miss the garden. It is a peaceful, simply laid out place which would scarcely deserve to be noticed were it not for the sundial. A young lady in seventeenth century costume, her fan in one hand and in the other a rose pressed against her bosom, stands on an octagonal platform and balances on her head a large polygonal sundial with seventeen faces. She came to Lennoxlove early in the twentieth century from a house in the west of Scotland, and carries the initials of one Donald MacGilchrist, who built the house in 1679. Her long hair falls to her shoulders, and her puff sleeves and the curves of her gown are firm and faultless. She is four and a half feet high, quite apart from the platform and the big sundial on her head, and she looks extremely pert.

Haddington is a small town and an old one that contrives to move with the times. The so-called Haddington Monument (1829) on a hill just north of the town marks its position for miles around. Haddington has several historic associations and numerous interesting buildings, but one of its most remarkable features is its shape. The medieval street pattern remains; and although a little obscured by later developments, these help to give a feeling of variety, and of the unexpected. The streets narrow and widen again, and the town unfolds most pleasingly; suddenly one comes on a new prospect, a calm enclosure, a wynd. There are trees and painted house-fronts, and all is made more agreeable by the River Tyne, flowing slowly past the great church – large enough for a small cathedral – and under the sixteenth century Nungate bridge.

The best way to see the town is to start from the west end (the street is called West End), as if you had come from Edinburgh. West End widens into Court Street, which is the apex of what was until the sixteenth century the long spacious triangle of the medieval High Street. There are no very old houses, because Haddington was reduced to ashes by Edward III in 1355 and sacked several times by

English armies in the following centuries. But all along here there are many Georgian houses, and many arched pends leading to old yards or closes at the rear. Some of the houses are as high as four storeys, pantiled or slated, and a few villas stand in their own gardens. The most imposing of these is now the Bank of Scotland (1803), with east and west wings, triple windows recessed in arches, a sphinx in the centre at roof level, and an elaborate iron work lamp-holder bridging the gate-piers. The County Buildings (1832) on the opposite side of the street are vaguely Tudor, with additions.

Looking down the widening street, and along a pleasant mid-street line of trees, the vista is closed by two blocks of building. That to the right, fronted by a white-washed pub, is of no great interest. But in the narrow lane alongside it is the entrance to a small pend which leads to the eighteenth century house where Jane Welsh lived before her marriage to Carlyle. The house is open to the public at certain times, and is a more cheerful place than it looks when you first see it. It was to this house that Carlyle came 'on a red, dusky evening' in June, 1821. He was a poor and unknown young writer. Jane Welsh was twenty years old, and in a modest way an heiress. She was also 'a beautiful, bright and earnest young lady, intent on literature as the highest aim in life'. It is probably not unfair to say that Carlyle talked her into marrying him five years later.

The other block of building is fronted by the Town House. The gable is well proportioned, there is a correct Venetian window in the centre, and a handsome slender steeple rises above. Admirers like to attribute the Town House to William Adam, who produced elevations in 1742. But there is little here from the 1740s. Assembly rooms were added at the west end in 1788, and the steeple, by Gillespie Graham, in 1831.

The Town House begins the division of what was once the spacious end of the old high street into two narrow streets, Market Street and High Street, connected by four still narrower closes. This area used to be a crumbling congestion of buildings, but it has been restored at least to stability. There is a fine confusion of uses and a still finer confusion of round-headed windows, pantile roofs, pedimented doorpieces, Ionic columns, Victorian shopfronts and at least two stair-turrets, one in what used to be the Bluebell Inn. The eighteenth century Castle Hotel, 'improved' in the nineteenth and twentieth centuries, makes a clamorous and deplorable eastern end to the High Street.

Pushing past two early nineteenth century pubs, which are close to a Palladian palace front of c1760, you emerge into Hardgate, which used to be the road to Dunbar. Turn right (Hardgate immediately becomes Sidegate) and in a hundred yards or so you reach Haddington House, an elegant mansion of three storeys, now owned by a local trust and used for concerts and exhibitions. Haddington House was built around 1650, an L-plan house with an octagonal stair-turret in the angle. The canopied doorway and balustraded stair are dated 1680, with the initials of the then owners. About 1800 a small extension with tall windows was added beside the turret, and the street front was lengthened by adding a low wing with a Venetian window looking onto the garden. Restored in 1969, the house retains some rooms and fireplaces of the seventeenth century, and the garden has been carefully re-made in the style of an old Scottish garden. Further down the road is Poldrate Mill, a three storey eighteenth century cornmill with an under-shot water wheel, reconstructed in 1842. It is on the site of the medieval Kirk Mill, and the granary, maltings and workers' houses are at the rear.

To reach the mill, however, you have already passed the entrance to Haddington's parish church, the church of St Mary the Virgin, the greatest building in Haddington. St Mary's is cruciform, long, large and lofty. In terms of size it comes second only to St Giles in Edinburgh among the burgh kirks of the Lothians – it is, in fact, a couple of feet longer than St Giles – and is comparable with some of the smaller Scottish cathedrals. It was completed about the middle of the fifteenth century, but in 1548 an English invasion force attacking Haddington destroyed the roof and the vaults. The nave was soon afterwards repaired and services were resumed, but the transepts and choir, i.e. the greater part of the church, remained roofless and decaying until an ambitious work of restoration was carried out in the early 1970s.

Because of repair and reconstruction, St Mary's is a difficult church in which to feel completely at ease. The exterior is certainly impressive. The west front, facing Sidegate, displays a very large window with good tracery, and the fine round-arched doorway below has foliage capitals and double round-arched doors. It is a handsome elevation, and the fact that the parapets and pinnacles above the cornice date from 1811 is of no great consequence. The crossing tower is massive, relieved by three closely spaced round-headed lancets on each face. It is commonly said that the tower once carried an open crown like the crown at St Giles, but there is no proof of this; if it did, it must have given added distinction to an already fine building. The window at the east end dates from 1877, and is said to resemble one at Iona. So far so good. The interior raises greater difficulties. It is extremely spacious, and rather empty; the altar, and probably a rood screen as well, went out at the Reformation. The nave is of a yellow/gray stone whereas the choir and the transepts are red, which looks odd, although it is original. But what is really off-putting is the roof. In the choir and transepts the 1970 vaulting replicates the shape of the original, but with fibre-glass; the vaulting in the nave on the other hand, was constructed in 1811, replacing a timber roof, but it is meagre-looking plaster-work. The result of all this is the uncomfortable feeling that one is in a building neither new nor old. Part of it is history, but part of it is, so to speak, fiction. And one's unease is not entirely dispelled by the fine stained glass window in the south transept by Burne Jones (originally in St Michael's, Torquay, and brought to Haddington *via* the V and A in 1970), by the dazzling Scicluna window by Sax Shaw (1979), also in the south transept, by the stone panel in the choir depicting a goat (the Haddington burgh arms, no less) surprisingly supported by angels, or even by the grave of Jane Welsh Carlyle with its sad and moving inscription penned by Carlyle himself:

> *In her bright existence she had more sorrows than are*
> *common; but also a soft invincibility, a clearness of*
> *discernment, and a noble loyalty of heart, which are rare.*
> *For forty years she was the true and ever-loving helpmate*
> *of her husband; and, by act and word, unweariedly*
> *forwarded him, as none else could, in all of worthy that he*
> *did or attempted.*

It reads as if he meant it, and perhaps he did. But it hardly prepares one for the lamentable truth that for Jane the marriage was catastrophic. In the course of it Carlyle referred to sensations of 'deep gloom and bottomless dubitation', and his wife described the married state as being, in general, 'extremely disagreeable'. Carlyle was self-centred and domineering, a stranger to gentleness and love, so it is little wonder that when Jane died she was worn out by drink and drugs, melancholy and isolation. There were no children.

The former sacristy projects from the north wall of the choir. It was largely rebuilt early in the seventeenth century, and stands over the burial vault of the Lauderdale family. It is now an ecumenical chapel and contains a remarkable Renaissance marble monument (c1675) to Sir John Maitland of Thirlestane (d. 1595) and his wife Jane Fleming, and to their son the first Earl of Lauderdale (d. 1638) and his countess Isabella Seton. (Sir John was a brother of Sir William Maitland; *see* p 270. For Thirlestane, *see* p. 291). The alabaster effigies of Sir John and his wife, and their son and daughter-in-law, lie in twin archways with Corinthian columns supporting a broken pediment overhead. There are low relief figures, busts above, large inscribed black tablets, and a great display of family heraldry. In so small a space the scale, the elaboration, and the sombre colours of the stone and the alabaster are truly depressing. But to those who built it, such a tomb as this was part of the personal greatness of the dead, a protection and perpetuation of their blessed memory.

It would be unjust, however, to leave this great church on an unsympathetic note. It is of noble proportions, and its setting is far better than that of most English cathedrals. Surrounded by an extensive and well-kept graveyard on three sides, the east end of the choir is only a few yards from the slow-moving waters of the River Tyne, which bends past St Mary's along tree-lined grassy banks. The best plan is to leave the churchyard by the path along the river and walk the few score yards to Nungate Bridge. The bridge is not as old as the church – it goes no further back than the sixteenth century – but it is a delightfully graceful construction of red sandstone, the gentle curves of its three arches as easy as the gentle flow of the river. (True, there are four arches; but the small arch on dry land was added in the eighteenth century to make the approach on the far side less steep, and does not intrude). The purpose of the bridge was to link Haddington to the ancient Barony of Nungate. Old cottages brought up to date and some modern additions are clustered on the east bank, while on the west side a castellated cylindrical Gothic doocot stands on the line of the bridge in what is called Lady Kitty's Garden. All is old and peaceful, and where renovation has taken place it has been done with good sense and discretion. Best of all, and what really ensures for these surroundings their old cathedral atmosphere, there is no passage of buses, or lorries, or motor cars. It is a village-and-river-and-church pedestrian precinct of a very superior sort.

One more surprise awaits the visitor. Go straight ahead and then turn, as you must turn, into Church Street. Suddenly, you are in urban surroundings, a street enclosed like an eighteenth century square; Holy Trinity church is on the north side, and on the south there are two fine blocks of housing, one with a central chimney gable and quoins, while the other is a lower whitewashed row with two chimney gables. The former began about 1750 as the burgh school. Holy

Trinity (1770) was brought up to date and Gothicized in the 1840s, and then made more Byzantine in 1930. (Who says that churches do not move with the times?). It stands on the site of the Franciscan friars' church known as the Lamp of Lothian, which was destroyed by the English in 1356. The old name is now frequently although unhistorically applied to St Mary's. Not far away, on the road to Whittingehame, is St Martin's church, a two-cell rectangular building of the late twelfth century which once belonged to a Cistercian nunnery at Haddington. Only the nave remains. The thirteenth century buttresses were presumably added in order to support the pointed tunnel vaulted roof.

From Haddington you can travel quickly back to Edinburgh *via* the A1 and the city by-pass. But if you have time to spare, **Athelstaneford** is worth a visit, only a few miles north of the A1. It is a planned village, laid out by a local landowner in the mid- eighteenth century. The site – which does not lack for fresh air – is a ridge of high ground, sloping gently to the east. Very low single-storey cottages step down for two or three hundred yards along the road, which is remarkably wide. The cottages are white-washed, roofed with the customary East Lothian pantiles, and although there are no front gardens roses contrive to grow and cover many of the cottage walls. In the churchyard beside the road there is a fine lectern-type doocot, dated 1583. Tradition has it that here or hereabouts in the tenth century the Picts and the Scots defeated the Northumbrian Athelstane, and a St Andrews cross appeared in the sky above the battlefield; this is the legendary origin of Scotland's national flag.

Finally, only a mile or two to the north-west lies the **Chesters hill-fort**, close to the village of Drem. It is not spectacular, an oval hillock encircled by two ramparts with three additional ramparts to the north; over twenty mainly circular stone buildings once occupied the enclosure. The attraction of Chesters is its situation, for it is easily visited, low-lying and not far off the road. Curiously, it is completely overlooked by higher ground immediately to the south, which makes viewing easy. It seems to have been occupied from the 2nd century AD or later.

Returning to Edinburgh by way of Dalkeith you pass close to a famous tower and a great house. The former is **Carberry Tower**, on an eminence overlooking much country and the sea. Over the centuries the building has grown. It is U-shaped in plan, the early sixteenth century tower being at the NW corner. This tower is decorated with winged heads and gargoyles, and a circular wrought-iron fire basket is mounted on the parapet. Late in the sixteenth century the tower was extended to the south, and further additions (with pepperpots) were made in the eighteenth and nineteenth centuries. Inside there are a couple of vaulted ceilings and some marble chimneypieces – nothing of great note. What is memorable is that it was here that the forces of Mary and Bothwell met those of the Protestant nobles in June, 1567, one month after her disastrous marriage. There was no battle – the Queen's supporters, of whom there were not at this point very many, quietly dispersed. Bothwell fled to Norway, and spent the last ten years of his life in a Scandinavian dungeon; Mary surrendered, to be imprisoned in Loch Leven castle on the other side of the Forth, and was compelled to abdicate in favour of her infant son. Almost exactly a year later she escaped, was defeated in battle, and at once crossed the Solway into England.

Dalkeith House (1711) which is now an educational institution and is not open to the public, is a much grander affair. It was built by James Smith for the Duke of Monmouth, later the Duke of Buccleuch, on the foundations of an old castle. The main façade of three storeys is pedimented over a giant order of Corinthian pilasters, and has two projecting wings. Some alterations were made by John Adam in the 1750s and by William Burn in 1831. The external appearance is grand, Classical and severe. Inside, grandeur is also the keynote – the heavy grandeur of marble. The hall has a marble floor, marble doorcases, marble pilasters and leads to a cantilevered marble stair. There are numerous marble fireplaces throughout the building, and a good deal of oak panelling. In Duchess Anne's Room, there is a marble fireplace with a white marble panel in the overmantel depicting the story of 'Neptune and Gallatea' (sic) by Grinling Gibbons. Clearly, no expense was spared. George IV was here in 1822. He is said to have caught a chill from the draughts. But the whole place is rather chilling, and must have been a shock to one accustomed to the Brighton Pavilion. The interior was disastrously damaged by the army during the 1939–45 war.

The grounds, which constitute Dalkeith Country Park, are less pompous. There is a large twelve-sided conservatory (1834) with Doric columns and a central support which is in fact the chimney; and a bridge (1792) by Robert Adam, a single semicircular arch which carries the west approach drive between massive parapets high over the North Esk. There are also lodges, gates, stables, other bridges, a coach house and all the rest of the apparatus of eighteenth century nobility. The park is open during the summer months, but the Palace is occupied by teaching staff and students from the United States.

THE BORDERS

21

The Borders: and to Peebles and the Tweed via Eddleston

FROM EDINBURGH SEVERAL roads lead to the Borders. But how shall we know when we have got there? Where, exactly, are the Borders?

The Border itself runs from Berwick-upon-Tweed to Gretna Green on the Solway Firth. For fifteen miles or so the River Tweed is itself the Border, and few would deny that the Tweed Valley is of the essence of the Borders, even although Berwick-upon-Tweed is an English town. But not many would say that Gretna Green, sixty miles to the west, or neighbouring Ecclefechan where Thomas Carlyle was born are Border towns, still less Dumfries, which is properly thought of as the gateway to the somewhat remote and self-contained province of Galloway.

The fact is that the Borders is a region without precise and agreed boundaries; yet it is certainly an identifiable region, and its distinctiveness and limits, however vague the latter, have been settled by the massive forces of geology, history, and the imagination of Sir Walter Scott.

Fundamentally, what distinguishes the southern counties of Scotland from the central plain where Edinburgh and Glasgow are situated is the physical make-up of the land itself. From Dunbar on the east coast to Girvan on the Firth of Clyde there runs a geological fault which sharply separates the newer Palaeozoic rocks of the central belt from the older rocks to the south. The central plain is mostly level and fertile ground, with many scattered coal seams. But south of the fault the hills are all but continuous, rounded and for the most part not very high, the fertility of the soil is poor, and the extensive uplands are composed mostly of rough moorland. Only in the valleys – and the Tweed is the only one of any size – are there richer alluvial soils where crops and forest trees grow well.

From Dunbar to the Solway Firth the southern counties are basically similar. So why not call the entire area the Borders? The geographical answer is that from where the Tweed rises near Elvanfoot and Crawford all the country to the east is drained by rivers flowing into the Tweed. The rivers of Dumfriesshire, on the other hand, flow south into the Solway, and the River Clyde, which rises only a few miles from the source of the Tweed, soon leaves the southern uplands altogether and turns north-west towards Glasgow. It is therefore possible to think in terms of two border regions, the East Border on the one hand and the West Border and Galloway on the other. But although they merge into one another they face, so to speak, in different directions, and belong to two different shores.

Nor is this all that separates east from west. When Edward I invaded and overran Scotland in 1296 – the country had already been an independent kingdom since the eleventh century – he began the War of Independence – or wars of independence – which lasted for the better part of three hundred years. Campaigns were fought all over the east and central borderlands. The main invasion route was Dere Street, the old Roman highway into Scotland which crosses the Border near Carter Bar and goes on to Jedburgh and Melrose. Alternatively, armies could come up *via* Coldstream, or even take the longer route by the east coast. What they did not do was to attack from Carlisle, because from there it is a long hilly moorland road to Edinburgh. From Carlisle invaders could more easily have reached Glasgow, but Glasgow in those days was a small place of little consequence. The capital, the principal towns, the abbeys, the wealth of Scotland all lay in the east. So the battlefields, the castles, and the tower-houses are also in the east.

Recurrent war in rough country made law and order difficult to maintain, all the more so because it bred a population accustomed to the use of arms – on both sides of the Border. So there was a good deal of anarchy, a good deal of raiding and thieving and killing; and men often found no need to cross the frontier to find enemies, or victims. Every one lived in a constant atmosphere of war. As a result, the great and necessary virtues of Border society were bravery in battle and loyalty to the group, which in the Borders meant the family – Scott, Elliot, Ker, Home, Armstrong and numerous others. Many of these families were a law unto themselves. And as is common in such a society the triumphs and disasters of enmity and war were made the subject of a vigorous epic or heroic literature which here took the form of ballads.

Because fighting belonged largely to the east, so did the ballads. Scott began to travel through the Borders in the 1790s and eagerly 'picked up from tradition' many old ballads which had been passed down orally from generation to generation. These he published, sometimes with 'improvements' of his own, in *The Minstrelsy of the Scottish Border* (1802–3). This publication had two effects; it started Scott on his literary career; and it brought to prominence the old Border feuds and battles as well as such remote and little-known places as the Ettrick Valley, Yarrow and Liddesdale. In 1805 he published his own wildly romantic *Lay of the Last Minstrel*, and his fame was assured. Equally, *The Lay* and *Marmion* (1808), not to mention the building of Abbotsford fifteen years later, turned the Tweed Valley and all the country round about into the heartland of romance. It became Scott country. subtly changed by his life and his imaginings. A new and special character was given to the broad river and its tributaries, to the rolling windswept moors and the grassy heathery hills, a character which it retains to this day.

The shortest route from Edinburgh to the Tweed is due south, passing between the Pentland Hills to the west and the Moorfoots a little further south and to the east. For those with minimum time this is the best way to go, returning by the slightly longer road through Lauder. That route and the two longer still are described in the following chapters.

Immediately south and south-west of the Edinburgh bypass the country is abandoned to a confused medley of dreary villages, small towns and would-be small towns, interspersed with agriculture. This area is on the coal seams, and coal was once its life. But that is gone now, leaving but a small legacy to treasure. The visitor may choose to speed through these places towards the beckoning hills, or spare an hour for a couple of houses and a famous chapel, islanded in this sea of uninterest.

The nearest of these three to Edinburgh is **Mavisbank House**, just south of Loanhead; and it must be admitted that there is not much to see, for it is a mere shell, burnt out in 1973. It was designed by the proprietor, Sir John Clerk, 'under the correction of Mr Adams, a skilful Architect', i.e. William Adam, in the 1720s, and is vaguely Palladian. The front elevation is rather square, with a flight of steps to the porch-style entrance and a large pediment overhead filled with 'large pieces of foliage' and a bull's eye window. Arcaded quadrants connect the house to the flanking pavilions, which are more Dutch than Italian. Mavisbank is a small house and it has been called beautiful; it has also been described as 'a gawky provincial mansion'. Perhaps it is chiefly interesting as an illustration of William Adam's belief that good architecture consisted of sound building plus surface decoration; cornices, coats of arms, balustrades, pediments and scrolls. This was, after all, in the Scottish tradition: as John Fleming observed: 'Behind his cumbrous pediments one may often discern the skeleton of a crow-stepped gable, and behind his wide Corinthian pilasters the ghost of a bartizan'.

Roslin is a couple of miles south of Loanhead, perched on the west side of Roslin Glen, 'a deep den with wooded eminencies' and now a natural park. **Roslin Chapel** itself is on the brow of a hill overlooking the River Esk. Writers from the fifteenth century to the present day have exhausted their store of superlatives in trying to describe it. Yet it is not large, nor astonishingly old, and few people, perhaps, find it remarkably beautiful; it was even dismissed by Pennant as 'a curious piece of Gothic architecture, ornamented with a multitude of pinnacles, and variety of ludicrous sculpture'. This, however, is the fascination. It is medieval-fantastical to the utmost degree, stone-carved to the limit, 'of most curious worke', without question one of the most amazing Gothic buildings in Britain.

It was established by William Sinclair, Earl of Orkney, in or about 1450, and was intended to be a large cruciform building; but only the choir was built, along with small sections of the transept walls; foundations for the rest of the transept and the nave were uncovered during the nineteenth century. The five-bay layout, with a clerestory and aisles on each side plus an ambulatory or transverse aisle at the east end, which is divided into four small chapels, is reminiscent of many Cistercian foundations of the twelfth century; it is essentially early Gothic. Externally, the buttresses, with niches and pinnacles and flying buttresses above them, are the most conspicuous feature. The flying buttresses, with pinnacles of their own, relieve the flatness of the clerestory, but according to the experts they are quite unnecessary to keep the walls in place, for these walls are very thick. The vestry at the west end was added in 1880.

On entering the chapel, one is struck by its height; in this respect it is like Trinity College Church in Edinburgh, which was begun at almost exactly the same time. The roof over the main span is a pointed tunnel vault, which is very much in the Scottish tradition; this one is unusual only in being set on a clerestory. The aisle and ambulatory roofs are likewise pointed tunnel vaults, which is not so usual. The pillars that support the main roof are bundles of shafts, undecorated, and they are very nearly the only undecorated items in sight.

The general impression is overwhelming, almost claustrophobic; the very structure of the building has all but disappeared behind the carving. The plain pillars are surmounted by elaborately foliaged capitals, and from them double lines of foliage grow up over the arches; each compartment of the vaulted roof has its own close pattern of stars, or squares, or flowers; angels, animals and satanic figures are in wait for you wherever you go. On a roof rib at the east end – to notice only one roof rib – there is the Dance of Death; in one of the aisles – to notice only one little scene – a fox carries off a goose and is pursued by a farmer. The eye has no rest. Every available space is decorated with intricate and often spirited carving – apostles, martyrs and parishioners, Samson, St Peter and the Prodigal Son, the keys of heaven and the gates of hell, enough angels playing musical instruments – one of them a bagpipe – to make an orchestra. The whole extravagant display reaches its climax at the east end where the roof bosses seem ready to fall off with the weight of carving, and the pillars, instead of being plain like the others, are laden with decoration. Best known is the so-called Prentice Pillar, where four strands of foliage start from the four base corners and spiral their way through 180° to the top; round the base winged serpents, their necks intertwined, bite their own tails. It is all very wonderful. It is also very overwhelming, rather as if the Fifth Symphony were being played in fifteen minutes, *fortissimo.*

How did this *tour de force* of stone carving come into existence? We really do not know. The Earl, its founder, is reported to have been much given to luxury and ostentatious display, and to have had 'so many titles that it would weary even a Spaniard to repeat them'. But this does not do much to account for the extravagance of Roslin Chapel. That would be remarkable anywhere, at any time, but it is especially remarkable in view of the plainness, not to say the austerity, of most late medieval Scottish buildings. To see similar encrusted Gothic, the experts tell us, we must go to the monasteries of Portugal or Spain, in which William Beckford saw 'the utmost exuberance of decoration – the richest and most gorgeous of spectacles, the earth and the heavens and all the powers therein'. But Roslin seems to predate these continental examples. And although it was reported at the time that the founder 'caused artificers to be brought from other regions and forraigne kingdoms', there is no reason to suppose that carving of this kind was beyond the skill of many Scottish masons, or that the Earl of Orkney could not imagine a whole church so carved, and have been prepared to pay for it. As for the Prentice Pillar, a legend has been attached to it – Scott bears some of the responsibility – which is a folk-tale in many countries. The story is that a master mason employed at Roslin, who had run out of ideas, went abroad to seek inspiration. When he returned, he found that his apprentice had carved the marvellous pillar. Overcome with jealousy, he struck the young man dead. The story came long after the carving. In Defoe's *Tour* of the 1720s the reference is to 'the Prince's Pillar'.

The nearby castle, a couple of hundred yards away at the end of an unsurfaced road, is an utter ruin except for the east range which is a private dwelling. The site is a spur of rock approached over a high narrow causeway, where once there was presumably a drawbridge. Attacked by the Earl of Hertford in 1544, much of the old masonry lies in Roslin Glen, far below. The east range is larger than appears, for a good deal of it is below courtyard level, built on to the rock. A fireplace bears the date 1597 and on a doorway there is an inscription which reads 'sWS [for Sir William Sinclair] 1622', so this part of the castle was restored, then and later. Roslin Glen, where there is ample space for parking and walking, is heavily wooded, which means that even the outlines of the castle can scarcely be seen from below.

From Roslin it is only a mile or two to Penicuik, a planned town which rose to prosperity in the nineteenth century on the basis of paper-making, of which nothing survives. The town is of little interest. **Penicuik House** however, a mile or two away, has been described as the Scots Palladian house at its best, with grounds generously planted and romantically diversified by architectural fancies in the approved fashion of the eighteenth century. The house was designed by the son of the builder of Mavisbank (*see* p. 281), and completed in 1778. The design was quite grand and was made even grander in the nineteenth century, and the interior once contained murals of scenes from *Ossian*; Sir James Clerk was an enthusiastic student of antiquity. There is, unhappily, a serious drawback. The house was gutted by fire in 1899, and only the shell remains.

But in a sense the phoenix has risen from the ashes. After the fire the family moved into the adjacent stables, converting them into a quadrangular domestic courtyard as elegant in its own way as was once the house itself. The front of the court is of eleven arcaded bays, and it is entered through a portico surmounted by a tall slender Gibbsian steeple. On the opposite side from the steeple there rises above roof level a hefty doocot, built in the 1760s as a reproduction of a Roman shrine or monument which once stood near the Antonine Wall. In every angle of the court there is a stair turret, and a fountain plays in the centre. It is all very charming, and vaguely Italianate. The erstwhile stables are now a living room, and the wall-niches are the old mangers; there are pedimented doorcases and a chimneypiece rescued from the ruined house.

The grounds were first developed not by Sir James, the builder of Penicuik, but by Sir John, the builder of Mavisbank. He began in the 1720s by planting trees – more than 300,000, it is said – and in 1730 he built the walled garden with its two-storey pavilion. In 1738 he built the Centurion's Bridge over the Esk, humpbacked, with two shelters like sentry-boxes; water features in 1743; and a Roman watchtower in 1751. In 1755 he died, but Sir James continued the work with a Chinese Gate in 1758, and in 1759 an obelisk over a round-headed archway, which is a monument to Allan Ramsay. What is interesting about Penicuik House and its surroundings is that they recall so clearly the creative spirit of the eighteenth century. The house and grounds are private property and are not open to the public.

South of Penicuik you are at once in the windswept open country between the Pentlands and the Moorfoots, at an elevation never less than six hundred feet, an area very liable to be blanketed in snow every winter. Soon the road joins the Edddleston Water, and begins to descend to that small village, where an old Border tower has blossomed into the Barony Castle Hotel. Beyond the village, on the right-hand side of the road, there is a memorial to the designer of the Scott Monument in Edinburgh, John Meikle Kemp (*see* p. 121), who worked for a time in Eddleston as a wheelwright. The valley is small, cultivated and enclosed; and very soon a rampart of hills ahead presages the outskirts of Peebles.

22

To Kelso and the Tweed via Lauder

FROM DALKEITH THE A68 sweeps up the hill and, before turning south towards the Moorfoots and Mellerstain and the Lammermuirs, crosses what is probably the line of Dere Street. A mile or two further south the road passes Oxenfoord School, hidden in its own extensive grounds. This was once Oxenfoord House. It began as a tower, was expanded by Robert Adam in 1782 into a large tall castellated block with turrets at the corners, and then in 1840 William Burn spoiled it by sticking on – there is no kinder expression – lower but extensive additions in a vaguely Tudor style. The best feature of this now enormous pile is the wide outward curve of the wall between Adam's corner turrets. The library (by Burn) and the drawing-room (by Adam) are separated only by folding doors; when these are open, there is a room with high white ceilings and bay windows, ninety feet long.

The school cannot be seen from the road and neither can the bridge over the Tyne at Pathhead, because the bridge carries the road. It is a handsome structure (1831) by Telford, built at the same time as the Dean Bridge over the Water of Leith, which it resembles. There used to be a ford here (hence the village of Ford almost beneath the bridge) and it was probably here that the Roman road crossed the river on its way to the Forth.

The partially eighteenth century village of Pathhead is immediately south of the bridge, and here a road to the right leads in a couple of miles to Crichton Castle, and then, in two more miles, to Borthwick Castle. This little detour is well worth while for anyone interested in Scottish history and Scottish buildings.

Crichton Castle is an outstanding example of a fourteenth century keep, subsequently extended to become a sixteenth century castle surrounding a courtyard. Built on open undulating ground above the steeply wooded banks that slope down to the infant River Tyne, the castle stands massive, roofless and forlorn. Although close to Edinburgh, its situation is extremely rural and retired.

To Kelso and the Tweed via Lauder

The original keep, now in the centre of the east side of the castle, was built late in the fourteenth century, with walls seven feet thick. During the fifteenth century three ranges were added so as to form a courtyard, and late in the sixteenth century the fifth Earl of Bothwell – not the consort of Mary, Queen of Scots, but a nephew – made such alterations as would turn the castle into an exceptionally up-to-date and impressive lordly residence.

The keep is of the usual form, one vaulted space above another, with a pit prison, and a stair in the thickness of the wall. The upper space was the hall, with large windows, and there were rooms above, which have long since disappeared. The fifteenth century extensions on the south and west sides of the courtyard were made so as to provide a new entrance (now built up) on the south side, new halls, new kitchens and other accommodation. The new great hall is above the closed entrance, its fireplace having shafts and foliated capitals which support a heavily moulded lintel and canopy; this hall was later divided by a partition. Above it is the second hall, or withdrawing room, which has a stone cornice carved with flowers and ball ornaments, and a handsome fireplace with an arched lintel. It probably had a timber roof. Kitchens and bedrooms were provided in the west wing; the main kitchen is very large, and the fireplace is enormous, 21 feet across and 10 feet deep, arched in two spans, with a pillar in the centre. The tall gable on this side of the castle, with windows directly beneath the chimney, was an addition made by the Earl of Bothwell in the 1580s, and the same is probably true of the corbelled bartizan and the highly decorative corbelling and machicolations which also appear on the east and south frontages.

The pride and curiosity of Crichton is the north range. Begun some time in the fifteenth century, it was altered in a most surprising way by the fifth Earl between 1581 and 1591. The wall facing the courtyard is arcaded at ground level, seven bays long, with a return bay to the west. The entire wall above the arcading is ornamented with a strong and distinctive diamond-pattern rustication, covering two storeys. And the large windows in the wall are most effectively positioned and are framed in smooth surrounds which perfectly show off the rustication. Nor is this all. The first steps of a handsome square staircase project invitingly into the court, and as one mounts this staircase one finds pillars at each landing and carved and flowered string-courses. How did all this architectural display and refinement reach a prison-like fortress deep in the Scottish countryside before the end of the sixteenth century? That it was decreed by the fifth Earl is certain; the monogram FSMD (for Francis Stewart and his wife Margaret Douglas), with an anchor, is above the two central columns of the arcade. But this in itself does not explain much. How came the Earl to make such a break with the past – and with his own day? The rustication is unique in Scotland for the period, and the staircase, the arcading, and the rhythmic distribution of the windows belong to the architecture of the Renaissance, which had hardly begun to reach Scotland in the 1580s. Part of the explanation must be that the Earl spent a good deal of his youth on the Continent; he is known to have been in Italy around 1580. So he probably saw the marvellous palaces newly built at Florence or Verona, and he resolved to produce the same effects at home. But the intention was not enough. He must have had a good architect to put his ideas into practice (some wandering Italian, perhaps, paid well to cross the seas), for there is nothing fumbling or ill-managed about these modern improvements. The architectural refinement in a grim old castle almost makes one gasp. For possibly the first time in Scotland, an elegant setting was provided for elegant, civilized life. It is not difficult to imagine the lords and ladies from a painting by Raphael or Mantegna descending the staircase at Crichton Castle.

Unfortunately, the fifth Earl was not only a patron of the most modern architecture, he was also a little mad. His military/political activities in the 1580s endangered the lives of the King and the King's enemies alike, and when he was only a little over thirty the Earl was an exile in France. Later, he settled in Naples, where he died in 1612. His castle fared little better, stumbling gradually to decay. It appears thrice in history. Within its walls, in 1440, Sir William Crichton devised the plan to invite the sixth Earl of Douglas and his brother to a feast in Edinburgh Castle and then murder them, which he did; this is famous as the Black Dinner. In 1562 Mary Queen of Scots came as a guest to the wedding of one of her (seven) natural brothers. And in 1567 the Queen again appeared, this time with Bothwell on her way to Dunbar.

Near the castle are the roofless stables, also built in the 1580s and now requiring buttresses to keep the walls in place. The church dates in part from the middle of the fifteenth century. It has a massive tower, is cruciform, aisleless and tunnel-vaulted, and remarkably cavernous.

A narrow, twisting and turning, up-and-down country road leads away from the lonely ruins of Crichton Castle to the most magnificent of all Scottish tower-houses, a building which is sometimes claimed to be the most imposing in Scotland, **Borthwick Castle**. Borthwick Castle is a private dwelling and is not open to the public; even so, it should not be missed.

Borthwick was built in the 1430s, and although restored it has never been altered; it is in a state of almost perfect – some may think almost too perfect – preservation. It is less dramatically situated than Crichton, on lower flatter ground, and it is not immediately obvious that it stands on a spur of land jutting out into a little valley, at the junction of two streams, towards which the ground slopes steeply. Most of the courtyard wall, with a round tower at one corner and the entrance gateway beside it, was rebuilt in 1892 on the old foundations.

The plan is a rectangle with two projecting wings on the west side, built so large and close together as to leave only a deep narrow recess between them; from three sides it looks like a solid block, from the west it looks like two adjacent towers. The walls, faced with expertly dressed stone, not mere rubble, rise sheer for an astonishing eighty feet. It is a severely feudal fortress, massive, bare and perpendicular. There are windows in the walls, not many of them and distributed with marked irregularity, but no gun-loops; the battlements are heavily machicolated. Above the parapet there rise steep stone-slated roofs, and sufficient chimneys to give a lofty, domestic touch. But these are only by way of contrast. The walls are the thing, as inhospitable as precipices. What is unforgettable about Borthwick is its size, its extreme verticality of aspect, and its general air of mighty indestructibility.

Inside, everything is of stone, even the ceilings, some of them barrel-vaulted and semi-circular. The main range, which has three vaulted stages, contains the principal rooms; the lesser rooms are in the projecting wings, the smallest in the walls themselves. This last causes no difficulty, as the walls are up to twelve feet thick; they accommodate the turnpike stairs as well.

The hall occupies the whole of the main building on the first floor. It has been described as the grandest medieval hall in Scotland, a princely apartment fifty feet long, twenty three and a half feet across, and with a pointed vault which soars up to almost thirty feet above the floor. Scott said that within it 'an armed horseman might brandish his lance'. It contains an enormous fireplace, with a huge pyramidal stone hood, and with mouldings and ornaments of the period. Borthwick is also provided with windows with stone seats, aumbries or cupboards recessed into the walls, and stone wash basins. For so formidable a fortress, a surprising amount of trouble was taken over the comfort of the inhabitants.

Borthwick has no history – that is why it stands as it always stood, imposing and sombre. Mary and Bothwell came here in 1567, but when their enemies approached they departed. Cromwell's guns opened fire on it in 1650, but after a few rounds Lord Borthwick prudently submitted and was allowed to withdraw. Never seriously attacked, it remains a complete building of the fifteenth century; few places in Scotland, certainly few within sight of a main road (it is just visible from the A7), look quite so out of sympathy with the concerns and manners of the present day.

From Borthwick the visitor may easily reach the A7 and travel down the valley of the Gala Water to Galashiels. But it is a winding road, not particularly interesting, and a better choice is to return to Pathhead and take the A68, which climbs over the Lammermuirs and immediately descends into Lauderdale, going south to the Tweed.

The crossing is over Soutra. The road is well engineered and easy, but is bleak and usually windswept, and sometimes blocked by snow in winter; for most of the year, however, it provides splendid prospects, looking north over the low, fertile, cultivated country that stretches through Haddington to Dunbar, with the crags and hills of Edinburgh to the west, or, on the other side, south over Lauderdale to the rolling Border hills.

Almost before the climb over Soutra begins, the B6368 leaves the main road on the right. A little distance up this minor road are the remnants of a twelfth-century hospice for pilgrims, other travellers and poor folk. The Reformation cut off its support, and as the years went by the fabric was carted away, bit by bit, to make walls elsewhere. Little remains. The B6368 was originally Dere Street, the Roman highway to the north, and the line of Dere Street can be traced southward from the hospice across the hills until it rejoins the A68 at Oxton.

The descent into Lauderdale is swift and easy. The Leader Water, which rather confusingly gives its name to Lauderdale, rises not far from the main road, which keeps close to it for almost twenty miles. The valley – an often-used invasion route – is narrow as far as Lauder, fine grazing country with beautiful lines of trees and small woods on the eastern slopes.

Lauder is a little town which once hoped to be important, for it was made a royal burgh in 1502. Possibly that was when the Tolbooth was built, in the middle of the High Street, a picturesque little building with a flight of steps ascending to the door. Much reconstructed, the Tolbooth splits the High Street into two; otherwise, the street pattern is almost certainly medieval. Apart from the Tolbooth, and taking for granted the lanes and the alleys and the well-built stone houses, the pride and eccentricity of Lauder is Lauder Kirk (1673); its pride because it was built by Sir William Bruce for the Duke of Lauderdale, its eccentricity because the plan is a Greek cross, with four pointed arches carrying a central tower above the crossing. Such churches are few in Scotland, and this is one of the best preserved. The tower is square to the roof-line, then octagonal, and with a pointed roof – what the Duke called 'a handsom litle steeple'. The pulpit is in the crossing. When built in the days of Charles II there was an altar in the eastern arm; and probably lofts (i.e. galleries) in the others. The church-yard contains a watch-tower, built after a body-snatching raid by 'resurrectionists' in 1830. Science was on the march, and the needs of the anatomists in Edinburgh must be met.

For Thirlestane Castle, turn off the A68 about half a mile along the road from Lauder. The original Thirlestane Castle stands a couple of miles to the east, a simple tower-house beside the Boondreich Water (visible from the A697). It is an utter ruin, having been abandoned probably in the late sixteenth century, when the present house was begun.

John Maitland, Baron Maitland of Thirlestane and Lord Chancellor of Scotland, began the first stage – now almost entirely concealed – of present-day **Thirlestane Castle**, and it was completed about 1600. He sited his castle on rising ground, close by the river Leader, which gave some protection on that side, while to the west the land seems once to have been under water, or at least boggy, which also would have hampered attackers. The site was possibly once occupied by the old Lauder Fort, which was in the hands of Edward II in 1324 when he was trying to hold down the country. But while defensive considerations may have carried some weight with the Lord Chancellor, his castle was built for comfort and convenience and without much regard for fighting.

It was a most unusual building, long and narrow, with four large round towers, one at each corner, a stair turret in one of the angles, and along each side three semi-circular towers projecting from the walls. In two of these there are staircases. This elongated and almost symmetrical plan is without precedent in old Scottish castle houses.

What was built in the 1590s became the stem of a much larger T-shaped building when John Maitland's grandson, the formidable second Earl and subsequently first and only Duke of Lauderdale, decided in the 1670s to make the old place more imposing and bring it up to date. Lauderdale was Secretary of State for Scotland from 1661 to 1680, and controlled the country in the interests of himself, his family, and Charles II. According to Clarendon he was 'insolent, imperious, flattering, dissembling, had courage enough not to fail when it was absolutely necessary, and no impediment of honour to restrain him from doing anything that might gratify any of his passions'. His portrait by Lely, a splendid piece of painting, is in the National Portrait Gallery in Edinburgh.

Having decided to build, Lauderdale commissioned the 'gentleman architect' Sir William Bruce, currently engaged in rebuilding Holy-roodhouse, to draw up plans. Bruce was an admirer of Classical architecture – about which little was known in seventeenth century Scotland – so he tended to favour pavilions and pediments and symmetry after the prevailing fashion in England and France. But he was also sympathetic to the Scots vernacular style. He therefore left most of the existing building untouched, but extended the west front with a pair of four-storey pavilion-towers with pointed roofs, created a terraced forecourt at first floor level reached by a wide flight of steps, raised the west elevation to five storeys and put a pediment centre-top. Thirlestane now looked much grander, and must have been an excellent example of what Horace Walpole called 'that betweenity that intervened when Gothic declined and Palladian was creeping in". Seventy years later the building was converted into a Victorian fantasy. Extra wings with towers and pointed roofs were added; oriel windows were supplied; balconies appeared on the west face where there never had been any; and the central tower was considerably raised, crowned with a very prominent ogee roof, and backed up by a pair of slim, sharp-pointed turrets. Looking over an extensive and well-wooded park, beyond which rise the easy slopes of Lauderdale, Thirlestane Castle now seems out of place. It would fit better into Beverley Hills.

Behind all the make-believe many of the old rooms remain, and most, if not all, of the seventeenth century ceilings. These latter, (by Dunsterfield and Houlbert), are the chief interest of the interior. They are, to speak frankly, overdone; 'heavily stuccoed', as an eighteenth century visitor laconically remarked. Perhaps the Duke and his craftsmen, who had just finished at Holyroodhouse, were resolved to have more than regal splendour. The Duke's Room is not inelegant. But in the two Drawing Rooms caution has been thrown to the winds.

Garlands of roses, fruit and other flowers, wreaths of laurel, coronets, lions and life-size eagles hang miraculously from the ceilings and round the friezes. The furniture and pictures are of little interest, although there are two handsome pedimented doorcases. Prince Charles Edward slept in one of the small bedrooms on his way south in 1745.

Return to the A68 and continue to Earlston. This is delightful country, a pastoral valley watered by a steadily widening river all the way; fine trees come close to the road as Earlston is approached. Here take the A6105 for Gordon. The road is not especially interesting, but just before you reach the village, on the left hand side of the road, stands **Greenknowe Tower**, perhaps the most attractive small tower in the Borders.

Although roofless, Greenknowe is well preserved; it was inhabited until about 1850, and one can easily imagine its conversion into an imposing home today. Built in 1581, it is L-plan, four storeys high, of pink and grey stone, with a turret stair corbelled out at first floor level in the angle of the L. The entrance doorway still has its iron yett, and the lintel above it is carved with the date 1581, two shields, and the initials I.S. (James Seton) and J.E. (Jane Edmondstone). The ground floor is vaulted, and a stair near the entrance doorway leads to the hall on the first floor, which has a large fireplace with side pilasters, and two little closets built within the wall on each side of the kitchen flue – good central heating. The gables are finished with crowsteps, and there are three circular angle-turrets, corbelled out.

What makes Greenknowe so delightful is partly its good order – it scarcely wants more than the roof – and partly its setting. It is indeed on a green knowe, or knoll, and thus stands a couple of metres above the further off surrounding ground, which is level but marshy. Ancient beech trees protect it from the west wind, and springy grass is all around. In the springtime there are snowdrops amid the trees, and a few daffodils. Celandine grows in the rough grass, and at any time of year you may see a heron keeping watch in the wet land, which was once Greenknowe's first line of defence. There is not a house in sight.

On to Gordon, and turn right for Kelso. After three miles of up-and-down green prosperous countryside you reach the grounds of **Mellerstain House**, generally regarded as one of the most distin-guished eighteenth century houses in Scotland.

Mellerstain has an odd history. In the seventeenth century there stood here or hereabouts 'ane old melancholick hous that had had great buildings about it'. In 1725 William Adam was commissioned to improve matters, and he built the two wings which today flank the forecourt. But nothing connected them until a subsequent owner, inspired, perhaps, by what he had seen during his Grand Tour, commissioned Robert Adam to build the house itself. This was in 1770. Adam's patron was George Baillie, ancestor of the present owner, the Earl of Haddington.

The design is simple and austere, excellently proportioned, in Adam's castellated manner. A central projecting keep of four storeys is connected to equally projecting wings, which in their turn connect to the lower 1720 wings. A stairway leads up to the central entrance door, and there are machicolations all round. The elevation to the garden is similar, but almost flat. The exterior is thus fairly plain, and certainly not overstated.

It is therefore a surprise to find that the interior is of the utmost sophistication. The Stone Hall, with which the tour of the house begins, has a simple William Adam fireplace with Dutch tiles, and the Small Sitting Room, which comes next, has a delicate Gothic-style ceiling all white. These hardly prepare one for the outburst of colour and Classical decoration on the walls, ceilings, doors and even the window-shutters of the next four rooms, which all overlook the garden. The Library and the Music Room are the most remarkable. In the Library, pale green predominates. Above the white carved-wood bookcases, filled with leather-bound eighteenth century volumes, are panels with low-relief Classical figures, white on a grey background, and antique busts in circular niches (two by Roubiliac). All these are set against the pale green wall. In the centre of the green ceiling is an oil painting of Minerva, surrounded by a large and elaborate plaster-work pattern in white, grey and old rose. In the Music Room the doors and doorcases (carved, as usual) are white against plum coloured walls, and the ceiling, delicately but extensively ornamented with scrolls, medallions and tracery of all kinds, is chiefly in soft greens and blues. The walls of the Drawing Room, by contrast, are hung with pink damask, but the ceiling, in shades of blue and lilac, is again most delicately decorated with lines of white filigree and panels of vases and griffins, a motif repeated in different colours in the cornice. In the small Drawing Room the ceiling is similarly decorated, and there is a white marble fireplace designed by Robert Adam.

In rooms of such colourful decoration the contents might pass unnoticed. But all these rooms contain very fine pieces of eighteenth century furniture, mostly English, some by Chippendale. The large

Aubusson carpet in the Drawing Room is quite splendid, and the Strasbourg faience turkey tureen (c 1755) in the Small Drawing Room could surely hold a gallon of soup. The paintings, mostly portraits, include half a dozen by Allan Ramsay, a small landscape by Ruisdael, an imposing 'Isabella d'Este' attributed to the circle of Parmigiano, and an early Gainsborough.

Inevitably, the other rooms are not decorated and furnished to the same standard, although the hand of Robert Adam reaches even to the Great Gallery at the top of the house; but his plans for the ceiling here were never implemented.

The gardens are twentieth century, but none the worse for that. They were laid out by Sir Reginald Blomfield in 1909. They consist of terraces, with balustrades and steps and urns, which skilfully lead down to an immense stretch of lawn which in its turn leads to an artificial wood-fringed lake. Beyond the lake, the long line of the Cheviot hills is blue in the distance. It is an excellent piece of design.

Mellerstain is thus a very unusual house. Its interior is insistent Robert Adam, insistently colourful, insistently correct to the last detail. If you like it, well and good. If you don't, pause to admire the Front Hall on your way out. It is in quiet, restful tones, beautifully proportioned with apsidal ends and two niches which contain marble busts of Apollo and Venus. Facing the door hangs the portrait of the most famous chatelaine of Mellerstain, Lady Grisell Baillie (1665–1746). She kept a 'Household Book' which is a document of some historical importance. What is a good deal more exciting, when she was twelve years old she was sent by her father, Sir Patrick Hume, to get in touch with Robert Baillie, owner of Mellerstain, who was at that time imprisoned in the Tolbooth in Edinburgh. To communicate with imprisoned covenanters was a dangerous game; and the young lady must have known that, once in the Tolbooth, she might find it very difficult to get out; but the mission was successfully accomplished. Soon afterwards Robert Baillie was executed. A few years later her father was in deep trouble, and had to take refuge from persecution in the vaults of Polwarth church, near Duns; there his daughter brought him food after darkness fell, passing alone through the chill churchyard. To complete the story, the family next had to flee to the Netherlands. While in exile, Grisell frequently saw George Baillie, son of the Robert Baillie once imprisoned in the Tolbooth. This young man she had first met when getting in touch with his father. On returning to Scotland in 1688 they were married, and Lady Grisell became the mistress of Mellerstain.

From Mellerstain it is only six or seven miles through rolling cultivated country to Kelso and the Tweed. On your left you may catch a
glimpse of **Hume Castle**, just beyond Sweethope Hill. (By a side
road you can be there in a few minutes). Hume Castle does not stand
very high, but it is visible over an astonishingly wide area, 'queening
it over the Merse'. Yet most guide-books studiously ignore it, and one
of the few entries likens it not to a queen but to 'a loathly and wrin-
kled hag". Poor old Hume Castle, once a great bulwark of the
Borders! Just because it looks bogus, it is cold-shouldered by the
connoisseurs! Admittedly it is bogus; those walls with their absurd
crenellations were erected about 1800, when the 'real' castle had
been almost entirely demolished. But they stand exactly on the foundations of the ancient castle, a nearly rectangular plan on a rocky
outcrop, almost certainly begun in the thirteenth century. It was taken
by Somerset in 1547 (after a determined resistance by Lady Home),
by Sussex in 1569, and by the forces of Cromwell in 1650. It was the
seat of the Lords Home, later Earls of Marchmont. (Hume, by the
way, is approximately the local pronunciation of the name correctly
spelt as Home). Travelling on almost any road between Berwick-
upon-Tweed and Kelso (*see* p. 321), you will be surprised how often a
look-out in Hume Castle would have you under surveillance.

23

To Berwick-upon-Tweed via Gifford and the Lammermuirs

TAKE THE A68 out of Dalkeith, and after four miles turn left for Ormiston and Pencaitland. (If you want to see two very inter-esting castles, Crichton and Borthwick, continue on the A68 to Pathhead and turn right. See Chapter 22). The hamlet of Ormiston was extended to become a planned village in the eighteenth century, its economy a careful mix of agriculture and industry. It lost money, and its founder had to sell it. In the wide tree-lined main street there stands one of the very few pre-Reformation cruciform mercat crosses in Scotland. It must have been brought here from somewhere else and re-erected, possibly to add dignity to the new foundation. But now its incisive edges have been worn to a kind of resignation of dulness. In later days Ormiston became a mining village ('the miners sit in the sun outside the inn'; but that was in the 1950s) and now it is largely a dormitory for Edinburgh.

Pencaitland – strictly speaking, Wester Pencaitland; Easter Pencaitland is on the other side of the bridge across the River Tyne – also has a mercat cross (c1700), this time with a sundial. There are attractive pantiled cottages, and one of them, once a school, has a bellcote and the stone figure of a pupil above the porch. The bridge across the river appears to date from soon after 1500. The church, which stands on medieval foundations, appears to contain building from every century from the twelfth to the seventeenth, except, for some reason, the fifteenth century. The school (1870) is one of those nineteenth century charitable fantasies which demon-strate the Victorians' sense of fun as well as their faith in education.

Continue through East Saltoun, once the home of Andrew Fletcher (1653–1716), a notable opponent of the Union of 1707, and then through pleasantly wooded rolling country to Gifford.

Gifford is a white-washed village with a spacious and somehow aristocratical air. The original village was demolished early in the eighteenth century so as to give the newly aggrandised Yester House more dignified surroundings, and the re-created village was laid out on one side of the avenue which leads towards the house; this avenue is at right-angles to the Edinburgh road. However ungenerous it was to evict people from their homes, the laird was generous enough in giving space to the new village; a large green or bleaching ground separates the line of cottages – the first to be built – from a splendid avenue of lime trees, on the other side of the avenue is an even larger green, now a recreation ground, and then comes the little river and bridge (1704, rebuilt early in the nineteenth century). The mercat cross of 1780 is where the avenue reaches the road. In due course, houses were built along the road, away from the bridge and up to and beyond the parish church (1710), making Gifford into an L-plan village.

Although it has been steadily added to, Gifford has not yet been spoiled. Many houses clearly belong to the eighteenth century, notably the Tweeddale Arms with an arched entrance to its courtyard and a handsome post-and-beam sign; and, near the gates of Yester House, Beechwood is of the same period, with a square projecting stair turret. But Gifford is attractive not because of individual houses but because of its general air of order and good proportions. The church is T-plan, white-washed like so much else, with a square tower and a short slated spire; inside there is a laird's loft and a seventeenth century pulpit. Gifford is further distinguished by the fact that John Witherspoon (1723–1794) was born in the manse here. He emigrated to America, became the first President of New Jersey College (now Princeton University) and was one of the signatories of the American Declaration of Independence.

Yester House, upon which the original hamlet of Gifford entirely depended, is not visible from the road and it is not open to the public. It was begun early in the eighteenth century, was modified by William Adam in the 1730s, further altered by Robert Adam late in the century, and altered again in the 1830s. It is a great block of a house, chiefly distinguished by pedimented attics north and south, a very large glazed porte cochere on the west front, and a prominent slated roof which is punctuated all round by recessed attic windows. No one could call it beautiful. But the interior, regular and symmetrical, is of a very high standard; the drawing room, indeed, has been described as the finest room of its kind in Scotland. It is basically

William Adam, with a deep coved ceiling and tabernacle doors. Robert decorated the coves with octagonal coffers, enlarged the windows, and provided an elaborate Rococo chimneypiece and over-mantel. This is all set off by the mural paintings (1761) by William Delacour, Classical scenes in cheerful colours. The square dining room, by William Adam, also has a Rococo chimneypiece and over-mantel and some excellent plasterwork.

The chapel, close to the house, is a startling mixture of old and new. It is vaulted, with stone roofs and ancient carvings, but all this lies behind the Rococo Gothic frontage applied by the Adam brothers in 1753; according to one critic this architectural medley provides the best realization that Robert Adam achieved of his early Gothic fantasies.

Yester Castle lies about a mile to the east, up the Hopes Water. There is very little of it left. It is supposed to have been built in the thirteenth century. Nearby is the underground Goblin Ha' or Hall, built by spirits, so it is said, acting on the order of Hugo Gifford de Yester, who raised the castle by more orthodox means. The Hall is the size of a large room, and vaulted. Like the castle, it is extremely diffi-cult of access.

From Gifford the road climbs rapidly into the Lammermuirs, and you are soon above the 1000 foot contour. After some five miles the road forks. If you turn right for Longformacus, you are immediately in a world of long rolling hills, covered entirely with heather and moorgrass. For ten miles there is not a habitation. The road rises and falls, twists and turns, a narrow ribbon of asphalt laid through country that has hardly changed since time began. There are some sheep and a very few pine trees, and there are little wandering streams at the foot of the slopes. Curlews possess this high ground. Longformacus is no more than a few houses, sheltered by beech trees in a quiet valley. The Southern Uplands Way passes through the village, which is a good centre for walks in the Lammermuirs.

Then, after only a few more miles (but you can divert to Abbey St Bathans; *see* below), you are in **Duns**, solid dignified Duns, a very Scottish small town. It is the administrative centre for Berwickshire District Council. Duns Scotus is said to have come from here; his statue is in the park. And Jim Clark, who won the World's Racing Drivers Championship in 1963 and again in 1965, grew up in Duns, and is remembered in a memorial room which houses mementoes and trophies of his career.

If, on the other hand, you take the left fork after leaving Gifford, you soon reach the Whiteadder Reservoir, where a road turns north to

Garvald. Those interested in pre-history should take this road, for in four miles it reaches **White Castle Fort**, which was occupied from about 400 BC to 100 AD. The ramparts and ditches are well preserved, and the fort is immediately accessible from the road. Over a dozen small forts and settlements are to be found on the north-western slopes of the Lammermuirs above the 700' contour; this is the easiest of them to visit, in a totally unspoilt hill setting, with a tremendous view to the west.

Return to the reservoir, and the road which takes you to Duns. (This road can be reached by a cross-country road from Longformacus). About nine miles from the reservoir a road climbs sharply to the left, signposted to Abbey St Bathans.

Abbey St Bathans is not so much a village as a collection of houses, some large and some small, strung along the west side of the Whiteadder Water. Approaching from the south, the road winds up through the trees, attains the open slopes above, and then after a mile or two descends to a small saw-mill and the Whiteadder River. Opposite the saw-mill there are parking facilities and cream teas, and the church and the youth-hostel beside it are just round the corner. Approaching from the A1, the road crosses rich agricultural country and then climbs steeply to the rolling, wind-swept hillsides further up, before descending to the river and the little hamlet, passing a small wood of ancient, stunted oak trees. Abbey St Bathans is hidden away in wild, empty country, sheltered where the hillsides slope steeply down into the valley.

The site was originally occupied by the Cistercian monastery of St Botha, founded in the later twelfth century. The monastery was dissolved in 1558. The church, easily seen because of its prominent octagonal spire, is mostly late eighteenth century, although the east wall with its round-headed windows is some four hundred years older. The church is not particularly attractive, but contains two rather fine items. The first, just inside the entrance, is a remarkably well-preserved gravestone inscribed with the names of George Home, died 1705, one time minister of the parish, and 'Jean Hamilton spows to the seid George Home', died 1719. The lettering is unevenly spaced, but of excellent quality. The second item is at the east end of the church, an effigy of a prioress, seemingly of the dimmest antiquity, but which the experts say dates from about 1500. The remains of a crozier are by her right arm – unusual for a prioress – and the lines of her tunic, which stretches to her feet, are long and flowing. This simple effigy, lying half-forgotten in a somewhat dismal little church amid the hills, has the quality – even if only in a small degree – of genuine art.

Just by the church, where there used to be a ford, an ugly but substantial wooden bridge crosses the river. It was built by the Gurkhas, which is a surprise, in 1987, and must have been much needed, for the river here is wide and fast flowing, and can be deep. The Southern Uplands Way runs along the east bank. The path climbs into the hills from Abbey St Bathans, going south, and leads, in a couple of miles, to the **Edinshall Broch**. (The easiest way to the broch is *via* a minor road which goes west from the A6112). This simple form of tower, or circular fort, belongs much further north; several hundred have been identified in Shetland, Orkney, Caithness, Sutherland, Skye and the Outer Hebrides, but there are very few indeed in the south of Scotland. This example stands within a pre-historic oval fortification above the Whiteadder Water. It has a fifteen feet long entrance passage and, as was usual, the stair and chambers are within the very thick walls. The walls are now of no great height, but the courtyard has a diameter of over fifty feet. Brochs were places of refuge, and were in use from about the last years BC until the arrival of the Vikings.

From Duns it is only a short distance along the A6105 to **Manderston House**, sometimes described as the grandest Edwardian country house in Britain. Certainly no expense was spared in its construction – or, rather, its reconstruction, for it dates back to the 1790s when it was built as a moderately large, severely Classical, stylish Georgian house. Just over a hundred years later its millionaire owner, Sir James Miller, (hemp and herrings made his fortune) set out to alter and enlarge it. Ostentatious opulence was the aim, but mercifully the Adam style was retained. The garden front is as it always was, well-proportioned, urns and balustrades in the right places; but a new wing was added, greatly increasing the size of the house, and a full-height entrance portico. Inside, there are domes, apses, columns, candle-sticks and urns, all very Classical and very correct. The palatial twentieth century public rooms – and there are plenty of them – have elaborate plasterwork ceilings of such excellent quality as to be a match for those in the original drawing room, morning room and tea room along the garden front. The first-floor corridor, impressively wide and lined with columns, is reached by a staircase which is modelled on that in the Petit Trianon at Versailles. This staircase is especially famous, because it has a silver-plated balustrade topped with brass rails. It is usually referred to as 'the silver staircase'.

Almost all the furniture is reproduction Louis XVI. Below stairs are the kitchens and five marble-clad larders.

The dairy and the courtyard stables are also worth a visit. Reconstruction began with the stables (Sir James was a racing man) where the horses' stalls are in teak; each has a brass-framed marble plaque for the occupant's name. The dairy is vaulted in the Gothic style, and the walls are surfaced with marble from seven different countries. The head-gardener's house is Neo-Scots-Baronial, and the grounds extend to 56 acres.

All in all, Manderston is a remarkable house. Strictly Adam and Neo-Adam in style, it could belong only to the Edwardian era, when there were men (and women) rich enough and socially ambitious enough to pay for such a house, and craftsmen skilful enough to build and make furniture for it.

The road from Duns to Berwick-upon-Tweed runs along the northern boundary of the Merse, that great stretch of undulating fertile country that lies between the Lammermuirs and the River Tweed, and extends from Berwick-upon-Tweed to Kelso. Merse has the same meaning as March; the Merse was once the East March, where the Warden of the East March struggled to uphold the law (when he was not breaking it himself), his opposite number over the Border doing the same. Much Border fighting took place in the Merse, although the situation was never as bad here as further west. This was partly because the open and level nature of the country made concealment difficult, and partly because of the line of English castles on the other side of the Border – Berwick-upon-Tweed, Norham and Wark (*see* p. 319). These are positioned along a fifteen-mile stretch of the Tweed. All were formidable fortresses in their day, although Wark has almost vanished, little remains of Berwick-upon-Tweed, and only Norham retains an appearance of strength and grandeur. Today the Merse is a spacious scene of fertility and high cultivation. Like East Lothian, it is a land of long views, full of splendid eighteenth and nineteenth century farm steadings, farmtowns where cottages cluster beside the farm buildings themselves, and wide green acres.

The A6105 passes through Chirnside, which is notable only as being a mile or two north of the estate of Ninewells, the family home of David Hume, author of *A Treatise on Human Nature*, and continues above the valley of the Whiteadder Water to Foulden. Here, immediately at the side of the road, is Foulden Teind Barn, probably built early in the seventeenth century. Like the similar but larger barn at Whitekirk (*see* p. 263), the purpose was to store the produce collected by the Kirk each year as tithes. The door at the west end is approached by stone steps, and there are crow-stepped gables.

Foulden looks across the Merse and across the River Tweed to the Cheviot Hills. The long mass of the Cheviot itself, 2,674 feet high and one of the highest hills in England, is due south, over twenty miles away. But England is just round the corner. A mile from Foulden the road crosses the border, and after passing the site of the battle of Halidon Hill (1333, yet another Scots defeat) and providing one final view of the extensive range of the Cheviot Hills, it descends to Berwick-upon-Tweed and the sea.

24

To Berwick-upon-Tweed via the coast

THE A1 GOES from Edinburgh to Berwick-upon-Tweed, by-passing, as is the wont of main roads, everything of interest. Sweeping south of the Aberlady/Tantallan promontory and thus avoiding all sight of the castles, the golf courses and the Bass Rock, it approaches the sea at Dunbar, and then passes south of the town by a mile or so.

Dunbar is on the very edge of the sea, in the 'red lands' of East Lothian. Its parish church (1821), of Dunbar Red sandstone, is a landmark to anyone approaching the town, either by land or sea, for it stands high. There was a church here in the fourteenth century. Fire almost destroyed the present building in the 1980s, but it has been restored, and remains as conspicuous as ever.

Robert Burns came to Dunbar in 1787. He described it as 'a neat little town', and although it has spread outwards like almost all towns, its centre, with three streets nearly parallel to one another and to the water's edge, remains much as it was, and the road from Edinburgh lands you, quite suddenly, almost in the middle of it. The High Street – 'so wide', according to Cobbett, 'as to be worthy of being called an oblong square' – is made up of characteristically Scots eighteenth century houses, three or four storeys high, and is diversified with several pends, porches and chimney gables.

The High Street contains two interesting buildings, the Tolbooth and Lauderdale House. The Tolbooth looks very old – one wonders if its rough red stonework ever looked new – but it appears to date back no further than 1650. The stair-tower, which looks hexagonal but has only five sides, is topped by a wood-framed spire, which is unusual in Scotland, and there is a sundial on the SW face, just below the roof. Lauderdale House, looking down the High Street, is altogether different. It is a 1740s house enlarged to a design which was probably sketched by Robert Adam before his death in 1792. The principal elevation consists of the original house plus a balustrade and a sphinx, with two pedimented pavilions added, one on each side.

Additional nineteenth century windows have spoiled the harmony of the design, and the half-round portico with Ionic columns looks out of place. For the better part of a hundred years Lauderdale House was a barracks, and it seems somehow never to have recovered.

Dunbar improves as you go seaward. Although it now depends a good deal on the tourist trade, it used to depend almost entirely on the sea. It was the port for Haddington, and was once a centre for whalers, and more significantly for herring boats. James Watt remarked that 'the whole coast of Scotland may be considered as one continual fishery', and he did not exaggerate; there was a time when tens of thousands of people in Scotland depended upon the herring, that 'shifting, ambulatory fish', which 'annually deserts the vast depths of the arctic circle, and comes, heaven-directed, to the seats of population'. Little enough is left of that now, but Dunbar's harbours – there are three of them – are well worth a visit. They are so clearly the product of human toil, built stone upon stone for the convenience of wooden vessels and the men who risked their lives in them. The oldest and smallest, which was in use in the sixteenth century, consists merely of a short causeway to an island, with wall-walks and cobbles. The eighteenth century harbour, on the other hand, is formed by a curving rubble pier and a short straight pier which turns sharply back; it was constructed early in the century, and in 1761 a quay for importing coal was built within the curved pier. The Victoria Harbour – they are all close together – is much larger. Begun in 1844, it is formed by a pier which connects outcrops of rock to seaward, and a quay along the shore. There are two entrances, one past the castle and another which gives access to the old channel, and is spanned by a curious little hand-operated drawbridge. Old warehouses, granaries and maltings, many of them now put to new uses, crowd close to the water. Pleasure boats monopolise the harbours, where the herring busses used to come.

The castle, cheek by jowl with the Victoria Harbour, is the ruin of a ruin. Mary, Queen of Scots came to stay here on three occasions, each one more disastrous than the last. She came with Darnley in March, 1566, two days after the murder of Riccio; she came again in April, 1567, this time with Bothwell, ten weeks after the murder of Darnley; and she came for the last time a month later, on her way to Carberry Hill where she surrendered herself to the rebellious nobles. She gave Bothwell the captaincy of Dunbar before she married him, and this caused the government to order the destruction of the castle at the end of the year. It was once a considerable fortress, but gales and the sea have added to the work of destruction, and the builders of the Victoria Harbour carried the process a little further. It is a dejected old place on a rough coast, strange company for the memory of a queen.

From Dunbar the A1 sweeps eastward, out of sight of the sea. Cultivation is everywhere, and trees are few; perhaps this is the part of the country that Dr Johnson was thinking of (like almost all eighteenth century travellers, Johnson travelled north *via* Newcastle and Berwick upon Tweed) when he said that the entry to Scotland was a treeless waste. On the higher ground a few miles back from the coast there are some attractive little villages, in varying shades of pink or pink-purple sandstone: Spott, with Spott House nearby, rebuilt in 1830 but standing on very old foundations; **Innerwick**, settled along two ridges, with fine nineteenth century farm buildings and cottages, and a remarkable stone tablet which reads as follows:

> *A man of kindness to his beast is kind*
> *But brutal actions show a brutal mind.*
> *Remember He who made thee made the brute.*
> *Who gave thee speech and reason made him mute.*
> *He cant complain but God's all seeing eye*
> *Beholds thy cruelty and hears his cry.*
> *He was designed thy servant not thy drudge.*
> *Remember his creator is thy judge:*

and Oldhamstocks, with a green, a mercat cross, and a church that dates back, although periodically altered, to the sixteenth century.

These little old peaceful villages look down on a grand temple of the nuclear age, the Advanced Gas-cooled Reactor at **Torness**. You cannot miss it; it is not far from Dunbar, quite close to the A1, and the main section is 90 metres high and 130 metres long. It is here because of sea water and bedrock, and is the largest technological project ever carried out in Scotland. The statistics are endless. It took nine years to build (1979–1988); it cost £1,800 million; it has two reactors, eight emergency diesel generators, and sufficient cables to go two and a half times round the world; the walls of the reactors are 5.8 metres thick; sea water is pumped in at the rate of thirty three million gallons per hour; the two turbo-generators can produce more than enough electricity for a city the size of Edinburgh. Anyone who wants more statistics, and to find out how it all really works, has only to go inside, for Torness is open to the public. No one can question that building this nuclear power station was a great engineering achievement. For example, a dock for barges was built on the shore so that enormous components could be brought in by sea; and then a sea-wall was constructed to prevent the highest possible tides and the wildest possible waves from reaching the site itself. We are assured that the station is safe; 'an accident of the type which occurred at Chernobyl could not happen at Torness'. We have to take their word for it. As regards its appearance, opinions are bound to differ. Look at it as a piece of sculpture. Its planes and proportions, projections and recesses; its severe but varied rectilinearity; its subtle grey-blue colour; its combination of concrete with amber-tinted solar glass; its imposing scale and stance; is not all this at least as good as the best of le Corbusier? or, some might say, a great deal better? No doubt about it, Torness sits well and naturally with the stern landscape, the inhospitable sea, and the sky.

A few miles further on and close to some very rocky coast the road reaches Cockburnspath (pronounced Co'path). Shortly before you come to the village, a minor road turns off to the **Collegiate Church of Dunglass**, which was founded in the fifteenth century. In some respects it is a poor little church, having been dreadfully knocked about after the Reformation. But fifteenth century churches, even in a poor state of preservation, are not common in Scotland, and Dunglass is distinguished by its roofs of overlapping flagstones and the barrel vaulting that supports them. It boasts little ornamentation – indeed, its antique style and simplicity provide much of its interest. There is, however, a delicate triple sedilia, or priest's seat, with corbels depicting winged and long-haired angels playing a harp and a lute, and there is a tomb with a lady in mid-fifteenth century dress. A spire once rose above the square tower. The post-Reformation damage is of some melancholy interest. A ragged opening in the east gable was made to allow the entry of carts, and holes in the stonework of the nave and choir were evidently made so that upper floors could be inserted. In short, the ancient church was used as a shed or barn or perhaps as a stable, doubtless by some eighteenth century 'improving' landlord. It is interesting to compare it with the slightly later but similar church at Ladykirk (*see* p. 315),which is remarkably preserved.

Cockburnspath itself is just at the side of the A1. (A side road from the village winds into the hills to Abbey St Bathans. See p. 300). The unusual round tower of the church is visible from the road. Some parts of the church may date from the fourteenth century, but the tower, which contains a wheel stair, was built around 1600. The mercat cross is of about the same date, and has a carved top showing thistles and roses. There was once a small keep to the south of the town, but its remains are fragmentary, If you turn aside here to **Pease Bay** you will find a beauty spot and a caravan park, as far as the two can co-exist; golden sands and toilet blocks are advertised.

A second interest of Cockburnspath is that it is the eastern terminus of the **Southern Uplands Way**, a sign-posted long-distance footpath, opened in 1984, that crosses Scotland from coast to coast. (Cockburnspath not being exactly on the coast, enthusiastic walkers should complete the 212 mile trip, starting at Portpatrick in Wigtownshire, by covering the extra mile to Pease Bay). This footpath is not for the faint-hearted. Some sections of the walk are very long (two are over twenty miles), accommodation along most of the route is scarce to non-existent, and the intrepid walker must traverse forests as well as long stretches of bleak high country. It is generally agreed that the hardest going is in the west, and that it is easiest to travel eastward, with and not against the prevailing winds. A comprehensive guide is available. We shall encounter the Southern Uplands Way at half a dozen other points in the course of our travels through the Borders.

From Cockburnspath the A1 continues through undulating lightly wooded countryside to the Pass of Pease, where the hill slopes are close to the road and in bygone days many a commander was able to halt the advance of forces superior to his own. But before this point there is a choice; to stay on the A1 or to take the scenic route (A1107) nearer to the coast. It has to be said that while the A1 hereabouts is not very interesting, neither is the scenic route very scenic. Its advantages are that it gives the motorist a close-up view of Coldingham Moor, an extensive, desolate, sodden, treeless bit of country which travellers in olden times were always careful to avoid. There are numerous pre-historic settlements in the area, preserved because never ploughed under. The road passes as near as most people are likely to get to Fast Castle, on the rock-bound coast, on the very edge of the sea. The castle, now a mere fragment, stands on an inaccessible peninsula of rock overlooked by towering cliffs. There was once a round tower, and there was a drawbridge over the chasm which separates the castle's rocky platform from the mainland; but little remains. There was fortification here in the fourteenth century, but its usefulness scarcely lasted two hundred years. The wretched ruins show only to what extremities men were sometimes driven in order to maintain their position in life during the Middle Ages, and even afterwards.

Coldingham itself is of no great interest; it lies in a little valley only a mile from a sheltered sandy beach. The attraction of the village is the **Priory**, a few hundred yards to the east, its remains now incorporated in the church. A religious house of some kind is mentioned here by Bede in the seventh century, but the Priory seems to have been built some time around 1200. It was at first cruciform, but only the choir and sanctuary remain. The north and east walls are original, and are a remarkable piece of Romanesque design. Externally, the walls are divided vertically by buttresses, and horizontally, by a string course, into two storeys. The string course is ingeniously lowered where it crosses the buttresses. In each bay there is a large pointed window above, and below it two round arches of a blind arcade. There are square turrets at the corners, one containing a wheel stair. Internally, the rhythm is particularly subtle, for the lower storey has an arcade of pointed arches, and the upper storey, which resembles a clerestory with lancet windows and arches between them, has a central passage in the thickness of the wall. The free use of multiple arcading gives an unusually vigorous and horizontal character to these ancient walls.

Nearby are some unusual graveslabs, one of them commemorating Radulphus, a prior who died in c1198, and another Emaldus, one of his successors who died early in the thirteenth century. There are also several incised cross-slabs which are certainly medieval.

From Coldingham it is only a short distance to **St Abbs**, a small village perched between the cliff tops and the sea, named after St Abba, a seventh century Northumbrian princess. St Abbs is popular with day visitors, so popular that driving into it is apt to be very difficult and driving out the same. More important, St Abb's Head is owned by the National Trust for Scotland (about 190 acres), and there is an excellent Visitors Centre by the roadside before you reach the village.

From the Centre a walk goes along the cliffs to the lighthouse, about a mile and a half away. Care is required, for the path is in some places very close to the cliff-edge. There is a great variety of flowers – pink thrift in early summer, rock rose, bird's foot trefoil and bluebells (harebells in England) as the days lengthen – and at all seasons the scenery is wild and spectacular. Not far from the village the path descends steeply to sea level, where there are rock pools; but soon you are again on the cliff tops, and have a view of the bird life that is everywhere along this rocky coast. Between St Abbs and the lighthouse there are cormorants, shags, fulmars, guillemots, and an estimated 15,000 pairs of nesting kittiwakes. Gannets are to be seen, but they prefer the even greater inaccessibility of the Bass Rock, twenty miles further west. The clatter and cacophony of bird life is sometimes louder than the sea. From the lighthouse the pre-historic Earn's Heugh Forts are about a mile further west, on the very edge of a cliff that drops 150 metres to the water. They are semi-circular – which means that in the last two thousand years or so a good deal of cliff has disappeared, for they must originally have been round or oval. There are the usual ramparts and ditches, and within them traces have been found of several circular stone-built houses. These forts are pre-Roman, but seem to have been occupied as late as the fourth century AD.

From the lighthouse you can return to St Abbs, passing either east or west of Mire Loch, or you can continue west from the lighthouse and join a track – if you can find it – which leads to the B6438.

Eyemouth, the next village along the coast, is a little fishing port and holiday resort, squeezed into a small area around the mouth of the only river in Berwickshire which flows directly into the sea. There is nothing very important about Eyemouth – and perhaps that is its attraction. The harbour was built in the later eighteenth century and extended in the nineteenth, and it is still a working harbour; there is a fish-market on the quay, and there are days when the fishing boats are tied up alongside two or three deep. Fishing used to be a cloak for smuggling. Wines, spirits, tea and tobacco were got ashore and stored in caves along the nearby cliffs, or in cellars and lofts in Eyemouth itself. Gunsgreen House, an eighteenth century mansion on the east bank of the river, is supposed to have been a good place for conceal-ment, and the tricky layout of the town ('a chaos of alleyways', it has been called) further facilitated this important trade. Some splendid stone-built warehouses and granaries remain to recall more legitimate activities. On the headland west of the harbour are the remains of a sixteenth century fort. Eyemouth is full of bustle, and for those who like crab, straight out of the ocean, there is no better place to go.

From Eyemouth it is only three miles to Ayton and Ayton Castle, on the inland side of the A1. The village is of no special note, although it has an old church, now ruinous, which dates back to the twelfth century, and is dedicated to, of all people, St Dionysius. **Ayton Castle**, however, close to the village, is much more interesting.

Designed by Gilllespie Graham and completed in 1848, the Castle was slightly altered and extended in 1861. It occupies a commanding position in lovely rolling country just north of the Lammermuirs. A delightful wooded drive above the Eye River leads round and up to the entrance on the north side. Built of red sandstone, the Castle has a central square tower with corbelled out turrets, and wings to each side. The south elevation, with a long line of regularly spaced windows, looks rather uninteresting, a sort of low-key Scottish baronial. But the interior is altogether another matter.

The two principal rooms on the ground floor, which look south, are large, lit by large windows, and have splendid geometrical plaster ceilings; the pattern is completely formal, repetitive and effective. These rooms open off a wide corridor, which is arched with a triple window at the west end, providing a most interesting internal vista. A stone spiral staircase in the heart of the building leads to the bedrooms on the upper floor. The stone of the staircase was originally painted with a small, colourful pattern, which was later painted over; but the original pattern and colouring are now partly revealed. The walls of the Gallery are similarly hand-decorated, and have never been altered.

What is especially interesting about Ayton is its perfectly preserved interior detail. Here is a Victorian castle that was built from scratch, has been continuously occupied since it was built, has never been neglected, and so has never required drastic restoration. The Victorian central-heating system (under-floor ducts) is still in place; the pictures (many of them not yet attributed) were mostly brought to the house when it was built; the doors and the panelling on the walls are Victorian woodwork at its most competent. Grand but not ostentatious, solid but never dull, this is a great Victorian family house as such houses were meant to be.

Rejoin the A1 and you are only a couple of miles from the border. But Scotland offers one last vista. As the road passes below the main-line railway to London and then climbs and swings right – suddenly, an immense liberating panorama of sea is spread before you. The cliffs go straight down from very close to the road, and the arc of the horizon is immense. Only the fishing boats are small, a few from Eyemouth, perhaps, or Berwick, pulling up their lobster pots, or fishing for white fish or crab. Traffic tears along regardless. But there is room to park. And as the poet said (more or less)

> *What is this life if full of care*
> *We have no time to park and stare?*

And after that, there is no reason not to pay a brief visit to England.

25

From Berwick-upon-Tweed to Kelso

INTERNATIONAL CONFLICT AND local government have combined to cause Berwickshire to be in Scotland and **Berwick-upon-Tweed** to be on the other side of the Border, in spite of its being on the north side of the Tweed. Throughout the Middle Ages the town repeatedly changed hands; its history 'was one red record of strife and bloodshed'. During the Wars of the Roses Henry VI came to Scotland (1461) and ceded Berwick to the Scots in return for promises of help. But then Edward IV became King of England, and took it back in 1482. At this point the Scots finally gave up their claim.

Little that is medieval remains in Berwick except the castle, and there is not much of that. It was built by Edward I of England around 1300, on the crest of the hill just north of the town and the river. Of the castle itself only a few fragments are to be seen; when it was already much the worse for wear and had resisted many sieges it fell in the 1840s before the onslaught of the railway; the down platform is where the great hall once stood. But a long line of curtain wall called the White Wall still goes down the east-facing slope of the hill from the railway to the river. This outwork was built to guard a steep flight of steps which leads down to the ruins of the Water Tower, on the banks of the Tweed, from which a chain or boom may have been carried across to the other side.

Far less old than the castle, but far more remarkable, are the Elizabethan town walls. These fortifications are on an enormous scale, and there is nothing else like them in Britain; Lucca, in Tuscany, provides the best comparison. They were built between 1558 and 1569 to keep out the Scots (naturally), they circle the town for a distance of a mile and a half, and they are almost perfectly preserved. It is nothing to say that they are twenty two feet high, twelve feet thick at the base and ten feet at the top, and backed by huge quantities of heaped up soil. What is more striking is that they are faced throughout by large blocks of masonry trimmed smooth and with square edges, and are themselves protected on the landward side by five very large projecting bastions, shaped like broad arrowheads. There is a calculated, daunting geometrical symmetry about these bastions. This was the very latest in the design of fortifications in the sixteenth century, and it was never superseded; the days of defensive walls were really over when these were built. They were never attacked. In the course of time the citizens turned them into a broad and easy promenade, and now they provide the visitor with good views of the town and the river where it flows into the sea.

The second construction which makes Berwick worth a visit is the **Old Bridge** over the Tweed. Its combination of length, strength and antiquity, to say nothing of its modest height and the easy rise and fall of its arches, must be hard to beat. James I and VI, when he crossed the earlier and shaky sixteenth century wooden bridge on his way to London in 1603, decreed that a new bridge be built; made of red sandstone, it was begun in 1611 and finished in 1624. It is almost three hundred yards long and carries a narrow roadway over fifteen arches. Angular recesses above the piers were provided to secure foot-passengers from being crushed against the parapet by wagons of wool, or herds of cattle; now, motor cars. At the south end the arches are small, but they increase in size up to the second most northerly arch, where the channel is deepest, and then diminish. It is like a cadence in music, seen instead of heard above the ripple of the water.

The Old Bridge carries modern vehicles, which is a surprise, because there is a broad 1928 concrete bridge just upstream. Partly because it is concrete this bridge is not particularly pleasant to look at, and as a piece of town planning it seems to be a mistake for it drives straight into the heart of the town and causes endless traffic problems. One advantage it does have, which is to provide a good view of the Old Bridge, and also of Stephenson's magnificent Royal Border Bridge or viaduct, opened by Queen Victoria in 1850. This is one of the greatest of all monuments of British railway engineering. It follows a long, slow curve for over two fifths of a mile, and carries the main line on twenty eight round-headed arches, of which twelve span the river, clearing the mean water level by 120 feet. An inter-city express looks small, even very small, on the Royal Border Bridge.

Besides these wonders (and they would be very famous wonders if located south of a line drawn from the Wash to the Severn) there are other good things in Berwick. The Town Hall dominates the skyline. Built in the 1750s, it is by no means a grand design, but the ground floor is arcaded, and from the four-column portico above the steps the tower, octagonal lantern and short spire rise 150 feet above the roadway. Much of the interior was once used as a gaol, and the dismal details now prove to be an attraction for tourists.

Holy Trinity Church, on the north side of town, is that uncommon thing, a church built during the Commonwealth. It is a long, low, rectangular building, with two turrets at the west end but neither tower nor spire. The main windows are Venetian (more or less), and those in the clerestory are also three-light but of two complex and unusual designs. Inside, there is a gilded reredos by Lutyens. Standing in a large and leafy churchyard, Holy Trinity is architecture of a high order. The nearby Barracks (1717–21) must also have been designed by someone who knew what he was about, although there is no evidence that that someone was Vanbrugh, as is often suggested. The south block and the gateway, with fine iron gates and a swaggering coat of arms above them, are full of confidence and good proportions – and also full of stone from Edward I's castle, like other buildings in Berwick. The barracks now houses a regimental museum for the King's Own Scottish Borderers.

Berwick also possesses a pleasing variety of Georgian domestic architecture, all in stone or faced with stone. The town is not on one level, which is a merit, and every street – almost every house within the walls – is different from every other, which makes it an interesting place to walk about in. Several houses have pretensions to grandeur. And yet, in spite of its cheerful red pantiled roofs, Berwick somehow gives the impression of being a little dejected, as if its best days were over. Burns described it as 'an idle town, but rudely picturesque'. That still seems to fit. Perhaps Berwick is too isolated, too much affected by the grey North Sea.

The A1 by-passes Berwick, and from the by-pass a road north of the river, signposted to Swinton, leads in a couple of miles to Scotland. One mile further on a road to the right takes you to **Paxton House** (1758–66). For several reasons this Palladian mansion is worth seeing. Paxton House was designed by John and James Adam, and Robert Adam worked on the interior c1773. It is built of red sandstone. It is a U plan, and the central porticoed section is connected by corridors to large wings, all very formal. The setting, which gives splendid views south to the Tweed, is superb. What makes Paxton House doubly interesting is that it contains an outstanding collection of Chippendale furniture, and also has a very handsome library and picture gallery. These were added early in the nineteenth century, and the picture gallery now serves as an 'outstation' for National

Galleries of Scotland. Over 70 paintings are on long-term loan from the Galleries.

Return to the B6461, continue towards Swinton, and in a mile or so, turn left down a side road signposted to Horncliffe. This road goes down to the **Union Bridge** across the Tweed. If you like out-of-the way places, or are curious about bridges, take this road. It is narrow and winding, between gently rolling fields; at one point a range of Border hills is on the horizon, with the massive Cheviot much above the rest. You descend to the bridge and to the river quite suddenly, amid trees. As far as traffic is concerned, this is a very unimportant bridge. But it has a little niche in history, because it was completed in 1820 and is the first full-scale suspension bridge erected in Britain designed to carry vehicles; Telford's bridge over the Menai Straits was not opened until 1826. The designer and builder was Captain Sir Samuel Brown, R.N. Having thus joined England to Scotland – for the Tweed is here the Border and continues so for ten miles – he attached a plaque to one of the pink stone pylons, bearing a red rose and the words *Vis unita fortior*. The pylons have a style to them, that Roman air of being built to last; that on the Scots side is pierced by a narrow round-headed arch (one car at a time), on the English side the pylon is built against the cliff, requiring an immediate right-angle turn in the road. The river here is wide, flowing in a long curve between grassy banks and ample green fields. There are trees, and there are almost sure to be sheep, and a quiet white house alongside its garden is reflected in the water. This sheltered spot makes an unusual impression, a conjunction of ancient peace and pioneering achievement.

Return the way you came and continue west for another couple of miles until you reach another side road on the left, marked to Ladykirk. This road is even more narrow and winding than the first, but it leads to a truly wonderful little church, a medieval building still in use, with a well-documented past and a very perceptible atmosphere of antiquity.

Ladykirk was founded by James IV, and was built between 1500 and 1513, entirely of stone, pews and all, so as not to burn. The king was in the church on several occasions, the last a few days before he was killed at the battle of Flodden (*see* p. 318). You have a good view of it as you approach, on the right of the road (for it stands on high ground), not a large church but certainly not a simple one, towered and buttressed; and as you come round the east end you may fancy for a moment that you are looking at a scaled-down and simplified version of Notre Dame. The resemblance is no doubt slight; but the twenty prominent buttresses and the apsidal east end and transepts make the church look bulkier than it is, and imposing.

Notre Dame was built about 1200, classic Gothic, of breathtaking height. Ladykirk is modest in size, but a remarkably complete example of the final phase of Gothic church architecture in Scotland. At no other time was church building north of the Border so distinctively Scottish in style. Too poor to aim for grand and soaring effects, the Scots could yet produce churches of superbly Gothic harmony and vigorous composure. 'The simple interiors,' wrote Sir John Stirling Maxwell,

> have great dignity and at their best real beauty, as well as a
> charming homeliness. Seen from outside, the design [of
> Ladykirk] is dominated by the roof. Nothing could be more
> satisfactory. The permanency of a stone roof supported by a
> stone vault appeals to the mind as peculiarly suitable for a
> place of worship, while the eye delights in the fine workman-
> ship and complicated perspective of the roofing slabs.

Every buttress is topped with a pinnacle, one of them carrying a sundial. The windows in the apse, transepts and north wall are pointed, with two or three lights; but in the south wall they have flattened, elliptic arches, which is most unusual.

The tower supplies a different kind of distinction. A marble plaque inside the church explains (in Latin) that 'due to the passing of time and the indifference of the inhabitants the church began to crumble and indeed almost to fall into ruin', but was restored, and the upper part of the tower, with its bell roof and lantern, was added in 1743. This addition is believed to have been the work of William Adam. A medieval church and an eighteenth century addition to the tower sound an odd combination; but they get on together very well, as good designs usually do. The tower was originally built to be defensible. The walls are a metre thick, and the only access is by a door within the church, below a nineteenth century bust of James IV. A narrow turnpike stair with extremely worn steps leads to the priest's rooms, which are on two floors and vaulted, and once had heavy doors; in one of these rooms a small window, now blocked up, looks into the church. It is likely that when the kirk was built it served also as a watch tower, for it commands an extensive view which includes the nearby ford across the Tweed – once of much military importance – as well as Norham Castle.

Norham Castle, often sketched and painted by Turner, (there is a superb oil painting in the Tate), is only a mile downstream, on the English side of the river. It stands on a steep bank just above the water, surrounded by a large shelving lawn and magnificent beech trees. Parts of the castle date back to the twelfth century. The keep was constructed early in the fifteenth century, and further improvements were made a hundred years later. For four hundred years it was a key point in the English defence system along the eastern marches. The village of Norham has a triangular green and some eighteenth century houses, and the long low church, dating from about 1170, contains a good deal of Norman work, but there are substantial nineteenth century additions. The nearness of these buildings to Ladykirk, separated from it only by the Tweed and centuries of past hatred, makes a moving and even a dramatic scene.

Coldstream is reached either by secondary roads in Scotland or by the main road from Berwick, through Cornhill-on-Tweed. Neither route is very interesting. The country hereabouts is good farm land, but rather featureless. Nor can much better be said about Coldstream itself, although it has seen history enough. It is the town of origin of the Coldstream Guards, for it was here that General Monck assembled a small force in 1659 which he took to London where he laid the ground for the restoration of Charles II. There is a regimental museum in Market Square, south of the High Street. Coldstream makes a second (and last) appearance in history in 1745, when General Cope, his army cut to pieces by the highlanders at Prestonpans, clattered into the town with his inglorious dragoons; vanquished that morning, he reached Coldstream the same night. Less than twenty years later, John Smeaton began work on his great bridge here across the Tweed, thus inaugurating a new era of bridge building in Scotland; so fast did times change in the eighteenth century. The Coldstream bridge has five arches and an unusual series of dummy flood-openings above the piers. The red-tiled toll house at the Scottish end was once the scene of runaway marriages, and was only a little less popular than Gretna Green itself. All was made easy. Once across the border and within the ambit of eighteenth century Scots law, the escaping couple required no more than a declaration before witnesses.

At the west end of town is the entrance to the **Hirsel**, seat of the Earls of Home. The house is not open, but there is an estate museum and craft centre at the end of the long entrance drive, and a loch that is a wildfowl sanctuary. The visitor is free to walk through a large part of the extensive, wooded grounds, which contain some exceptionally fine beech trees. Dundock Wood (also accessible from the A697) has a very colourful collection of long-established azaleas and rhododendrons, many of them fifteen feet high or more, growing one into another amid tall pine trees and looking as if they were native to the country. It is a very special place to wander through, and in late May and early June the scents and colours are sensational.

Although there is nothing else notable at Coldstream, the road across the river into England will conveniently take the visitor, if he wishes, to **Flodden field**. In Scottish history, Flodden is at least as famous a defeat as Bannockburn was a victory; in song and story it is even more famous – the Scots sometimes seem to have a romantic relish for disaster. Numerous books have been written about the battle, although reliable information is scanty. Briefly, the facts are as follows.

Pope Julius II (1503–1513) (his enthusiasm for leading his forces on the battlefield scandalised even contemporaries) arranged, purely in the interests of power politics, a so-called Holy League against France, the ancient ally of Scotland. Henry VIII joined the League, and invaded France in 1513. Louis XII of France appealed to James IV for help, and James, although married to Margaret Tudor, sister of Henry VIII, invaded England. It was a terrible mistake. He reduced three castles, and when an English army arrived he positioned his forces on Flodden Hill. This was a sound move. But when the Earl of Surrey unexpectedly led his forces across the River Till at the Twizel Bridge (built in the fifteenth century – a mighty span for its day) and thus got between the Scottish army and the border, James left the hill and prepared to fight a battle near the village of Branxton. Even then the prospects seemed reasonably good. But when the engagement began the Scottish heavy guns, although numerous and up-to-date, were ineffective because the best gun crews had been sent to France; and when the English artillery compelled the Scots to leave their higher ground and attack across a nearby bog, the king went with them. 'Refusing advice to stay where he could retain command, he rushed on with his men, leaving the leaders of the other divisions to act without any concerted plan'. In the conditions, the Scottish long spears were no match for the English bowmen and the English bills – shafts with broad blades which could cut through the shafts of spears. The result was a massacre, at least for much of the Scots army. The English claimed that 10,000 Scots were killed. Battle and exaggeration usually go together, but certainly the losses were extremely serious. James himself was killed, along with one of his natural sons, an archbishop, a bishop, two abbots, over twenty lords and earls, many knights and gentlemen and many thousand men.

Sir Walter Scott, who wrote much second-rate poetry, rose to epic heights when he described the battle in the last canto of 'Marmion':

> *But yet, though thick the shafts as snow,*
> *Tho' charging knights like whirlwinds go,*
> *Tho' bill-men ply the ghastly blow,*
> *Unbroken was the ring:*
> *The stubborn spearmen still made good*
> *Their dark, impenetrable wood,*
> *Each stepping where his comrades stood*
> *The instant that he fell.*

As a distinguished critic observed, 'Scott is with his countrymen, locked in the struggle'.

At Branxton there is not much to see, but the battlefield, just west of the village, is clearly marked and signposted, and there is a small car-park. There is also a simple celtic cross, erected in 1910, inscribed: 'Flodden 1513. To the brave of both nations'. Every August, during Coldstream's Civic Week, a cavalcade of horsemen rides the marches, and a standard is carried to the top of Branxton Hill, where a short service takes place.

Return to the Tweed – it is only a few miles away – and head for **Kelso**, surely the most attractive small town in the Borders. It is attractive because it is the most architectural, the most charming, and the most complete – complete in having its river, its ruined abbey, its market square, its ancient streets still with their old names, and of course a large number of historical associations.

As you approach Kelso, the river keeps you company, a wide river and never far off, traditionally a paradise for salmon fishermen. The country is rich and well wooded. On the far bank, soon after leaving Coldstream, you may be able to pick out the ruins of Wark Castle, another of the great Border fortresses built to defend Northumberland from the Scots. What little is to be seen stands on a ridge above the river, less noticeable than the cottages beside it. Soon after Wark the border turns sharply south, and the Tweed ceases to be the dividing line between England and Scotland.

Once in Kelso, bear left for the car park; it is next to the Church-yard of the Old Parish Church, and scarcely a minute's walk from the

Abbey. A churchyard does not sound like a good beginning, but this one is different, an extensive piece of ground with great beech trees, lofty Wellingtonias, yew trees, cypresses and limes. The church is different too, for it is octagonal, an unusual form in Scotland. Built in 1773 it has attracted some severe criticism; sixty years after it was built it was dammed as 'a mis-shapen pile ... being, without exception, the ugliest and least suitable in Architecture of all the parish churches in Scotland – and that is saying a good deal – but it is an excellent model for a circus'. Unconventional, that is its trouble; the critic quoted would doubtless have been better pleased if it had been built to look more like a barn. The Italianate wooden belfry over the north porch was added in 1833. The Old Parish Church is no masterpiece, admittedly; but it is pleasant enough.

The **Abbey** – what is left of it – is altogether another matter. There are four abbeys in the Borders, all of them once superb and glorious constructions, all different, all ruined. Kelso Abbey is perhaps the least easily admired of the four. Not that it lacks fine details and a memorable aspect; but it is much spoiled, and is rather hemmed in and pushed up against by roads and later buildings, so that the imagination has to make more effort than usual to re-create it and bring it to life.

It was founded in 1128 by David I. During the next several centuries it became one of the wealthiest and most influential monastic churches in Scotland, but it suffered repeatedly in the wars with England. It was sacked in 1544 and again in 1545 and finally in 1547, when a group of monks and laymen attempted to hold out against the cannon-fire of the Earl of Hertford's army. (Some survivors escaped from the ruins under cover of darkness). Its spoliation was completed by the mob at the Reformation. It then served as a quarry, for the most part, for local landowners and townspeople. The statues were largely demolished in 1649, when a new parish church was created by securing a thatched roof over part of the eastern transept (now demolished). In the late eighteenth century a small school ('Lancelot Whale's seminary') was attached – literally – to the east end of the abbey. Walter Scott was one of the pupils. Not until 1805 was ruination slowed down. In 1866 the Duke of Roxburghe undertook extensive repairs, and thereafter its gradual decay was brought to a halt.

The Abbey is essentially a late twelfth century Norman building. The plan is unusual, in that there were transepts at both ends of the nave. Only the west end of the nave survives, and the most complete elevation is of the north transept, which you pass to reach the entrance gate to the grounds. It is five storeys high, with arched windows, a circular window, and a pediment on top flanked by round towers. The doorway is extremely stylish, and hints at what the overall effect must once have been. It consists of three recessed arches, an interlaced arcade above them, and on top a strong triangular pediment with lattice decoration. What a superb subject this would have made for the art of John Piper! Internally also there is much decorative arcading. When the abbey was complete its height relative to its floor space must have been astonishing, made all the more impressive by the fact that the triforium and clerestory are treated as continuous arcades. The best general views are looking along the ruined nave, either from east or west; the tremendous height of the central arch and the tower are then evident.

Leave the Abbey and go left, towards the river, passing two conspicuous blunders. The first is the Memorial Cloister, erected to the memory of the 8th Duke of Roxburghe by his widow in 1933 and attached to the Abbey. It is no excuse that the Dukes of Roxburghe at one time owned the Abbey; the family should have considered that it was held in trust. And to be told that the cloister 'is in a modern version of the Abbey's Norman style' merely adds insult to injury, as does the inclusion in the Memorial of a doorway taken from the original buildings. Poor Abbey! shut in, mutililated and despised, it has barely escaped with its life. The other blunder used to be on the other side of the street – a large white concrete garage, with petrol pumps, dominating the approach to Kelso Bridge. The garage and the pumps have happily been removed, and nothing, so far, has taken their place. Is it too much to hope that this empty space will become a planted area, with a few low-growing evergreens and perhaps a couple of rowan trees (mountain ash to non-Scots) or white-barked birches to decorate the scene?

Pass on. The War Memorial next to the abbey is by Sir Robert Lorimer, a tall shaft with a cross in a well-kept little garden. And then, quite suddenly, you are on the bridge, one of the delights of Kelso. It was designed by John Rennie and opened in 1803, replacing an earlier bridge which was swept away by floods in 1797. It has five semi-elliptical arches, twin columns rise above the piers, and the roadway is level – a novel feature for a bridge in the eighteenth century. It is fairly plain, in the sense of being extremely elegant. This bridge was the model developed by Rennie for his famous Waterloo Bridge in London, once described by a good judge as 'the only monument in

London of the nineteenth century which commands world-wide admiration' – and demolished in the late 1920s. Two of the lamps on the parapet of Kelso Bridge came from the demolition.

The bridge now has to carry far too much traffic (a new bridge has recently been built just east of the town), but it is worth walking across Rennie's bridge in order to enjoy the views. The confluence of the Tweed and the Teviot is just west of the bridge with eighteenth-century Ednam House close by and Floors Castle beyond; on the east side there are wide grassy banks and willow trees in a small island in the river, and perhaps a fisherman in his boat with a man at the oars to hold it steady against the current. This is the famous Junction Pool, one of the most expensive stretches of salmon-fishing in the world (although the salmon grow scarcer every year). The Tweed here is wide and shallow, overlooked by Victorian villas and cottages in Maxwellheugh, on top of the steep, wooded south bank, and next to these is Pinnacle Hill, well-named.

At the south end of the bridge, close to the road, there is a grand triumphal arch leading nowhere. It was once the gateway to a vanished mansion designed by Gillespie Graham in 1822. It looks as if it might have something to do with the nearby showground, but that is entered from a road alongside the river. Kelso is the centre of a rich agricultural district, and it needs its showground, most of all for the big agricultural show in July, but also for horse sales, ram sales, the pony show and other country events.

Re-cross the bridge, pass the little toll-house (1803) and turn left into Abbey Court, which used to lead to the 1754 hump-backed bridge across the river. Turret House is the local Information Centre, a seventeenth century building, white-washed like the row of old cottages nearby. The pavement is cobbled, so it too is old, probably made at least a hundred and fifty years ago. These cobbled pavements are pleasant to look at (few of them remain) but they are not liked by ladies with high heels. St Andrew's Church (1861) provides a somewhat startling contrast to its neighbours in this quiet cul-de-sac.

Continue along Bridge Street to the gates of **Ednam House**, now a hotel. It was built in 1761, and was for long known as Havannah House, because the proprietor had made his fortune as an agent for the Royal Navy in Cuba. It is a plain Classical design, with a heavy cornice and a central pediment. An objectionable north wing was stuck on in the mid-1950s – precisely the period when architectural taste in Britain reached rock bottom. The principal rooms contain some features of high quality. Many doors are made of hardwoods from Havana, and still have the original brass handles, locks, and hinges, and there is a good deal of rococo plasterwork. There is also, as a rule, a good display of fishing rods in the entrance lobby. Although from the street it looks rather shut in, Ednam House must enjoy as fine an outlook as any hotel in Scotland. It stands on the riverbank, facing south-west, separated from the broad flowing Tweed only by its own terrace and parterres. Beyond the river the view is all of woods and hills. Ednam House has a long frontage to the river, and its grounds suggest what the French call intimate pleasures – walks after dinner, or dances on autumn evenings, or quiet conversations by moonlight.

Soon after Ednam House you reach the Square. A visitor in the Days of George III well described Kelso as 'that neat place built much after the manner of a Flemish town, with a square and a townhouse'. The commodious little Square is still the focal point of the town, and looking onto it there is still a town-hall – not the old thatched one, but a Georgian-Edwardian one, built in 1816 and altered in 1906, with Ionic columns and a pediment and a domed octagonal belfry. It is a little heavy in appearance, a little too self-important, but dignified and all in stone, as is the surface of the nearby streets and the Square and all the buildings around it. Of these, the most imposing is the Cross Keys Hotel (1761), a coaching inn, where Turner stayed during one of his tours of Scotland. This inn is one of the few four storey buildings in the town centre. It owes its top storey and its Italianate style to a reconstruction carried out in 1880. The central arch used to lead to a yard and extensive stables, required to service coaches travelling between Edinburgh and Newcastle. In spite of its height and non-Scottish appearance, the hotel front does not disturb the harmony of the square or of the streets leading into it. Wherever you look there are well-proportioned, formal Georgian houses, some of them painted, or pedimented, or with pilasters or round-headed windows. Kelso is remarkably unspoiled and unified; a complete little town. And, what is equally pleasing, its spacious Square is not entirely given over to parked cars.

Apart from Bridge Street, three streets enter the Square. Horsemarket and Woodmarket have the usual agreeable mix of small shops and good buildings, while Roxburgh Street leaves the Square almost surreptitiously and heads towards Floors Castle. It is worth going along this street a short distance (remarkably bumpy stone setts), and then turning left on foot to the riverside walk, a broad grassy stretch which gives fine views of the river and the country to the west.

Finally, if you are in Kelso at the right time you may go to the races. The racecourse lies north of the town, on the way to the little village of Ednam, birthplace of the poet Thomson, author of '*the Seasons*'.

Two places of interest remain, one just south of the river and one on the north. The first of these, Roxburgh Castle, might be described as one of the region's all but invisible attractions. To reach it, cross the Tweed, turn right past the show-ground, cross the Teviot, and you are there, in the angle of the confluence of the rivers. The site is very beautiful, and wild, a long rocky knoll scattered over with trees, looking down on a bend of the Teviot. To walk over the castle – you can only walk over it, not through it – is not easy, for the few remaining fragments of masonry are confused with the rocks and grass and saplings growing out of the foundations. As a castle it is unrecognisable. Yet this was one of the four great fortresses of Scotland in the twelfth century; the others were Berwick-on-Tweed, Edinburgh and Stirling. Protected by water, like most early Scots castles, it was a fortified enclosure with towers set at intervals in the curtain wall, a rude imitation of contemporary castles in France and England. Not much is known of its history, but it was still an important place in the middle of the fifteenth century, when it was in the hands of the English. James II determined to recover it, but during the assault a cannon exploded and the king was killed instantly. A holly tree – or is it a yew? – in the grounds of Floors Castle is supposed to mark the spot where he fell. Also according to tradition, his widow, daughter of the Duke of Gueldres, continued the attack, pressed it to a successful conclusion, and then razed the castle to the ground.

The old town of Roxburgh once stood in the shadow of the castle. It was a walled town, where priests and sometimes courtiers lived, a town large enough and prosperous enough to contain three churches, more than one school, and the Royal Mint. It has completely disappeared.

Floors Castle, looking directly across to Roxburgh Castle from the other side of the Tweed, could hardly be more different. To nineteenth century writers it was all that a great house should be: the princely residence of Floors, the ducal domain of Floors, or, according to Sir Walter Scott, 'the modern mansion of Fleurs, with Its terrace, its woods, and its extensive lawns ... a kingdom for Oberon or Titania to dwell in'. What building produces these ecstasies? The answer is, two buildings.

The Floors that Scott saw was built between 1721 and 1726. Stories that it was designed by Vanbrugh can be discounted; it was almost certainly the work of William Adam. Contemporary prints show it as a large oblong four-storey block of no great elegance, with square corner-towers and a low roof broken by regularly spaced chimneys. In 1838 the 6th Duke of Roxburghe – the family has been here since the Reformation – commissioned Playfair to turn it into a nobleman's residence in the grand manner. Playfair was working at the time on Donaldson's Hospital in Edinburgh, which was supposed to be Elizabethan in style; but at Floors there are scarcely more than reminiscences of the Elizabethan style; and although Playfair claimed that there was a Gothic element in his designs, the building is neither Gothic nor Elizabethan nor Classical nor particularly Scots but is a far-flung, flamboyant extravaganza, picturesque and entertaining in its own way. There is about Floors an operatic, an almost fabulous quality.

Playfair's policy was to keep what was there, extend it, and ornament it. So he built an east pavilion and a west pavilion, each large enough to surround its own courtyard, and linked them to the main block; added a ballroom on the east side; and stuck on – it looks stuck on – a porte-cochère to the entrance, which is on the side facing away from the river. These additions more than doubled the size of the old house, and trebled its frontage. He then ornamented everything. Hood moulds were added above all the windows; corbelled pepper-pot turrets and castellated parapets, in quantity, were strung along the roof line; and water spouts looking like gun barrels were designed to project from the wall-heads. The effect is certainly striking, and Floors has been likened to Chambord. But where Floors is studiously playful, Chambord is more truly fantastic.

Inside, a series of rooms on the ground floor, looking onto the river, is open to the visitor. These rooms display a great quantity of antique furniture, pictures, china and tapestries. The tapestries are of exceptional interest. In the Ante Room, an early fifteenth century Brussels tapestry hangs over the fireplace; woven with wool and gold thread, it depicts The Pentecost and is crowded with figures. In the Drawing Room there is a magnificent set of late seventeenth century Brussels tapestries. These were brought to Floors by Duchess May, the American wife of the 8th Duke (d. 1932) from her family's Long Island home. They are known as the Triumphs of the Gods, and depict the Feast of Bacchus; a garden scene with Flora and her attendants; a whirling scene of Neptune, the sea, and attendant nymphs and goddesses; Venus at the forge of Vulcan; and Apollo and the Muses. The colours are marvellously preserved, the designs are grand and energetic, and the spectacle of these large colourful tapestries on three walls of a room decorated (by Duchess May) in the manner of the early eighteenth century is not soon forgotten. More is to come. Play-fair's ballroom was redesigned and repanelled in American oak, again by the Duchess, so as to show to advantage two Gobelins yellow-ground tapestries, one of them very large indeed. Woven after designs by Claude Audran le jeune in 1699, they form part of a famous series known as Les Portières des Dieux, and depict some of the gods framed in elaborate arabesques. More restrained in colour than the Brussels Tapestries, they are beautiful pieces, and are mounted in panelling carved by a local craftsman after the manner of Grinling Gibbons.

As well as these exceptional tapestries there is much to see. In the Entrance Hall a large painting by Hendrick Danckerts showing Charles II walking in Horse Guards Parade; in the Drawing Room a set of eight Louis XV gilt chairs and a settee, covered in Beauvais tapestry depicting scenes from La Fontaine's Fables, as well as a commode by Joubert from the bedchamber of the Comtesse d'Artois at Versailles; in the ballroom a fine Gainsborough and portraits of the first Earl of Roxburghe (d.1650) and his second wife, Jane, both attributed to George Jamesone. There are also several Reynolds, much Chinese and Meissen porcelain, an extensive display of mostly French furniture, carved and gilded, and other items too numerous to mention.

Once outside, do not fail to walk round to the front in order to admire the view. Perhaps it is the setting which causes people to be so enthusiastic about the house. It stands on a wide sweep of ground which declines very gently to the river. There are trees on the left (a small wood which constitutes an unusual car park), and the spires and roofs of Kelso are distinct but unobtrusive a mile away, beyond the long line of the river; just opposite is the tree-studded knoll on which linger the last remains of Roxburgh Castle; and the delicate line of the grey-blue Border hills is on the horizon. It is a wonderfully soothing pastoral scene, and does much to restore one's confidence in the goodness of the universe.

26

From Kelso to Melrose

FROM KELSO TO St Boswells and Melrose two routes are possible, the A6091 south of the Tweed or what starts as the A6089 and keeps north of the river. The latter is to be preferred. At first it runs alongside the great grey wall which surrounds the policies of Floors. This wall is several miles long, and has the melancholy interest of having been built by French prisoners of war during the time of Napoleon. Then the wall turns south, and the road to follow is now the B6397. The country hereabouts, said an early traveller, 'is full of gentle risings, covered with corn, and resembling Picardy'; and it has not much changed. There are potatoes in vast fields, and cabbages in large tracts, and of course sheep and cattle, most of the latter black and white Ayrshires. Tributaries of the Tweed run down the slopes, and there are numerous small plantings of wood and lines of trees along the roads.

After a few miles turn onto the B6404, and soon you are in sight of Smailholm Tower, closely associated with Walter Scott, and almost a symbol of Border warfare.

Smailholm Tower is visible from far off, bold, stern and solitary. It is small as towers go, and not on a hill top. But it stands on a rocky eminence which is the highest in a broad spreading area of volcanic rocks and knolls, and so it commands the surrounding countryside even to the grey waving hills on the horizon. The area round the Tower is rough uncultivable ground, unattractive in winter but delightful in spring and summer in its own way, when the yellow gorse is everywhere and wild thyme, tormentil, ladies' bedstraw and violas grow among the rocks, and a pair of swans, perhaps, or some duck, cruise silently in the little tarn nearby.

Smailholm is so plain and unornamented that no one can tell its date. It was attacked in 1546, and its small windows and six feet thick walls suggest that it was then already fifty or a hundred years old. The entrance is in the south front, by a low round-headed door. There are few windows, only two gun-loops, and there is a battlemented parapet on the north and south sides only – a not uncommon sixteenth-century arrangement. Chutes in the north wall served the garderobes at first and second floor level. It could hardly be plainer. Inside, a spiral staircase in the angle of the south and east walls leads up to the hall, which has a substantial fireplace and windows with stone seats, and thence to the top floor. This level was considerably altered in the sixteenth century. Doors give access to the wall-walks, and the north parapet wall is provided with a watchman's seat and a recess for his lantern. These are doubtless connected to the fact that in the later sixteenth century Border towers were required to 'keip watch nyght and day, and burn baillis [bonfires or beacon-fires] according to the accoustomat ordour observit as sic tymes upoun the bordouris'. A beacon at Smailholm would have been seen over a very wide extent of country.

Smailholm was once surrounded by a barmkin, or defensive wall, as well as later domestic buildings, of which traces remain. Within the tower there is an exhibition of costume-figures and tapestries bearing upon Scott and his writing.

In itself, Smailholm Tower is not very remarkable. But it stands undamaged in what Scott called 'the very nakedness of the land,' and tower and moorland make it easy to imagine the Middle and West Marches as dangerous country, which they certainly used to be. Smailhom is near the centre of an area – it extends north to Lauder and south to the Border – which, however peaceful and pleasant it looks today, has a history saturated with blood and vengeance.

Even when England and Scotland were not at war, brigandage and fighting were endemic, and theft was the rule. A code of Border law, agreed by both kingdoms, existed throughout the Middle Ages, and Warden Courts were held to try to enforce it. But enforcement was often impossible. One practice indicative of the way of life was the 'Hot Trod' which allowed an injured party to cross the Border in pursuit of stolen goods 'with Hund and Horne, with How and Cry'. A burning turf on the point of a spear was to indicate the horsemen's mission. But raiding across the Border was often much the same as stealing from and murdering one's neighbours.

An eighteenth century traveller saw in the horse-races at Kelso (which still take place) a benevolent kindly means of 'conciliating the affections of two nations', and horse-racing may indeed have helped the union of the Crowns. But there were long centuries *when revenge at one time dictated an inroad, and necessity at another; when the mistress of a castle has presented her sons with their spurs to remind them that her larder was empty; and that by a foray they must supply it at the expense of their neighbours; when every evening the sheep were taken from the hills, and the cattle from their pasture, to be secured in the lower floor from robbers prowling like wolves for prey, and the disappointed thief found all in safety, from the fears of the cautious owner.*

The picture provided by the ballad-makers is the same:

Then Johnie Armstrong to Willie 'gan say,
Billie, a riding then will we:
England and us have been long at feud,
Perhaps we may hit on some bootie.
Then they're come on to Hutton-ha,
They rade that proper place about;
But the Laird he was the wiser man,
For he had laft nae geir without.

This way of life was romanticised by Sir Walter Scott, whose poems obscure the fact that it was anarchic and destructive; 'noblest knights do kill most men'. The reivers – the word comes from the Old English 'reifian' meaning 'to plunder' – were not knights but for the most part freebooters, the equivalent of present-day bank-robbers and gunmen, who 'did all by force'. Scottish kings struggled to control them, as well as those supposed upholders of the law, the Wardens of the Marches, and they began to get the upper hand only in the sixteenth century. James V was perhaps unwise in having almost all the Border lords in prison at one time or another – Scott of Branxholme, Ker of Ferniehurst, Lord Home and several others like them – but the barons and the freebooters had much in common. Little wonder that for several centuries 'every house was made defensible, and each owner garrisoned against his neighbour'.

Besides these, Smailholm has other, later associations. In 1635 it came into the possession of the Scotts of Harden, who were ancestors of Sir Walter Scott, and when they left it they moved to the new farm-house of Sandyknowe, only a stone's throw away. In due course Sandyknowe came to be farmed by Scott's grandfather, and it was to Sandyknowe that Scott was sent as a very small child to live with his grandparents and aunt, in the hope that fresh air and farm food would cure his lameness. There was no cure; he was a victim of poliomyelitis. But the years at Sandyknowe changed his life. Carried as a little lame boy over the rocks and rough grass and laid down, sometimes wrapped in a sheepskin, to watch the ewes being milked; listening to his aunt or the old 'cow-baillie' read or recite old ballads and tell tales of raids and battles in the countryside all around; exploring, as best he could, the old tower itself, and looking out from the battlements; here he began to acquire his unsurpassed knowledge of Scottish history, legend, and topography, and here was the start of his inspiration and imagination. Many years later, when he was already a successful author, he recalled his years at Sandyknowe, and Smailholm Tower:

> *And still I thought that shatter'd tower*
> *The mightiest work of human power;*
> *And marvelled as the aged hind*
> *With some strange tale bewitch'd my mind*
> *Of forayers, who, with headlong force,*
> *Down from that strength had spurr'd their horse*
> *Their southern rapine to renew,*
> *Far in the distant Cheviots blue,*
> *And, home returning, filled the hall*
> *With revel, wassel-rout, and brawl.*

It is stirring stuff, now quite out of fashion. But Scott's vivacity and force were to be put to better use when, in the novels, he recalled events from the past and depicted characters such as he had met in the wynds and law courts of Edinburgh and all over the Borders, and set scenes such as he had first known at Smailholm and Sandyknowe.

Before St Boswells, turn off to the right to **Bemersyde**. The road is narrow, and winds steeply up through oak and larch trees. In a mile or so you reach Scott's View, where there is room to park, and an indicator. This is probably the most famous viewpoint on the Tweed, if not in the Borders, and Scott took a particular pleasure in the place. The ground slopes steeply down to an almost complete loop of the river; within the loop there are superb trees, and others no less fine crowd down the outside banks; the river, dark and quiet, glints between them as it winds its way from the sloping fields that lead up to the triple peaks of the Eildon Hills beside Melrose. It is a panoramic and dramatic view, nature as luxuriant and beautifully laid out as anywhere in Scotland. The original monastery of Mailros

(Melrose), believed to have been founded by St Aidan in the seventh century, stood within the bend of the river; but nothing remains.

Bemersyde House, between Dryburgh and Earlston, is the home of Earl Haig. There were Haigs here in the twelfth century, and the original tower was standing in 1535. Like most towers it has grown; some of the stones for its growth are said to have come from the ruins of Dryburgh Abbey – but that was before 1800. The house passed for a time into the hands of another branch of the family; in 1921, however, it was purchased by the nation and given to Field Marshal Earl Haig. It is not open to the public.

Return down the hill and turn right for **Dryburgh Abbey**, very old, very damaged, and in a setting as nearly perfect as any setting could be; 'in picturesqueness and seclusion of situation perhaps the most charming monastic ruin in Great Britain'. Enormous cedar trees signal your approach – the first of them are not actually within the abbey grounds – and then you walk down a narrow pathway to the custodian's hut. Beyond it, more trees; cedars, wellingtonias, yews and hollies, all marvellously well grown, the cedars and wellingtonias of outstanding height. Many of these trees have been here for over a hundred years, some perhaps for over two hundred. Stories go about that one of the yews is coeval with the abbey itself, and although this may be an exaggeration it conveys the ancient spirit of the place. Among the trees are headstones, not thickly placed, but scattered; and then the walls and windows, doorways and arches come in sight, carved stones among the ruins, all mysteriously peaceful and beautiful.

Dryburgh Abbey was founded in 1150 for White Friars of the Premonstratensian Order. It became prosperous, and perhaps for no better reason was burned by the retreating forces of Edward II in 1322. In 1385 Richard II raided Scotland, and Dryburgh, along with the other Border abbeys, is reported to have been again 'devastated by hostile fire'. It seems never to have fully recovered, although it remained in normal use until 1507, when the position of abbot began to be treated as a sinecure and a convenient source of income for rich clerics and noblemen's illegitimate sons. In 1544 an English raiding party sacked and burned the abbey again, and it was never rebuilt.

The Abbey is best understood as a late twelfth and early thirteenth century church, with monastic buildings attached. These latter make Dryburgh peculiarly interesting, because at Kelso and Jedburgh the monastic buildings have disappeared, and at Melrose only the foundations remain. But at Dryburgh enough still stands for the visitor to be able to imagine something of the surroundings and the secluded life of a fraternity of medieval monks.

Built of a soft-coloured, grey-pink sandstone, the abbey was cruciform, with short transepts, an aisled nave, and side chapels. The six-bay nave has almost completely vanished; low walls and the foundations of pillars are all that remain. (Scratched onto a stone on the north side is a merelles board. This game, which resembles noughts and crosses, was introduced into England by the Normans. Examples are very rare). The entrance doorway at the west end is well preserved; round-headed and heavily moulded, it dates from after the destruction in 1385 and is a good example of the persistence of Romanesque design in late medieval Scotland. The most complete part of the church consists of the chapels in the north transept. These must have escaped serious damage when the tower fell, and they were no doubt maintained afterwards by the well-known families for whom they were a burial place. There are post-Reformation tombs of the Erskines, the Haliburtons and the Scotts. Sir Walter Scott is buried here, as of right, because his great-grandfather was Thomas Haliburton of Newmains, who at one time owned the abbey lands of Dryburgh. Scott's wife and relatives also lie here, as well as Field Marshal Lord Haig and Lady Haig.

Although only a fragment, the north transept is dignified with elegant arches, window openings and arcading. In the gable one lancet window survives out of two storeys of triple lancets. The dog-tooth decoration and the arch mouldings are masonry work of high quality. The gable of the south transept, seeming so strangely detached from the rest of the church, rises to a considerable height and retains part, but only part, of its great window. Set beside the mighty, brooding cedar trees these fragments still communicate something of the spiritual intensity of the Gothic world.

From the nave a stair, known as the night-stair, led through an arch in the south transept to the canons' dormitory. (Wooden steps now help out). There was originally a timber roof over the dormitory, but this was burned, probably in 1544. By that time alterations had been made on the east side so as to provide accommodation for the commendator, i.e. the person appointed in lieu of an abbot.

Due to the fall of the ground, the monastic buildings on the south side of the nave are at a lower level. The square open space known as the cloister garth would once have been surrounded by a covered walk, but no roofing remains. The garth is entered from the church through the east processional doorway, a very fine example of medieval design and carving, round-headed and recessed, with multiple shafts and dog-tooth ornament. The eastern range of monastic buildings is well preserved. Next to the processional doorway is a wall-press, or aumbry, once fitted with doors and shelves for books. Then there is a barrel-vaulted chamber which seems to have been a library or vestry, but which was appropriated as a burial place by the Earl of Buchan in the eighteenth century – after all, he was an enthusiastic antiquarian and he had bought the abbey in 1730. The second doorway leads into a barrel-vaulted 'parlour', where the canons were allowed to converse, and the third doorway, similar to the processional doorway but flanked by two windows, leads to the chapter-house. This is barrel-vaulted and lit by five windows at the east end. There are stone benches for the canons all round the room, and a stone basin decorated with strange long-necked birds. The east wall is crossed by intersecting arches on shafts, and there are clear traces of painted mural decoration, mostly simple geometric patterns executed in black and red on a white plaster ground. Painting like this was undoubtedly common in Scots medieval churches, but very little has survived. Finally, there is a plain entrance to a stair which once led to the canons' dormitory, and at the south-east corner of the cloister a stairway and passage which lead down to the warming-room, the only place in the abbey where the canons were allowed the comfort of a fire.

On the south side of the garth there are barrel-vaulted cellars. The refectory used to be above them, but all that is left is the west gable with a particularly fine rose window, a rare example to have survived from medieval Scotland. Beyond this south range there is a ditch, which used to be the old water-channel, – and beside it a ruined gate-house, built after the Reformation. Beyond the gatehouse a carved memorial pillar tries to look medieval, but not very successfully; it was erected by the afore-mentioned Earl of Buchan some time in the eighteenth century.

If there is a water-channel, where did the water come from? You have only to walk along to find out. It came from the Tweed, not visible from the abbey but less than a hundred yards away. This is another of the delights of Dryburgh, for it lies within a sweeping bend of the river, 'as if in the crook of a protecting arm', and a minute's walk will take you to the river bank. From there you can see the suspension footbridge that leads across to Newtown St Boswells. It is not far to go, but unfortunately the path terminates on the side of the re-routed A68, and further progress is hazardous.

Although so close to a main road, Dryburgh is entirely separated from it. The Abbey and its grounds lie deep in the countryside. A visit to this quiet haugh when the banks of the water-channel are thick with snowdrops, or early on a spring morning when the dew has not yet vanished from the daffodils, is an experience not to be forgotten.

Return to the B6404 and turn right for **St Boswells**. Almost at once you cross the Tweed, very wide here, with high banks on the right and on the left a grove of young poplar trees in lines like soldiers. St Boswells is an unusually attractive little village, without having anything in it of particular note. It is said to be named after St Boisil, the first prior of an abbey that stood near Bemersyde in the Dark Ages, and on the extensive village green one of the largest livestock fairs in the Borders used to take place. Cricket is played at St Boswells, and it has the distinction of being the centre of the Buccleuch Hunt.

Turn north onto the A697 for Melrose. If you continue through Newtown St Boswells on the A697 you soon reach the place where three bridges cross the Tweed within a few hundred yards of one another: the old road bridge (1780), four spans and very handsome; the railway viaduct (1865), nineteen arches, tall and graceful; and the modern road bridge (1974), steel box girders and reinforced concrete, very dull. The railway bridge is now an historic monument and is open to the public. You can go from this point to Melrose – but follow the signs with care. Alternatively, fork left at the Newtown St Boswell's by-pass, and either go straight on into Melrose or turn right again in order to reach the site of the Roman camp of **Trimontium**, so named after the three peaks of the Eildons.

Of the camp there is nothing to see except a memorial stone in the shape of a Roman altar, erected in 1928, which simply states, 'Trimontium. Built by the troops of Agricola in the first century A.D'. These words conceal the fact that an important complex of Roman forts and camps once occupied this commanding position, looking down on the Tweed close to where the river could be forded, and north into Lauderdale. Dere Street, the military road from York, led straight to Trimontium and then on over the hills to Edinburgh; we shall see this road further south, near the Border and where it crosses the River Teviot. Trimontium was begun about 80 AD and continued to be occupied and extended until about 180 AD, after which time the Romans finally withdrew from Scotland. In its hey-day it covered almost seventeen acres, which is three times as large as Chesters, the best known fort on Hadrian's Wall. Numerous artefacts recovered during excavations are on display in the Museum of Scotland in Edinburgh.

From Kelso to Melrose

The road to **Melrose** descends through the ancient hamlet of Newstead and immediately enters the Market Square. Melrose is a pleasant little town which contains, apart from the Abbey, surprisingly little of note. There is a sixteenth century market cross in the square, which is overlooked, as is most of the town, by Gallows Brae – not the happiest reminder of the good old days. The George and Abbotsford Hotel, an old coaching inn, was well-known to Sir Walter Scott, and William and Dorothy Wordsworth visited it during their tour of Scotland. Just off Market Square a road leads to the railway station, opened in 1849, closed in 1969, and re-opened as a restaurant with craft workshops in 1985. The building is quite handsome (and like all Victorian railway stations, very well built), in a sort of Flemish-Jacobean style, designed by the same railway engineer who was responsible for the very different Haymarket Station in Edinburgh. Further afield, towards the west end of the town is the Greenyards, home of the Melrose Rugby Football Club, an important place not only because rugby is a passion as well as a game in the Borders, but also because seven-a-side rugby began here in 1883, whence it has spread to Australia, Latin America, Hong Kong and many other places too numerous to mention.

Returning to Market Square, go down Abbey Street past the Abbey, leaving it until later. In a short distance you reach what is now a woollen shop, housed in a building which was originally a corn mill. This mill, built in 1640, was erected on the site of a medieval mill; water diverted from the river was brought along a channel cut through the abbey grounds. Near the mill is the Melrose Motor Museum, which contains a score or more vintage cars as well as numerous motor cycles and bicycles. Beyond is the river, and a very short walk will take you to the Chain Bridge, built in 1826. The road on the other side has particularly fine views looking south across the valley. Where the bridge is there used to be a ford, and one surmises that this is where the Romans crossed on their way to the most northerly and exposed outposts of their empire.

Of the four Border abbeys, Jedburgh and Melrose are the most nearly complete; and being on flat ground without other buildings nearby, Melrose is the most easily understood. For a brief description, lines written in the late eighteenth century by Thomas Pennant cannot be improved upon:

> *The south side and the east window are elegant past description; the windows lofty, the tracery light, yet strong. The*

> *church had been in form of a cross, and of considerable*
> *dimensions; the pillars clustered; their capitals enriched*
> *with most beautiful foliage of vine leaves and grapes. A*
> *window at the north end of the transept represents the crown*
> *of thorns. The rich work of the outside is done with*
> *uncommon delicacy and cunning. The spires or pinnacles*
> *that grace the roof; the brackets and niches, that, till 1649,*
> *were adorned with statues, are matchless performances.*

Dedicated to the Blessed Virgin Mary, Melrose was founded in 1136 by monks from the Cistercian Abbey of Rievaulx in Yorkshire. The original buildings were destroyed by Edward II when he invaded Scotland in 1322, and the rebuild was burned and wrecked by Richard II in 1385. Melrose as it stands was built between 1385 and 1505, and is the finest example in Scotland of the late medieval Decorated style. It was sacked by an English force in 1544 and again in 1545, was desecrated by fanatical presbyterians a hundred years later, functioned, in part, as the parish church during the seventeenth and eighteenth centuries, and then became a useful source of stone for local builders until fairly recent times.

The church consists of a long nave, which was intended to be longer, transepts, and a short choir. It is built of a pink sandstone quarried in the Eildon Hills. Approaching from the entrance gates, you cross the foundations of the west gable, all that remains of the original twelfth century church, and pass a series of eight aisle-chapels on the right. These chapels were completed at the beginning of the sixteenth century and have piscinae in the outer wall, some of them scalloped and ornamented. A stone screen separated the nave from the choir, but the appearance of this part of the church is hopelessly damaged by a massive rubble wall built up against the north arcade, helping to support a plain stone vault. This was part of the arrangements made after the Reformation to adapt the ruined Abbey so as to serve as the parish church. When this use ended in 1810, the rubble wall and stone vault remained to convert the approach to the crossing into what has been well described as 'a dismal tunnel'.

When the central tower fell it destroyed almost all the vaulting in the north transept and reduced the south transept to two bays and a chapel. Within the north transept there are statues of St Peter and St Paul in niches high up on the west wall, the former with key and book, and there is part of a flat ceiling lavishly ornamented with leaf carvings. The south transept retains its splendid traceried window, and there are two mural inscriptions, one of them a replica, referring to John Morow, a master-mason of French extraction who was probably responsible for the whole south gable. The square (replica) panel reads as follows:

> *John Morow sum tym callit was I and born in Parysse*
> *certanly and had in kepying al mason werk of Santandroys ye*
> *hye kyrk of Glasgw Melros and Paslay of Nyddysdayll and of*
> *Galway I pray to God and Mari bathe and swete sanct Johne*
> *to kepe this holy kyrk fra skathe [harm].*

The square east end of the church, the presbytery, is lit by a splendid Perpendicular window in the east wall. The ceiling is vaulted and has an intricate pattern of ribs and bosses. The central boss is carved with a representation of the Holy Trinity attended by two angels, and the other bosses show figures of saints or are carved with rose or leaf ornaments.

Seen from almost anywhere in the surrounding graveyard, the splendid proportions of the Abbey and the richness of its decoration are easily appreciated. The flying buttresses which support the vaults have been described as the finest examples in Scotland. Some of the pinnacles with their recessed niches and panelling are reminiscent of York Minster, while others, in a distinctively Scots style, have figures supported on brackets and below canopies, but set against plain stonework without niches. The most remarkable of the figures is an effigy of the Virgin and Child set in a niche high up on the western-most buttress on the south side of the nave. The Virgin holds the Infant on her left arm and in her right hand she holds a flower. The drapery of her robes falls in graceful curves, and she stands in the swaying pose one associates with the best carved Gothic Virgins of the fourteenth century. (These were the Virgins who caused Lord Clark to ask, perhaps a little wistfully, 'Did the ladies of the four-teenth century really look like this?'). The supporting corbel and the canopy overhead are elaborately carved, and on each side of the central niche there are four small niches for statues. Sadly defaced, the entire composition is still a brilliant work of art.

The gable end of the south transept is also rich in decoration. The great window is a perfect example of 'decorated' tracery; a niche above its highest point probably contained a figure of the Virgin. The figures for the beautifully disposed niches which flank the window have all gone, but the niche-corbels are carved with finely modelled figures. The doorway is deeply recessed and moulded, with the Royal Shield and supporting unicorns above the point of the arch. Between the doorway and window-sill is a line of arches with figures, now all headless. On other walls and buttresses angels play musical instruments, a monk tells his beads, the grotesque figure of a mason holds his chisel and mallet, and a pig plays the bagpipes. All this delicate carving is in the grey-pink sandstone of the rest of the Abbey and retains much of the sharpness it was given five hundred years ago. The whole building has a graciousness and splendour which are probably unique in Scottish churches.

The monastic buildings are (unusually) on the north side of the church, because that made it easier to use the waters of the Tweed for drainage purposes. Very little stonework remains above ground, but the south-east corner of the cloister is clear enough, next to the church, with stone benches and decorated wall arcading. The joist-holes and corbels above the arcading would once have supported the lean-to roof of the cloister walk. The main drain is also worth noticing. Melrose is in a bend of the river, and it was not too difficult to cut a water-channel through the grounds of the Abbey. The water powered the corn mill, and from it water was diverted into the cloister buildings and used to assist in sanitation. A stretch of this drain or sewer is now exposed. It was built of stone, the floor was cobbled, and large stone lintels covered it except where it passed beneath buildings, where it was arched.

Close to the Abbey but now behind a wall stands the Commendator's House. It was built in the fifteenth century as a palace for the abbots, but was considerably altered in 1590, when the square tower with very small windows, crow-stepped gables and loop-holes for hand guns was added. It now contains a display of items found during excavations in the abbey grounds.

After so much magnificence and destruction it may prove a welcome change to visit Priorwood Gardens, next door to the Abbey, hidden away behind a high wall decorated with wrought-iron railings by Lutyens. The house is the local Information Centre. The gardens, which include a small orchard and picnic area, specialise in plants and flowers grown for drying. The range of suitable grasses, roses, herbs and herbaceous plants is surprisingly large, and the resultant products are for sale, as well as leaflets explaining how to do it yourself.

High above the town, the great grey-green bulk of the Eildons heaves itself into the sky. There are four ways of regarding the

Eildons. You may think of them geologically, as a steep outcrop of volcanic rock, almost fourteen hundred feet high, shaped into three distinct peaks, forming the most conspicuous landmark in the Borders. Or you may think of them pre-historically, because Eildon Hill North was a fortified settlement before the Romans came to Britain; it was possibly the tribal capital of the Votadini, the Celtic people who at one time occupied the whole region from the Tyne to the Forth. Three concentric ramparts, clearly visible although they now appear as terraces, enclose an area of about 16 hectares, within which some 300 hut circles have been found. This would indicate a population of approximately 2,000 people. The Romans built a rectangular wooden signal tower on the north side, in a small enclosure surrounded by a ditch. Eildon Hill North was of great strategic importance, because it commands much of Lauderdale and the Tweed Valley, and can be seen from the Cheviots.

Or again, your attitude may be circumnavigatory, for you can drive all round the Eildons in a car in thirty minutes. But allow more time than this, for at the foot of the south-facing slopes there lies the village of **Bowden**, surely one of the most attractive in the Borders. There is a small green and a much-damaged late sixteenth century mercat cross, and there are numerous pleasant late eighteenth and nineteenth century houses along the slightly winding main street. The church is exceptional, down a steep narrow road and over the Bowden Burn. It seems to have been rebuilt some time in the fifteenth century, but by 1793 was described as old, long, narrow and somewhat ruinous. Repairs were made, and further alterations and extensions were carried out in 1909. The external appearance of the church is strange, because the transepts which once existed have disappeared, emphasising the length of the building, and the chancel stands distinctly higher than the nave; this is because of a burial vault constructed beneath the chancel in the seventeenth century. The oldest part of the church now standing is the north wall, which dates in part from the fifteenth century. Internally, there is an arched wooden roof and a large pointed arch-way which opens into the choir and organ loft. The most remarkable feature, however, is the Laird's Loft, a large dark wooden construction, supported by iron pillars against the north wall, panelled and canopied. There is a coat of arms in the centre of the painted decorations, and below are the following words:

Behold the axe Lyes at the Tree's Root
To hew doune these that Brings not forth good fruit

And when theyre Cut The Lord into his Ire
Wil them Destroy and Cast into the Fire.

1661 has been suggested as a likely date. The Loft is still in use, and no doubt this contributes to the spirit of the place, the spirit of a church that is old, but still alive and active.

Another practical approach to the Eildons is to climb them; provided that you are energetic and healthy and have plenty of time. There are a number of routes to choose from, but the paths can be steep and the going heavy – Scottish hillsides often retain a surprising amount of water. Starting from the square in Melrose, or from the golf-course above the town, an hour or more will see you to the top. Stand there and you will stand where Scott stood in 1817, pointing out 'forty three places famous in war and verse' to Washington Irving. 'I have brought you', he told his guest, 'like the pilgrim in *The Pilgrim's Progress*, to the top of the Delectable Mountains, that I may show you all the goodly regions hereabouts'.

Finally, you may think of the Eildons poetically, as has been done for many hundreds of years. Their division into three, by old report, had nothing to do with geological turmoil, but was the work of a wizard, Michael Scott. King Arthur, Merlin, and the Knights of the Round Table knew the Eildons well, and are even at this hour asleep in a great hall deep in the hill, ready to rise again in the hour of Scotland's need. (Who thought that Arthur was exclusively an Englishman? or exclusively Welsh?). And it was at the Eildon Tree, on the eastern slope of the Eildons, a spot once marked by the Old Eildon Stone and now by another one placed there by the Melrose Literary Society in 1929, that Thomas the Rhymer disappeared for seven years. He had met a lady of exquisite beauty mounted on a dapple-grey horse, whom he had at first thought to be the Virgin. But she had told him that she came from 'another countree', and she led him down into the hill to the Court of Fairy. Ancient writers are not as explicit as might be wished about exactly what happened next, but when Thomas returned seven years later he brought with him the gift of prophecy.

There are many legends, and they cannot all be right; perhaps none of them is right. History, however, records that a Thomas of Ercildoune, also called Thomas the Rhymer, lived in the Borders in the thirteenth century, and may have been the author of a poem entitled 'sir Tristram'. Certainly the poem exists, and Sir Walter Scott thought that it was genuine. There must be connections going far back. As for the story about the prophecies and the lady from 'another countree', they are now said to date from 1401 at the earliest. So what is one to believe? Romance, alas! is always being spoiled by modern research.

27

From Melrose to Peebles

FROM MELROSE TO **Abbotsford** is only a step, but it takes one from the Middle Ages to the nineteenth century, from Thomas the Rhymer to the Wizard of the North. There is no making sense of Abbotsford without an understanding of Sir Walter Scott, and there is no understanding Sir Walter Scott without taking due account of Abbotsford. If ever a famous man was bound up with his house, that man was Scott.

It is not easy now to sympathise with the nineteenth century view that Scott, a working lawyer for most of his life, was also a towering literary genius; he is probably not much more read today than Mary Shelley or Thomas Love Peacock, perhaps not as much. But in his own time his reputation was enormous, and it spread far beyond Scotland. His writing broke new ground; he was hailed as a great poet as well as a great novelist; and his output by any standards was prodigious. Moreover, his life itself was an extraordinary story, for he wrote his way to great wealth, went spectacularly bankrupt as men did in the early nineteenth century when there was no such thing as limited liability, and vowed to pay off his debts with a stream of further novels. He died in the attempt, but his honourable resolve proved to his contemporaries that he was not only a great author, but a hero and a gentleman.

His literary career began with ballads, historical or romantic. He made expeditions from Edinburgh into the Borders and 'picked up from tradition' old songs and ballads which he 'corrected' and 'improved'. The results were popular, although those from whom he got the originals did not always care for the final versions; 'ye hae spoilt them a' thegither', one old lady told him; 'they're neither right spell'd nor right settin' doun'. From these ventures he went on to ballads of his own, and at an early stage his popularity was such that he received an advance of a thousand guineas for *Marmion*, although it had hardly been begun. The novels came next, and swept all before them. They reminded industrializing Britain of more chivalrous, more picturesque ages, and were filled with a spirit of adventure and a homely and warm-hearted affection for all kinds and degrees of decent people. He could portray kings and queens ('No historian's Queen Elizabeth', wrote Thomas Hardy, 'was ever so perfectly a woman as the fictitious Elizabeth of *Kenilworth*') and he could also, with the same genial and convincing naturalness, give the character and speech of shepherds, lawyers' clerks, serving women and ale-house keepers. Only passion is wanting in these books. Love, hatred and revenge (so essential to present-day popularity) do not leap out of his pages, and his work makes no strenuous comment on life.

This easy, romantic fiction with antiquarian undertones made an immediate appeal. The market for everything he wrote was immense, and he became popular as no novelist had ever been popular before. For the better part of twenty years he could obtain several thousands of pounds for a novel which he had not yet begun to write. 'It is not fair', Jane Austen wrote to her sister. 'He has Fame and Profit enough as a Poet, and should not be taking the bread out of other people's mouths'.

Scott wrote because, to begin with, he enjoyed writing, and he also wrote for money. In 1804, when his great successes were still to come, he left Edinburgh and rented a house at Ashiestiel, a moderate house 'approached through an old-fashioned garden, with holly hedges, and broad, green terrace walks. On one side, close under the windows, is a deep ravine, clothed with venerable trees, down which a mountain rivulet is heard, more than seen, in its progress to the Tweed'. He wrote much at Ashiestiel and was happy, and he should have been content. But his consuming aim was to become a landed gentleman and an improver; although a friend on equal terms to high and low, he valued extremely 'baronial towers and aristocratical distinction'. So when the lease of Ashiestiel ran out in 1811, he purchased the little cottage and estate of Cartleyhole, on the banks of the Tweed three miles from Melrose. The estate consisted of 110 acres of poorish land, literally in a hole (it was known locally as Clarty Hole), and Scott's friends described it as 'the ugliest spot on the Tweed'. But the runaway success of the novels made possible land acquisition and home improvement on a big scale. 'Land was my temptation', he said afterwards; land and his dream house, in which 'the hand of the builder was never at rest'.

Land and improvements cost money, and a great deal of money was spent. It was constantly being borrowed and spent before it was earned, borrowed on the prospects of the next book, and in 1826 the interlocked publishing houses of Constable and Co, and Ballantyne, in which Scott was a 'sleeping' but in reality a very active partner, one on whom both enterprises depended, failed for well over £100,000. Scott was aghast. 'The feast of fancy is over', he wrote. 'I can no longer have the delight of waking in the morning with bright ideas in my mind, haste to commit them to paper, and count them monthly as the means of planting groves and purchasing wastes'. He resolved that all his creditors would be paid in full. He was allowed to keep his salary as Sheriff of Selkirkshire, along with Abbotsford and the home farm, and he at once began on a further torrent of novels, biographies, histories and articles. He even tried to limit his always generous hospitality: 'I dare say my kind friends will not quarrel', he wrote, 'if they find at Abbotsford port and sherry instead of claret and champagne'. But the pace was too much and he died seven years later, prematurely worn out. Lord Cockburn summed up what everyone felt: 'Scotland never owed so much to one man'.

Given this extraordinary background, it is hardly surprising that Abbotsford is an extraordinary house. The original farm-house of Cartleyhole was improved, extended in 1818, and then entirely demolished in 1822 and replaced by the present main block, which was completed in 1824. The small west wing was added in the 1850s. Scott changed the name to Abbotsford, the property having once belonged to the Abbey of Melrose and a ford close to the house having been used, so it was said, by the monks.

The best that can be said for the exterior of Abbotsford is that it consists of a jumble of disconnected effects. There are crow-stepped gables, conical turrets, bay windows, a battlemented tower, prominent chimneys and an entrance porch copied from one at Linlithgow Palace which was built in the 1530s. A lady from London described it in the 1820s as

> *finely finished in every part according to the Gothic style ...*
> *so many towers and turrets and pinnacles and bartizans and*
> *all that I ever read of in ancient story ... ceilings, passages*
> *all encrusted with roses, leaves, fruit, groups of figures*
> *imitated in plaster like oak with such exactness that it is*
> *impossible to detect it from the finest oak carving without*
> *scraping it etc. etc.*

Such praise is not a little damning. Other writers have referred to its 'vaguely Tudor appearance' or described it as 'a kind of attenuated Neo-Tudor'. Ruskin, too well-informed to suppose that the house had any particular style, pronounced it 'perhaps the most incongruous pile that gentlemanly modernism ever designed'. There is no doubt that Abbotsford is an undistinguished derivative hotch-potch of architecture. An expert critic has described it as 'not even predominantly Scottish', in spite of its incorporating several old inscribed stones 'from various sources', a lintel from the old Edinburgh College, a niche from the Edinburgh Tolbooth ('better a niche *from* the Tolbooth than a niche *in* it', Scott wrote), and, set into the wall at first floor level and to the left of the porch, what was once the main door of the same ancient prison.

The visitors' entrance is at basement level, at the east end of the house, which means ascending a spiral stair and starting with the study. The study is not a large room, full of books, part of Sir Walter's collection of 9,000 volumes most of which are in the library, and a gallery runs round it. Scott's elaborate writing desk and large leather chair occupy most of the floor space. This is where almost all his writing was done after the crash of 1826.

The library is the biggest room in the house, again lined with books. It is on the north side, with a view of the Tweed and the handsome beech trees on the further bank. The well-known bust of Scott by Chantrey (1820) looks down the length of the room, and a large portrait of Scott's eldest son hangs above the fireplace. The heavily moulded ceiling was designed after the fashion of Roslin Chapel. Not high enough for the room, it does a good deal to confirm one's impression that Queen Victoria was right when she declared that Abbotsford was 'rather gloomy'. Yet this room and the drawing room next to it were the scene of numberless occasions of happy and generous hospitality. This is where distinguished guests gathered to go fishing or coursing or hunting; and if they were lucky it might be 'on a clear bright September morning, with a sharpness in the air that doubled the animating influence of the sunshine'. Here also took place the grand dinner after the Abbotsford hunt, attended by neighbours and tenants as well as family and guests. And here there were dances – 'a dance of neighbours which began without music and ended at five in the morning without light – the whole stock of gas being burned out just as the company broke up', or 'Christmas gambols' which 'came off gaily and they danced till moonlight and starlight and gaslight were one'. So Scott wrote, delighted to have been the host and to have been part of it all. The house is so solemn and quiet now. But it was the revelry and the company that reflected the man himself, as much as the books that remain.

The drawing room is more intimate, hung with a very decorative green hand-painted Chinese wallpaper, a design of leafy branches, flowers and birds, with figures at the foot. A portrait of Scott by Raeburn hangs on the wall. There is a Portuguese ebony roll-top desk and chairs to match, given to Scott by George IV, and in the wall-cases are pieces of silver, including an urn presented by Byron. This urn contains bones found at Athens in 1811. Here we see another side of Scott, Scott the compulsive collector. (And, it may be added, Scott the uncritical antiquary). As you go through the house, more and more bric-a-brac (the weapons and armour we shall come to in a moment) surrounds you: a small iron box said to have belonged to Mary of Guise; a hunting bottle said to have belonged to James VI; a bunch of keys said to have been thrown into Loch Leven during Queen Mary's escape from Lochleven Castle; two cannon balls said to have been fired at the siege of Roxburgh Castle in 1460; a model of the skull of Robert the Bruce; the head of an elk found in Abbotsrule Moss in Roxburghshire; two highland swords found at Culloden; and so on. It is all a tremendous, enthusiastic muddle.

The armoury contains knives and guns of all descriptions, broadswords and dirks, flintlocks and pistols. Some are Scott's own, including his yeomanry sword and pistols, some were gifts, such as a double-barrelled carbine from the Tyrol. In the dining room, which is next to the armoury, there is a superb set of Louis XIV couteaux-de-chasse mounted in silver gilt; these once belonged to Prince Charles.

The armour, which includes a very fine suit of Augsburg tilt armour of about 1580 and two French cuirasses from Waterloo, is in the entrance hall. This extraordinary hall has a wooden roof, down the middle of which run shields bearing the arms of Sir Walter's ancestors. The panelling on the walls, some of it richly carved, came from the old parish church within the walls of Dunfermline Abbey, and perhaps also (but this is not said too loudly) from Holyroodhouse itself. The huge stone fireplace is modelled on the most elaborate of the arches above the stone benches in the north-facing cloister wall of Melrose Abbey. It contains a basket grate which is said to have belonged to Archbishop Sharp, who was murdered near St Andrews in 1679. Statues of saints on the east and west walls are copied from Melrose Abbey. Referring to this entrance hall Scott said that when he planned it he had 'gambolled a little', even admitting that 'I knew it was not in very good taste when I did it, but why should a gentleman not be a little fantastic as Tony Lumpkin says 'So be he is in concatenation accordingly?'

Poor Scott, he loved it all, passionately; and he very nearly lost it. To modern taste Abbotsford is apt to seem something of a Gothic nightmare, a gloomy house of dark wood and ancient weapons and long-unopened volumes. But it should also be seen as the very foundation and embodiment of Scottish historical romanticism. If Scott had not built Abbotsford, it is hard to believe that Prince Albert would ever have built Balmoral.

Finally, if you do not like the inside of the house, see what Scott's antiquarianism did for the court, which you can reach from the entrance hall. The porch, as already mentioned, is copied from one at Linlithgow Palace, and the design of the screen on the east side of the court is based on the cloisters of Melrose Abbey. The wall which faces the house has set into it six carved rectangular stones from the Roman camp at Old Penrith, and between them are five medallions which were once part of the old Mercat Cross in the Royal Mile. When the Cross was pulled down in 1756 these medallions were built into Deanhaugh House in Edinburgh, which came later into the possession of Raeburn; and in 1822 he presented them to Scott. The bowl of the fountain in the middle of the court was also once part of the Cross. Beside the doorway is a stone effigy of Scott's deerhound, Maida, with a Latin inscription which says, in Scott's own translation,

> *Beneath the sculptured form which late you wore*
> *Sleep soundly, Maida, at your master's door.*

It is only right that the last word should be his.

Galashiels, almost opposite Abbotsford, is the industrial town of the Borders: woollen goods and micro-electronics are its business. It mostly lies close-pent along the narrow valley of the Gala Water, just above its junction with the Tweed; but in recent years Galashiels has crept out of its confined space and has spread, not very attractively, closer to Melrose.

Woollen goods were made here in the Middle Ages, and the Caerlee Mill in Galashiels was the first factory in Scotland to use water power to produce woollen yarn. At the beginning of the nineteenth century the cloth produced was 'shepherd tartan' for trousers and travelling cloaks (like those on show at Abbotsford), but the national boom in picturesque tartan which was begun by Scott and

George IV was the driving force for subsequent expansion in several Border towns. There was plenty water power, new machinery was brought in, the blackfaced sheep were replaced by Cheviots which had a better fleece, and the word 'twill' or 'tweel' became misread as 'tweed'. Galashiels expanded faster than anywhere else, and is plainly a nineteenth century mill town. For high quality goods, however, the old 'putting-out' system, with knitters working in their own homes on yarn delivered to them, is also in operation in the Borders.

The War Memorial in the town centre is Galashiels' principal landmark, and an unusual one. It takes the form of a life-size figure of a mounted Border reiver, or moss-trooper. It is a very spirited piece of statuary, the horse abruptly pulled up, the rider helmeted, with a sword by his side, looking intently towards some suddenly noticed movement ahead. The Memorial as a whole was designed by Lorimer, who was also responsible for the fountain in nearby Cornmill Square. The shaft is surmounted by a capital and frieze carrying the town's coat-of-arms. The latter is unusual, for the device is a fox trying to reach some plums hanging on a tree, and the legend reads 'soor Plums'. The reference is to a song, 'soor Plums o' Galashiels', the words of which have been lost but which was written to commemorate a Border foray of 1337, when, so the story goes, some English raiders were trapped while picking wild plums, and slaughtered. It is more cheerful to remember another song connected with Galashiels, Burns's 'Gala Water' and its refrain 'Braw braw lads o' Galashiels'.

Continue west to Clovenfords, where Scott (frequently) and Wordsworth (once) stayed (but not in the hotel now standing), and on past Ashiestiel just visible on the opposite side of the river. Now the rolling fertile lands of the lower Tweed valley have disappeared, and the hills are closing in, some of them fifteen hundred feet high and more. The road is winding, crossing streams and burns (the larger are usually 'waters' in this part of the world) that tumble down the hillsides, and conifer forests that stretch from the road far up the slopes; Yair Hill Forest and Elibank and Traquair Forest are east and west of Ashiestiel Hill, and Glentress Forest is just north of Peebles.

The only settlement between Galashiels and Peebles, a distance of some twenty miles, is **Innerleithen**, a small town where the Leithen Water reaches the Tweed, and the hills are steep. It was once a scarcely known hamlet of thatched and white-washed cottages. Then in the 1790s it was discovered by the woollen industry, and mills were built. More surprisingly, a mineral spring was found, with waters said to resemble those at Harrogate, and Innerleithen became a spa, complete with a pump-house, reading rooms, and a verandah. Scott used it as the setting for a novel, and the spring became St Ronan's Well. But Innerleithen's day was not a long one; it has subsided into a small mill town of no particular interest, notable chiefly for the excellent salmon fishing in the vicinity. A road going south over the hills from Innerleithen is a short cut to St Mary's Loch (*see* p. 360).

But there is something else close to Innerleithen, not quite as old as the salmon fishing but more accessible. Turn south in the village, cross the river, and in about a mile, where the small stream of the Quair joins the Tweed, you reach **Traquair House**, often said, and perhaps rightly, to be the oldest continually inhabited house in Scotland. Certainly there was a royal hunting lodge here in the twelfth century, and in the summer of 1566 Mary, Queen of Scots visited the tower-house – now part of the present building – with her infant son James VI. Much of Traquair was built after Mary's time, but no changes or additions have been made to it since the end of the seventeenth century, with the result that it not only has the appearance of unaltered, authentic antiquity, but to a remarkable extent preserves the very atmosphere of a long past age. From that point of view it is one of the most interesting of all Scottish houses.

Traquair is in a low-lying position, denied extensive views because of the encircling hills, and guarded by innumerable trees; those along the avenue which leads in a straight line for half a mile from the old entrance gates – the Bear Gates – to the front of the house are, like the house itself, old and lofty. The Tweed flows through the grounds, and flowed at one time so close to the house that the laird, it is said, was able to fish from his windows. But this convenience was not worth the risk of a flood, so the river was diverted into a new channel a quarter of a mile further away, and all that remains of the old course is a densely wooded backwater, popular with waterfowl. There are woodland walks and a maze and a walled garden, reserved for visitors and peacocks.

It seems likely that a rudimentary tower stood here early in the twelfth century; but the first explicit reference to Traquair Castle is in 1512, when the first stage of the present building, an L-plan tower-house three storeys high, had probably been standing for at least ten or twenty years. This tower was added to during the sixteenth century by extending it to the south-east (i.e. to the right, looking from the avenue), and making a new entrance door. The extension was the full depth of the L-plan, so Traquair became a long rectangular house, the newer part extending from as well as continuing the forward line of the tower. The fact that there are two parts to the main block was then further concealed by raising the old tower to four storeys, the same height as the extension, building further to the south-east, and putting a new slated roof right across from gable to gable. Finally, at the very end of the seventeenth century, the low wings towards the avenue, the forecourt, the grand entrance gateway, and the terraces and the two pavilions to the rear were added, doubtless in order to make Traquair look more up-to-date.

There is little on the outside to indicate that the main block was not built as one, for the stonework is covered with roughcast plaster, and the windows were altered so as to be more uniform in size, and almost regular in distribution. The square bartizan at the outside end of the old tower may not be original, although it looks very old; the old tower probably ended near the chimney stack, one third of the way along. The sixteenth century extension has a round bartizan at one corner, and on the right a round tower rising from the foundations. On the central dormer window, facing the courtyard, there is carved the date 1642. The side wings of around 1700 have only one storey, with attics. Along the back of the building is a high wide terrace, with a stair which leads down to a second terrace, and then a second stair to the level park which stretches to the Quair, not far off. To describe the house is to make it sound plain. And in a way it is plain, with its many small windows, large areas of grey-white wall, and steep roof. But it is impressive partly because it is so plain, and so honestly old. Virtually unaltered since 1700, it preserves its antique air, is contemptuous of ornament, and strives neither for symmetry nor asymmetry. Intensely Scots in appearance, it fits perfectly into its surroundings of woodland and Border hills.

The main entrance door, iron-studded and pierced by two small windows, is clearly as old or almost as old as the walls that surround it; the massive door-knocker is dated 1705. Inside, there is nothing grand and overwhelming, for Traquair is not a grand and overwhelming house. It is personal and intimate. It has palpably grown into what it is, and not been made or contrived for public display. There are items of interest all over the house. At the foot of the main (turret) stair there is a superb carved oak door dated 1601; it shows two animals locked in combat – the Scottish unicorn and the English lion. The High Drawing Room, a delightful room, has eighteenth century *trompe l'oeil* overdoors and a *trompe l'oeil* overmantel, and part of a seventeenth century beamed ceiling has been exposed, painted with grotesques and floral motifs. There is also a harpsichord dated 1651, and among the numerous pictures is a portrait of John Dryden. The Library, which is on the top floor and dates from the first half of the eighteenth century, has a coved ceiling with heads of philosophers painted on it, and the very valuable collection of books includes a copy of the Nuremberg Chronicle, printed in 1493, and an illuminated bible of 1479. In the Museum Room, also on the top floor, there is a section of mural decoration of about 1530 which shows a hound and other animals against a background of grapes and vine leaves. In the King's Room there is a four-post bedstead said to have been slept in by Mary, Queen of Scots. Other articles associated with the Queen include her rosary and crucifix, and a cradle in which she laid her son. The Chapel contains a set of carved Flemish wood panels which once belonged to Mary of Guise.

Traquair also possesses the oldest licensed brewing premises in Scotland; operations are conducted in a tiny brew-house beneath the chapel. The recipe was discovered by the 20th laird in the early 1960s among family papers, and is thought to date from the late eighteenth century. Traquair House Ale is said to be 'unspoilt by modern technology or inferior ingredients', and is available in the shop. It is not cheap, but it is potent. Most of the small output (200 barrels) is exported. Bear Ale, not quite so strong or so traditional, is more widely available.

Why is Traquair so atmospheric? Perhaps because, as described by one of its own Lairds, it is 'a symbol of lost causes'. It has been in the same family since 1491. When Mary was Queen, it was the home of Sir John Stewart, captain of the Queen's bodyguard and second cousin to the Queen. She visited Traquair, with Darnley, in August 1566. During the seventeenth century successive Lairds developed a lasting commitment to Roman Catholicism, and during the first half of the eighteenth century they schemed for the restoration of the Stewarts; the fifth Earl spent two years in the Tower as a result of his support for the '45. When the Stewart cause was finally proved hopeless the family's influence in religion and politics fell to zero. Traquair became a backwater, 'forgetting the world and by the world forgot'. In this happy condition it survived into the twentieth century, a home undamaged by progress, redolent of historical continuity.

Before leaving Traquair, be sure to look at the gates, for they are at least as famous as the house itself. There are two gates, one at the top of the avenue by the road, and the other at the foot of the avenue, forming part of the screen in front of the forecourt. This screen is totally unlike the house, fashionable and sophisticated. The gate itself has sideposts of rustic stonework, each topped by a large Baroque vase; these sideposts are joined by elaborate floral ironwork with a coat of arms and a coronet in the centre; and the railings to each side have fleur-de-lis finials and Baroque urns on top of the supporting posts. How the old house must look down on all this finery! It came into existence because the fourth Earl of Traquair, very late in the seventeenth century, resolved to modernise his property, and was advised by James Smith (*see* p. 55), an architect sympathetic to the latest Palladian developments south of the border, and not at all the man for Traquair.

The other gates are Georgian, the sideposts surmounted by toothy bears holding heraldic shields. The story about them is that they were closed when Prince Charles passed through them in 1745, and the Laird – a firm supporter of the rebellion, for he was a Roman Catholic – vowed that they would never again be opened until a Stewart was on the throne. Alas for romance! There is no evidence that Prince Charles ever visited Traquair. But Sir Walter Scott did, and the house is sometimes said to have been the model for Tully-Veolan in *Waverley* which was, he says, 'built at a period when castles were no longer necessary, and when the Scottish architects had not yet acquired the art of designing a domestic residence'. We must count ourselves most fortunate that this 'artless' building survives, undamaged and unimproved.

From Traquair village – another staging post on the Southern Uplands Way – one of the better-known Border walks goes south-east over Minch Moor to Selkirk. It is an old drove road, described in Sir Walter Scott's tale '*The Two Drovers*'. It now passes through parts of Elibank and Traquair Forests, and for most of the way is in high country with Traquair to the west, the Tweed and Sir Walter Scott's Ashiestiel (*see* p, 343) to the north, and Yarrow Water and Newark Castle (*see* p. 363), to the south. Traquair to Selkirk is only about ten miles – as the crow flies.

For those who prefer to drive, it is only a few miles to **Peebles**, travelling either on the north or on the south side of the river. Both roads afford excellent views of the narrow valley; the flood plain here is the last sizeable stretch of level ground before Lanark, twenty five miles to the west over the rolling almost uninhabited lowland hills. The main road, north of the river, is the faster and more open. The lines of the hills are flowing and easy, the Tweed winds between green steeps, and sheep are scattered everywhere on the level ground, and up the green hillsides. Glentress Forest stretches up the hillside, behind the Peebles Hydro, just before you enter the town. The forest is threaded by a network of narrow roads, and its highest point, almost 2,000 feet above sea level, commands a panoramic view of the Moorfoot Hills. The road on the Traquair side, narrow and winding, is equally attractive. The river keeps it very close company. From the roadside, walks start into Cardrona Forest, and nearer Peebles are the Kailzie Gardens, 17 acres of woodland and rhododendron garden sloping up the hillside, and a large walled garden with walls almost twenty feet high.

Peebles is a county town and a holiday town. Situated amid the hills, where the Eddleston Water, the Manor Water and the Glensax Burn flow into the Tweed, it is an excellent walking centre. For those who do not wish to explore the countryside on foot, the town itself, although not especially beautiful, has much to offer. Its remarkably wide High Street, said to have been laid out in the sixteenth century, has a welcoming air, with buildings of various heights, styles and ages along each side and the Old Parish Church (not so old really, 1885) looking along it. The river is only one street away from the High Street, and it too is wide, with riverside paths along each bank. Although now something of a dormitory town for Edinburgh (the dormitories are mostly on the south side of the river), Peebles maintains an agreeable mix of bustle and quiet, and the old tag comes readily to mind, 'Peebles for pleasure'.

It does not look it, but Peebles is an old town. A medieval fort or castle once stood where the Parish Church now stands, and a fragment of the sixteenth century town wall can be seen, along with one of the 'blok houssis', on the north-west side of town near Venlaw Road. Peebles was frequently visited by early Scottish kings, and there are some grounds for supposing that it was James I who wrote '*Peblis to the Play*', a poem which describes boisterous merrymaking in the streets, 'a daft abandon, beyond English comprehension'. (In case the attribution should seem absurd, it is worth adding that James certainly wrote '*The King's Quair*' which contains some poetry that Chaucer would not have been ashamed of. The author tells how he looked from his prison windows (James was a prisoner in England from the age of twelve until he was thirty) into a garden where a nightingale was singing, and saw a lady with whom he fell instantly in love:

The fairest and the freschest yonge floure
That ever I sawe, me thought, before that houre,
For quhich sodayn abate, anon astert
The blude of all my body to my hert.

The lady was Joan Beaufort, daughter of the Earl of Somerset. They were married before James returned to Scotland in 1424).

Pilgrims also came here in the Middle Ages. The attraction was the Church of the Holy Cross, or Cross Kirk, founded in 1261. A monastery was added in 1473. The church was built on the spot where an 'ancient and venerable' cross had been discovered, lying on a stone inscribed with the name of St Nicholas; or so it was said. Pilgrims came to celebrate the Feast of the Finding of the Cross, an occasion which was cleverly grafted onto the old pagan Beltane Festival of the Celts. The church was abandoned in 1783, and what is left of it can be seen in peaceful grounds on the north side of town.

In the High Street the old Mercat Cross stands where the market used to take place and where the revived Beltane Festival is held at midsummer. The head of the sixteenth century shaft displays the three fish of Peebles; the sundials and windvane were added in 1662 to mark the restoration to the throne of Charles II. The nearby Tontine Hotel (1808), set back in its own little cobbled square, has an elegant dining room, with an Adam-style fireplace and a musicians' gallery. The County Hotel, almost next-door, has an eighteenth century façade, but incorporates within itself a thick-walled, barrel-vaulted room which seems to have been part of a 'bastel-house'. These bastel-houses were not so much forts as secure places into which a community could retreat in time of danger. Few have been identified, but they existed in many burghs and townships in the Borders. Finally, to end on a more peaceful note, appropriate to Peebles, there is the Old Town House (1753) only a few yards further down the street. A simple two-storey rectangular block with a pediment bearing the burgh arms, it shows what can be achieved with good proportions and robust detail. During the Napoleonic War French officers who were on parole were billeted in Peebles, and they used the upper room of the Town House as a theatre, giving performances of plays by Molière and Corneille. With all respect to Peebles, one wonders how often works by these authors have been performed in this pleasant little town since the French officers went home.

28

From Peebles to Moffat, St Mary's Loch and Selkirk

A MILE OR SO upstream from Peebles stands **Neidpath Castle**, for centuries the home of the Hays of Yester. Its situation is very striking, for it is built on a high projecting rock above a sudden bend in the Tweed, where the river, abruptly emerging from a thickly wooded gorge, forms a deep pool at the base of the rock and, towards the other bank, flows wide and shallow across pebbles.

Neidpath dates from the late fourteenth century and was originally a fortress of great strength; the walls are over ten feet thick in some places. It is the usual L-plan, but owing to the shape of the site is not rectangular. Designed above all to withstand attack, the original door was on the side where the rock falls steeply to the river, and the upper floors were reached by a turnpike stair within the wall. The castle consists basically of three lofty vaulted compartments, the great hall occupying the entire first floor, with the kitchen in the now ruined wing. The principal compartments on the ground and top levels were subdivided by wooden floors, and a pit prison, as gruesome as all other pit prisons, was provided below the short wing.

In this form the castle remained for some two hundred and fifty years until, when some sort of peace seemed at last to be settling on the country, the Earl of Tweeddale decided to make it less like a castle and more like a house. The courtyard on the east side was extended and the courtyard buildings were remodelled. The entrance was moved to the courtyard side (which meant that the visitor arrived on the level of the first wooden dividing floor, not absolutely in the dungeons), and an ornate gateway was built in the forecourt wall, with the crest of the Earls of Tweeddale (a goat's head) carved on the keystone. Inside, a wide, square, convenient staircase was built, making access to the hall and private upper apartments easy, instead of as difficult as possible. To complete the effect, the 'gairdene' was probably tidied up and extended. A garden of some kind seems to have existed even in the late sixteenth century. Parallel terraces can still be seen to the east of the castle, although their retaining walls are ruinous, and these terraces doubtless formed the garden. According to one of Neidpath's more imaginative historians, there were days when 'the orchard on the hillside basked in the rays of the summer sun, and the garden was brilliant with flowers; when the terraces along the banks of the silvery stream formed the favourite promenade for the ladies and their attendant maids, and a rude hospitality was dispensed within'. But it is not easy to imagine it. Scottish history seldom sounds like that.

Just beyond the castle a road leaves the A72 and descends to cross the now narrowing Tweed. This road offers two possibilities. One is to circuit **Cademuir Hill** and return to Peebles. The circuit is short but interesting. After Old Manor Bridge, a graceful single arch built in 1702 over the Manor Water, the road runs close to the steep unfenced slopes of the hill. The climb to the top, for those who have the energy, is worthwhile; the severest part is the beginning. The view over the valley of the Manor Water and the surrounding hills is of the utmost peacefulness; sheep are almost the sole inhabitants of this entire region. Along the ridge there are several prehistoric sites. South-west of the summit there are two fortified settlements, within which traces of at least 35 timber-framed houses have been found. The ruins of the protecting walls cannot be missed. On the north face there are the remains of cultivation terraces. Similar fortified hilltop settlements are to be found all along the upper Tweed Valley.

If you go further up the Manor Water – the road ends after seven miles so you are spared the annoyance of 'through' traffic, and are in unusually peaceful country – you come first to the Black Dwarf's Cottage, with date 1802 and the initials DR above the door. The initials stand for David Ritchie, an unfortunate cripple whom Sir Walter Scott met and who appears, with the most enormous distortions, as the principal character in *The Black Dwarf* (1816), one of Scott's most nonsensical novels. Further up the valley there are the remains of several tower-houses, the best of them at Posso, where the outbuildings and what may even be the remains of a garden or orchard can be discovered. Enthusiastic climbers can go on to ascend Dollar Law, the second highest hill in the Borders, just west of the valley; or walkers can go over the hills to Glengaber, six miles to the south, and thence easily to St Mary's Loch.

West of the Manor Water take the B712 signposted to Drumelzier and Moffat. The road passes **Stobo Kirk** on the right, a twelfth century building with a tower which was clearly defensible. The nave and chancel were 'improved' in the fifteenth–sixteenth centuries by providing a porch and larger windows. There is an unusually good assemblage of eighteenth-century gravestones in the churchyard.

The country is now quite different, the valley narrow and enclosed, with many trees along the road and on the hillsides.

Everywhere hereabouts is good tree-growing country, as the Forestry Commission has proved – plenty rain – and near Drumelzier there is the finest arboretum in Scotland, **Dawyck Botanic Garden**. The garden extends to 1,000 acres of woodland, and they rise to an elevation of 1,500 feet, offering the visitor an opportunity for delightful walks.

The property was gifted to the nation in 1979, when selective tree-planting within its bounds had already been going on for three hundred years. Linnaeus is said to have visited Dawyck in 1725. One of the first larches in Scotland was planted in the grounds in that year, and one of the earliest Douglas firs in 1835. In 1838 the house (which is not open to the public) was described as having been transformed from 'a lonely mansion in the bosom of a gloomy mountain to the extreme reverse'. There are many magnificent specimens of Douglas fir (one of them over 150 feet high), giant redwoods, and the dark, pendulous Picea breweriana, all from the west coast of North America. In spring thousands of daffodils flank the drive to the house, and in early summer the rhododendron walk exhibits such treasures as Rh. lacteum ('very beautiful, very difficult' say the books), Rh. forrestii, Rh. oreodoxa, and innumerable others, all growing in natural woodland conditions. A small stream goes through the estate, crossed by an antique bridge; mature woodland clothes the steep slopes, and wild life abounds. For garden enthusiasts, as well as tree enthusiasts and rhododendron enthusiasts, this is a spot not to be missed.

Leaving Drumelzier you are suddenly on the open uplands of the Tweed. Join the A701 and turn south for Moffat. The road winds along amid rolling hills, sheep on the green slopes but many hillsides bare and in places rock-strewn. The ascent is gradual, and the great beech trees near Drumelzier are now replaced by fir and spruce. At the very small village of **Tweedsmuir**, close to where John Buchan (Lord Tweedsmuir) was born, an easy five-mile walk westward leads to the top of Broad Law (2,754 feet), the highest hill in the Borders. Above Tweedsmuir it is wonderful moorland country. All the way the road accompanies the Tweed, which flows on a rocky bed from its source at Tweedswell, a shallow boggy depression close to the road, 1,300 feet above sea level.

Just after the watershed the **Devil's Beef Tub** appears suddenly on the left. The Devil's Beef Tub is a great scar gouged by nature out of an already precipitous hillside. It is fenced off, a dangerous place; people have been killed here, for once rolling down over the loose stones, no one could stop, and it is a long way to the bottom. The name comes from the idea (and possibly the practice) of hiding stolen cattle here. There are other deep sudden hollows like this in the Border hills which are said to have been used for the same purpose.

From this high point there is a superb view looking south. The moorland is all behind you, and, stretched out the better part of a thousand feet below, are the fertile upper reaches of Annandale, the little town of Moffat amid its trees, and all the country down towards Dumfries, the Solway and even as far as Cumbria.

Moffat is eight miles south of the Devil's Beef Tub. It is sited on cross-roads amid fine mountains and is a remarkably smart little place, a stopover on the way from Carlisle. Its mineral springs became well known in the eighteenth century, and they did so much for the place that the Spa Building was put up in 1827. Now serving as the Town Hall, it is a Classical design, severe but somehow cheerful, and rather a surprise in rural Dumfriesshire. Even more surprising is the Colvin Fountain in the wide main street, erected in 1875. Sheep have always been the main business of Moffat (although now perhaps overtaken by tourists), so here is a sheep, or more accurately a ram, a big bronze ram on top of its own little mountain, looking confidently on all who pass by. Better a sheep than a Lord Provost, one traveller remarked. Hill walkers as well as sheep are catered for in Moffat. Numerous walks up the nearby valleys lead to high ground and superb views. The summit of Hart Fell (2651 feet) can be reached up the Birnock Water, going north; and for those who make light of twenty kilometres it is possible to follow the Southern Uplands Way, which climbs to the top of Bodesbeck Law and then runs along the ridge for several miles until the path descends to the Loch of the Lowes and Tibbie Shiels' Inn (*see* p. 362).

Moffat is the extreme western limit of what can reasonably be called the Borders. Those who drive up the A74 are travelling on the line of an old Roman road which passes just west of Moffat; a few miles further north the A74 comes close to a Roman camp before reaching Crawford and Abington. One would not stray out of the Borders in order to see Crawford or Abington, which in any case are sited amid the headwaters of the River Clyde – and *that* decidedly belongs to the west of Scotland. But it is tempting, nevertheless, being so far west already, to go a few miles into the Lowther Hills and visit Leadhills and Wanlockhead.

Wanlockhead, at 1383 feet, is the highest village in Scotland; **Leadhills**, a couple of miles distant, is only a little lower. The country is high, remote, heather-covered moorland, a common refuge for Covenanters during the religious persecutions of the seventeenth century. Oats and potatoes grow badly at these altitudes, and it is rough country even for sheep. Why, then, does one find a pair of centuries-old villages in these inhospitable surroundings? The answer is gold – gold first, lead later. Gold from Wanlockhead was important in the sixteenth century, mostly alluvial. Lead mines opened in 1680 and were worked continuously until 1934. The resulting hummocks and hollows are scattered about the area, and at Wanlockhead a water-bucket pumping engine (flooding of the mines was a perpetual problem) is still in place.

The two villages – the Earls of Hopetoun promoted Leadhills, while the Dukes of Queensberry did the same for Wanlockhead – were further developed in the nineteenth and early twentieth centuries, when the existing short rows of miners' cottages were built. The library buildings are older. The poet Allan Ramsay was born at Leadhills in 1686, and he went to Edinburgh to be apprenticed to a wig-maker in 1700. Forty one years later he founded at Leadhills one of the first circulating libraries in Scotland; the building now serves as a tourist Information Centre. A similar library was founded a few years later at Wanlockhead, and this now houses a Museum of Scottish Lead Mining. Furthermore, railway enthusiasts will rejoice to see what is left of the Leadhills and Wanlockhead Light Railway, which opened in 1901 and closed in 1938. Plans are afoot to construct a narrow-gauge railway line on the existing track-bed, and once again to connect the two villages. Thus enterprise still exerts itself amid the mountains, and a small fragment of industrial and transport history is preserved.

Return to Moffat, and head north-east on the A708 up Moffat Water. This is a delightful highland-style road, unfenced, going up and up into the hills, with cattle-grids (for sheep) and flats by the riverside which make it easy to stop and picnic. The steep slopes on the right prevent even a glimpse of the extensive forests of Craik and Eskdalemuir, which stretch a long way to the south. These belong to the Forestry Commission and have greatly expanded during the last twenty years; except for those in the south-west, they are the largest forests in Scotland. They lie just south of Ettrick Water and of the area which is still sometimes referred to as Ettrick Forest, which you are now approaching.

Ettrick Forest was once a royal hunting ground, famous for its majestic oak trees and wild deer. According to an old ballad,

> *Ettrick Forest is a fair forest*
> *In it grows many a semelie trie*
> *The hart, the hynd, the dae, the rae*
> *And of a' beasts great plentie.*

But now the area is one of the least wooded in Scotland, with only a scattering of pine plantations and the occasional cluster of hazel rooted in a patch of scree. Responsibility for the disappearance of the forest – much of the Borders was once covered by more or less open woodland – is variously ascribed to the monks, the English, James V and 'progressive' estate-owners and farmers. Doubtless all played a part, for the forest went gradually, and through the centuries sheep were undoubtedly the great instrument of destruction. In medieval days the forest was useful as a hiding place for outlaws, marauding bands and even small armies; but when more peaceful times came after 1600, this function disappeared. By the start of the eighteenth century only fragmentary areas of the original forest remained, and the word itself began to mean no more than the open ground beyond the reach of cultivation, whether it was pasture, moorland or woodland.

After climbing in ten miles to just over 1,000 feet, the A708 passes close to the **Grey Mare's Tail**, a narrow 200 foot waterfall formed by the Tail Burn as it plunges down a rocky chasm in the hillside on its way to join Moffat Water. The burn comes from Loch Skeen, a lonely mountain tarn set high above the road in a circle of dark cliffs and rough hillsides. Even if the visitor decides against the very steep climb to the loch (steps are provided, but these hillsides are tremendously abrupt), it is worth following the track that leads to the foot of the waterfall. A distant view of the Grey Mare's Tail is not enough; no one should miss the full sound and sight of the ever-cascading curtain of white water.

Once over the watershed – the road snakes swiftly through a narrow cleft in the hills – the descent to the Loch of the Lowes and St Mary's Loch (they are separated by only a narrow stretch of ground) is swift. The Loch of the Lowes is rather bare and not very interesting, but **St Mary's Loch** is one of the best-known beauty spots in the Borders. The loch itself is quite large, three miles long by up to half a mile in width, and is 800 feet above sea level; Yarrow Water flows from it, going east to Selkirk. Surrounded on all sides by high but gently-sloping green hills, which are often mirrored in the water, St Mary's Loch conveys at almost all times a remarkable sense of tranquillity and repose. Here if anywhere is life without hurry, peace without monotony, remission from the problems of today. There is now a sailing club at the west end of the loch and sometimes there are too many motor vehicles. But one still sees why 'a complete day's idleness' meant for Sir Walter Scott a visit to

> *These crystal shores*
> *Set among bare rounded fells;*

and why a celebrated churchman, Lord MacLeod of Fuinary, once remarked that his

> *highest idea of earthly happiness was to spend a long*
> *summer's day in Yarrow, with a few choice friends, stretched*
> *at full length on the grassy sward, amidst the blooming*
> *heather, looking up to the bright sky and leisurely smoking a*
> *cigar, when the rest of the world was completely shut out,*
> *and the first person who spoke of Church affairs should be*
> *bastinadoed.*

From the literary point of view, **Yarrow**, **Ettrick** and **St Mary's Loch** are the heart of the Borders. Scott made the district famous. It was here, more than anywhere else, that he collected ballads which he then patched up and published. Yarrow and Ettrick were often their setting. He befriended James Hogg, the so-called Ettrick Shepherd, who also collected ballads. Hogg had been born at Ettrickhall in 1770. Shepherd, farmer, land-agent and poet, he once described himself as 'king of the faery school' of ballad writers, leaving the 'raiding ballads' to Scott. Where Scott and Hogg led, others followed, and a severe outbreak of balladitis swept the country. The best of the old ballads, not many, are real poetry, old traditional stories about family feuds, treachery, desperate fights in gathering darkness, death and doomed lovers. Their unadorned, matter-of-fact style gives them their force:

Fa on them, lads! can Simmy say;
Fy, fa on them cruelly!
For or they win the Ritter ford
Mony toom [empty] saddle there shall be.

One of the best tells how Lady Margaret elopes with Lord William, to be pursued by her father and seven brothers. In the ensuing moonlight fight Lord William kills his opponents while Lady Margaret looks on, torn between her loves. But Lord William is mortally wounded;

Lord William was dead lang ere midnight,
Lady Marg'ret lang ere day –
And all true lovers that go thegither,
May they have mair luck than they!

The lovers are buried, according to the poem, in the churchyard of St Mary's Kirk which lies just out of sight above St Mary's Loch itself.

The imitators of the old ballads mostly wrote sorry stuff. But no matter; Yarrow and St Mary's Loch were the places to visit. Scott brought parties across from Abbotsford. Wordsworth came more than once, and wrote three poems about Yarrow. A widow who occupied a cottage at the head of St Mary's Loch turned it into an inn – **Tibbie Shieil's Inn**, still popular – and when she died many years later her hospitality had been extended to de Quincey, Thomas Carlyle, Robert Louis Stevenson, Sir James Simpson, Gladstone, and numberless other eminent men.

These and far more romantic associations have faded now, which possibly adds to what Wordsworth called the 'pastoral melancholy' of the scene. Tibbie Shiel's Inn (it has become a stopping place on the Southern Uplands Way) is the principal link with the past. On the hillside nearby is a monument to James Hogg. His ballads are mostly forgotten, but his *Private Memoirs and Confessions of a Justified Sinner*, is still read, an astonishing exploration of religious fanaticism carried to the brink of insanity. The site of St Mary's Kirk, built in the thirteenth century, is not far above the loch shore. Of the little church nothing remains. There are a score of tombstones, and an old wind-blown ash tree, and sheep find shelter within the churchyard walls. Many ballads refer to this deserted spot. But St Mary's Loch has no need of the past. It is one of those peaceful places that seem to be set apart, well above and far from the everyday cares and activities of the world.

Half way along the loch a road turns sharply back to the Megget Reservoir. Reservoirs are rarely an attraction, but from this one a track goes north over the hills to the head of the Manor Water (*see* p. 353), and thus to Peebles.

If you are not for walking but yearn to see more 'ballad country' continue to Mountbenger, cross the Yarrow, and go over the hills to Tushielaw Inn; grassy hills and sheep and a well-surfaced little-used road. Tushielaw is on the Ettrick Water. The Ettrick rises far up in the hills near Moffat, and is not a great stream even at Tushielaw. A short distance above the inn, at Ettrickhill, a tall sandstone monument occupies the site of the cottage where Hogg was born, and in the nearby churchyard is the grave of Tibbie Shiels. For all its fame, the Ettrick Valley is disappointing. There are numerous ancient ruined towers in the valley, not easily accessible, and vague associations with Michael Scott the Wizard (1175?–1234?), who was astrologer to the Emperor Frederick II and whom Dante saw in Hell.

Returning to the Yarrow Water, the A708, now only six miles from Selkirk, passes Broadmeadows on the left, a property that Scott once hoped to purchase, and Foulshiels, birthplace of Mungo Park, the explorer of Africa; and then, almost immediately, Newark Castle appears on the other side of the river.

Newark Castle is a tall, massive, rectangular keep standing on top of a steep bank that rises above the Yarrow. It was built early in the fifteenth century and was at first a royal hunting lodge, the principal among many towers and fortified places in Ettrick Forest. The walls are ten feet thick, and contain several small rooms as well as the turret staircases. The royal arms are on a shield on the west gable, and the building is surrounded by a barmkin or defensive wall. Newark was taken by an English force in 1548, and by Cromwell's troops a hundred years later. Scott was particularly fond of the old place, which appears in his '*Lay of the last Minstrel*'. Doubtless he habitually saw it peopled by knights in armour and ladies in distress, all of them, of course, Scotts of Buccleuch, by whom it was and still is owned. Entry is by application to the Buccleuch Estates.

Bowhill, Border home of the Scotts of Buccleuch, is half a mile down the road. It has been described as 'a princely dwelling in the Italian style, girt by gorgeous plantations', and 'perhaps the ideal baronial residence in the south of Scotland'. The Duke of Buccleuch's principal residence is Drumlanrig Castle in Dumfries-shire, another treasure-house of art and objets d'art.

If architectural merit were the only criterion, Bowhill would not rank very high. It was originally a modest eighteenth century country house of two storeys. Early in the nineteenth century it acquired a new façade, a west wing, and a separate stable block. In the 1830s William Burn added an east wing, a front porch, and a third storey to the central block; and further alterations were made in the 1870s. It is a large rambling house, in dark whinstone, and there is about it an easy-going largeness of effect; but in appearance it is neither very elegant nor very grand. It has, however, a beautiful situation. And better still, the relaxed un-stuffy interior looks decidedly comfortable, and shows to advantage a truly superlative collection of furniture, pictures and tapestries.

The Entrance Hall leads directly into the rectangular Gallery Hall (1812), which is the most imposing space in the house. The Gallery Hall rises through the first floor, with a balcony all round at that level, and is lit from above. High up, the walls are covered by four splendid Mortlake tapestries woven in 1670, three of them depicting 'the Triumph of Julius Caesar' after Mantegna's cartoons in Hampton Court. At gallery level there are eighteenth and nineteenth century landscapes, and at ground floor level several large portraits by Lely, and others attributed to the School of van Dyck. There are also elaborate Louis XV chairs with Aubusson covers, a Boulle bracket clock of about 1710, and a Louis XIV mirror of ebony, tortoiseshell and ormolu, given by Charles II to the Duke of Monmouth and Buccleuch.

Splendid as these items are, they hardly prepare the visitor for what is to come. The Italian Room contains no fewer than eight Venetian scenes by Guardi, as well as five other high-quality eighteenth century paintings of Venice. To back these up, there is a large interior of the Pantheon in Rome by Pannini. Only a few yards away (as the house is presently arranged) is the astonishing Buccleuch Collection of Portrait Miniatures. What is displayed varies from time to time, but there are always a large number to be seen. Among the most interesting from a historical point of view are those of Henry VIII, his daughters Queen Mary and Queen Elizabeth (by Nicholas Hilliard), and Catherine Howard (by Hans Holbein the younger). There is also the famous unfinished portrait of Oliver Cromwell by Samuel Cooper. Most of these are jewel-like objects, as well as being portraits of astonishing intimacy and vitality. To see two or three together would be remarkable enough; to see twenty or thirty at once really takes the breath away.

This by no means ends the catalogue of artistic treasures. In the Dining Room hangs a spacious Canaletto which some may regard as the greatest masterpiece in the house: 'Whitehall', a famous view looking along past Downing Street to the Banqueting Hall, with St Paul's Cathedral just visible on the other side of the river. But nearby are portraits by Gainsborough and Reynolds, including the latter's 'Winter', which is a portrait of a little girl in a chilly landscape; she is Lady Caroline Scott, wearing a black cloak, a black bonnet, and a red muff; for spontaneous charm it would be hard to beat. In the Drawing Room are two landscapes by Claude and an especially fine Ruysdael, as well as one of Reynolds' very grandest compositions, a portrait of the wife of the 3rd Duke of Buccleuch along with her daughter and two dogs, the heiress who united the families of Montagu and Scott in the later eighteenth century.

These are only a few of the many pictures of the highest quality which this great house contains. And of course there is the furniture – a silver wine cistern (1711) which weighs over nine stone, Meissen china made for Madame du Barry in 1771, more chairs and settees covered with Aubusson tapestry, Louis XV tables, Boulle cabinets, and in the very comfortable looking Morning Room four walls of delightful Chinese hand-painted wallpaper of the late eighteenth century. Nor is history forgotten. The Duke of Monmouth was the natural son of Charles II and Lucy Walters. In 1663 he married Anne Scott, Countess of Buccleuch in her own right, and he was created Duke of Buccleuch and Earl of Dalkeith. When his father died in 1685 he made his ill-judged bid for the throne. Utterly defeated at Sedgemoor, he was executed in London ten days later. The titles and lands of the Duchess, however, could not be touched because of her lineage, and she lived on at Dalkeith Palace until her death in 1732. Items on display include the Duke's cradle, and the shirt he wore on the day of his execution.

29

From Selkirk to Hawick to Jedburgh

SELKIRK IS NOT uncommonly described as 'a typical Border town', meaning, perhaps, that it is not as big and industrialised as Hawick or Galashiels, but less attractive than Kelso or Jedburgh. It is situated amid rolling hills, just east of the junction of the Ettrick and Yarrow Waters, and occupies a steep hillside above the Ettrick. Until recently there were many tweed mills in the valley below the town, but now Selkirk depends as much on electronics and tourism as on wool.

The town has a long history, although few traces of it are to be seen. An abbey was founded here in the twelfth century, but within a few years it was removed to Kelso and building was not proceeded with. There was an early medieval castle, but only a green mound remains to mark the site. A strong tradition avers that in 1517 eighty men marched to join James IV at Flodden and that only one returned; true or not, this supports other evidence that Selkirk was of some importance in the later Middle Ages.

The Common Riding at Selkirk is a link with the Flodden tradition. The detail of the story is that the sole survivor from the battle brought with him a captured English banner. When he was asked about his companions he could not speak, but cast the banner on the ground to tell the news. Selkirk's Riding of the Marches recalls this dramatic gesture. After the horsemen and horsewomen have ridden round the North Common and returned to the town, the Royal Standard Bearer, who carries the Burgh flag, mounts a platform in the Market Place and 'Casts the Colours', i.e. lowers his flag to the ground before him. The Standard Bearers of the old craft guilds do likewise, and there is then a minute's silence in memory of the fallen. The ceremony ends with the playing of 'the Flowers of the Forest', sometimes entitled 'A Lament for Flodden'. The last verse is as follows:

We'll hear nae mair lilting at our ewe-milking;
Women and bairns are heartless and wae;

From Selkirk to Hawick to Jedburgh

Sighing and moaning on ilka green loaning –
The Flowers of the Forest are a' wede away.

This fine poem was written by a woman, Jane Elliot (1727–1805), and gives, it has been said, 'perfect utterance to the unforgotten pain which even in Scott's day made old men in Ettrick Forest burst into tears at the mention of Flodden'. Such involvement in the past has no doubt something to do with Selkirk's relative remoteness in the Border hills.

It is the Market Place that gives Selkirk its visual character. Many of the old houses and shops are painted or whitewashed, and have a sturdy air. But it is the Town Hall, which was Scott's courtroom during the thirty three years when he was Sheriff of Selkirk, that attracts attention; a statue of 'the shirra' stands in front of the old courtroom. It is not a grand building – a corner of it has become a coffee shop – but the bench and chair used by Scott are still on view and there are other items of interest. Some of these relate to Mungo Park, the explorer of Africa who first earned his living as a surgeon's apprentice in Selkirk, and who was often a visitor at Ashiestiel. In Halliwell's Close there is a local museum, occupying premises which were once the home and workshop of, surprisingly enough, a maker of periwigs.

From Selkirk the A7 winds over the hills to Hawick. To the north-east there are good views of the fertile Teviot basin, fields and mansions and stretches of woodland; while to the south-west the land forms one great rolling sea of grassy sheep pastures, leading up to the high ground of Craik Forest and Eskdalemuir Forest.

Hawick, like Galashiels, is a nineteenth century mill town. Frame knitting has been its business for two hundred years, and it is the home of famous companies such as Pringle and Lyle and Scott. Most of its production is for the top end of the export market.

As regards architectural interest, Hawick has little to show apart from St Mary's Church, on a grassy knoll overlooking the town. Built in 1763, the present structure replaced a much older building. It is whitewashed, curiously Scots and informal in appearance, perhaps because of its unusual fenestration – it has windows which are round, rectangular or dormer, but not a single one pointed or round-arched, and the tower has no window at all. Surrounded by a grassy grave-yard, its air is unpretentious, a sort of domestic/ecclesiastical. The Tower Hotel in the High Street is the oldest building in town. It incor-porates the 'Black Tower of Drumlanrig' which is of great but uncertain antiquity. The house was once the home of the Duke of Monmouth, illegitimate son of Charles II, who was 'provided for' by marriage to the Duchess of Buccleuch. The name is due to the fact that the seat of the Buccleuch's is Drumlanrig Castle, not far north of Dumfries.

Hawick can boast, however, of having one item of unquestionable antiquity. This is the motte, on high ground above the older part of the town. Mottes were an early form of castle, introduced by the kings and the Anglo-Norman aristocracy in the twelfth century. There are about two hundred known sites, most of them in the south-west. A motte consisted of a small circular earthen mound, defended by a ditch, and surmounted by a palisade and a wooden tower. Because of their construction they did not last, and they are seldom easy to see or identify. In the Hawick example the ditch has almost disappeared, but the mound is still a prominent, flattened cone, about thirty feet high. It was excavated in 1912, and the search produced *inter alia* a bone needle, numerous pieces of pottery, and a coin belonging to the reign of Henry II (d. 1189). Construction was almost certainly some time in the twelfth century. The items discovered are in the museum in Wilton Park, where there are picnic areas among the trees, along the banks of the Teviot.

Hawick's Common Riding ceremony takes place in the early part of June. It too is connected with Border fighting, and indirectly with Flodden. The Hawick story is that in 1514, the year after the fateful battle, a party of youths, or 'callants', surprised and routed a band of English marauders who had entered the district ('slew them almost to a man' is one version). They then returned to town with a captured flag. This story and the Galashiels story are clearly similar. The skirmish near Hawick is commemorated by rides and ceremonies involving the Burgh flag, which is finally attached by the Cornet (no longer on horseback but on an extendable ladder) to the Horse Monument in the High Street, which is itself a memorial to the post-Flodden affray. Such ceremonies grow more and more contrived and commercial. But at Hawick there is a battle-cry of which the first line may well be, in some mysterious way, genuine enough, derived from some pagan invocation to Thor and Odin:

> *Teribus, ye Teri Odin,*
> *Sons of Heroes slain at Flodden,*
> *Imitating Border Bowmen,*
> *Aye defend your rights and common.*

It is good fighting stuff. And the distribution of oak leaves may have some shadowy druidical origin.

From Hawick the A7 goes south-west to Branxholme, Teviothead, and then the watershed at the Mosspaul Hotel.

Branxholme Castle is a private residence. There was a castle here in the fifteenth century, and at that time it was the chief seat of the Buccleuch family. It guarded the pass from Carlisle to the Tweed Valley, was repeatedly sacked, and in 1570 was wrecked first by the Scots, to prevent it from falling into the hands of the English, and then by the English, to complete the job; they 'cawysed powder to be sett, and so blew up the ane halfe from the uther'. It was rebuilt in 1576, a rectangular building on a salient overlooking the River Teviot, with projecting towers at opposite corners, i.e. on the familiar Z plan. It was subsequently greatly altered and extended, but the south-west tower has the original parapet mouldings, and a narrow newel staircase gives access to rooms on each floor and to the parapet, which was at first open for purposes of defence. Scott converted Branxholme Castle into Branksome Hall, and put it into *The Lay of the Last Minstrel*, his first enormously successful work (1805). It has been described as 'a metrical romance, in the mouth of an ancient minstrel, the last of his race', and it involves the lady of Branksome Hall, a visit to the tomb of Michael Scott, the wizard, in Melrose Abbey, an elfin page, magical impersonation, single combat (fatal), and the reuniting of star-crossed lovers. Its sales before 1815 broke all literary records; but who reads it now?

From Mosspaul return to Hawick and take the A698 for Jedburgh. (Alternatively, go two miles further south and take the road over Geordie's Hill to Hermitage Castle. See p. 378).

The village of **Denholm** is only five or six miles from Hawick. There is nothing sensational in Denholm, which is part of its attraction. But it is unusual in being an eighteenth century planned village, like Athelstaneford (*see* p. 276), or Gifford (*see* p. 298), and it is further unusual in being built round an exceptionally large village green, after the manner of an English village. The houses, however, are in the usual severe Scots style. In one of these – the only house still thatched – Dr John Leyden was born; an obelisk on the green is to his memory. Few now could say why he should be remembered, but he was one of those many Scots who, born in humble circumstances, rose to fame. Who would suppose that the son of a Border shepherd, born in Denholm, would become a doctor, a translator of Persian and Arabic poetry, a professor of Hindustani at Calcutta – and die in Java at the age of 36? Denholm began as a village of stocking-weavers, but it has some older buildings, notably Westgate Hall, a house at the SW end of the village, built in the seventeenth century; the lintel above the door is dated 1663.

The easy road forward from Denholm is straight on to Bonjed-ward, and then right to **Jedburgh**. The final approach is past the famous rugby ground, and also past the wool-outlet shops which are a feature of the Borders towns. But if you can leave these till later, go by Dunion Hill. You climb to 800 feet (but remember that Denholm is not exactly at sea level), begin the descent, pass the inevitable golf course – and suddenly the houses of Jedburgh are below you. Most of them are at the foot of the hill; but the steep slope of the Castlegate, where you have arrived, is lined continuously with buildings.

There was once a castle here, guarding the town – Jedburgh is only ten miles from the Border, on the preferred invasion route. But the castle was as often held by the English as the Scots, and in 1406 it was demolished by the men of Teviotdale in order to keep it out of enemy hands. This did not, alas! make Jedburgh a safer place. It had always been a regular target for English armies – 'often their first destination on crossing the border and their last visit before leaving' – and it remained so; it was sacked in 1305 (when a good deal of the lead roofing of the Abbey disappeared), 1410, 1416, 1464, 1523, 1544, and 1545. Throughout the Borders it is the same story; always the spectre of warfare, the destruction of whatever was beautiful and precious.

The town-plan of Jedburgh follows, or followed, a pattern common all over western Europe in the Middle Ages; the castle at the top of the hill, the great church down below, and the houses in between. Edinburgh is on the same plan, and Jedburgh's Castlegate is strongly reminiscent of the Royal Mile. What is different is that in this case the Abbey is near the centre of the town, and the principal car parks are conveniently close to it.

Like Holyrood, the church at Jedburgh was founded by David I. It began as a priory in the early years of the twelfth century, and building was started soon after 1138. Some ten or twenty years later it was raised to the dignity of an abbey, and by the middle of the next century the fabric of the church was complete. It is in some ways the best preserved of all the Border abbeys, and is the only one to retain its tower; 'fine old ruins', wrote Burns, who visited Jedburgh in 1787, 'a once magnificent Cathedral'.

The visitor enters the Abbey grounds near to where the cellars and the Abbot's house used to be, and approaches the church itself from the south, with the cloister on the left and the chapter-house on the right. The cloister is now laid out as a late medieval garden, and the plants include some grown for their medicinal or culinary properties – such plants were probably growing here in the Middle Ages. The chapter-house is a poor affair, and probably dates from the later fifteenth century; excavations have shown that there were previously larger chapter-houses on the same site, and this probably reflects some decline in the Abbey's size and fortunes.

The steps bring you to where the south transept once was, and you enter the nave close to the tower. It is the nave, a powerful design and remarkably well preserved, although roofless, that gives the feeling of a great abbey interior more completely than any of the other Border abbeys. It belongs to the second phase of building at Jedburgh, which seems to have begun about 1180 and to have been pressed on to completion with remarkable speed. The nave is on a grander scale than the choir to the east. It is flanked by aisles north and south, is nine bays long and three storeys high, and has richly moulded arches opening into the aisles. The galleries above the arches have themselves round-arched openings, each containing two pointed arches, and the clerestory is a continuous arcade of four pointed arches to each bay. Great masses of stone seem to be lightly and effortlessly raised up. It is a most harmonious and flowing composition, full of variety in uniformity, as like music as architecture can be.

Move into the choir and you go back half a century, from early Gothic to late Romanesque. Whereas the nave is unusually long, the choir is unusually short. The peculiarity of its design is that the pillars are carried right up to the middle of the second storey; the decorated arches then enclose the double openings, which themselves have double columns, at that level. This very unusual arrangement makes the choir seem loftier, and gives to the triforium almost the appearance of a balcony. No other Scottish church has this design, but it is found occasionally in the south and west of England. Romsey Abbey, built early in the twelfth century, is an example. And it is tempting to connect Romsey to Jedburgh, for David I, who passed his youth in England, knew Romsey. His aunt, Christina, was a nun there, and his sister Matilda had stayed there before her marriage to Henry I. This was in the peaceful days, before the wars began.

The other great feature of Jedburgh Abbey is the splendid west façade, in three stages. At ground level is the processional entrance, deeply recessed. The shafts flanking the door are much damaged, but the rich variety of carving on the capitals and above the door, including numerous bird-like creatures, is very fine. The door is surmounted by three gablets, with empty niches. The second stage has a single tall window, once flanked by arcading. And in the gable, above it all, is a perfectly intact rose window, inserted some time in the fifteenth century.

Reconstruction work went on through much of the fifteenth century, and in the early sixteenth lower roofs were built over the nave and aisles; signs of this are to be seen on the tower, which has itself had to be a good deal repaired throughout the centuries. The lower roofs were doubtless built to make good damage done by English armies. After the Reformation, part of the Abbey – or to be more accurate, different parts at different times – became a new parish church. The crown arch and vault of the crossing collapsed in 1743, but in spite of this the parishioners persisted in keeping a roof over their heads and did not leave the crumbling ruin until 1875. To their persistence, without doubt, we owe the fact that Jedburgh is the best preserved of the four Border Abbeys.

To reach the Castle Gaol from the Abbey, you have to walk along Abbey Place, past the eighteenth century steeple of Newgate, which once served as a prison, and turn up Castlegate. This street was here in the Middle Ages, and markets were held in it and in Market Place, where the Mercat Cross used to stand. Castlegate is lined with houses, some of them dating back to the eighteenth century (when most of them were thatched), and there are narrow pends and closes, just as in Edinburgh. It has many historic associations. Prince Charles came to Jedburgh on his march into England in 1745, and stayed a night in a house at the corner of Blackhills Close. Scott made his first appearance as a defence counsel in Jedburgh in 1793 and secured the acquittal of a local poacher. (According to the story, Scott whispered to the accused when the verdict was announced, 'You're a lucky scoundrel', and received the reply 'I'm just o' your mind, and I'll send ye a maukin (hare) the morn, man'). William and Dorothy Wordsworth came in 1803, and stayed in Abbey Close, just off the Castlegate. Scott visited them, and read part of his as yet unpublished *'Lay of the Last Minstrel'*. Dorothy's entry in her journal says, 'We had our dinner sent from the inn, and a bottle of wine. ... The Sheriff stayed late, and repeated some of his poem'. Do we detect a hint of *ennui*? Girtin painted the view from the top of the Castlegate in the 1820s. Burns was also a visitor, although he 'put up' in the Canongate. He seems to have been better pleased than Dorothy, for he blessed the place: 'Jed, pure be thy crystal streams, and hallowed thy sylvan banks!' But then, he had met 'sweet Isabella Lindsay, a good humour'd amiable girl, beautiful hazel eyes full of spirit and sparkling'. About her we know very little; but Burns, perhaps, knew much. (He also met an older spinster whom he was ungentlemanly enough to wish 'curst with eternal desire and damn'd with endless disappointment').

About the gaol, when you reach it, there is nothing very exciting. It was built in 1823, when there was much interest in new-style prisons which would be hygienic, cheap to operate, and productive of moral reform. It looks like a fortress, and has a complicated radial lay-out. Whether it produced moral reform or not we do not know, but it ceased to be a gaol in 1886 and is now a museum of local history, well worth a visit. Devotees of penal institutions are sure to like it.

Return down the Castlegate, and, if you wish to see the shops and the life of the town, continue into the High Street, where almost everything is new except the rather dismal-looking Spread-Eagle Hotel, which is claimed to be the oldest continually occupied inn in Scotland. But if you turn into the Canongate you can reach Canongate Bridge, on the other side of the main road. Now used only as a footbridge, it is an attractive design, narrow, with ribbed arches and massive piers. Only about a score of these fifteenth and early sixteenth century bridges survive in Scotland.

The Canongate will also take you to **Queen Mary's House**. (If you prefer, you can reach it from the High Street). This is Jedburgh's second most notable building, notable because it is old, and notable because of the Queen. She was certainly in Jedburgh in 1566, and the house is big enough and looks old enough – but, nagging thought, is it *quite* old enough? – to have been the house in which she stayed. The story itself is well authenticated. Queen Mary came here in 1566 in order to preside at the Justice Aire, or Circuit Court, and to see that some authority was put into the treatment of 'thieves and malefactouris'. While in Jedburgh, she learned that Bothwell, who was Warden of Hermitage Castle and Lieutenant Warden of the Marches, had been wounded in an affray, and was lying at Hermitage. She therefore set out with a few companions to ride over the hills to Hermitage, almost twenty five miles away. It was a bright October morning. She remained only two hours at the castle, and when she returned it was through heavy rain and across a sodden, wind-swept and rough countryside. She must have been in the saddle for at least seven hours, possibly ten or eleven; her ride was an outstanding feat of horsemanship and endurance. But on her return she fell ill, developed a fever, and fears were even entertained for her life. She recovered. But not many months afterwards, when affairs were slipping hopelessly out of her control, she was wont to say – or so it is reported – 'Would that I had died at Jedburgh'.

Queen Mary's House is a fortified town-house rather than a tower-house proper. It is a tall rectangular structure, with a tower projecting from the centre of the south side, and prominent crow-stepped gables. The ground floor is vaulted, and the main staircase leads, as was usual, only to the first floor, where the wheel-stair in the corbelled angle-turret commences. Until modern times the house was thatched. What is now the garden – and an excellently kept garden – was probably once a courtyard with enclosing walls. The house now serves as a museum, and contains items which relate to numerous aspects of the Queen's life.

Like other Border burghs, Jedburgh has its annual festival (in July), but with a difference. It dates from 1947, and instead of riding the marches as the other Burghs do, there are rides to places of historic interest; the principal ride follows the roads and tracks taken by the Queen to Hermitage Castle. Another is to Redeswire, near Carter Bar, where in 1575 one of the last of the Border affrays was turned into a Scots victory, so the story goes, by the timely arrival of a contingent from Jedburgh. Of vastly older origins is the Ba' Game, played around mid-February between the 'Uppies' and the 'Doonies'. The object of the game is to get the ball, by fair means or foul, to the Castle Gaol (if you are a Doonie, born below the Market Cross) or to Townfoot Bridge (if you are an Uppie, born above the Cross). It sounds very medieval and looks, as the Middle Ages were, pretty rough.

Close to Jedburgh are two other attractions, one just south and one just north of the town.

The first of these is **Ferniehirst Castle**, only a few miles south along what Burns called the 'Eden scenes on crystal Jed'. Ferniehirst Castle is the ancestral seat of the Kerr family. There was a castle here in the fifteenth century and probably earlier, but it was destroyed by English forces in the 1570s. The present building dates from 1598.

As you approach it, the Castle is very picturesque; it contrives, somehow, to have the general air of a house with a history. A long wing with a massive projecting chimneystack faces the drive; a tower, probably the oldest part of the castle, projects to the right, having a circular stair-turret in the angle, a handsome doorway, and smaller turrets and crow-stepped gables above; and a fine arched gateway adjoins the tower. Facing the castle is a long narrow building two storeys high, thought once to have been a chapel. It now serves as an information centre.

One hundred years ago this rather elegant sixteenth century house, with some quite fanciful stonework around its doors and windows, was 'in a state bordering on ruin ... the ivy has it in its deadly embrace". It was rescued just in time, and was turned into a youth hostel. Fifty years later it had to be rescued again, and the Marquis of Lothian and his family came to live in it. Internally, extensive alterations have been necessary. The old kitchen wing, now thatched, has been turned into living quarters. The entrance stairway is new, and most of the first floor is now a fine hall, lit from both sides, with two large fireplaces. The gem of the building is the library, a very small (seven foot six inches in diameter) twelve-sided apartment, panelled, with a wooden ceiling divided into thirty six compartments and having a central pendant boss. There are three levels of shelves going most of the way round the room. When the castle was crumbling, this unique little library was 'in a most deplorable state of ruin ... the ceiling in such a threatening condition that it may fall any day'. It has been completely restored. Once again it is 'fitted up with the most fastidious taste and care', and contains numerous ancient volumes. Purists may say that it is not quite as it was. But it is very near. And how many libraries can demonstrate their antiquity by having genuine gun-loops? This one has two.

Ferniehirst Castle cannot, as a rule, be entered by the public, but the exterior of the castle can be seen, there is access to the vaulted cellars (one now a simple chapel), and there are extensive wooded walks in the grounds.

Finally, **Peniel Heugh**, reached off the B6400 on the other side of the Teviot. This 800 foot high hill carries the 156 foot high Waterloo Monument erected by the Marquis of Lothian in 1820. It took five years to build. The path or track which leads up to it is a very pleasant walk or scramble through the trees, and there are several hillforts nearby which date from the early-iron age to Roman times. Needless to add, from the monument itself there is a fine sweep of view over the surrounding country. And if you should afterwards want a cup of tea or coffee, the Lothian Estates Woodland Centre is on the road back to the B6400.

30

The deep south: Carter Bar, west and east

CARTER BAR IS one of the major Border crossings, and certainly the most spectacular. Coming to it from the south, the A68 climbs gradually up the Rede Valley from near Otterburn, passes numerous Roman roads and camps to the east, skirts the Catcleugh Reservoir, attains and crosses the 1,300 foot contour – and suddenly the whole landscape ahead of you falls away. Here, from the ridge of the Cheviots, is one of the most extensive views in Scotland: abrupt detached hills nearby, moorland, woods, undulating farm land, the triple peaks of the Eildons a mere twenty miles to the north, forty miles to the north-west the high hills beyond St Mary's Loch, and far ahead the shadowy and ill-defined outline of the Moorfoots and the Lammermuirs. A car park and an indicator of the hills are by the roadside.

Carter Bar is an ancient crossing, six miles west of the point where Roman Dere Street enters Scotland. There are many of these old Border 'gates', usually at the head of little burns flowing down the hillsides, places once well-known to moss-troopers and cattle-thieves, and where the Wardens of the Marches might meet to sort out their problems. They have curious names – Butt Roads, Black Brae, Windy Gyle, Gamel's Path (the Dere Street crossing), the Wheel Causey and others. Close to Carter Bar is the site of the Redeswire Fray, which was fought in 1575, when a meeting between the English Warden of the Middle Marches and the Deputy Keeper of Liddlesdale turned sour, and many men suddenly died. This is sometimes described as the last Border battle, the end of a three hundred years war.

No tour of the Borders is complete without a visit to Hermitage Castle, so take the A6088 to Chesters and Bonchester Bridge. They are both very small places. In the church at **Chesters**, however, there is a stained-glass window dedicated to James Thomson (1700–1748), author of '*the Seasons*'. Thomson was born at Ednam, near Kelso, but he was only two months old when the family moved to Chesters. He was educated at Jedburgh (the school was conducted within the ruins of the Abbey) and he subsequently attended Edinburgh University. It was Thomson who wrote the words for '*Rule, Britannia*'.

The approach to Bonchester Bridge from Chesters is dominated by the prominent pointed summit of **Ruberslaw** (1391 feet). A fortified pre-Roman settlement crowns the hill. Within the pre-historic rampart a circling stone wall has been built, probably by some community re-occupying the site in the fourth or fifth century AD. South of Ruber-slaw and west of Bonchester Bridge old cultivation strips can easily be seen on the hill slopes; they look medieval, but they are thought to be no earlier than the eighteenth century.

From Bonchester Bridge cut across to the B6399, and turn south. You are now on the edge of **Liddesdale**, only twelve miles north of Hermitage, the greatest fortress in the Borders. As soon as you are over the watershed, it is apparent why this region was so hard to control. It is even now very thinly inhabited, extensive rolling moor-land country, over which horsemen could travel at great speed, and where concealment would be easy; it is the Forestry Commission which has planted thousands of trees, but there were always forests, and these were a further help to outlaws and raiding parties. It was for long dominated by the Elliots and the Armstrongs, and it was one of the latter, Johnnie Armstrong, 'feared as far off as Newcastle', whom James V sought out and summarily hanged from a tree, along with his followers, in 1530. The resultant ballad is not without merit:

> *To seik heit water beneath cauld ice*
> *Surely it is a great folie –*
> *I have asked grace at a graceless face,*
> *But there's nane for my men and me!*

No doubt the outlaws were the curse of the country; on the other hand, James V was never a merciful king.

From the viewpoint of peace-loving people, Liddesdale had an evil reputation for several centuries, and the burnings, plunderings and killings were not brought to an end until the days of James VI.

Today, the traveller may be startled to see, not a band of cut-throats (although it is easy to imagine them), but a remarkable relic of a later age, a tolerably well-preserved fifteen-arch railway viaduct in the middle of nowhere. This is the *Shankend Viaduct*, complete with a group of uncosy-looking cottages and a two-storey timber-built signal box. What is a railway doing in these desolate moors – or rather, what was it doing? This was the Carlisle-Hawick-Edinburgh line, long known as 'the Waverley route' (more a reference to Sir Walter Scott than to the station in Princes Street), and it was opened in 1862, closed in 1963. It was a scenic route, but never important; and according to one passenger it was 'singularly notable for the unpunctuality of its trains'.

As the road descends from Sandy Edge it becomes very winding, hemmed in by the rocky declivities of the Liddel Water. A side-road leads off to the Castle, which, however, is nowhere to be seen. Then over a rise it suddenly appears, only a few hundred yards away. The approach is along the Hermitage Water, running shallow over a remarkably stoney bed, overhung by alders. In springtime there are primroses (south of Hawick is first-class primrose country), and you may be lucky enough to see a heron at his patient watch beneath the trees.

Unlike so many old castles today, **Hermitage** does not have comfortable little houses, busy roads, and all the paraphernalia of the twentieth century lapping round its walls. It stands alone, bare and perpendicular, among the high hills and in tracts of moorland that have hardly changed since the times when it was built. Hermitage Castle is one of the greatest, grimmest, and most isolated of all the medieval fortresses in Scotland.

It is situated almost at the head of Liddesdale, a short valley which goes south to the Solway, and it is only sixteen miles from Hawick and less than five miles from the Border – a fact which caused much concern to several Scottish as well as English kings. The site is on the north bank of the Hermitage Water, within earthworks which are probably older than the castle itself, but which were subsequently altered and enlarged so as to serve as gun emplacements. Further protection is provided by two small streams and the generally boggy nature of the surrounding terrain. Hermitage was described in the middle of the sixteenth century as 'an oulde house not strong, but evill to be wyn by reasone of the strate [difficult] grounde aboute the same'. During much of the fourteenth century possession of Liddesdale alternated between England and Scotland, and until 1594, when Hermitage reverted to the Scottish crown, it was held successively by the great families of de Soulis, Dacre (subjects of Edward III), Douglas and Bothwell.

Hermitage is really two buildings, one inside the other. The internal one, constructed in the fourteenth century, is a small rectangular building which encloses a very small courtyard. Its entrance is the present entrance to the castle, and a turnpike stair in the wall facing the entrance gave access to the upper floors on the east and west sides of the courtyard. This design is characteristic of English fortified manor houses of the period, so one concludes that the house within the castle was built by the Dacre family, which dates it to about 1360. It undoubtedly replaced an earlier building which has almost completely disappeared.

Late in the fourteenth century the Douglases built the extended castle which has dominated the countryside for six hundred years. First a rectangular keep was built, four storeys high, incorporating the old manor house, and forming two new courts east and west of the small central court; then square projecting towers were added to three corners of the rectangle and, early in the fifteenth century, a much larger fourth tower was added to the remaining corner, and carried a good way south of the castle entrance. Hermitage thus has an irregular ground plan, but its roofline is perfectly flat, except for three small and rather incongruous gable ends perched on top, which belong to restoration work of the nineteenth century. There are no windows in the external walls at ground floor level.

This description, however, omits the castle's most striking feature, two great pointed flying arches, one on the east and one on the west side. They look like entrances but are not; they relieve the monotony of the sheer forbidding walls, but only to make the whole place look more forbidding than ever. They are there for good defensive reasons. High up on the walls there are large rectangular openings, above a long series of stone corbels. The corbels were to support a wooden gallery, to which the openings gave access. Because it would have been awkward to build this gallery in the deep and narrow recesses formed by the corner towers on the east and west fronts, these faces were made continuous by building what is in effect a bridge between each pair of towers. The gallery was then built straight across. The purpose of the gallery was to facilitate various defensive operations, from shooting arrows to pouring unpleasant boiling liquids on the heads of attackers. It was quite an elaborate arrangement. But firearms made it antiquated, and during the sixteenth century gunloops were inserted in the walls.

The south face is the nearest that Hermitage comes to looking domestic; there is actually a two-light window beneath a pointed arch, with a circular opening above it; but this is a nineteenth century reconstruction, more or less. The low pointed arch to the left of the ancient doorway is genuine enough, however; it was built to allow the latrines to empty into an external vaulted cesspool, from which the effluent was led by a culvert into the Hermitage Water.

Within the great walls not much remains, except for the little central courtyard of the mid-fourteenth century manor house. Its enclosing walls are beautifully built of squared red sandstone, and three round-arched doorways open off it; there are well-cut masons' marks, Gothic style, of the fourteenth century. Beyond the central courtyard all is ruin and speculation. In the court to the left a carefully constructed well survives, still with water, and the bakehouse was clearly in the basement of the large south-west projection. The hall is thought to have occupied most of the western part of the building, at first floor level, and the lord's apartment may have been above the right-hand court. But the all-destructive hand of time and ill-advised restoration have left little more than a few fireplaces and windows, and vast amounts of undecipherable masonry.

A couple of hundred yards to the west lie the ruins of an ancient chapel. It was a single-cell building, buttressed and vaulted, and probably built, or re-built, in the fourteenth century. Some of its windows have been re-erected nearby. Fields and a sunken track extend a little way up the hillside. The chapel is sited within a graveyard, which is itself within a defensive bank and ditch. Could these earthworks once have surrounded a still older castle, known to have existed hereabouts before 1250? Or was the first castle where Hermitage is now, and the slight embankments are all that is left of a moated homestead on these lonely, desperate moors?

From Hermitage cross to the B6357 and make towards Jedburgh. This is a pleasant road, through some cultivation and much forest. At Saughtree (a saugh is a willow in Scots) you are only two miles from the Border, which is presumably why Queen Mary chose the safer route *via* Sandy Edge when she rode between Jedburgh and Hermitage in 1566. Beyond Saughtree you are in Wauchope Forest which, over the Border, becomes Kielder Forest. These two forests form a large part of the great **Border Forest Park**, an expanse of almost 200 square miles. Wauchope Forest is planted almost exclusively with Norway and sitka spruce and a little lodgepole pine – no other trees care for the combination of peaty soil, exposure, and high rainfall. Some people feel hemmed in by trees. But a great range of hills borders the forest to the south, their summits above the level of timber-growing – good walking country; and the entire Park is home to a great variety of wild life. There are roe deer, red squirrels and mountain hare as well as short-eared and long-eared owls, buzzards, sparrow-hawks and kestrels.

Join the A6088 and turn right for Chesters. From Chesters there are two side roads which lead across to the A68. Take either, for the object is to leave the A68 on the first side road going east on the descent from Carter Bar, the road which leads to Hownam, More-battle and Kirk Yetholm.

This narrow road starts by winding up and down through surprisingly wooded country, and past hidden farms, but after a short time it emerges into the open moorland and the hills. Farms and fences disappear, and instead there are cattle grids and passing places. For several miles the Cheviots rise like a wall to the south. Beyond the first cross-roads, where a road leads off to Oxnam, the road you are on crosses **Dere Street**. This pre-historic route, of the dimmest antiquity, was the main Roman road to the north, still used in medieval times and by drovers in the eighteenth century; on your left it is an obvious track, leading up between drovers' dykes and past prehistoric cairns and a stone circle to Whitton Edge, and on to Newstead (*see* p 355). Turn right, between the scarcely discernible remains of Pennymuir Roman camps – vague outlines and inconsequent mounds – and go down over the ford to **Woden Law**. Here you have the rare privilege of parking, literally, on Dere Street unimproved – not on a metalled road built on top of Dere Street, but on Dere Street itself, stones and grass and heather. You are less than two miles from the Border.

Dere Street comes off the Cheviots in a long curve round the east side of Woden Law, which was a British fort before it was occupied and developed by the invaders. The climb to the ramparts and ditches on top is not difficult, and the view is superb; Woden Law commands a great stretch of Border country, and for this reason, its possession was for centuries essential to the safe use of Dere Street. Now, all hereabouts is the most deserted country imaginable, a world apart from ancient war as well as from modern life. The Kale Water flows quietly by, and curlews call across the moors. There are many larks in summer time, and wildflowers, and unusual grasses. Sheep are on the great green hillsides. In this solitude it is remarkably easy to feel that the centuries have slipped away, and to visualise the passage of Roman soldiers, and the coming and going of those whom they called barbarians.

The road now turns north, going up the narrow valley of the Kale Water. At **Hownam** you may branch left over an old, narrow, one-arched bridge and rejoin Dere Street; at this point it is easy to walk along the ancient track, and there are extensive views towards Jedburgh and the Eildon Hills. North of Hownam the little valley gradually begins to be cultivated; trees appear, and clumps of mimulus are to be seen at the water's edge. Near Hownam Law there are extensive cultivation terraces. And Hownam Law itself is noteworthy, both for the number of huts and enclosures which have been traced on its summit as well as for the long period of its occupation – the evidence suggests that a simple palisaded enclosure was built here in the 6th or 7th century BC, and that stone-built houses were erected on the same spot late in the 3rd century AD.

After many twists and turns, still with the Kale Water for company, you reach more level ground, and Morebattle. What a suitable name, one thinks, in this part of the world! But no. Morebattle is a corruption of Merebotle, the village by the mere. The mere has disappeared, and Morebattle has not much of interest to offer. But only three miles to the west **Cessford Castle** stands on high ground overlooking the Kale Water, with an extensive view of the Cheviots to the south.

Built of red sandstone, Cessford Castle is a most massive construction, It was originally surrounded by an earth and stone rampart and a moat or ditch; marshy ground nearby, drained in later times, gave additional protection.

Now dangerously ruinous, Cessford was a place of extraordinary strength. It appears to have been built about 1400, the wing of the L-plan raised from four to six storeys some time in the sixteenth century. The walls vary in thickness from 12 feet to 13 feet 6 inches, and in the castle's heyday they contained much of the accommodation. There were two entrance doorways, the principal one fifteen feet above the ground, reached by a moveable ladder, and the other at ground level. The arrangements for the latter entrance give a good idea of the life of the place. There were two outer doors, one opening outwards and one (probably an iron yett) opening inwards; these gave access to a passage 13 feet 6 inches long through the wall which was secured at the inner end by another pair of doors. It would clearly not have been easy to get in, unless you were welcome.

The ground and first floors were vaulted. The hall and kitchen were on the first floor, the former having four windows, three of them with stone seats. The kitchen was provided with only one window, which cannot have helped the cooking.

Cessford was attacked by the Earl of Surrey in 1523. He had 'a numerous army, well provided with powerful ordnance', but could not make much impression; unluckily, the castle was surrendered on a misunderstanding. In 1544 it was taken and 'thrown down' (i.e. made indefensible) by the Earl of Hertford. Nevertheless, it remains a most impressive, lonely ruin. There are fissures in the walls, and doubtless the whole place is crumbling inch by inch; but inches of decay will take a long time to make an impression on so many tons of masonry.

Cessford was the seat of the Kers – not the Ferniehirst Kerrs but the Cessford Kers, whose chief representative is now the Duke of Roxburghe at palatial Floors Castle. The family appears to have left their old home some time after 1650.

From Cessford Castle through Morebattle to Town Yetholm is less than ten miles – ten miles of green, undulating, easy country. A mile or so before Yetholm the **Bowmont Water** comes down from the hills. This is a most pleasant little valley; a side road goes up it for seven or eight miles and then stops at Cock Law, two miles from the Border. To begin with there are flat haughs, with some cultivation, but soon the valley narrows, and is entirely the domain of shepherds, sheep dogs and sheep. The water runs clear and shallow over a stoney bed; dippers are often to be seen on the stones, or darting through willows that hang over the stream. Except for parked cars at week-ends, it is all totally unspoiled. History has passed the Bowmont Water by (mercifully), but not pre-history. As is usual in the Southern Uplands, Iron Age forts are common on the hilltops round about, and in the valley itself there are some evidences that cultivation seems to have taken place, perhaps intermittently, from Roman times until the coming of the Anglo-Saxon invaders.

Town Yetholm is a pleasant village, with a green at the east end and tidy houses around it in the usual front-gardenless Scottish small town manner. Its chief claim to notice nowadays is as a walking centre. Along with Kirk Yetholm it was once the capital of the Scottish gypsies, home of the once famous Romany family of Faa. That has all gone now, but Kirk Yetholm has renewed its youth as the terminus of the **Pennine Way**. At the end of 270 miles from Edale in the Peak District National Park the resolute walker reaches Kirk Yetholm and probably proceeds immediately to the Border Hotel, on the edge of the admirably unlandscaped village green, to celebrate his achievement. Less resolute walkers (having perhaps arrived by car) may decide that if they walk a few hundred yards out of Kirk Yetholm, going south, they can justly claim that they have walked on the Pennine Way.

From Town Yetholm it is only a short distance back to Kelso and thence to Edinburgh. Or for those returning to England it is but a mile to the Border, and then round the shoulder of the Cheviots, past Yeavering Bell, and on to Wooler.

Appendices

Brief Lives

The House of Stewart

James I [b.1390 – ruled 1424–1437]. Captured by the English in 1406 on his way to France, James spent eighteen years in captivity. He was treated as an English gentleman, living at court, and Henry IV saw to it that he received an excellent education. [He may have been the first Scots King who could write]. In his absence, Scotland was governed – if that is the word – by regents whose policy was to keep things ticking over, even if that meant steady erosion of the powers and wealth of the Crown. As soon as James was released in 1424 he took control: 'If God give me life, tho' it be but the life of a dog, then throughout all Scotland, with His help, I will make the key keep the castle and the bracken bush the cow'. Within a few years several leading noblemen had been arrested and some were executed, and machinery was put in place to revive the royal authority and to enforce law and order. High rank ceased to mean that great families were above the law. As a ruler he was, if anything, too firm; but he had to make up for the laxity of preceding years, and he was not unin-terested in the lives and the fate of ordinary people. But there were nobles who looked back to the 'good old days' before 1424, and James was assassinated in the Dominican friary at Perth in 1437. The conspirators were savagely put to death.

James II [b.1430 – ruled 1449–1460]. Son of James I. Scotland was governed by regents until the young King suddenly took matters into his own hands in 1449. His reign was almost fully occupied with fending off the powerful Douglas family, who were strongly placed in the line of succession. In 1440 two Douglas children were treacher-ously seized in Edinburgh Castle and executed. In 1452 the Earl of Douglas was in Stirling Castle, where he was murdered by the King himself. In 1455 the Douglas's rebelled, but civil war lasted for only a few months. The King's military successes were partly or largely because of his fondness for 'gret bombards' [the most up-to-date military technology] which his opponents did not have and which readily made large holes in their medieval castles. He was also successful in playing off 'old lords' against newcomers, while acquiring valuable estates in the process; and land meant power. But in the end, it was modern technology that was his undoing: at the seige of Roxburgh Castle [held by the English] in 1460, one of his 'gret bombards' blew up and killed him. The Queen then brought the siege to a successful conclusion.

James III [b.1452 – ruled 1469–1488]. Eldest surviving son of James II. Scotland had yet again to endure a period of rule by untrustworthy nobles who all wanted the throne for themselves, and when James's minority ended in 1469 rivalry and violence intensified. Two of the King's brothers were imprisoned. One died in prison, possibly murdered, and the other escaped, fled to England, and persuaded Edward IV to invade Scotland on his behalf in 1482. Resistance was weak, and the English seized Berwick-on-Tweed, which they have held ever since. In 1484 Scotland was again invaded, this time by Scots nobles based in England. The insurrection failed, but four years later a home-based revolt ended with the death of the King, murdered as he left the scene of battle. In spite of all these misfortunes, the country made some progress, for James III seems to have been an enlightened ruler, more attracted to the arts than to bloodshed. The economy expanded, and several ambitious building schemes were begun – Seton Collegiate Church, for example, Rosslyn Chapel, and Trinity College, Edinburgh, for which the extremely costly alterpiece by Hugo van der Goes was commissioned in the 1470s; some Scotsmen, clearly, were in touch with the cultural life of the Continent. James III was the first Scottish king who appears as a patron of learning and the arts.

James IV [b.1488–1513]. Often called 'Scotland's Renaissance King', James had the great advantage of ascending the throne [aged seventeen] almost immediately after his father died; there was no regency, and very little strife. Reconciliation was the heart of his policies, and he was widely popular, even approachable; we read of 'a wife that brocht strawberries to the king … a wife that brocht cherries to the king and criit on him for silver'. He was strongly in favour of the 'new learning' and was a patron of the arts. The Royal College of

Surgeons of Edinburgh received its charter in 1506; the Universities of Aberdeen and St Andrews were founded during his reign; and work was begun on the royal palaces at Edinburgh and Linlithgow. He was a patron of William Dunbar, the greatest poet writing in English between Chaucer and Spenser. His sons were sent to Padua, Sienna and Rome for their education. He sought peace abroad, and in 1503 a diplomatic marriage took place between James and Henry VIII's sister Margaret. This arrangement seemed to bring to an end the 'Three Hundred Years War' between the two countries (can be dated from the 1290s), and to leave Henry VIII free to attack France. For reasons which are too complex to summarise, James broke his word, sided with France [Scotland's traditional ally], and the disastrous battle of Flodden was fought in 1513. The King was hacked to death in the melee.

James V [b.1513 – ruled 1528–1542]. 'James the ill-beloved' succeeded to the throne when he was one year old, and the unfortunate country had to endure fifteen years of regency. It was rule of a sort. Noble intrigued against noble, while the Queen Mother struggled to maintain her official position as head of the government. She was a formidable opponent, for although her affections were fickle she commanded support as the sister of Henry VIII. Pacifying the country and extracting money from those who had it were James's constant preoccupations as soon as he ascended the throne; almost all the heads of powerful Border families were in gaol at one time or another. From 1517 onwards much depended on the progress of the Reformation. James married Mary of Guise in 1537; the marriage brought in a useful sum of money, and also put Scotland on the side of France and the Papacy, and against the heretic Henry VIII. Both sides wanted Scotland to be helpful. France and the Papacy were both great secular powers, and schemes were afoot to attack England. So for once Scotland was well-placed to secure something out of European antagonisms. The Pope paid well for Scottish promises of co-operation, and Henry VIII responded by becoming almost friendly. But James's position in domestic affairs was growing almost untenable. His greed for money became paranoid; 'This King inclineth daily more and more to covetousness". Cruelties and unjustifiable executions became far too common. And when Henry lost patience and struck at Scotland in 1542, James could not muster an adequate army. He died two weeks after losing the battle of Solway Moss.

Mary, Queen of Scots [b. 1542, – ruled 1561 until abdication 1567 – d. 1587]. Mary's life and times were of truly labyrinthine complexity. When she succeeded to the throne, she was only one week old, and the regency lasted for nineteen years. As usual, great families schemed and murdered to be uppermost. To complicate matters further, Roman Catholic France was always at or on the brink of war with Protestant [most of the time] England, and it was important to each of these countries to keep Scotland on the 'right' side. So each aimed to control Scottish affairs. A peace treaty was signed between England and Scotland in 1543 but was repudiated by new Scots counsellors in 1544, with the result that a large English army immediately invaded Scotland and, on strict orders, destroyed everything within reach – buildings, chattels, crops and animals. In 1548 Scotland agreed to send Mary to France with a view to marrying the heir-apparent after [say] ten years. To get possession of the Scottish Queen was a real *coup* for France. But it settled nothing. At one time or another France or England were occupying St Andrews, Leith, Dunbar and Haddington. In 1560 both countries agreed to withdraw their troops. Mary still lived in France, having become Queen of France in 1559. But late in 1560 her husband died and she returned to the turmoil of Scotland. For several years she pursued a policy of moderation and conciliation with much skill and success. She remained a Roman Catholic but did not press Catholicism on others. Her policies mattered, because although Scotland was a small poor country, Mary herself was an important international figure; she was a grand-daughter of the sister of Henry VIII, and should Queen Elizabeth have no children, Mary would have a very strong claim to the English throne. She was thus a key figure in the business of royal alliances, and everyone expected her to marry. At this crucial moment Mary seems to have lost her bearings completely. Infatuation seems the most likely explanation; but no one knows. She chose to marry Lord Darnley, whose only qualification was that he sat well on a horse. They were married by Protestant rites in July, 1565. Within a few months everyone, including the Queen, knew that it was a disaster. In June 1566 Mary bore a son, and in February 1567 Darnley was murdered. Many suspected that Mary knew about the plot. She then turned to the Earl of Bothwell, who had taken part in the murder of Darnley, and married him in May, 1567. But the game was up. She now had more opponents than supporters, and was compelled to abdicate. A year later, she fled to England.

James VI [b. 1566 – ruled Scotland c1596–1603; ruled as King of England and Scotland 1603–1625]. James VI was crowned when he was a year old. The usual regency ensued. There were several regents, of whom the first was assassinated, the second was killed in an affray, and the third gave up in despair. What amounted to civil war between supporters of the young King [the Reformed Church party] and the supporters of Mary [the Roman Catholic party] went on for a few years, but lust for power and resort to violence were declining. With Henry VIIIs version of the Reformation imposed on England, and John Knox encouraging attacks on religious houses in Scotland, the Roman Catholic cause was losing support. James gradually gained control of the situation from the mid '90s. Always cautious, he destroyed the political importance of one faction after another. He chose new advisers well. Church lands were not annexed to the Crown but distributed among families whose loyalty could be counted on. Lands seized in earlier reigns were confirmed to their present owners. Peace, justice, and no illegal executions or seizures of property made the monarchy respected. James engaged in no foreign adventures, and he succeeded in a remarkable way in establishing domination over both the Reformed Church and the nobility. He built little, except for enlarging the palaces at Edinburgh, Dunfermline and Linlithgow, for he was a thrifty man. He was also far-sighted; he was astute; he detested violence; he was just a shade tricky. These were the qualities that at last brought peace and stability to Scotland.

A Few of the Famous

Adam, Robert [1728–1792]. Architect. Born in Kirkaldy, Fife, and educated at Edinburgh University. Spent eight years in Italy studying architecture and cultivating the acquaintance of m'lords on the Grand Tour – possible future clients. Published a handsome volume on the ruins of the Palace of Diocletian at Spalatro (i.e. Split). Among his finest works are Kedleston Hall in Derbyshire; Newby Hall in Yorkshire; Syon House west of London; Register House in Edinburgh; and Mellerstain near Melrose. His achievements as an interior decorator were equally noteworthy: he introduced a refreshing lightness and grace into the classical style, designing his interiors to the last detail. Many great houses besides the above have superb Adam interiors. He was buried in Westminster Abbey.

Adam William [c. 1690–1748]. Architect, father of Robert Adam. Worked in Scotland, mostly in the south-east. Admirer of Vanburgh. Built several country houses, but his masterpiece is undoubtedly Hopetoun House, near Edinburgh, which was begun by Sir William Bruce [q.v.]

Anne of Denmark [1574–1619]. Married James VI in 1590. Fond of an extravagant life-style [unlike her husband]. She is chiefly remembered for having commissioned the Queen's House at Greenwich, designed by Inigo Jones.

Boswell, James [1740–1795]. His *Life of Johnson*, whom he first met in 1763, has been described as 'a work of extraordinary originality and genius' and has gained him an international reputation. He was born in Edinburgh, son of a Scottish judge, and was educated at Edinburgh University. He did little as a lawyer, but soon became well-known for his sychophantic approaches to famous men. He cultivated their acquaintance, but never ceased to work on his *Life* which was published in 1791. He lived mostly in Edinburgh, visiting London only occasionally. Drink and brothels played a large part in his leisure hours.

Bruce, Sir William ([630–1780]. Architect. He was a prominent supporter of Charles II, and spent two periods as a member of parliament. In addition, he held a series of important government appointments in London. He restored and extended Holyrood Palace (q v), and designed the central core of Hopetoun House, later greatly enlarged and completed by Robert Adam.

Cockburn, Henry Lord [1779–1854]. Lawyer, son of an Edinburgh lawyer. Well known in his lifetime as an advocate of political reform. Best remembered now as the author of *Memorials of His Time* which brilliantly depicts life in the Edinburgh of his day.

David I [c1084–1153]. King of Scots after 1124. He was an Anglo-Norman, and when he died he was the greatest baron in England. His rule extended at one time as far south as the Tees. He built a number of castles and founded several abbeys, including Kelso and Jedburgh.

Darnley, Henry Stewart, Lord [1546–1567]. Born and brought up in England, he was one of the many possible successors to Queen Elizabeth. He was briefly married to Mary, Queen of Scots.

Forbes, Duncan [1685–1747]. Edinburgh lawyer. Became an MP in 1722 and rose to high legal positions in the administrative system as it was reorganised after 1707. He exercised extensive powers from 1725 onwards, powers which he often used against interference in Scots affairs by London. When the Jacobite rebellion began he was the principal architect of resistance, and spent some time in the Highlands, where he persuaded several clans not to join the rebellion. His home was Culloden House, near which the final battle was fought.

Gillespie Graham, James [1777–1855]. Architect. Designed and remodelled country houses in south and east Scotland. His greatest achievement, after Moray Place, is Brodick Castle in Argyll. In later life he occasionally worked with Pugin.

Haig, Field Marshall Earl Douglas [1861–1928]. Born at Bemersyde on the Tweed. Became a cavalry officer. He went to France in 1914 in command of the First Army and at the end of 1915 he became Commander-in-Chief of the British forces in France. He held this position to the end of the war. Late in 1918 his final offensive broke the Hindenburg line. His strategy and tactics have been severely criticised and strenuously defended. In spite of appalling casualties, he never lost the confidence of his men.

Hume, David [1711–1776]. In the history of philosophy, Hume must be ranked among the very greatest. He was born in Edinburgh, and attended Edinburgh University. He worked for a few years in France, and in 1739–40 published his *Treatise on Human Nature*. This book was a bombshell. Hume asked such questions as What is meant by perception? What is the nature of cause and effect? What is mind but a series of impressions? All later philosophy has had to consider Hume's arguments. His was a supremely powerful and penetrating intellect, which questioned all established faiths and conventions. Other books worth mentioning are his *History of England* (1754–61), for many generations a standard work, and his *Enquiry concerning Human Understanding* (1748). Perhaps surprisingly, this most intellectual of men was excellent company and a very good cook.

Knox, John [?1512–1572]. Priest. First appears in 1546 among a group of extreme Protestant reformers who had murdered a Cardinal and were holding out in St Andrews Castle. A French force relieved the castle, but Knox ended up in one of the galleys of Henri II. On release, he was for a time a preacher in England, where he declined a bishopric, but fled to the Continent when Mary Tudor (a Catholic) came to the throne. At Geneva he was under the influence of Calvin, but returned to Scotland in the 1550s; his preaching stimulated the revolt which gave the Protestant party final control. He was 'anglicised in speech and outlook' and was not nearly so extreme as many of his successors.

Lister, Joseph Lord [1827–1912]. English surgeon. Lister was responsible for the greatest break-through ever made in the history of surgery. He came to Edinburgh from London in 1854, a newly-qualified young doctor, and almost immediately began research into the causes of post-operational inflammation and suppuration. These conditions caused the death of many, probably most, of those who survived a mid-nineteenth century operation. Lister proved, and was able to prove in practice, that the trouble was caused by bacteria entering the wound, and that the remedy was 'the antiseptic system'. He developed his ideas for thirty years, first in Edinburgh and then, after 1877, in London. He was made a baronet in 1883.

Mary of Guise-Lorraine [1515–1560]. Queen of James V and mother of Mary, Queen of Scots. Married James in 1538 (he died four years later) and as a co-regent allied herself with the Roman Catholic party. She showed excellent political judgement, but in 1559 French policy became strongly anti-Protestant, and Mary followed suit. The Scottish reformers rebelled, and Mary was driven back to Dunbar. She recovered, but English intervention put the Protestants in control in 1560. Mary died that year in Edinburgh Castle.

Pennant, Thomas [1726–1798]. Born in Wales, Pennant was an eighteenth century gentleman; an antiquary, a naturalist and a traveller. His interests ranged wide, and his knowledge was very extensive. He was one of the most eminent naturalists of the eighteenth century. He made two tours in Scotland, which resulted in two books (1771 and 1774), and in 1790 he published *Of London*, a volume twice reprinted in three years. He corresponded with Linnaeus, met Voltaire, and was made a Fellow of the Royal Society.

Playfair, William [1789–1857]. Born in London, son of a Scots architect, Playfair became an apprentice in a London office and came to
Scotland in 1817. All his work, excepting his country houses, is in the
classical style, and is to be seen all over Edinburgh, both public buildings and private houses. The detail work is always meticulously
drawn in his plans.

Raeburn, Sir Henry [1756–1823]. Portrait painter. Raeburn was born
in Edinburgh. His father died when he was six, and he was educated
at George Heriot's Hospital. At the age of twenty two 'fortune
assisted him in taking a firmer footing' when he met and then married
a lady of means. Before he was thirty he was the leading painter in
Scotland. He went to Rome for a couple of years, and then settled in
Edinburgh in 1787, remaining there until his death. Even in London
he was regarded as a rival to Sir Thomas Lawrence. His portraits 'are
distinguished by great breadth, both of treatment and character' and
have 'a certain appearance of facility'. He was knighted by George IV
during the latter's visit to Edinburgh in 1822.

Ramsay, Allan [1686–1758]. Poet. Born in the west of Scotland,
Ramsay came to Edinburgh and set up as a wig-maker about 1700.
Scoottish vernacular poetry was then in vogue, and Ramsay revived
some old poems and wrote some new ones of his own. The best
known is *The Gentle Shepherd*, which was published in London in
1731. He also engaged in bookselling and publishing. Later, he
started a circulating library and attempted to establish a playhouse,
which was declared illegal. He made money, and was welcome in
Edinburgh society. He built a prominent house on the north slope of
Castle Rock.

Ramsay, Allan [1713–1784]. Son of the above. At an early age he
showed outstanding talents as a painter. He went to London for a year
in 1734, and spent two periods studying in Italy in the later 1730s and
the 1740s. His father's connections in Edinburgh gave him access to a
wealthy clientele. In 1737 he moved to London, where he was an
instant success. He further developed the baroque style of portraiture
– all drama and magnificence – and became Painter in Ordinary to
George III. Reynolds and Gainsburgh learned from him. But after
1755 he concentrated on his sitters as individuals rather than types,
and he moreover developed a style of lightness and delicacy. His
portraits of David Hume, Jean-Jacques Rousseau and his own second

wife Margaret Lindsay are masterpieces of his later style. If portraiture is the art, not of flattering the sitter or producing an attractive canvas but of delineating character, Ramsay has few equals.

Scott, Sir Walter [1771–1832]. Son of an Edinburgh lawyer. Studied law at Edinburgh University, and was called to the bar in 1792. He began his literary career in 1802 by publishing a collection of Scots ballads. His first novel appeared in 1815 and twenty one others before the end of 1831. All this was done in tandem with a busy professional life, and in addition to writing several other substantial works – e.g. a *Life of Napoleon*, for which he received the prodigious sum of £18,000. His popularity was enormous and so was his income. In 1826 his publishers failed, owing a little over £100,000. Scott undertook to pay the debts, and, in effect, wrote himself to death in the next five years.

Simpson, Sir James Young [1811–1820]. Physician. Came to Edinburgh in 1825, a poor boy, fourteen years old. He entered the University's Medical School, then the leading institution of its kind in the world. He qualified in 1832, published his first paper in 1836, and was appointed Professor of Midwifery in 1839. He liked people, and he believed in work. At that time, many doctors were using ether as a short-time anaesthetic, but it was thought to be too risky to be used in midwifery. The hunt was on for a new agent. Chloroform had been discovered in 1831, and Simpson tried it (on himself) in 1847, with satisfactory results. The same discovery was made in America at about the same time. After a few years of debate, the use of chloroform anaesthesia became common practice in all surgical operations as well as midwifery, and an incalculable blessing had been bestowed on mankind. (It is interesting that he criticised Lister, but campaigned for fresh air in hospitals).

Stephenson, Robert [1803–1859]. English engineer. Son of George Stephenson, he helped his father to build the 'Rocket' steam engine in 1827, and subsequently built the first railway to reach London (the London-Birmingham, completed 1838). He then turned his attention to bridges, and built some of the finest Victorian bridges, such as the Menai Straits bridge, the Conway bridge, the long viaduct at Berwick-on-Tweed, and the high-level bridge at Newcastle.

Stevenson, Robert Louis [1850–1894]. Writer. Born in Edinburgh, Stevenson was persuaded by his father to become a lawyer. He qualified, but his passion was to be an author, and before he was twenty six he had established his position with *An Inland Voyage* and *Travels with a Donkey in the Cévennes*. Thereafter he moved about incessantly, living in Scotland, Switzerland, Provence, California and elsewhere. He also wrote incessantly (novels included *Treasure Island* and *Dr Jekyll and Mr Hyde*). In 1888 he cruised with his wife in the Pacific, and in 1889 they settled in Samoa, where he bought an extensive property. Stevenson died five years later.

Tijou, Jean [fl.1689–1712]. French metalworker and designer, Tijou came to England as a Huguenot refugee in 1689. He seems never to have worked in France or the Netherlands. His work is remarkable for the extravagant use of elaborately modelled leafwork. He was extensively employed at Hampton Court, and also at Chatsworth and at St Paul's Cathedral under Wren.

Architectural Glossary

Acanthus	Stylised decoration in the form of a leaf.
Anthemion	Ornament like a honeysuckle flower.
Apse	Semi-circular or polygonal end to a church.
Arcade	A series of arches supported on columns.
Ashlar	Hewn or squared stones.
Astragal	Wooden glazing bar between window panes.
Barbican	Outer defence to a wall or castle.
Bartizan	Corbelled turret at the angle of a building.
Bay window	A window in a recess, i.e. with a projection out from the wall.
Cartouche	Elaborate ornamentation round a shield or coat of arms.
Chancel	East end of a church which contains the altar; can be all the nave east of the crossing.
Clerestorey	Upper storey of a church, usually with a row of windows.
Corbel	A projecting piece of wall supported on carved blocks of stone or wood; hence corbelled out.
Cupola	A spherical roof covering a circular base.
Curtain wall	Wall that connects towers in a castle.
Crowstepped	A gable that goes up in a series of vertical-horizontal-vertical upward steps.
Doorcase	Case or frame lining a doorway, in which the door is hung.
Fenestration	The arrangement of windows in a building.
Fluting	Vertical channelling on the side of a column.

Garderobe	Medieval privy.
Hammerbeam roof	A vaulted roof, supported by horizontal brackets projecting from the wall itself supporting uprights which are joined to the roof approximately half way up.
Imperial stair	A stair dividing half way up through 180° right and left.
Jettied out	The arrangement whereby an upper storey projects beyond the storey below as a result of the beams and joists of the lower storey oversailing the external wall.
Mullion	Vertical member dividing a window.
Newel stair	Circular or winding stair held up by a central post.
Oriel window	A bay window above ground level.
Pediment	Triangular shape in classical architecture resembling a gable end.
Pilaster	A rectangular-shaped column not standing free of the building.
Piscina	Basin in a church for washing communion vessels.
Reredos	Painted or sculptured screen above the altar.
Rusticated	Stone treated so as to give it a rough or knobbly surface.
Spandrel	Surface between an arch and the straight lines enclosing it.
String course	A moulding running horizontally along a wall.
Tolbooth	In more recent times called the Town House, this building was the regular meeting place of the burgh court and of the town council; it was also frequently used as a municipal prison.
Transept	The side parts usually running north and south of a cruciform church, set at right angles to the nave and choir.
Triforium	The first floor above ground-level in a church, designed as a passage or arcade.

Tunnel vault   The simplest form of vault, a continuous semicircular arch. Also called a barrel vault. More complicated vaults have surfaces at several angles, usually joined by ribs.

Turnpike stair   See newel stair.

Vault   Arched overhead covering, usually of stone.

Index

The Index is in three sections:

A Persons, including their statues and memorials
B Edinburgh – places, streets, buildings and subjects
C East Lothian and the Borders – places, streets, buildings and subjects.

A INDEX OF PERSONS

Index

Index

415

C EAST LOTHIAN AND THE BORDERS – INDEX OF PLACES, STREETS, BUILDINGS AND SUBJECTS

Index

419